Commercial Nationalism and Tourism

ASPECTS OF TOURISM

Series Editors: Chris Cooper, *Oxford Brookes University, UK*, C. Michael Hall, *University of Canterbury, New Zealand* and Dallen J. Timothy, *Arizona State University, USA*

Aspects of Tourism is an innovative, multifaceted series, which comprises authoritative reference handbooks on global tourism regions, research volumes, texts and monographs. It is designed to provide readers with the latest thinking on tourism worldwide and in so doing will push back the frontiers of tourism knowledge. The series also introduces a new generation of international tourism authors writing on leading edge topics.

The volumes are authoritative, readable and user-friendly, providing accessible sources for further research. Books in the series are commissioned to probe the relationship between tourism and cognate subject areas such as strategy, development, retailing, sport and environmental studies. The publisher and series editors welcome proposals from writers with projects on the above topics.

Full details of all the books in this series and of all our other publications can be found on http://www.channelviewpublications.com, or by writing to Channel View Publications, St Nicholas House, 31–34 High Street, Bristol BS1 2AW, UK.

ASPECTS OF TOURISM: 77

Commercial Nationalism and Tourism

Selling the National Story

Edited by
Leanne White

CHANNEL VIEW PUBLICATIONS
Bristol • Blue Ridge Summit

Library of Congress Cataloging in Publication Data
Names: White, Leanne, editor.
Title: Commercial nationalism and Tourism: Selling the National Story/Edited by
    Leanne White.
Description: Bristol: Channel View Publications, [2017] |
Series: Aspects of Tourism: 77 | Includes bibliographical references and index.
Identifiers: LCCN 2016041192| ISBN 9781845415891 (hbk : alk. paper) |
ISBN 9781845415884 (pbk : alk. paper) | ISBN 9781845415921 (kindle)
Subjects: LCSH: Tourism--Political aspects. | Nationalism—Marketing.
Classification: LCC G155.A1 .C53355 2017 | DDC 910.68/8—dc23 LC record available at
https://lccn.loc.gov/2016041192

British Library Cataloguing in Publication Data
A catalogue entry for this book is available from the British Library.

ISBN-13: 978-1-84541-589-1 (hbk)
ISBN-13: 978-1-84541-588-4 (pbk)

Channel View Publications
UK: St Nicholas House, 31–34 High Street, Bristol BS1 2AW, UK.
USA: NBN, Blue Ridge Summit, PA, USA.

Website: www.channelviewpublications.com
Twitter: Channel_View
Facebook: https://www.facebook.com/channelviewpublications
Blog: www.channelviewpublications.wordpress.com

The policy of Multilingual Matters/Channel View Publications is to use papers that are
natural, renewable and recyclable products, made from wood grown in sustainable forests. In the manufacturing process of our books, and to further support our policy, preference is given to printers that have FSC and PEFC Chain of Custody certification. The FSC
and/or PEFC logos will appear on those books where full certification has been granted
to the printer concerned.

Typeset by Nova Techset Private Limited, Bengaluru and Chennai, India.
Printed and bound in the UK by Short Run Press Ltd.
Printed and bound in the US by Edwards Brothers Malloy, Inc.

Contents

Conclusion

Acknowledgements

I hope that you will be energised and engaged by the diverse international cases that examine commercial nationalism and how this phenomenon engages with tourism or events. As editor of this collaborative international body of work, I am delighted that, from the tremendous collegial work of scholars around the globe, we have produced a volume that advances the academic debate surrounding commercial nationalism and tourism. All 26 contributors have combined an applied approach with solid academic and critical analysis. I would like to thank all of the authors who made this book possible. They have been wonderful to work with, extremely responsive to my many emails and always highly cooperative.

On a personal level, I am extremely grateful for the immeasurable support from friends and families. In particular, I would like to thank Clarke Stevenson for his unconditional love, ongoing support and understanding.

I would like to thank my publisher, Channel View, along with the wider production team involved in seeing this book come to fruition. In particular, I thank Elinor Robertson, Sarah Williams and Florence McClelland. I would also like to thank the anonymous reviewer who provided very useful comments on the first draft of the manuscript to myself and a number of the contributors. The comments helped make for a more robust book.

This book builds upon two earlier books which I edited with Associate Professor Elspeth Frew: *Tourism and National Identities: An International Perspective* (2011) and *Dark Tourism and Place Identity: Managing and Interpreting Dark Places* (2013) by narrowing the focus of study to commercial nationalism while broadening the discussion of national identity to encompass both tourism and events.

This book is a reference text aimed principally at the academic market. It is designed to address the void that currently exists in the discursive space where commercial nationalism and tourism or events intersect. However, it should also prove interesting reading to anyone who has been a tourist or attended a major event in an increasingly commercial world.

Leanne White
Victoria University, Australia

Contributors

Dr Marie Avellino Stewart is an Anthropologist and Lecturer in the Institute of Tourism, Travel and Culture, at the University of Malta. Marie has brought 30 years of tourism and management experience to academia. She is involved in collaborative research such as the Lifelong learning projects: Socialising Tourism and Heritage Interpretation for Senior Audiences. Her main research interests are: Heritage, Consumer Behaviour and Tourism.

Dr Michael Basil grew up in California in the 1970s. He received his PhD from Stanford in 1992. He is currently a Professor of Marketing at the University of Lethbridge in Alberta, Canada. His main research interest is in marketing communications. Mike developed his international interests having lived and worked in five different countries on four continents and in Hawaii. He also lived in Japan for several months in 1985 and 2005, and revisited Japan for this research in 2009. Currently Mike is most interested in food choice – especially the influence of culture on food choice.

Dr George Cassar is an Associate Professor in the Institute for Tourism, Travel and Culture of the University of Malta. He is a historical sociologist who researches the History and Sociology of Education; the Pedagogy of Heritage, History and Social Studies; the History of History Teaching; the Study of the Order of St John; the History and Culture of Malta; Heritage and Culture; Cultural Tourism; and the Sociology of Food. He is the author or editor of books and academic journals, and has published numerous papers in journals and chapters in books related to his areas of interest.

Dr Alan Clarke has been travelling the world trying to unravel the meaning behind cultural heritages. He works as a Professor in Hungary at the University of Pannonia and is encouraged to reflect on his journeys wherever possible. As a result, he has published widely in the fields of International Hospitality Management, tourism and most recently on community festivals and events. His curiosity is not yet sated – hence his growing interest in routes and pathways. He was awarded a medal for his contribution to Hungarian Science despite being neither Hungarian nor a scientist!

Dr C. Michael Hall is a Professor in the Department of Management, Marketing and Entrepreneurship, University of Canterbury, Christchurch, New Zealand; a Docent in the Department of Geography, University of Oulu, Finland; and a Visiting Professor in the Linnaeus University School of Business and Economics, Kalmar, Sweden. Current research includes Finnish short-breaks in Stockholm, World Heritage short-breaks, and return visits to the Icelandic wilderness.

Dr John Harris is Reader in International Sport and Event Management within the Department of Business Management and also heads the Sport and Identities Research Cluster at Glasgow Caledonian University. He is the author of *Rugby Union and Globalization,* co-editor of *Sport and Social Identities* and editor of *Sport, Tourism and National Identities.* His research interests cover sport, tourism and events; sport communication; national identities and globalisation; and social identities. He is Leisure and Events Subject Editor of the *Journal of Hospitality, Leisure, Sport and Tourism Education.*

Dr Svitlana Iarmolenko received her undergraduate education in commercial tourism from Kyiv National University of Ukraine, and continued on to earn a Masters degree from East Carolina University and a PhD from Pennsylvania State University, both in recreation and tourism. Dr. Iarmolenko's twofold research program focuses on immigrant issues, heritage, acculturation, transnationalism, and mobilities on the one hand, and heritage tourism development through collaborative community-scholar processes and stakeholder involvement.

Dr Anna Irimiás has been an Associate Professor in Tourism Geography at Kodolányi János University of Applied Sciences Hungary since 2008. She graduated from the University of Messina in Italy in 2004 in English and Spanish language and literature. She was awarded her PhD in Human Geography in 2008 in Messina. Her research interests include tourism destination management, cultural tourism, film induced tourism, warscapes and heritage management and the nexus between migration and tourism. She has published several scientific articles in different languages.

Dr Deborah Kerstetter is a Professor and Professor-in-Charge of the Graduate Program at Pennsylvania State University. She received her Bachelor's degree from California State University and her graduate degrees from Pennsylvania State University. Her principal research interests are in the areas of tourism marketing, decision-making behavior, and the benefits of travel. She has published more than 70 articles in scholarly journals and has co-authored multiple book chapters.

Dr Pascale Marcotte is a Professor in the Department of Geography at Laval University in Canada. She holds a management position for cultural and tourism organisations where she heads studies in the field of tourism. Between marketing and sociology, she is particularly interested in the behaviour of tourism and cultural consumers.

Dr Jean Martin holds a doctorate in historical geography. He is an historian with the Directorate of History and Heritage, National Defence, Canada. His research interests include: military geography, tourism, commemoration and the First World War.

Dr Brent McKenzie is an Associate Professor, in the Department of Marketing and Consumer Studies, in the College of Business and Economics, at the University of Guelph, in Ontario, Canada. Dr McKenzie is an expert on management and business-related issues in the Baltic States of Estonia, Latvia and Lithuania. He has engaged in extensive research fieldwork and conducted a number of academic and industry workshops, presentations and seminars in these countries. His research on the Baltic States has been widely published in both academic and practitioner journals.

Dr Patrick Naef is a postdoctoral scholar in the Department of Anthropology at the University of California, Berkeley. His main areas of research are memory, tourism and violence. He holds a PhD in Geography from the University of Geneva and his dissertation looked at conflicts of memory in the cultural heritage management and tourism sectors in Sarajevo, Srebrenica and Vukovar. His research in Eastern Europe and Southeast Asia lead him to examine concepts such as identity and nationalism.

Dr Leighann Neilson is Associate Professor, Marketing, at the Sprott School of Business, Carleton University. Her research interests include marketing history, Canadian tourism history, and marketing in not-for-profit, arts and heritage organisations. Her current work focuses on the ways that consumers 'use' history, especially family history, in their everyday lives.

Dr Kelly Phelan is a Senior Lecturer at The University of Queensland and a Fulbright Scholar at the University of Botswana. Her current research focuses primarily on tourism development in Africa and approaches the topic from a multidisciplinary angle. Some of her publications have examined volunteer tourism, conservation efforts, challenges associated with sustainability and ecotourism, and the host-guest interaction. She is currently working on a book about the growth of the tourism industry in Africa and the political, economic and social implications of that phenomenon.

Dr Maya Ranganathan teaches in the Department of Media, Music, Communication and Cultural Studies at Macquarie University, Australia. Her research interest and expertise lie in the area of 'mediated identities', particularly political identities in South Asia. Her works relate to the ways in which media in Asia have evolved in the age of globalisation. She has authored *Eelam Online: Negotiation of Political Websites by Diaspora in Australia* (2011) and has co-authored *Indian Media in a Globalised World* (2010) and *From Observer to Partaker: Indian News Media* (2015).

Dr Tamara Rátz is Professor of Tourism and Director of the Institute of Tourism and Business Studies at the Kodolányi János University of Applied Sciences, Székesfehérvár, Hungary. She has taught various tourism-related courses in Finland, Norway, the Netherlands, Poland, Bulgaria, the Ukraine, Romania, Spain, Turkey and Kazakhstan. She is the author or co-author of more than 180 publications on tourism, including a number of books on the impacts of tourism, attraction and visitor management, and health tourism and quality of life. Her current research interests include cultural and heritage tourism development and management, creativity and innovation in niche tourism development, and the role of tourism as a catalyst in European integration.

Dr Kathleen Rettie is an adjunct professor in Geography at the University of Calgary. Her work focuses on the human aspects of protected areas, in particular Canada's mountain national parks and the Cairngorms in Scotland. Kathy was a social scientist for the Parks Canada Agency prior to retirement from a 35-year career as a Parks Canada employee. She has resided in Banff National Park for 38 years.

Dr Juan Sanin is a Lecturer in Industrial Design at Royal Melbourne Institute of Technology University in Melbourne, Australia. His doctoral research looked at the commercial construction of Australianness by analysing manifestations of commercial nationalism in the history of Australia. He also has studied the commercial construction of Colombianness through nation branding campaigns and manifestations of commercial nationalism in popular culture. Results from his research on this topic have been presented at conferences held in Australia, Latin America and England and have circulated in Colombian and international publications.

Dr Sagar Singh has been associated as an editor with the Centre for Tourism Research and Development, Lucknow, India, since 1984. He has also been associated with the centre as a researcher in the anthropology of tourism since 1996. He has written some 23 research papers/book chapters and two books on tourism management, including *Shades of Green: Ecotourism for Sustainability* (2004). His research interests also include tourism and ecology/ conservation, the economic anthropology of tourism, and tourism education. He is currently Editor (honorary) of the 40-year-old international journal, *Tourism Recreation Research*.

Mojtaba Shahvali is a PhD candidate at the Department of Recreation, Park and Tourism Management at the Pennsylvania State University. He was introduced to the world of tourism during his Masters degree at Allameh Tabatabai University, Tehran. His earlier research interest was in visitor management and evaluation of services satisfaction. However, pursuing his PhD Penn State opened his eyes to a new perspective in tourism studies, humane and psychological perspectives on travel, and travel for the benefit of the traveler. His most recent research stream deals with how the internet and user-generated content impact travelers' experiences.

Dr Aaron Tham is a Lecturer in Tourism, Leisure and Events Management within the School of Business, University of the Sunshine Coast. His primary research is focused on social media and its impact towards destination decision-making. Other research interests include destination marketing, tourism networks and cultural and heritage studies. Aaron currently serves on the editorial board with the *eReview of Tourism Research* as a conference news editor, and as a reviewer on several leading tourism journals.

Dr Leanne White is a Senior Lecturer in the College of Business at Victoria University in Melbourne, Australia. Her research interests include: national identity, commercial nationalism, popular culture, advertising, destination marketing and cultural tourism. She is the author of more than 50 book chapters and refereed journal articles. Along with editing this volume, Leanne is a co-editor of the following research books: *The Palgrave Handbook of Dark Tourism Studies* (2017), *Advertising and Public Memory: Social, Cultural and Historical Perspectives on Ghost Signs* (2017), *Wine and Identity: Branding, Heritage, Terroir* (2014), *Dark Tourism and Place Identity: Managing and Interpreting Dark Places* (2013) and *Tourism and National Identities: An International Perspective* (2011).

Dr Nicholas Wise is Lecturer in Sport and Events, and is currently the programme leader for the Master of International Events Management and Master of International Tourism Management at Glasgow Caledonian University. His current research focuses on sport, events and tourism, and his academic background and PhD is in human geography. He brings an international perspective to the programme having completed research focusing on the Dominican Republic, Argentina, Croatia and Serbia. His current academic interests deal with interdisciplinary approaches to globalisation, urban regeneration and place image/identity. Nicholas has travelled extensively in over 80 countries as a student, an instructor, for research/fieldwork, to present at conferences, as a volunteer and for leisure.

Yang Yang is a PhD student in human geography at the University of Colorado Boulder. Her research interests include ethno-religious politics, urban studies, cultural heritage, and Islam in China. Her doctoral dissertation concerns how China utilises urban planning to make connections with global Islamic financial powers while not being involved in political Islam. She focuses on two comparative cases in Xi'an and Yinchuan to examine the interplay between ethnic identity and the production of ethnoreligious spaces in second tier inland Chinese cities. Since 2009, she has conducted a longitudinal study in the Hui Muslim communities in Xi'an, China.

Dr Yujie Zhu is a Postdoctoral Research Fellow in the Australian Centre on China in the World at Australian National University. His research in heritage cities of China includes heritage politics, tourism, cultural consumption and production, and the practice of everyday life. His work has appeared in leading tourism, heritage and anthropology journals. He co-edited the book *Sustainable Tourism Management at World Heritage Sites* (2009). Since 2013, he has served as the Vice Chair of the Commission on the Anthropology of Tourism for the International Union of Anthropological and Ethnological Sciences.

Introduction

1 Commercial Nationalism: Mapping the Landscape

Leanne White

Introduction

This chapter provides a brief introduction to the book, an examination of the theory surrounding commercial nationalism, an overview of the three sections of the book and the chapters within them. Nation branding and national imagery can be explored using a range of methodologies. The aim of this book is to show how particular narratives are woven to tell (and sell) a national story. By deconstructing images of the nation, one can closely examine how national texts create key archival imagery that can promote tourism and events while at the same time helping to shape national identity.

The topic of 'commercial nationalism' (the use of national signifiers to sell products or services, and the selling of the national story for purposes such as tourism) is both interdisciplinary and of international importance. The concept engages with a wide range of research areas, including tourism, events, hospitality, marketing, history and cultural studies. The complex relationship between commerce and the nation has attracted the interest of scholars in recent years and warrants further investigation.

The aim of this book is to demystify the various ways in which the nation has been imagined by key organisers and organisations and then communicated to millions. The meanings conveyed in the presentation of signifiers of nation will be investigated. This edited volume investigates the concept of commercial nationalism as it relates to the presentation of national tourism stories and campaigns, along with key national events. The book explores the relationship between state appropriation of marketing strategies and the commercial use of nationalist discourses.

A theoretical context to commercial nationalism, nation branding and tourism is expanded upon to provide a further background to the research

Figure 1.1 The three themed sections of this book

undertaken in this volume. This chapter also examines how commercial nationalism differs from other forms of nationalism such as 'official nationalism' and 'popular nationalism'. Chapters 2–19 then investigate case studies from around the world, exploring commercial nationalism and tourism or events. The book draws on studies from the following countries: Australia, Belgium, Bosnia and Herzegovina, Canada, China, Colombia, Croatia, Estonia, France, Hungary, India, Japan, Malta, New Zealand, Singapore, South Africa, Ukraine and the United States, to consider commercial nationalism as it relates to tourism or events. Chapter 20 concludes the book, summarises some of the arguments made and points to some further research in this area.

This volume is divided into three sections: National Narratives, Heritage and Tourism; Tourism Branding and Promotion; and Festivals, Events and National Identity (see Figure 1.1). These three themes emerged from the collection of abstracts that were submitted by scholars from around the world. This research book combines academic analysis and critical input with fresh perspectives from a range of experts.

Exploring Nationalism, Tourism and Events

While numerous theorists have analysed nationalism, Anderson's ground-breaking 1983 work *Imagined Communities: Reflections on the Origin and Spread of Nationalism* reconceptualised the way scholars have come to think about nationalism. Anderson popularly conceptualised the nation as an 'imagined political community'. Of the academic literature produced on theories of nationalism over the past 30 or so years, Anderson is among the most frequently cited (Culler & Cheah, 2003: vii). Ozkirimli argues that Anderson's work 'constitutes one of the most original accounts of nationalism to date' (Ozkirimli, 2000: 151), while James claims that Anderson's key text 'remains the most insightful book written in the area' (James, 1996: ix).

Commentators understand the imagined community of the nation as being maintained by cultural artefacts and institutions such as literature, art, media and the education system, and argue that a sense of nation is established and sustained 'by the quotidian rhythms of print and electronic media output, along with periodic national ceremonies' (O'Sullivan et al., 1994: 196–197).

Indeed it is the daily ritual, undertaken by individuals of the nation separately, of reading about the events that have been selected as newsworthy that cements the concept of a common national identity. Billig refers to the way in which symbols of the nation are reproduced on a daily basis as 'banal nationalism' (Billig, 1995: 6). An example of Billig's concept of banal nationalism can be seen in the words and logo of the masthead of the nation's daily newspaper *The Australian*. The concept of the 'homeland' or 'heartland' (as the nation is sometimes referred to) is doubly reinforced in both the title of the newspaper and the image of the Australian landmass. As Billig explains, banal nationalism is evidenced not by the flag but by the flag that might be relatively unnoticed in a public space (see Figure 1.2).

Gammon has argued that heritage has the ability to 'guide and cement national identities' (Gammon, 2007: 1). When exploring our past, we are delving deeper into our own heritage and also that of the nation or nations. Underlying this suggestion is the proposition that heritage is a 'cultural and

Figure 1.2 Billig's theory of banal nationalism is evidenced by everyday displays of patriotism that may go largely unnoticed

social process' that is 'ultimately intangible' (Smith, 2006: 307). This book explores some of the ways in which heritage is imagined and celebrated. By examining some of the rituals surrounding national celebrations, we can rethink our understanding and awareness of national heritage and tradition 'in our everyday lives' (Waterton, 2010: 206). For the individual celebrating national festivals and events, heritage becomes somehow embodied and personified by their own experiences and those of others – along with the many photographs of the experiences that may be taken and shared. If we understand heritage as a process that constructs meaning about the past, then the construction of the related rituals and traditions is illustrative of this process. It is, essentially, a construction of national heritage based on stories, memories, reports and photographs that have been documented and passed down through the ages by family and friends.

Hall suggested that, 'Events are those things out of the everyday which punctuate, mark, and identify collective and individual social realities' (Hall, 1997: xi). The mega-event describes that activity undertaken on a large scale such as world fairs and expositions, significant cultural events and major sporting events. Also referred to as hallmark events, mega-events generally consist of 'major fairs, festivals, expositions, and cultural and sporting events' and have come to assume 'a key role in international, national and regional tourism marketing strategies'. These events may 'leave behind legacies' and 'are the image builders of modern tourism' (Hall, 1997: 1).

At the Barcelona Olympic Games in 1992, archer Antonio Rebollo released a blazing arrow to light the flame, while at the 1996 Atlanta Games, it was arranged for world champion boxer Muhammad Ali to light the cauldron. As Tomlinson argues, 'No one witnessing this Ali–an act of reaffirmation could forget it. And it was great television. Like no sportsman before or since, Ali has had a political, historical, worldwide resonance' (Tomlinson, 2000: 169). Kociumbas argues that the choice of Indigenous Australian athlete Cathy Freeman to light the Olympic flame in Sydney was foreshadowed at the Atlanta Games when Ali was chosen (Kociumbas, 2003: 128).

Many of the spectators who attended the mega-event that was the Sydney Olympic Games were tourists – be they from other parts of New South Wales, other states of Australia or other parts of the world. Most of these tourists would have carefully planned their itinerary – which included attending particular Olympic events. At a mega-event such as the Sydney Games, the industries of tourism, sport and the media were intimately connected and contributed to the overall experience that was consumed by the visitor.

As Roche has argued, events such as opening ceremonies can be both a cause and effect of the development of tourist cultures (Roche, 2000: 125). The search for representations of Australianness can be discovered through a close examination of the momentous event that was the Sydney opening ceremony. While some may argue that Australia has matured as a nation in recent times, our widespread and constant questioning of our identity seems to suggest that we still have some way to go before we can step forward as a confident and proud self-assured nation that appreciates who we are and what we stand for. National texts work to perpetuate certain myths in a range of industries such as tourism.

Falassi argues that festivals modify our normal sense of time with various ritualistic movements that are carried out from the beginning to the end of the festival. This modification creates a so-called 'time out of time' – with a respectfully observed temporal dimension devoted to each key activity (Falassi, 1987: 4). Celebrations can indeed place our 'normal' sense of time in something of a holding pattern, while festival (atypical) time is taken to focus on others – especially family and friends. Festivals usually consist of a number of ritual acts or rites. As Falassi contends, an unavoidable element of many festivals is conspicuous consumption.

Studies in tourism have considered the role of attractions and events in helping create a national identity. Pretes (2003) contends that tourists obtain messages from the various sites they visit, and that these sites, presented as aspects of a national heritage, help to shape a common national identity amongst a diverse population. He also argues that a shared identity is often an official goal of countries comprising many different cultures where there exists a common urge to create a national identity to overcome diversity and difference within the nation-state. Another perspective on diversity is offered by Spillman (1997), who argues that, in a diverse country, diversity itself can become an aspect of national identity.

Commercial Nationalism

One of the earliest references to the term 'commercial nationalism' in the academic literature came about in the early 1980s. In an article published in *Arena* titled 'Australia in the Corporate Image: A New Nationalism', James analysed corporate advertising techniques used by multinational companies in Australia along with other key promotions such as the government-sponsored 'Advance Australia' campaign. James traced the initial stages of a phenomenon that he described as the 'commercial manifestations of nationalism'. He also explored the connection between 'government-sponsored nationalism' and 'commercial nationalism' (James, 1983: 79) and suggested that government and corporate advertising played 'mutually reinforcing' roles in underpinning the national outlook. It is from James's article of 1983 that I have developed and explored the terms 'official nationalism', 'popular nationalism' and 'commercial nationalism' further in a range of published and unpublished work which I will draw upon here.

The James study was a useful critique in conceptualising an analytical framework for an early research thesis, 'The Selling of Australia', which investigated the uses of Australian imagery in the advertising of five Australian-based and five overseas-based organisations (White, 1984). Further work that I undertook has contributed to this developing field. I have previously defined 'commercial nationalism' as follows:

> The term commercial nationalism was chosen to describe the style of nationalism promoted by advertisers, advertising agencies and other sections of popular culture, as it encompasses the idea that commerce and the nation are deliberately constructed entities. The term alludes to the notion that the once clearer boundaries of these two domains have been eliminated and that the broader concept of nationalism which deals with ideas and beliefs, has combined with the economic forces in the world of commerce which compete for the consumer dollar. Thus, commercial nationalism is essentially a paradox – two potentially conflicting sectors combining their influences and occupying the same space. (White, 1994: 1)

In 2004, in a contribution to the book *National Days/National Ways: Historical, Political and Religious Celebrations around the World*, I also compared commercial nationalism with official nationalism in a chapter focusing on the ways in which Australia celebrates its national day. I argued:

> Commercial nationalism – the adoption of national signifiers in order to generate profit – is a continuation and extension of the overall theme, style and symbols of the official nationalism. Commercial nationalism and official nationalism are directly related, and both contribute to the total discourse on nationalism. The official and commercial strands of nationalism are not binary oppositions; there is a significant degree of overlap between the areas ... Commercial nationalism operates like a paradigm; it continues the pattern that has been firmly established by the official body. It is not in the interest of the private company to create conflict between these two types of nationalism; they are merely used for different purposes. (White, 2004: 28)

A diagram and explanation of the relationship between official nationalism, popular nationalism and commercial nationalism is outlined in Figure 1.3. Official nationalism is the civic, formal and ceremonial nationalism such as the Australian Government's planning of the Bicentennial celebrations in 1988 or the Centenary of Federation celebrations in 2001. National anthem, flag and official symbols are part of official nationalism. The concept of popular nationalism was examined by Ward and can include nationalist messages and images as depicted in popular culture texts such as Australian film,

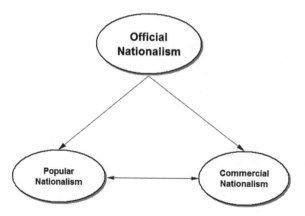

Figure 1.3 Official nationalism primarily emerges from the nation-state. Popular and commercial nationalism fall under the larger umbrella of official nationalism

television drama, popular songs and sport. Commercial nationalism refers to consumer-related uses of these national symbols, images and icons. It is the material, everyday nationalism represented by companies and products such as Qantas and Vegemite.

For many years, the phenomenon of commercial nationalism has been evidenced in advertising slogans that occasionally develop into popular jingles such as *Aussie Kids are Weet-Bix Kids, I'm as Australian as Ampol* and *Football, Meat Pies, Kangaroos and Holden Cars*. While popular and commercial nationalism generally play a subservient role to official nationalism, these forms of nationalism occasionally overlap. An example of all three forms of nationalism intersecting in Australian culture would be the kangaroo being displayed on the Australian coat of arms and the one dollar coin, the popular boxing kangaroo flag being flown frequently at sporting events, and the use of the kangaroo as the Qantas airline logo (see Figure 1.4).

It may well be the case that the exploration of this more aggressive form of nationalism is more likely to emerge from a 'young' country such as Australia. Countries such as Australia tend to be more likely to question their history and identity. Indeed, Australia celebrated its Bicentenary of European settlement in 1988 with much advertising that year incorporating Australian themes (White, 1994).

While a more thorough academic interest in commercial nationalism emerged in the 1980s, commercial nationalism – as practiced by corporations – has existed since at least the 1890s. Along with the general interest in all things Australian, books representing early uses of commercial nationalism (from the 1890s) by advertisers were produced from the mid 1970s. These types of book were compiled and written by a number of authors, including Carroll (1974 and 1975), Cozzolino (1980), Bryden-Brown (1981) and Shoebridge (1992).

Figure 1.4 Australia's airline Qantas displays the flying kangaroo as the carrier's logo

The persuasive and pervasive nature of commercial texts make them fascinating subjects for close analysis. Texts that contain national signifiers are particularly engaging and may also hold some information about the state of the nation at the time. Having examined the phenomenon of commercial nationalism for many years, I am particularly interested in how these nationalist messages traverse and are interwoven with other forms of nationalism such as official nationalism and popular nationalism.

From the 1990s, a number of exhibitions also served to raise the profile of commercial nationalism as depicted in a range of popular media products such as travel posters and tourist brochures. Since 1990, 'Refreshing: Art off the Pub Wall' has been exhibited at Sydney's Powerhouse Museum. In 1991, the National Centre for Australian Studies at Monash University staged 'Trading Places: Australian Travel Posters', while in 1992 it presented 'The Lie of the Land', which was exhibited at the Powerhouse Museum, the National Library of Australia and the National Wool Museum. The exhibition explored the way 'Australian landscapes have been presented and massaged for mass consumption' (Spearritt, 1992: iv). In 1993 the National Gallery of Australia's 'Poster Art of Australia' continued to raise the profile of popular Australian cultural artefacts, and in 2001 the State Library of Victoria staged 'All the Rage: The Poster in Victoria, 1850–2000', displaying posters with a political message alongside those from the advertising and travel industries.

As outlined above, an academic interest in commercial nationalism started to emerge in the 1980s. Following general interest books in the area, a more rigorous debate came about as a result of the works of Sinclair, Willis and Crawford, the latter having written on the history of Australia's advertising industry and its growth and development during the 20th century, including the book *But Wait There's More: A History of Australia's Advertising Industry, 1900–2000* (Crawford, 2008).

Sinclair argued in *Images Incorporated: Advertising and Ideology* that multi-national corporations foster various local identities to conform to particular markets (Sinclair, 1987: 168). He explored advertising campaigns which were transformed to suit 'each nation and its culture in commercial terms' (Sinclair, 1987: 169). Observing that visual images are always embedded in texts, Willis in *Illusions of Identity: The Art of Nation*, examined 'how visual imagery becomes enmeshed in processes of the construction of national identity' (Willis, 1993: 9). She contended that, in Australia in the late 1980s, a form of 'hyper nationalism' emerged (Willis, 1993: 26) and distinguished the 'cultural nationalism' of the Whitlam years from the 'corporatised figural nationalism' (Willis, 1993: 88), which she referred to as the 'consumer nationalism' (Willis, 1993: 180) of the Bicentenary.

Turner contributed to the debate on national representations in 1986 with the text *National Fictions: Literature, Film and the Construction of Australian Narrative* (Turner, 1986). He acknowledged that 'the nation' as a subject had not been a particularly 'fashionable undertaking' at the time (Turner, 1993: xiii). Turner examined 'the ways in which the nation is constructed through its stories' (Turner, 1993a: xiii) and spoke about 'our repertoire of definitions of the nation' (Turner, 1993: xiv). Following on from Anderson, Turner's argument was that 'nationalism is immensely flexible' (Turner, 1993: 154). He examined similarities between the genres by identifying preferred meanings, and their prevailing patterns of communication in Australian culture. Turner stated:

> The key issue in talking about the role and nature of the presence of nationalism in Australian narrative is thus not so much the range of meanings made available but the fact of the dominance of one set of terms, one body of myth or discourse, as the accepted mode of representation of the meaning of the nation. (Turner, 1993: 109)

One writer who acknowledged official and unofficial factors in telling a nation's story is Seal. He stated in the preface of *Inventing Anzac: The Digger and National Mythology* that his book 'demonstrates how the official and the unofficial, the formal and the folkloric, the institutionalised and the communal have colluded – and continue to collude – in the construction of a potent national mythology' (Seal, 2004: vii). Mackay argued that, 'Our belief in a distinctive, homogenous set of Australian characteristics – an essential Australianness – is sustained by the rural myth' (Mackay, 1999: 44). Such rural myths are evidenced in texts such as the 1895 poem *The Man from Snowy River* and the numerous related texts which have been produced since that time, along with associated commercial industries. Consequently the connected texts work to perpetuate the myth amongst Australian and over-seas visitors in industries such as fashion and tourism (White, 2009).

Khamis has also explored the relationship between corporate advertising and national identity in a range of papers. One company she has explored in detail is Bushells tea – the subject of her doctoral thesis (Khamis, 2007). Foster is a scholar who has examined the commercial construction of nations in the Pacific region (Foster, 1995). More recently, Volcic has explored commercial nationalism with particular relevance to the Balkan television and national advertising campaigns in the region. With Andrejevic, Volcic's latest contribution to the discussion of commercial nationalism is the edited volume *Commercial Nationalism: Selling the Nation and Nationalizing the Sell* (Volcic & Andrejevic, 2015). The title of the book reveals how commercial nationalism can be viewed from two distinct perspectives. It is the former (selling the nation) that is principally explored in this book.

Nation Branding

Nations have branded themselves throughout history and reinvented themselves as their circumstances or regimes have changed (Olins, 2002). It is also recognised that a positive country brand is also expected to boost exports and enhance product country image (Dinnie, 2012). Nation branding is rooted in the realities of a nation's culture (Dinnie, 2012). Dinnie's defini-tion of a nation brand as 'the unique, multi-dimensional blend of elements that provide the nation with culturally grounded differentiation and rele-vance for all of its target audiences' (Dinnie, 2012: 15) is a useful one. The fundamental features of national identity comprise the place, culture, people, politics and economy (Dinnie, 2012). The visual features of national identity are landscapes, cultural artefacts, the flag and other symbols (Dinnie, 2012). Some cultural artefacts and symbols of Turkey as a nation are displayed in a selection of Turkish souvenirs in Figure 1.5.

A nation brand is dependent on factors that are not amenable to direct control, can be situational or are limited by boundaries (Gnoth, 2002). Anholt (2012) has described the nation branding concept as 'competitive identity'. He argues that it is important to analyse the core identity of the nation being branded (Anholt, 2010). A nation's brand image is based upon people's previous knowledge, beliefs and experiences, or on the stereotypes of its people and the social, political and economic conditions (Akotia *et al.*, 2011). A strong stereotype for Taiwan that is actively promoted at Taipei's Taoyuan International Airport is the 'Made in Taiwan' slogan (see Figure 1.6).

Branding is a powerful marketing weapon available to contemporary destination marketers confronted by tourists who are increasingly seeking lifestyle fulfilment and experience (Morgan *et al.*, 2004). With increasing

Figure 1.5 Souvenirs from Turkey capture some of the iconic symbols of the nation

Figure 1.6 As visitors and locals leave Taipei, the slogan 'Made in Taiwan' is proudly displayed

competition, however, destinations must differentiate themselves from competitors and establish a compelling and legitimate basis for consumer preference more than ever. Anholt argues that a good national image can only be earned, it cannot be constructed or invented, and 'imagining that such a deeply rooted phenomenon can be shifted by so weak an instrument as marketing communications is an extravagant delusion' (Anholt, 2007: 6). Anholt also acknowledges that tourism promotion is often the loudest voice in 'branding' the nation, as the 'tourist board usually has the biggest budgets and the most competent marketers' (Anholt, 2007: 25). In the book *Branding the Nation: The Global Business of National Identity*, Aronczyk has explored how nation branding has become a global phenomenon (Aronczyk, 2013). Kaneva has examined nation branding with a particular focus on post-communist European nations (Kaneva, 2012).

Having provided an overview of some of the theories of commercial nationalism and nation branding, this book aims to demystify the various ways in which the nation was imagined by key organisers and organisations and then communicated to millions. The meanings conveyed in the presentation of signifiers of nation will be investigated. As outlined earlier in the chapter, this edited volume investigates the concept of commercial nationalism as it relates to the presentation of national tourism stories and campaigns, along with key national events. The book explores the relationship between state appropriation of marketing strategies and the commercial use of nationalist discourses.

About this Book

As previously outlined, this book is divided into three sections: National Narratives, Heritage and Tourism; Tourism Branding and Promotion; and Festivals, Events and National Identity. A brief summary of each chapter follows.

Part 1: National Narratives, Heritage and Tourism

The first part of this book begins with Rettie's chapter on Canada. The author examines the contemporary role of Canada's national parks with respect to nationhood and tourism. Chapter 2 examines how national parks evoke values of conservation versus development, livelihood economics, environmental stewardship and personal enrichment. They also fulfil positions in relation to the national and the international stage. Canada's first national park was created as a means to generate the financial resources needed to complete the trans-continental railway that united the country and secured confederation. Today, aggressive tourism marketing strategies are designed to increase visitation as a means to support critical infrastructure reinvestments and shore up sparse federal funding. From the beginning, tourism has been the cornerstone of national parks existence in Canada. Rettie explains how the links between tourism and nationhood are historic, complex and, at times, controversial, and how the timeless debate over 'use versus preservation' continues.

In Chapter 3, Naef addresses the links between tourism and nationalism in the former Yugoslavia after the wars of the 1990s. Some conceptual insights into this broad issue are proposed, showing how post-conflict tourism can be exploited as a vector for nationalism. Naef explores this dynamic in Sarajevo, the capital of Bosnia–Herzegovina, and in Eastern Croatia, where a developing tourism sector is appearing, often involving narratives presenting the construction of the nation. These places are now experiencing a boom in the construction of museums and memorials linked to the recent wars. Furthermore, the memory of war is often mobilised in local tourism promotion, presenting some sites as symbols of resistance, sacrifice or independence. By looking specifically at two case studies, the Alija Izetbegović Museum and the management of tourism in Vukovar, Naef examines how nationalist narratives can clash with the multicultural image promoted in some developing tourist sites.

In Chapter 4, Iarmolenko, Kerstetter and Shahvali examine the process associated with developing a collective narrative of nationhood and heritage. This includes a discussion regarding how the results of in-depth interviews with fourth-wave Ukrainian immigrants were interpreted and combined into a narrative with a behavioural example of diaspora tourism. The authors also discuss how a sample of Ukrainian immigrants in the US responded to the resulting narrative. They close the chapter with a thoughtful examination of what was learned from individual Ukrainian's narratives of nationhood and heritage, the process of creating a collective narrative and the implications of using a collective narrative as a form of diaspora tourism promotion.

In the following chapter, Zhu and Yang look at how the ethno-religious identity of the Hui people is constructed within New Silk Road initiatives and the United Nations Educational, Scientific and Cultural Organization (UNESCO) Silk Road heritage project designed to link China and global Muslim communities through economic and cultural exchanges. Along the new trade route, cities in northwest China are transformed from inland second-tier cities to strategic points that extend China's frontiers beyond the territory of the People's Republic of China. Specifically, the city of Xi'an has become a site to revitalise memories of Muslims in Central Asia. In Chapter 5, the authors explore how local governments use the process of claiming Hui ethno-religious identity as an expedient resource to legitimise initiatives in tourism development and nation-building. Zhu and Yang examine how the Chinese central and local governments use storytelling as a strategy to realise the objective of becoming a global power.

Chapter 6 focuses on the changed narratives of the nation following the re-emergence of Hindu nationalism in India. The resounding victory of the Bharatiya Janata Party (BJP) in the 2014 national elections to form a majority government for the first time in three decades signalled the end of the era of coalition governments. More importantly, it marked a clear break with 'Nehruvian Consensus', the policy of inclusiveness and state action that directed nation-making since the country's independence in 1947. The ensuing debates on 'secularism' in the public space have impacted the 'national story'. Post-election, the efforts to invoke a new national imagery by the BJP government riding high on its electoral victory are evident. Ranganathan teases out the meta narrative of the 'imagined' nation through an examination of events relating to national history, culture and geography prior to and since the 2014 Indian elections.

In Chapter 7, the final one in Part 1: National Narratives, Heritage and Tourism, Clarke examines the complex challenges for the Silk Road. The project to relaunch the Silk Road has the task of repositioning the many claims and counterclaims for the route(s) as it promotes a coherent brand to hold together disparate nations bridging Europe and Asia. There is much talk about the need to create the new narrative for the Silk Road and within that narrative will emerge the basis for new commercial national-isms. The chapter examines the attempts to bring established identities together and forge a further dynamic identity for the route. The idea of routing through competing and disparate heritages raises issues of peace, tolerance and understanding. There are also some who question the authen-ticity of any/all claims for the route as Marco Polo is said to have written that he had only shared fewer than half of his stories from the journeys. Identities have been constructed and deconstructed and nations changed over time.

Part 2: Tourism Branding and Promotion

The second part of this book begins with Hall's chapter exploring the New Zealand 100% Pure brand campaign that is widely portrayed in the tourism branding literature as a highly successful campaign. In Chapter 8, Hall argues however that this is not the case. While 100% Pure is undoubt-edly a very successful tourism brand, it was never intended to be the national brand. Yet its very success meant that it has assumed that de facto role for many. The chapter examines the shifting fortunes of branding New Zealand and its association with tourism and events. It highlights the difficulties that governments have had in shifting perceptions of New Zealand in the inter-national arena compared with how many New Zealanders like to think of the value of how they are positioned with respect to a green landscape and the All Blacks. Such issues raise concerns not only for tourism but also, and perhaps more importantly in the longer term, for many of New Zealand's other industries.

In Chapter 9, Phelan examines the branding of nations in Africa. Brand South Africa was a government initiative launched in 2002 to attract tour-ism. It was based on the principle that the country was a unified entity, willing to overlook apartheid injustices and move forward for the greater good. Heritage tourism has become a significant sector among the African diaspora. In particular, many African Americans have travelled back to 'the

Motherland' to visit slave tourism attractions in an attempt to reconnect with their roots. West Africa, especially Senegal and Ghana, are significant slave tourism destinations. Many tourists to these areas are disappointed when they realise that locals do not associate themselves with the slave history. Thus, residents are profiting from tourism that they consider unrelated to their national identity. Perhaps the most recent, yet curious, example of African national identity being utilised for tourism purposes is Kenya. Since the election of US President Obama, Kenyans have promoted tourism as an opportunity for visitors to experience the hospitality of 'Obama's people'. The chapter utilises a case study approach to illustrate these three opposing methods by which different regions in Africa embrace or dismiss national identity in an effort to attract tourism.

In Chapter 10, Avellino Stewart and Cassar explore, through socio-historical and anthropological lenses, how the Maltese islands are being branded for tourism purposes. The authors focus on two main markets for Malta – Britain and Italy. They explore to what extent Malta's national texts and imagery used in the local tourism industry are borrowed from the culture of Britain, its ex-coloniser, and from Italy, its influential and culturally close neighbour. In today's Malta, the locals live out a dual reality based on the old political and cultural divisions: language, politics, economy and food. Research conducted by the authors indicates that, although the two extra-national references (Britain and Italy) are counter-poised to polarise Maltese identity, this same polarity is usefully managed to form the Malta nation brand so as to create that particular pull factor that serves to attract more tourists from these countries, culturally diverse but traditionally close to Malta, each in its own peculiar way.

Chapter 11 examines Brand Estonia. As a former Republic forcibly incorporated into the Soviet Union in 1944, Estonia has engaged in numerous campaigns to both define and market the nation since their return to independence in 1991. In parallel to Estonia's formal endeavours to brand itself, there also existed the branding and identity efforts of the Estonian diaspora. Because the Estonian nation was subsumed within the Soviet Union during more than four decades of the 20th century, it was the Estonia diaspora that helped to lead the shaping and branding of Estonia to the Western world. McKenzie selected Canada as the country to better understand the impact of that diaspora on nation branding and national imagery, as there are approximately 24,000 Canadians that identify themselves as of Estonian heritage, one of the largest populations outside of Estonia. In order to address the research question as to the influence that migration has played in shaping activities that have been shown to impact nation branding and the national image of Estonia, a case study is undertaken.

In Chapter 12, Singh examines controversies surrounding the 'Incredible India' tourism campaign which was launched in 2002. Singh argues that a lack of internal marketing of tourism and tourists led to the failure of the

'Incredible India' campaign. The chapter explores how this clearly shows that selling tourism should always involve selling the idea of what is expected of both guests (codes of conduct) and hosts (ethical behaviour), and that education about tourism should not be confined merely to universities, research institutes and guide-training centres, but also include the public at large. Education of the masses through public campaigns on the rights of women and stringent laws regarding crimes against them are also essential for the internal marketing of tourism.

In Chapter 13, the final chapter in Part 2: Tourism Branding and Promotion, Sanin examines how consecutive Colombian governments have used nation branding campaigns for advancing their agendas. These initiatives have attempted to improve the country's reputation, aiming to attract foreign investment, find markets for exports and attract international tourists. As part of these efforts, in 2013 the national government launched 'Colombia is Magical Realism'. The campaign alludes to the work of Colombian author Gabriel Garcia Marquez to convince travellers that they can have 'unique and magical experiences' in Colombia. According to government organisations and advertising agencies involved in the tourism campaign, its objective is to consolidate the achievements of previous campaigns by showing the charms of Colombian tourist destinations as well as the progress achieved in terms of 'security and stability'. Drawing on the notion of commercial nationalism, the chapter shows how this campaign combines elements from nationalism and consumer culture to reinvent the nation, its symbols and national identity. In particular, the chapter argues that 'Colombia is Magical Realism' attempts to construct a sense of Colombianness in which reality and fiction merge.

Part 3: Festivals, Events and National Identity

The third section of this book begins with a chapter by Rátz and Irimiás that examines the National Gallop – a horse race which was created in 2008 with the aim of reviving Hungary's ancient horse riding traditions in the form of a modern, urban cultural event. Horses have always played an important role both in Hungarian history and in the nation's tourist image: historically, Hungarians were renowned for their equestrian expertise. Traditional horse riding skills are regularly exhibited in the programme of organised tours to rural areas, and the country offers favourable conditions for equine tourism. Based on interviews with the founders, the organisers and representatives of the Hungarian tourism industry, content analysis of the event's media coverage and a survey undertaken by respondents who have visited the event, the authors analyse the history and the transformation of the National Gallop, a highly publicised and controversial commercial event, its role in helping create a national identity and its contribution to the tourist image of Hungary.

In Chapter 15, Basil examines Cherry Blossom celebrations – a ritual dating back more than 1000 years in Japan. Many marketing scholars believe that our contemporary celebrations often undergo commercialisation and globalisation. Basil conducted an analysis of cherry blossom celebrations in Japan and around the world to examine the extent to which this celebration reflects these forces. Hanami celebrations in Japan still centre on the search for cherry blossoms and finding ways to capture the ephemeral aspects of the blossoms and the season. There are also established 'sakura' activities such as the consumption of sake and seasonal foods, and quasi-pilgrimages to sacred sites as venerated parts of the celebration. In other parts of the world, cherry blossom celebrations morph from a private observance of nature and the season to a more formalised and commercial celebration of Japanese culture. In essence, cherry blossom festivals tell a different but related story domestically and internationally, yet demonstrating commercialisation, globalisation and 'glocalisation'.

In Chapter 16, Martin and Marcotte examine Canadian memorial tours of the centenary of the First World War – a war that was considered a defining moment in the creation of the national identity of former British colonies. These emerging countries considered the building of war memorials as a way of embodying the part played by their young nations in the establishment of the new world order. For the centennial of the First World War, these countries' memorials, cemeteries and battle sites were restored, and brand new museums and interpretation centres opened to describe and explain the part they played in the war. The authors found that Canadian memorials, however, focus on an exclusively national memory, a memory of battle, sacrifice and victory. This is obviously at odds with the memory of wars in Europe. Moreover, the strong national symbols presented in those battle sites contrast with the popular and social memory preserved in the surrounding towns and villages. The chapter begins with an analysis of the contemporary representation of Canadian nationalism in the symbolism of First World War memorials. The authors then explain how those two opposing kinds of memory, the military and the popular, are expressed in memorial tours of the centennial.

In the following chapter, Tham explores how Singapore's Golden Jubilee event (SG50) was celebrated both in Brisbane and Singapore in 2015. Drawing on a mixed-methods approach of participant observation and content analysis from online sources, Tham examines how commercial nationalism can apply to the notion of hot authenticity within tourism and events. Singapore's Golden Jubilee provided the stage to showcase what the country has achieved over 50 years. SG50 took more than two years to plan and execute because of the consultative approach taken by all stakeholders to ensure that the country's success story was reflective of the multi-racial fabric of its citizens. The chapter constructs an appreciation of commercial nationalism from an Asian perspective. The emergence of Asia as a pillar of today's economy will undoubtedly compel other nations to strengthen their national brand.

In Chapter 18, Wise and Harris examine the national story of Clint Dempsey, who is referred to as 'Captain America' based on his role and performance at the 2014 Fédération Internationale de Football Association (FIFA) World Cup in Brazil. It is difficult to imagine that an American athlete who plays soccer (football) might be granted the title 'Captain America' in a sport that ranks quite low in the sporting milieu of the US. However, every so often, realistically every four years when the country qualifies and competes in the FIFA World Cup, the nation seems interested in the other type of football (soccer). The authors' analysis consists of a qualitative content analysis of major US newspapers and other sporting media outlets that were available during the 2014 FIFA World Cup. Moreover, the chapter critically frames the role of Dempsey as 'Captain America' as a way of re(imagining) the nation every four years when the media attention in the US focuses on soccer and away from what are considered the big four (American Football, Baseball, Basketball and Ice Hockey) professional sports in the country.

In Chapter 19, Neilson examines a Canadian music festival, the Folksong and Handicraft Festival for the New Canadians at Winnipeg, and how it served to influence ideas about new immigrants. The events that led to the publication of the award-winning book *Canadian Mosaic* and the subsequent influence of the book on Canadian politicians and immigration policy are also explored in this chapter. In Canada, the expression 'Canadian mosaic' suggests a way of thinking about the citizens of the nation that marks them as distinct from other nations, in particular, the 'melting pot' of the US. Neilson argues that, although Canadians acknowledge that the ideal is often not attainable, many still choose to see their country as a place where multiple cultures live in relative unity, each contributing the best of its ethnic heritage to the nation's brand equity. Yet many Canadians would be surprised to learn that the phrase, or self-sustaining myth, was popularised not by a politician or cultural policy maker, but by a marketer – John Murray Gibbon, general publicity agent for the Canadian Pacific Railway.

In the concluding chapter, I summarise the book's contents and main themes by contrasting the chapter contents and some of the key conclusions. The chapter also suggests future research themes and topics.

Conclusion

Visits to sites of significance play an important part in a nation's image and identity. Thus, this book provides a range of case studies to illustrate various aspects of commercial nationalism, tourism and events through the lenses of national narratives, national identity and branding.

This book – a reference text aimed principally at the academic market – is designed to address the significant void that currently exists in commercial nationalism as it relates specifically to tourism and events. This edited volume of 20 chapters might serve as a prescribed text for postgraduate coursework units and/or a recommended reading for advanced undergraduate and postgraduate students in a number of discipline areas such as marketing, tourism or events. The book will also be of interest to the many academics around the globe and other interested stakeholders including those in the tourism industry, event organisers, marketers, government bodies and community groups.

I trust that you will be inspired by the diverse international cases of national identity, tourism and events as they relate to commercial nationalism that are enthusiastically explored in this volume.

References

Akotia, M., Spio, A., Frimpong, K. and Austin, N. (2011) Country branding: A developing economy perspective. *International Journal of Business Strategy* 11 (2), 123–131.

Anderson, B. (1983) *Imagined Communities: Reflections on the Origins and Spread of Nationalism.* London: Verso.

Anholt, S. (2007) *Competitive Identity: The New Brand Management for Nations, Cities and Regions.* Basingstoke: Palgrave Macmillan.

Anholt, S. (2010) Definitions of place branding – Working towards a resolution. *Place Branding and Public Diplomacy* 6, 1–10.

Anholt, S. (2012) Practioners insight: From nation branding to competitive identity. In K. Dinnie (ed.) *Nation Branding, Concepts, Issues, Practice* (pp. 22–30). Oxford: Butterworth-Heinemann.

Aronczyk, M. (2013) *Branding the Nation: The Global Business of National Identity.* London: Oxford University Press.

Billig, M. (1995) *Banal Nationalism.* London: Sage.

Bryden-Brown, J. (1981) *Ads that Made Australia: How Advertising Has Shaped our History and Lifestyle.* Lane Cove: Doubleday.

Carroll, B. (1974) *The Australian Poster Album.* Melbourne: Sun Books.

Carroll, B. (1975) *The Australian Advertising Album.* South Melbourne: Macmillan.

Cozzolino, M. (1980) *Symbols of Australia.* Ringwood: Penguin.

Crawford, R. (2008) *But Wait, There's More… : A History of Australian Advertising, 1900–2000.* Carlton: Melbourne University Press.

Culler, J. and Cheah, P. (eds) (2003) *Grounds of Comparison: Around the work of Benedict Anderson.* New York: Routledge.

Dinnie, K. (ed.) (2012) *Nation Branding, Concepts, Issues, Practice.* Oxford: Butterworth-Heinemann.

Falassi, A. (1987) Festival: Definition and morphology. In A. Falassi (ed.) *Time out of Time: Essays on the Festival* (pp. 1–10). Albuquerque, NM: University of New Mexico Press.

Foster, R. (1995) *Nation Making: Emergent Identities in Postcolonial Melanesia.* Ann Arbor, MI: University of Michigan Press.

Gammon, S. (2007) Introduction: Sport, heritage and the English. An opportunity missed? In S. Gammon and G. Ramshaw (eds) *Heritage, Sport and Tourism: Sporting Pasts – Tourist Futures* (pp. 1–8). Abingdon: Routledge.

Gnoth, J. (2002) Leveraging export brands through a tourism destination brand. *Brand Management* 9 (4–5), 262–280.

Hall, C.M. (1997) *Hallmark Tourist Events: Impacts, Management and Planning*. Chichester: John Wiley and Sons.

James, P. (1983) Australia in the corporate image: A new nationalism. *Arena* 63, 65–106.

James, P. (1996) *Nation Formation: Towards a Theory of Abstract Community*. London: Sage.

Kaneva, N. (2012) *Branding Post-Communist Nations: Marketizing National Identities in the 'New' Europe*. Abingdon: Routledge.

Khamis, S. (2007) Bushells and the cultural logic of branding. Doctor of Philosophy thesis, Department of Media and Communication, Macquarie University, Sydney.

Kociumbas, J. (2003) Performances: Indigenisation and postcolonial culture. In H. Teo and R. White (eds) *Cultural History in Australia* (pp. 127–141). Sydney: University of New South Wales Press.

Mackay, H. (1999) *Turning Point: Australians Choosing their Future*. Sydney: Macmillan.

Morgan, N., Pritchard, A. and Pride, R. (2004) *Destination Branding: Creating the Unique Destination Proposition* (2nd edn). Oxford: Butterworth-Heinemann.

Olins, W. (2002) Branding the nation – The historical context. *Journal of Brand Management* 9 (4–5), 241–248.

O'Sullivan, T., Hartley, J., Saunders, D., Montgomery, M. and Fiske, J. (1994) *Key Concepts in Communication and Cultural Studies* (2nd edn). London: Routledge.

Ozkirimli, U. (2000) *Theories of Nationalism: A Critical Introduction*. Basingstoke: Macmillan.

Pretes, M. (2003) Tourism and nationalism. *Annals of Tourism Research* 30 (1), 125–142.

Roche, M. (2000) *Mega-events and Modernity: Olympics and Expos in the Growth of Global Culture*. London: Routledge.

Seal, G. (2004) *Inventing Anzac: The Digger and National Mythology*. St Lucia: University of Queensland Press.

Shoebridge, N. (1992) *Great Australian Advertising Campaigns*. Sydney: McGraw-Hill.

Sinclair, J. (1987) *Images Incorporated: Advertising and Ideology*. London: Croom Helm.

Smith, L. (2006) *The Uses of Heritage*. Abingdon: Routlege.

Spearritt, P. (1992) Foreward. In A. Shiell and A. Stephen (eds) *The Lie of the Land*. Clayton: National Centre for Australian Studies, Monash University.

Spillman, L. (1997) *Nation and Commemoration: Creating National Identities in the United States and Australia*. New York: Cambridge University Press.

Tomlinson, A. (2000) Carrying the torch for whom? Symbolic power and olympic ceremony. In K. Schaffer and S. Smith (eds) *The Olympics at the Millennium: Power, Politics and the Games* (pp. 167–181). New Jersey: Rutgers University Press.

Turner, G. (1986) *National Fictions: Literature, Film and the Construction of Australian Narrative*. St Leonards: Allen and Unwin.

Turner, G. (1993) *National Fictions: Literature, Film and the Construction of Australian Narrative* (2nd edn). St Leonards: Allen and Unwin.

Volcic, Z. and Andrejevic, M. (2015) *Commercial Nationalism: Selling the Nation and Nationalizing the Sell*. Basingstoke: Palgrave Macmillan.

Waterton, E. (2010) *Politics, Policy and the Discourses of Heritage in Britain*. Basingstoke: Palgrave Macmillan.

White, L. (1984) The selling of Australia. Minor thesis, Humanities Department, Footscray Institute of Technology, Footscray.

White, L. (1994) Commercial nationalism: Images of Australia in television advertising. Master of Arts Research thesis, Humanities Department, Victoria University, Footscray.

White, L. (2004) The bicentenary of Australia: Celebration of a nation. In L. Fuller (ed.) *National Days/National Ways: Historical, Political and Religious Celebrations around the World*. Westport, CT: Praeger.

White, L. (2009) The man from Snowy River: Australia's bush legend and commercial nationalism. *Tourism Review International* 13 (2), 139–146.

Willis, A. (1993) *Illusions of Identity: The Art of Nation*. Sydney: Hale and Ironmonger.

Part 1

National Narratives, Heritage and Tourism

2 Canada's National Parks: Nationhood, Tourism and the Utility of Nature

Kathleen Rettie

Introduction

As the name implies, national parks are for the nation. The link between national parks and nationhood, especially in Canada, is a relationship that permits one to associate pride in the protection of nature with national importance, and to address other universal concepts such as preservation for future generations. As the mandate dictates, national parks are for use and for preservation; the utilitarian aspects extend beyond this. Founded in the worthless land hypothesis, the aesthetic values of the national park landscapes soon translated into tangible economic benefits that were later recognised for their social, political and ecological values. Throughout history, tourism has played an essential role in the growth and continuance of national parks. As important elements of the nation's story and ensuing image on the international stage, the 'selling' of Canada's national parks through tourism constitutes a unique form of commercial nationalism.

In the late 1800s and early 1900s, the majority of new Canadian national parks were created in the west and the Rocky Mountains because of the aesthetic value of the landscape and the desire of government and the railroad companies to develop the western provinces through tourism (Hall & Shultis, 1991). Between 1938 and 1957, five national parks were created in the maritimes, the primary purpose being to act as regional economic growth poles, as well as becoming recreation spaces for citizens. In 1972, a formal park expansion system was announced, the main objective being the representation of each unique natural quality in Canada (Parks Canada, 2015a). The expansion of the system since 1973 to the present day has witnessed the development of 24 parks, primarily in Yukon and the Northwest and Nunavut Territories with limited establishment on the west coast,

Newfoundland and Labrador (Boyd & Butler, 2009: 109). To date there are 40 national parks and national park reserves representing 24 of the 39 distinct land types identified; the system is just over 60% complete (Parks Canada, 2015a). This chapter examines aspects of nationhood, tourism, utilitarian values and 21st century controversies associated with Canada's national parks.

Nationhood

While there is some debate over the origin of the term 'national park' (Boyd & Butler, 2000; Frost & Hall, 2009a; Sellars, 1997), ranging from Catlin's reference to Yosemite as a 'national public park' (Runte, 1990: 33) to Wordsworth's guide to England Lake District as a 'sort of national property' (quoted in Frost & Hall, 2009b: 23), there is sufficient evidence that national parks have a role in defining national identity and, in the case of Canada, even securing the confederation of a nation. In many ways, national parks tell the nation's story.

In the mid-1880s, the Canadian Pacific Railway (CPR) was constructing a rail line across Canada to open the west to settlement and to ensure that the territory of British Columbia was encompassed within Canada's confederation. The section of track through Canada's Rocky Mountains was exceedingly expensive to build. In 1883, railway workers discovered sulphur hot springs at the base of a mountain adjacent to what is now the town of Banff. To offset the costs of rail line construction the Prime Minister provided the CPR with an opportunity to build a luxury hotel near the hot springs. The scheme was simple: wealthy tourists from Europe and eastern Canada and the United States, attracted by the Rocky Mountain scenery and the health benefits of the hot springs, would pay to ride the train and stay in the hotel; the CPR would reap the monetary benefits (Bella, 1987; Boyd & Butler, 2000: 16). The venture worked out well for the CPR; the rail line that connected Canada from coast to coast was completed, opening the west to settlement and the development of extractive industries such as lumbering and mining (Frost & Hall, 2009a: 33). In 1885, lands adjacent to the hot springs were designated the Rocky Mountain National Park, Canada's first national park.

Since the 1860s, North America's natural beauty has attained symbolic value in what it could mean to the national culture by rivalling Europe's grandeur in built heritage and art, affirming that that the new nations are not inferior to Europe (Runte, 1990: 15). The CPR's promotional materials and commissioned artists depicted the majesty of the Canada's Rocky Mountains and the west coast, representing 'the first significant instance of a widespread acceptance in Canada of the myth of the land as the basis of national art' (Reid, 1979 in Frost & Hall, 2009c: 69). Landscape serves as a source of shared heritage and collective identity (Frost & Hall, 2009a; Meining, 1979), particularly in nations, like Canada, where peoples of disparate ethnic backgrounds came together to make the new nation. 'Landscapes are compelling symbols of national identity, and each person treasures those unique physical features that are distinctly theirs' (Lowenthal, 1997: 198).

Early concepts of national parks expressed the importance of nationalism and, as expressed by President Taft in support of the world's first national park in Yellowstone, the 'consideration of patriotism and the love of nature ... the accessibility and usefulness that would bring all these natural wonders within easy reach of our people' (American Civic Association, 1912). In more recent nationalistic verbiage, the parks are symbols of national heritage and evoke a sense of pride in what it means, in this case, to be Canadian. 'Our parks are the birth-right of every Canadian. Banff National Park will always be a place to visit, to experience, to discover and learn about. [It is] a place where one truly feels what it means to be Canadian' (Parks Canada, 1997a).

Parks serve as important vehicles for spreading messages about national identity. The social and political capital attached to the title 'national' is significant; one could say they are 'consciously created as national parks because of their significance to the national identity' (Frost & Hall, 2009c: 76–77). This political capital is not lost on politicians who 'use' national parks to their advantage; for example, at a time when Canadians were divided over unity (the Quebec issue), it was politically expedient to hold up a proud (and unified) Canadian heritage. The administration of national parks was moved to the Department of Canadian Heritage with the accompanying rhetoric about presenting our proud heritage to the world. Parks Canada-sponsored surveys between 1994 and 2003 demonstrate that national parks are consistently third or fourth on Canadians' list of 'important symbols of being Canadian'. According to the surveys, national parks are less important than the Canadian Health Care System, the Charter of Rights and Freedoms and the flag, but more important than the national anthem and the Royal Canadian Mounted Police (Parks Canada, 2015b).

National parks are used to mark disputed territories as belonging to a particular country. National parks developed in the Canadian north were, in part, the result of a political gesture of sovereignty. They also mark the emergence of national parks on lands where native peoples live, thereby necessitating negotiations that lead to the co-management of nature reserves in line with national park policy (Boyd & Butler, 2009: 108). One example of this is the establishment of Ellesmere Island National Park Reserve in 1988. Covering much of the northern part of Ellesmere Island, it represents the eastern high Arctic natural region with a mandate to protect its constituent species and to conserve the ecology. In 2000, the Reserve was elevated in status to Quittinirpaaq National Park, a process accompanied by re-populating this remote region with a Canadian presence (Dick, 2001: 267–307). Importantly, there is an agreement to work closely with the local communities (Dick, 2001: 489–490).

When discussing nationhood, one should not overlook the more tangible connections between Canadians and their national parks. Lands within the national parks are the property of the federal government and allocations drawn on general tax revenue constitute the key source of funding; therefore, the parks belong to the citizens of Canada. The parks are managed on behalf of Canadians by the Parks Canada Agency. Public opinion sometimes sets the tone for management actions; in 1960, in response to the outcry of Canadian citizens opposing extensive development at Lake Louise, in Banff National Park, Canada's National Parks Act (NPA) was amended to include a provision for public consultation on all park management plans; henceforth, the public has a legislated mechanism for direct involvement in the future of their national parks.

Tourism helps to construct national identity as it encourages people to visit sites of national importance and reinforces their national pride and sense of connection (Frost & Hall, 2009c: 64). The international attraction to these places affirms their importance as iconic destinations and showcases the nations' treasures to the world. Commercial nationalism emerges in the form of national park-based tourism.

Tourism

The Canadian national parks system is founded on the economic benefits of tourism (Bella, 1987: 1–3). Chapter 32 of the original Rocky Mountain Parks Act (1887) states that there would 'not be issued any leases, license or permit that would impair the usefulness of the park for the purposes of public enjoyment and recreation. There can be few clearer statements of the importance of the place of recreation (tourism) in a new park' (Boyd & Butler, 2000: 17).

As noted earlier, the profits from tourism were connected to the completion of the railway and the confederation of the country. The motto, 'If we can't export the scenery, we will import the tourists', was touted by the General Manager of the CPR (Hart, 1983: 7). The scenic and natural values of landscape soon evoked monetary meanings as well as aesthetic ones. Designated in 1885, Banff National Park was truly a park for profit (Bella, 1987). As noted by John Shultis:

The first national parks were created at a time in Canadian history where the development of natural resources was governments' main objective. Liberalism was the dominant ideology, and the 'doctrine of usefulness' the primary driver of government land-use policies. Early national parks focused on attracting visitors to generate public and political support for these areas. (Shultis, 2012)

There is a long history of tailoring the attractions to suit the visitor (Sellars, 1997: 88). The general impression of tourists visiting parks at the end of the 19th century was of affluent, privileged individuals, frequently foreign, often on long trips of several months' duration with visits to the new parks as one feature of an exploratory journey to the 'New Worlds'. Often trains served as travelling hotels (Butler & Boyd, 2000: 6). In her history of Banff National Park, Eleanor Luxton (1975) details the early days of hunting, outfitting and alpinism attracting an elite clientele. This was followed in the early 1900s by the construction of roads, a golf course, ski hills, campgrounds, affordable accommodation and even a zoo to attract a broader range of visitors who, owing to improved labour conditions and wages, could afford a national park experience. Tourism growth remained incremental during the post-Second World War period as North Americans sought the respite of nature-based leisure and recreation. Many families could afford an automobile and the annual family camping trip to a national park gained popularity (Wilson, 1991). Since the 1960s, the earlier park systems have struggled to accommodate ever-increasing numbers of visitors expecting to enjoy and participate in new forms of tourism and recreation activity (Butler & Boyd, 2000: 9).

Visitation to national parks can reasonably be regarded as a form of heritage tourism (Banff Heritage Tourism Corporation, 2004; Butler, 2000: 330; Parks Canada, 1997b). In the mid-1990s, following a comprehensive study on the impact of tourism on the ecosystem, heritage tourism took root in Banff National Park. Ideally, heritage tourism would highlight the purpose of the park as a place for nature and a place for people. The strategy aligns with the theory that 'tourism dollars foster community and national support for economic and conservation benefits' (March, 2000: 131). The strategy has four broad aims:

(1) Make sure visitors are aware they are in a national park.
(2) Encourage opportunities, products and services that are consistent with heritage values.
(3) Foster environmental stewardship.
(4) Strengthen employee knowledge of heritage values through training and accreditation. For example, train front-line hotel and restaurant staff in the natural and human history of the park (Banff Heritage Tourism Corporation, 2004).

The strategy was written into the 1997 Banff Park Management Plan; to date, a measurement of its success has not been undertaken.

The ongoing debate over use versus preservation, the 'dual purpose' in the national parks mandate, pits tourism and its tangible benefits against the more altruistic benefits of nationhood, conservation and preservation for future generations. Competing and complementary aspects of national parks are discussed next.

The Utilitarian Nature of National Parks

In 1916 the United States invoked the Organic Act (1916) in an attempt to balance tourism and conservation in its parks. The Act was mimicked in the NPA in 1930, and has been adopted almost verbatim by numerous nations since. The Canadian version is as follows:

> The National Parks of Canada are hereby dedicated to the people of Canada for their benefit, education and enjoyment, subject to the Act and regulations, and the National Parks shall be maintained and made use of so as to leave them unimpaired for the enjoyment of future generations. (Government of Canada, 2000)

This mandate exemplifies the utilitarian aspects of national parks (Sellars, 1997: 188) that translates into conservation and ecological standpoints as well as the aesthetic, recreation and tourism perspectives (Hall & Frost, 2009a: 7).

National parks are historically seated in the 'worthless land hypothesis' described by Alfred Runte as follows: '[early] national parks protected only such areas as were considered valueless for profitable lumbering, mining, grazing or agriculture' (Runte, 1979 in Hall & Frost, 2009b: 47). There were several boundary changes to the Rocky Mountain National Park (later Banff National Park) to remove resource rich-exploitable lands, the final being in 1923 to remove lands for a hydro-electric project (Johnston & Marsh, 1986). In 2012, the boundaries for Naats'ihch'oh National Park Reserve in the North West Territories were re-drawn to purposely exclude sites with mineral deposits (Canadian Broadcasting Corporation, 2012).

The national park mandate speaks to the use and preservation of national park resources; neither is exclusive. As once stated by J.B. Harkin, Canadian Commissioner of National Parks: 'The parks will pay not only in the strictly commercial dollars and cents way but they will also pay in a still more important way by adding to the efficiency and vitality of the nation' (Lothian, 1979: 16). National parks were key in meeting railroad company and government goals to develop the western provinces through tourism. 'The economic value of tourism provided a valuable weapon for preservationists in the development of more parks and the protection of others. Tourism gave parks a material value' (Frost & Hall, 2009b: 49).

When considering the preservation or existence value, there is an enormous felt or emotive difference between feeling that a place should be valued or respected for itself, for its perceived beauty and character, and feeling that it should not be defaced because it is valued by one's fellow humans, and provides pleasurable sensations, money or convenience for them (Routley & Routley, 2000: 141). This is usually coupled with an altruistic motive, where nature takes on yet another value, that is, the bequest of natural environments to future generations. In biocentric thinking it is the mere existence of the asset that is being bequeathed. The expectation is that the asset will be appreciated and valued in the same way by that future generation (Pearce et al., 2000: 178).

The equation, simply stated, is: intrinsic value = existence value. Assigning economic value to something's existence, and not use, seems superfluous. However, concepts of nature preservation comprise the core of environmental funding and of campaigns for the protection of endangered species and natural environments. As human use increased from 1980 onwards, extra provisions were made for the protection of native species including restricted access to popular trails and seasonal area closures to allow for wildlife migration. Under these policies, 'existence value' legitimates the taxpayers' dollars and entrance fees that go towards the preservation of non-usable or non-convertible-to-cash resources.

There is a convincing argument that one cannot put a value on the environment (Pearce et al., 2000: 181). The utilitarian measure is one of rating human preference with respect to the environment. Here environmental economists have developed a taxonomy of economic values reflected in the following formula: Total use value = Actual use value + Option value. Actual use value refers to direct benefit, for example fishing, bird watching and photography. Option value refers to potential benefit as opposed to actual present use value. It is an expression of preference, a willingness to pay for the preservation of the environment against the probability that the individual will make use of it at a later date. It relates to the availability or supply of the environment, and the theory is that this optional value is likely to be positive (Pearce et al., 2000: 175–176).

In the 1990s, public debates ensued over 'use versus preservation' or more to the point 'development versus conservation'. A moratorium on development was instituted while a series of government-sponsored studies assessing the environmental impacts of the ever increasing use in national parks were conducted. As a result of the studies' findings highlighting concerns over the impairment of natural resources, the NPA was amended in 2000 to include Section 8.2:

Maintenance or restoration of ecological integrity, through the protection of natural resources and natural processes, shall be the first priority of the Minister when considering all aspects of the management of parks. (Government of Canada, 2000)

Ideally this would make decision-making easier for park superintendents by giving them the power to err on the side of conservation when new developments were proposed. The emphasis on ecological integrity (EI) was reinforced when CDN$20 million (US$15 million) was allocated for the identification of EI indicators and new staff positions dedicated to EI research and monitoring.

Beyond use and preservation, the utilitarian nature of national parks extends to a role in reinforcing national sentiments. It also permits a positive government presence in the public domain, as opposed to the chronically unpleasant one associated with taxes, audits and restrictive policies. National parks are also a symbol of a nation's environmental ethic and as such can present either a positive or negative image to the world at large.

As discussed next, Canadians' views and attitudes, shifts in management policies, fiscal realities and the ongoing debates over use versus preservation are the face of Canada's national parks in today's world.

National Parks Today

Public attitudes towards national parks have been the focus of recent studies. With respect to national identity, a survey in Waterton Lakes National Parks revealed that, when asked 'In your view, what is the key purpose(s) of national parks?', all participants provided at least one view (N = 450). The majority (69.8%) felt that the protection of wildlife and natural resources was a key purpose. Providing recreational opportunities such as hiking, picnicking and camping were also high on the list. The least significant purpose was to promote national identity; only 1.8% of those surveyed thought it was a key purpose (Parks Canada, 2012a)

The 2009 Environics survey of over 3,700 Canadians revealed that, in terms of national parks, almost 6 in 10 Canadians (59%) believe that these parks are created mainly to protect natural wilderness areas threatened by human development. Canadians are most likely to indicate that ensuring these places are available for present and future generations should be very important to Parks Canada (87%) while two-thirds (68%) believe that providing opportunities for Canadians to discover and experience national parks and providing important examples of Canada's geography and ecology should also be important. Support is highest for using tax dollars to maintain existing national parks (95%); less than half (47%) support the use of tax dollars to create new parks (Environics, 2009).

Canadians' debatable enthusiasm for new national parks is evident from the ongoing efforts to establish a new national park in the Southern Okanagan region of British Columbia. The aversion to federal interference, new restrictions and questionable economic benefits (Oliver Daily News, 2015) is countered by proponents who see the creation of a park as protecting a legacy in a unique desert landscape (Mason, 2014; Canadian Parks and Wilderness Society, 2015). Others anticipate an increase in regional employment through Parks Canada-based jobs (personal communication, J. Wyse and D. Olson). The province of British Columbia remains unsupportive and the debate continues.

Parks Canada has recently shifted its focus away from maintaining or restoring ecological integrity as the first priority. Since 2005, annual budget allocations for visitor experience have increased while allocations for resource conservation have decreased. Scientists and research support staff were negatively affected by job losses and depleted resources. Under the new regime, connecting Canadians with their parks, through increased visitation, has become a critical goal.

> Canada's treasured natural and historic places will be a living legacy, connecting hearts and minds to a stronger, deeper understanding of the very essence of Canada.

> Parks Canada will pursue this vision and accomplish its strategic outcome by ensuring Agency activities are relevant to Canadians and thus strengthen and deepen Canadians' understanding and appreciation of their national heritage places. This will, in turn, build a strong sense of connection to these places in the hearts and minds of Canadians. (Parks Canada, 2010)

The Agency has set the target that 60% of Canadians report a personal connection to Parks Canada-administered places by March 2015 (Parks Canada, 2014). Support for this shift in focus lies with building a constituency of support and a culture of conservation. However, there are serious undertones that this refocusing of resources and the accompanying rhetoric has more to do with increasing visitation as a means to exploit 'use' value for economic gain. The first priority presented in the Parks Canada's 2014–2015 Report on Plans and Priorities is: 'Increase revenue through more visitors and more revenue per visitor' (Parks Canada, 2014). The current annual visitation target is 22.4 million visits to Parks Canada-administered places by March 2015; this is equivalent to an 8% increase in visitation over the approximately 20.8 million visits in 2008/2009 (Parks Canada, 2012b).

Logically, Parks Canada is concerned over flagging attendance to United States' national parks, fearing the trend will move north to Canada. As reported by Stevens et al. (2014), since 1997 the US National Parks Service has recorded stagnant and, in some cases, more than a 7% decrease in visitation to its national parks. Entrance and user fees comprise a major share of the funds required for Parks Canada's operations; a decrease in visitor revenue would therefore have serious implications across the national parks system.

Across the Agency, discourse focuses on goals to reach what are perceived to be under-represented sectors of the visiting population, primarily youth and ethnic minorities. Efforts to draw first-time visitors include 'oTENTiks' (canvas wall tents with beds and private barbeques for first-time campers). New activities have been introduced including Via Ferrata climbing routes and zip-lines. Special events such as 'Gran Fondo' bike races, runners' marathons, music concerts and cultural activities that bring participants, along with family and friends, to the park are promoted. As well, Parks Canada is focusing on the development of facilities that will attract new audiences, often relying upon the private sector as proponents. This has resulted in 'new and significant impacts upon the environments of parks [and] a mismatch of demand and supply. Visitors coming to parks … find facilities which are inappropriate for national parks purposes' (Butler, 2000: 328). The development of new facilities or disappointed visitors can cause problems in terms of maintaining a park's ecological quality and diversity (Butler, 2000; Canadian Parks and Wilderness Society, 2012; Wright, 2012). Expansion of certain tourist attractions sparks considerable public criticism, a recent example being the construction of the Glacier Skywalk (a suspended viewing platform) at the Columbia Icefield in Jasper National Park. 'No Glacier Skywalk' was an aggressive, but unsuccessful, campaign focusing on potentially negative ecological impacts.

In step with efforts to increase visitation, Agency funding for 2014/2015 was higher for visitor experience and marketing than for resource conservation (Parks Canada, 2014). Visitation targets and the shift away from a 'nature conservation first' approach to management has raised serious concerns over the future of the national parks and sparked controversy over whether or not the Agency is contravening the Canada National Parks Act (Canadian Parks and Wilderness Society, 2012). At stated by John Shultis:

> More than a century later, after the national parks had re-focused their policies towards the preservation of ecological integrity, several shifts in political and social forces have meant that park management has once again swung towards neo-liberalism and a focus on use versus preservation. The role of declining visitation in national parks has played a key role in this recent shift, although the rise of neo-liberal ideology has also had significant impacts on the recent shift towards an emphasis on use over preservation in Canadian national parks. (Shultis, 2012)

There is recognition for value in a trade-off analysis that would fairly weigh use and non-use values of parks. Tom Nudds, University of Guelph (Department of Integrative Biology) and a member of the 1998 Panel on the Ecological Integrity in Canada's National Parks, advises that:

> Recent studies suggest that non-use values of national parks to Canadians outweigh potential use values that could be realized without

undermining EI. These studies call into question whether Parks Canada needs to open its collective gates to greater visitor use, and put at risk parks' important roles as ecological baselines against which to measure ecosystem change. (Nudds, 2012)

The economic (use) value of Canada's national parks has been measured in dollars and cents. As reported by Outspan Groups Inc. (2011), national parks contributed CDN$2.405 billion (US$1.732 billion) to Canada's gross domestic product and CDN$1.5 billion (US$1.08 billion) to labour income in 2008/2009. Employment attributable to national parks was calculated at 32,757 FTEs (full-time employment equivalents) along with over CDN$161 million (US$115.9 million) in tax revenue. National park visitors spent CDN$2.269 billion (US$1.634 billion) on goods and services in and while travelling to national parks, thereby regionally expanding the economic impact. Overall, revenues substantially offset Parks Canada's CDN$383 million (US$275.7 million) in national park-based expenditures for 2008/2009 (Outspan Groups Inc., 2011).

Ironically, while increased park visitation is targeted as a source of extra revenue, federal allocations for the operation of parks have been significantly reduced, thereby reducing the services that attract visitors. Budget cuts at Parks Canada have been ramping up since 2012 to reach a total of over CDN$50 million by 2015. Cuts are being addressed by reducing staff, shortening operating seasons and replacing interpreter-guided tours with self-guided tours. The government's CDN$2.8 billion (US$2.02 billion) for infrastructure investment announced in spring 2015 is targeted at the maintenance and refurbishing of existing roads and buildings, many built in the 1950s and 1960s (Parks Canada, 2015c), and therefore will not offset shortfalls in operating budgets.

Conclusion

National parks evoke values of conservation versus development, livelihood economics, environmental stewardship and personal enrichment; they fulfil positions in relation to the national and the international stage.

Since their inception, Canada's national parks have been subject to management regimes that respond to economically and politically driven agendas. Commercial nationalism was evident early on as tourism was promoted to increase the value of the land and secure confederation. In the early 1900s, under Harkin, conservation was added to the agenda. After the Second World War, attractions and infrastructure, such as roads, campgrounds and ski areas, were developed in response to the dramatic increase in visitation accorded by North Americans' search for nature-based leisure activities and family-owned automobiles that mobilised new sectors of the population.

Public response to 'over development' in the late 1960s invoked an amendment to the NPA to include provisions for public consultation on national park management plans. In the 1980s, the term 'ecological integrity' appeared in Parks Canada policy documents, introducing a shift towards research and monitoring of species that would determine the state of parks' natural resources. Public debates over conservation versus development in the 1990s prompted a series of national studies focused on the future health of national parks. In 2000, the NPA was amended to declare the maintenance or restoration of ecological integrity as Parks Canada's first priority. Most recently, there has been an enthusiastic return to the development of new attractions and infrastructure as a means to promote tourism accompanied by a lesser focus on resource conservation.

Conservation is the tool that sustains the natural heritage and environment that attracts the tourists, subsequently increasing the landscapes' use and non-use value. Tourists have unique expectations when they visit national parks: natural beauty, peace and solitude, safe well-maintained services (i.e. campgrounds, roads, washrooms, visitor information centres), recreational opportunities, wildlife sightings, adventure and communing with nature in its natural state. Funding, secured through tourism and government allocations, supports conservation-based and visitor experience-based management practices. Recent government cutbacks to Parks Canada budgets are forcing a shift to a tourist economy that will offset parks' operating deficits. The emphasis on marketing and visitor experience over resource conservation, as evidenced in current plans and priorities documents, raises serious concerns over the future state of the ecological integrity of the parks' resources.

National parks matter to Canadians. They value access to their national parks and all that the parks have to offer. Canadians who do not exercise direct access still have a strong affiliation through a sense of pride in their nation's choice and ability to showcase and protect their country's natural treasures. It is not surprising, then, that decisions affecting the future of national parks attract public interest and controversy. The roots of controversy, often, are in the uneasy balance between use and preservation where use is linked to tourism and economic gain and preservation – or non-use – is linked to nationhood, pride, ecological integrity and the nation's approach to conservation. The two are not exclusive; what is often at issue is the over emphasis on one or the other.

References

American Civic Association (1912) President Taft on a National Parks Bureau, address to the American Civic Association. In *National Parks – the Need of the Future*. Washington, DC: Department of National and State Parks.
Banff Heritage Tourism Corporation (2004) *Banff Bow Valley Heritage Tourism Strategy*. Banff: Heritage Tourism Corporation.

Bella, L. (1987) *Parks for Profit*. Montreal: Harvest House.

Boyd, S. and Butler, R. (2000) Tourism and national parks: The origin of the concept. In S. Boyd and R. Butler (eds) *Tourism and National Parks: Issues and Implications* (pp. 13–27). Chichester: John Wiley and Sons.

Boyd, S. and Butler, R. (2009) Tourism and the Canadian national park system: Protection, use and balance. In W. Frost and C.M. Hall (eds) *Tourism and National Parks: International Perspectives on Development, Histories and Change* (pp. 102–113). Abingdon: Routledge.

Butler, R. (2000) Tourism and national parks in the twenty-first century. In S. Boyd and R. Butler (eds) *Tourism and National Parks: Issues and Implications* (pp. 324–335). Chichester: John Wiley and Sons.

Butler, R. and Boyd, S. (2000) Tourism and parks – A long but uneasy relationship. In S. Boyd and R. Butler (eds) *Tourism and National Parks: Issues and Implications* (pp. 3–11). Chichester: John Wiley and Sons.

Canadian Broadcasting Corporation (2012) Harper leaves room for mining near norths new national park. See http://www.cbc.ca/news/politics/harper-leaves-room-for-mining-near-north-s-new-national-park-1.1157611

Canadian Parks and Wilderness Society (2012) *Parks Under Threat: The State of Canada's Parks 2012 Report*. See www.cpaws.org

Canadian Parks and Wilderness Society (2015) *South Okanagan Similkameen National Park*. See http://cpawsbc.org/campaigns/south-okanagan-similkameen

Dick, L. (2001) *Muskox Land: Ellesmere Island in the Age of Contact*. Calgary: University of Calgary Press.

Environics (2009) *National Survey of Canadians Final Report*. Prepared by Environics for Parks Canada December, 2009.

Frost, W. and Hall, C.M. (2009a) American invention to international concept: The spread and evolution of national parks. In W. Frost and C.M. Hall (eds) *Tourism and National Parks: International Perspectives on Development, Histories and Change* (pp. 30–44). Abingdon: Routledge.

Frost, W. and Hall, C.M. (2009b) Reinterpreting the creation myth: Yellowstone National Park. In W. Frost and C.M. Hall (eds) *Tourism and National Parks: International Perspectives on Development, Histories and Change* (pp. 16–29). Abingdon: Routledge.

Frost, W. and Hall, C.M. (2009c) National parks, national identity and tourism. In W. Frost and C.M. Hall (eds) *Tourism and National Parks: International Perspectives on Development, Histories and Change* (pp. 63–78). Abingdon: Routledge.

Government of Canada (2000) *The Canada National Parks Act*. Ottawa: Queens Printer.

Hall, C.M. and Frost, W. (2009a) Introduction: The making of the national parks concept. In W. Frost and C.M. Hall (eds) *Tourism and National Parks: International Perspectives on Development, Histories and Change* (pp. 3–15). Abingdon: Routledge.

Hall, C.M. and Frost, W. (2009b) National parks and the worthless hypothesis revisited. In W. Frost and C.M. Hall (eds) *Tourism and National Parks: International Perspectives on Development, Histories and Change* (pp. 45–62). Abingdon: Routledge.

Hall, C.M. and Shultis, J. (1991) Railways, tourism, and worthless lands: The establishment of national parks in Australia, Canada, New Zealand and the United States. *Australian–Canadian Studies – A Journal for the Humanities and the Social Sciences* 8 (2), 57–74.

Hart, E.J. (1983) *The Selling of Canada: The CPR and the Beginnings of Canadian Tourism*. Banff: Altitude.

Johnston, M. and March, J. (1986) History of the Alpine Club of Canada's role in conservation 1906–1930. *Canadian Alpine Journal Alpine Club of Canada* 69, 16–18.

Lothian, W.F. (1979) *A History of Canada's National Parks Volume II*. Ottawa: Parks Canada under the authority of the Hon. Warren Allmand, Minister of Indian and Northern Affairs.

Lowenthal, D. (1997) Environment as heritage. In K. Flint and H. Morphy (eds) *Culture Landscape and the Environment: the Linacre Lectures 1997* (pp. 197–217). Oxford: Oxford University Press.

Luxton, E. (1975) *Banff Canada's First National Park, A History and Memory of Rocky Mountain Park.* Banff: Summerthought.

March, J. (2000) Tourism and national parks in polar regions. In S. Boyd and R. Butler (eds) *Tourism and National Parks: Issues and Implications* (pp. 125–135). Chichester: John Wiley and Sons.

Mason, G. (2014) South Okanagan national park proposal just makes sense. *The Globe and Mail,* Tuesday, 14 October.

Meinig, D. (1979) *The Interpretation of Ordinary Landscapes: Geographical Essays.* Oxford: Oxford University Press.

Nudds, T. (2012) Wither Parks Canada's ecological integrity mandate? Presented as a member of the Plenary Panel on Canada's National Parks (UWS2012). See http:// skies.mtroyal.ca/plenary-panel-on-canadas-national-parks

Oliver Daily News (2015) No national park movement grows in Similkameen. See http:// oliverdailynews.com/no-national-park-movement-grows-in-similkameen/

Outspan Group Inc (2011) *Economic Impacts of Parks Canada.* Prepared for Parks Canada Agency, Gatineau Prepared by The Outspan Group Inc., Amherst Island, Canada.

Parks Canada (199a) Ministerial press release announcing the downsizing of the town of Banff, March 1997.

Parks Canada (1997b) *Banff National Park Management Plan.* Ottawa: Parks Canada Agency.

Parks Canada (2010) *2010-2011 Parks Canada Agency Corporate Plan.* See http://www. pc.gc.ca/eng/docs/pc/plans/plan2010-2011/sec01/index.aspx#ia

Parks Canada (2012a) Restoring terrestrial ecosystems in Waterton Lakes National Park: External relations baseline study of regional audiences. Parks Canada Agency internal document.

Parks Canada (2012b) Internal audit and evaluation documents, evaluation of Parks Canada's visitor service offer, 31 January 2012. Office of Internal Audit and Evaluation, Report submitted to the Parks Canada Evaluation Committee, 9 February 2012. Approved by the Agency CEO, 5 March 2012. See http://www.pc.gc.ca/docs/ pc/rpts/rve-par/78/index_e.asp

Parks Canada (2014) 2014–15 Report on plans and priorities. See www.pc.gc.ca

Parks Canada (2015a) National parks system plan. See http://www.pc.gc.ca/eng/docs/ v-g/nation/sec1.aspx

Parks Canada (2015b) Internal audit and evaluation documents: Parks Canada – National performance and evaluation framework for engaging Canadians: External communication at Parks Canada. See http://www.pc.gc.ca/docs/pc/rpts/rve-par/26/ table9_e.asp

Parks Canada (2015c) Harper Government announces new investments to Parks Canada sites. See http://www.pc.gc.ca/APPS/CP-NR/release_e.asp?id=2215&andor1=nr

Pearce, D., Makrandya, A. and Barber, E. (2000) Economic valuation of environmental goods. In J. Benson (ed.) *Environmental Ethics: An Introduction with Readings* (pp. 171–184). London: Routledge.

Routley, R. and Routley, V. (2000) Environmental ethics in practice. In J. Benson (ed.) *Environmental Ethics: An Introduction with Readings* (pp. 139–141). London: Routledge.

Runte, A. (1990) *Yosemite: The Embattled Wilderness.* Lincoln, NB: University of Nebraska Press.

Sellars, R.W. (1997) *Preserving Nature in the National Parks: A History.* New Haven, CT: Yale University Press.

Shultis, J. (2012) The past is present: Linking the dual mandate, declining visitation and political ideology. Presented as a member of the Plenary Panel on Canada's National Parks (UWS2012). See http://skies.mtroyal.ca/plenary-panel-on-canadas-national-parks/

Stevens, T.H., More, T.A. and Markowski-Lindsay, M. (2014) Declining national park visitation: An economic analysis. *Journal of Leisure Research* 46 (2), 153–194.

Wilson, A. (1991) *The Culture of Nature: The North American Landscape from Disney to the Exxon Valdez.* Toronto: Between the Lines.

Wright, P. (2012) Impaired for future generations. Presented as a member of the Plenary Panel on Canada's National Parks (UWS2012). See http://skies.mtroyal.ca/plenary-panel-on-canadas-national-parks/

3 Tourism and Nationalism in the Former Yugoslavia

Patrick Naef

Introduction

This chapter looks at the links between tourism and nationalism by ana-lysing war heritage touristification in the young states of Bosnia–Herzegovina and Croatia. Reflecting the widely shared assumption that the memories attached to the wars of the 1990s in the former Yugoslavia are often associ-ated with nationalist narratives, it maintains that tourism can also be con-sidered as a vector for nationalism, especially when it is related to cultural heritage.

Two views are generally put forward when cultural heritage is at issue. On the one hand it can be conceptualised as a form of legacy from the past: what contemporary society chooses to inherit or to pass on (Graham *et al.*, 2000). However, it can also be looked at as a production of the present, fulfilling present-day purposes (Lowenthal, 1998). Following this second interpretation, the main argument advanced here is that cultural heritage can serve various contemporary needs, among them tourism development or the production of a place image, but also others, such as the diffusion of nationalist discourses. As stated by Pierre Nora (1989), heritage can be considered as a relic of a time gone by, but it may also be transformed and assume a particular value for a community. The narratives associated with heritage can thus serve to transmit certain values, like patriotism, bravery or heroism, that can be specifically associated with a national group. By looking at some case studies in ex-Yugoslavia, the objective is to determine if the narratives produced in the tourism sector can lead to a shared vision of the history of the war or on the contrary produce a unilateral interpreta-tion of it, enhancing the nationalist dynamics already at work in the region.

A study of the new states of Bosnia–Herzegovina and Croatia offers a particularly interesting context in this regard. These two countries are now experiencing strong nationalist currents, especially in politics and in the media, following their independence a little more than 20 years ago. Nationalist trends were previously repressed by Marshal Tito until his death in 1980. The 1980s saw the emergence of important nationalist currents leading to the wars of independence in several republics of the former Yugoslavia. This chapter will first examine how nationalism, war heritage and tourism can interrelate. It will then look at the specific context of the former Yugoslavia, focusing on two specific case studies: the tourism promotion of the town of Vukovar in Eastern Croatia and the museum dedicated to the first president of Bosnia–Herzegovina – Alija Izetbegović – in Sarajevo.

Tourism, War and Nationalism

If war, and particularly wars of independence, can generate nationalist dynamics in the post-conflict development of tourism sectors, these trends can also be observed in non-war-related settings. Examples such as the Scottish National Portrait Gallery or the Mount Rushmore monument certainly represent a type of nationalism expressed in tourism, by featuring elements attributed to the greatness of the Scottish or the American nation. Yet when a country has to reconstruct itself after a war, or if a country is born following a war (e.g. wars of independence), nationalist trends are even more likely to appear in various elements of society, such as school curricula, textbooks, political programmes, newspapers, museums and monuments.

Benedict Anderson (1983) describes nations as 'imagined communities' and points to different elements contributing to their development, such as maps, censuses and museums. However, if the latter represent a major object of tourism, the links between tourism and nationalism have been little explored, especially where war heritage is at issue.

Bui et al. (2011) have studied the role of heritage in the construction of national identity, looking at national museums in Vietnam. They present these institutions, and particularly the Ho Chi Minh Museum, as 'guiding fictions' (Shumway, 1991). For them, national museums are agents of nationalism and the presentation of national heritage is thus an ideological process. In a similar vein, Pretes (2003) analysed the heritage site of Mount Rushmore, demonstrating that monuments can serve as a means to representing something shared by citizens, especially in contexts where diverse cultures coexist. This is confirmed by Hall (2001: 100), who points out that this process is likely to accompany the creation of a new state: 'the resurgence of nationalist expression alongside a (re-)creation of new state systems has encouraged some countries to employ the heritage industry as a means of reinforcing national or particular ethnic identity'.

The issue of inclusion (and exclusion) is therefore fundamental when looking at case studies in the former Yugoslavia, where various national groups share a territory. It is stated here that, if heritage sites like monuments or museums can help popularise a hegemonic nationalist message of inclusion (Pretes, 2003), some citizens can identify with – and be included in – these national narratives, while others are excluded and even stigmatised as the 'other'. In some places of Bosnia–Herzegovina and Croatia, the war memory often points out the bravery of one group, in opposition to the barbarianism of the 'others'. This can partly represent what Doss (2010) conceptualises as the nationalisation of bodies. Through memorial practices like tourism and museum production, the dead and some of the living are mobilised to fulfil national imperatives.

These processes can join forces with other dynamics particular to tourism, such as trivialisation and simplification, enabling history to fit into specific nationalist narratives. As stated by Ashworth (1991), when nationalistic ideology is at stake, trivialisation can lead to selective simplification in order to present a sanitised and idealised past. Adopting a historical perspective, Rodriguez (2014) has shown how nationalism can be diffused through the tourism sector with some cases dating as far back as the First World War. She demonstrates how, during the Great War, French authorities were already promoting a kind of 'Battlefield tourism' invested with a strong sacred and patriotic dimension: 'they have to be named French battlefield pilgrimages. Furthermore, the discourses of the guides have to demonstrate the spirit of the national defence. Thus, it is a matter of showing 'our bravery' against 'German Barbary'' (Rodriguez, 2014: 3).[1] The battlefield descriptions appearing in the same period in the famous Michelin guidebooks are also seen as unilateral: 'Acts of violence are essentially attributed to the German army, which allows the tourism sector to occupy an important place in the nationalist arsenal used by the French state for its patriotic propaganda' (Rodriguez, 2014: 7).[2]

Still in the context of the Great War, some authors (Carlyon, 2001; Inglis, 2005; Winter, 2011) have also discussed the importance of the First World War events in the construction of the Australian nationality. For Inglis (2005), although most of the Australians were killed on the Western front, it is the Gallipoli Peninsula campaign in Turkey that is now central in Australian popular war remembrance, an event conceptualised as 'Australia's Homeric tale' by Carlyon (2001). Finally, later in the 20th century, the tourism authorities of General Franco's Spain invited tourists from all over Europe to visit Spain in order to discover the tranquillity and prosperity of the regions conquered by the General, allowing the battlefields to enter the 'heroic narrative of European civilisation' (Rodriguez, 2014). These various examples demonstrate the selections and adaptations of war history through its touristification, mechanisms that enable the construction of specific nationalist narratives.

Nationalism and the Post-Yugoslav Arena

After the collapse of the Soviet Union and Yugoslavia, the question of national identity became significant in the region (Smith & Puczkó, 2011) and Eastern European countries are now often seen as paradigmatic cases when nationalism issues are paramount. Appadurai (1996) mentions for instance that, in the United States, Bosnia–Herzegovina is almost always designated as the main symptom revealing that nationalism is 'alive and sick'. However, he warns us against this fascination with Eastern Europe, which some consider is the illustration of the complexity of all nationalisms. As Appadurai (1996: 21) states, scholars need to be sceptical when experts claim to have encountered ideal types in actual cases.

Nevertheless, Smith and Puczkó (2011: 39) demonstrate that, in the post-Communist era, political, cultural and tourism agencies face the challenging task of deciding how to redefine their nation and determining which cultural elements to select and promote. Moreover, after the bloody wars of the 1990s, countries such as Bosnia–Herzegovina, Croatia, Serbia and Kosovo are now confronted with dissonant types of heritage (Tunbridge & Ashworth, 1996). In this contentious setting, an increasing number of scholars are considering the management of the past as a new battlefield (Baillie, 2011a; Viejo-Rose, 2011; Naef, 2014), where symbolic wars are going on in places conceptualised by Ashplant et al. (2000) as 'commemorative arenas'. They define these arenas as socio-political spaces in which particular memories of various social actors with different experiences and political agendas are propagated.

Several authors (Szilagyi, 2014; Duijzings, 2007) use the Srebrenica–Potočari Memorial Centre and Cemetery to illustrate the concept of 'commemorative arena'. The commemoration of the collective suffering and martyrdom nurtured by many Bosnian Muslim nationalists confronts the Bosnian Serb counter-commemorations often associated with the relativisation and even denial of the Srebrenica massacre (Szilagyi, 2014: 74). Miller (2006), for instance, criticises the one-dimensional narrative produced by Bosnian Muslims that turns the massacre of Srebrenica into a 'Bosnian Muslim Holocaust': '[It] seems to me to be manufacturing a fixed and didactic narrative that leaves little room for exploring the broader context of both the recent war and of Bosnian history in general' (Miller, 2006, in Szilagyi, 2014). War memories and commemorative narratives can be selective and hegemonic and, as stated by Ashplant et al. (2000: 10), they produce 'patterns of exclusion and inclusion that determine which aspects of the collective and individual experience are acceptable for public recall and commemoration'.

The case of the Srebrenica–Potočari Memorial Centre and Cemetery can be enlightening in the context of this chapter, as the site is now also associated with tourism. The former Potočari United Nations military base is now a museum centre where photographs and personal items belonging to the victims are exhibited and a small boutique sells souvenirs. Some survivors of the massacre act as local guides. More than 100,000 people visit this memorial site every year and many tour operators in Sarajevo offer day trips from the capital.

If several dynamics – mourning, commemoration, tourism – characterise the Srebrenica–Potočari Memorial Centre and Cemetery, tourism entrepreneurs are included in the arena and are therefore also present in the front lines of these conflicts over memory. Tourism as a memorial practice thus constitutes a key dimension in the production of narratives associated with nationalism; tourism entrepreneurs are producing specific discourses on the war and on the nation, depending on their identity and their role in the wars.

The second part of this chapter will focus on two case studies, in Sarajevo and in Eastern Croatia, in order to examine in more detail how the tourism sector can support nationalist narratives.

Vukovar: Symbol of a Nation

Vukovar is a small town situated in Slavonia, next to the Serbian border, a region devastated during the Croatian War. In 1991, Vukovar was besieged for three months by the Yugoslav federal army and Serbian paramilitary groups. During the siege, the local population, a majority of Croats cohabiting with other national groups, including Serbs, defended the city with minimal means until they surrendered on 18 November 1991. This struggle, often compared with David against Goliath, transformed Vukovar into a symbol of heroism, martyrdom and independence (Vukovar was the last place reclaimed by Croatia after the country took back the territories it had lost at the beginning of the 1990s). Today, many museums and memorials of the last war characterise this town of less than 30,000 inhabitants where a majority of Croats share the territory with a large Serbian minority. For Baillie (2011b), Vukovar and Slavonia contain the most monuments associated with the Croatian War (see Figure 3.1).

This effervescence in memorial construction is certainly due to the traumatic siege the town lived through, but it can also be linked to the symbolic dimension Vukovar acquired, just as Srebrenica now represents the 'Bosnian Muslim Holocaust' in some nationalist narratives. Images and mentions of Vukovar are present in many elements of Croatian society and culture (stamps, banknotes, popular songs, street names, hip-hop music, etc.), and are also heavily featured in the local tourism promotional efforts.

In 2013, the Croatian tourist website 'Croatia at a Glance' described the sacred status of Vukovar, 'acquired by the selfless sacrifice of its defenders', as part of its promotion of Slavonia as a wine-producing and archaeological

Figure 3.1 Memorial to the Croatian soldiers facing the Republic of Serbia on the Sava River

region, but also as an important place of memory (Naef, 2013). Furthermore, the tourism office produced a free leaflet for visitors portraying different aspects of Vukovar such as nature, history or architecture. Two pages focused specifically on memories of the war, showing pictures of ruins and memorials; a Croatian flag floating on the rear of a boat illustrated the back of the brochure. The pictures of these sites of memory were also associated with a poem dedicated to the glory of the town: 'Vukovar is a miraculous town … Vukovar is pride … Vukovar is defiance … It is a tear in one's eye, sorrow in one's heart … And a smile on one's lips … Vukovar is both past and future' (Vukovar Tourist Board, 2006: 3).

Another particular feature of Vukovar tourism promotion is the involvement of Croatian veterans. In 2011, free maps of the town available to visitors in the local tourism office bore the logo of the Croatian Association for Prisoners in Serbian Concentration Camps, one of the main Croatian veteran groups in the region (Naef, 2013). The same group is also in charge of the Ovčara Memorial Centre, a heavily promoted detention and execution site where recent history and tourism intertwine, and also one of the most visited sites in Vukovar (see Figure 3.2). Finally, this veterans group also triggered an initiative in 2003 to build a 'Homeland War' Memorial Centre, an institution managed by the Croatian army and the Ministry of Defence since its construction in 2007. This site proposes, in a former military barracks, exhibitions, a documentation centre, some replicas of Serbian concentration camps and a simulation of a battlefield. All the diploma ceremonies of military cadets take place here and the main public target seems to be essentially military, although the Ministry of Defence would like to open it to a wider audience: 'The purpose of the centre is to connect the military with civilian society, principally through educational means and with other Croatian institutions which would study the material or show interest in the usage of that space' (Ministry of Defence of Croatia, 2009: 45).

In Vukovar city centre, a sign presents a map of the town and some historical information on its recent and bloody history. The war is described as a 'Serbian aggression' aimed at creating 'Greater Serbia'. Limiting the causes of the Croatian War to the creation of 'Greater Serbia' illustrates an

Figure 3.2 The personal belongings of victims exhibited at the Ovčara Memorial Centre

important mechanism of simplification within the framework of nationalist narratives. It also represents a one-sided interpretation of memory, especially if one looks back at the history of the country and its first president Franjo Tuđman's objective of creating a 'Greater Croatia'. This simplification process is also obvious in other sites of memory in Vukovar. The Ovčara Memorial Centre is described as follows:

> The Serb Aggressors turned those hangars into concentration camp for non-Serbian prisoners that were captured in Vukovar. ... Even the mayor of Vukovar, a Serb S. Dokmanović, beat his fellow-citizens.[3]

In this narrative, that Serbian prisoners were detained and killed in Serbian detention camps is something that is omitted. Moreover, as mentioned by the director of the Ovčara Memorial Centre himself, 'among those killed at Ovčara there were five Serbian people ... Five Serbians were also executed there'.[4] Serbian victims do not fit in the frame of Croatian nationalist narratives, where they are depicted only as 'aggressors', 'drunks' or 'Chetniks'.

These examples demonstrate that a simplification process appearing alongside touristification and musealisation leads to the production of uniform and clear-cut categories of victims and perpetrators. These categories are linked to national groups and only a little space is left for nuance. The Serbian community is associated with notions like 'Greater Serbia', 'aggression' and 'concentration camps' and the Croatian community with opposite elements, such as 'heroism', 'bravery' and 'resistance'. Although these latter qualities could also be attributed to all of those Serbian individuals who defended the city with the Croatian resistance, this interpretation does not fit into the hegemonic discourse of the war in Eastern Croatia. Thus, some members of the Serbian community who chose to stay in Vukovar during the siege, and were among the victims of the paramilitaries who besieged their city, are now victims of conflicts over memory and are stigmatised as bloody and drunk barbarians. Finally, the status of memorial entrepreneurs managing these sites of memory is also fundamental to understanding some of the mechanisms involved in the production of these unilateral narratives. In Vukovar, the army and the veterans are still deeply implicated in memory enterprises.

The Alija Izetbegović Museum: Between Nationalism and Multiculturalism

The capital of Bosnia–Herzegovina is presented as a multicultural city and most of the tourism actors remind the visitor that Sarajevo comprises a Catholic church, an Orthodox church, a mosque and a synagogue within a few hundred metres of each other. Although a multicultural image of the city is promoted in marketing material, in guides' discourses and in some museums, other institutions tend to present a more unilateral interpretation of history, especially when the recent war years are evoked.

The structure of Sarajevo's touristscape hampers the diffusion of different points of view. Bosnia–Herzegovina is divided into two entities: the Federation of Bosnia–Herzegovina administered by Bosnian Croats and Bosnian Muslims; and the Serbian Republic ruled by Bosnian Serbs. An invisible demarcation line also runs through Sarajevo; the historical core of the city is part of the Federation of Bosnia–Herzegovina and the eastern suburbs are part of the Serbian Republic. Most of the governing bodies are divided and tourism is administered by different ministries and organisations, depending on the entity concerned. In this divided context, all of the main museums are located in the Federation of Bosnia–Herzegovina, and therefore administered without the Serbian authorities' participation. The establishment of a state institution that would involve the three main national groups in the interpretation of war heritage seems far away. A Bosnian museum curator described the complex situation of some of Sarajevo's museums in 2011:

> The problem with projects related to the siege is linked to the politics issued from the Dayton agreement. The state is very reluctant to support such projects because half of our state has been given to the people that attacked us. And they do not want to accept anything related to the history of the siege. That is why the Tunnel Museum is private. So the Siege Museum is going to be also a private initiative. And this is unfortunate because it is history and we cannot close our eyes on it. The tunnel Museum could go to the cantonal level, but never to the state level because the Serbs would never accept it.[5]

This view was confirmed by a tour guide, Zijad Jusufović, who also insisted on the impossibility of creating a state-owned war museum and criticised the funding mechanisms in cultural heritage management: 'A big war museum will never be established, because Serbs will never allow it. I call it money cleaning. Projects, projects, projects ... And the result is nothing. It is easy to get money from the budget to ... do money'.[6]

However, half a dozen museum projects associated with the history of the last war are present in the Bosnian city, managed privately or at the level of the Canton of Sarajevo (dependent of the Federation of Bosnia–Herzegovina). In the following lines, the objective is to analyse one of them – the Alija Izetbegović Museum – as it relates to the multicultural image promoted in the local tourism sector. Can this multiculturalism narrative persist in the context of war museums or does a unilateral and hegemonic discourse emerge when war memory is at issue? Makas (2012: 13) supports the idea that the museums of Sarajevo, in reaction to the various national-isms in the country, tend to develop a multicultural discourse on the city: 'Even within the exhibits focused specifically on these violent political rup-tures and conflict within the city, curators at Sarajevo museums in the past decade have managed to insert narratives or include content that reinforces this idea of a multicultural Sarajevo'.

The Alija Izetbegović Museum was established in memory of the first president of Bosnia–Herzegovina. It opened its doors on 19 October 2007, four years after the president's death. Initially managed by the city and the Canton of Sarajevo, the museum became independent in 2012. Its focus is entirely on the former president, describing his life, his implication in the war and his political involvement through the presentation of explanatory boards and memorabilia. One of the museum consultants insisted in 2011 on the importance of highlighting the multicultural dimension of the first presi-dent of the nation: 'We want to show the multi-ethnic politics he developed. He is the most important person in the creation of Bosnia and he was a multi-ethnic president, representative of the three communities'.[7] This mul-ticultural reference can also be observed on the museum's website describing the architecture of the edifice built between the Ploča and Širokac towers: 'the symbolism of the tower wall makes the visitors sense the struggle of good against evil; the feelings which permeate the work of Izetbegović. This symbolism speaks of his constant commitment to connect people, nations and cultures'.[8] However, good and evil are also clearly defined and this Manichean dichotomy is present in other parts of the museum narrative:[9]

> The war in Bosnia was not a classical war, if we consider that to be a clash of two armies. It was the attack of one powerful military machin-ery against the bare-armed people. The goal: creation of the Greater Serbia.

> We are the moral winner! There are no military victors. We have both won and lost.

In opposition to Bosnian Muslim bravery, Serbs are assimilated with 'Chetniks', a 'genocide threat' and 'aggressors motivated by Nazi propaganda'.

Of course, responsibilities have to be acknowledged and the majority of Sarajevo besiegers were of Serb origin, or at least identified themselves with a Serbian culture. Nevertheless, victims were of all origins during the Bosnian war and all three national groups involved were perpetrators of atrocities. Moreover, as in the case of Vukovar, many Serbians stayed in Sarajevo during the siege (unofficially about 12%) and some defended the city, as for example the former Bosnian Serb General Jovan Divjak, who fought on the front lines against besiegers. Yet references to a share of guilt or opponent victims are completely absent in a museum dedicated to the father of the nation, as well as any solidarity expressed by those supposedly seen as the enemy. If this is not particularly surprising or unique in the context of a war museum, it contradicts the multicultural dimension advocated by the managers of the site.

In a specific reference to the Alija Izetbegović Museum, Makas (2012: 13) acknowledged the multicultural dimension of the museum: 'Multiculturalism is a privileged theme even in the museum dedicated to Alija Izetbegović, a highly controversial figure in Bosnia associated quite specifically with the Bosnian Muslims'. The thematic of multiculturalism is certainly present in this museum. However, the question remains whether the objective is to enhance coexistence between national communities or to valorise Izetbegović's personality. In regard to the present analysis, the recurrent stigmatisation of the Serbian community and the unconditional glorification of Bosnian Muslims seem to leave little room for promoting a real dynamic of coexistence. As in the case developed by Bui *et al.* (2011) in Vietnam, the museum presents a particular interpretation of history, together with specific values, in order to propagate a Bosnia–Herzegovina nation-state narrative. By 'showing some elements and not showing others' (Ashley, 2005 cited in Bui *et al.*, 2011), the museum participates in the dissemination of a hegemonic discourse of inclusion and exclusion.

Conclusion

Tourism can be seen as a means to alleviate community tensions by supporting cooperative projects and enhancing qualitative contacts among groups. On the other hand, it can also be seen as a weapon in conflicts over memory, a means to propagate nationalist discourses of hate. Where war heritage is concerned, one of the main challenges is to manage to strengthen people's identification with a nation while at the same time integrating groups considered as antagonistic into the commemorative arena.

This chapter presents only some of the elements of the touristic and museum landscape in the former Yugoslavia, and some institutions certainly support cultural coexistence. However, the tourism promotion of Vukovar and the Alija Izetbegović Museum cases show that, in two cities often represented as multicultural, when war heritage is involved, the tourism sector can produce strong nationalist narratives. In both cases, a simplified and hegemonic discourse presents victims and perpetrators in clear-cut categories often associated with specific national groups. A myth of national bravery confronts another of national guilt.

The objective here was to throw light on certain mechanisms associated with nationalism and tourism, especially in relation to war heritage. Simplification, very often present in tourism narratives, leads to categorisation, a form of essentialism that produces groups of victims – Barbarians, heroes, etc. – and contributes to creating the 'guiding fiction' outlined above. With the de-individualising of victims and perpetrators, a great national narrative is fabricated, strengthened by the transformation of places (Vukovar) and figures (Izetbegović) into symbols.

Notes

(1) Translated from French by the author.
(2) Translated from French by the author.
(3) Illustrated information booklet provided at the *Ovčara Memorial Centre*.
(4) Interview by the author in Vukovar (August 2011).
(5) Interview by the author in Sarajevo (July 2011).
(6) Interview by the author in Sarajevo (July 2011).
(7) Interview by the author in Sarajevo (August 2011).
(8) http://www.muzejalijaizetbegovic.ba/en/page.php?id=9
(9) Museum's desciption boards.

References

Anderson, B. (1983) *Imagined Communities: Reflections on the Origin and Spread of Nationalism.* London: Verso.
Appadurai, A. (1996) *Modernity At Large: Cultural Dimensions of Globalization.* Minneapolis, MN: University of Minnesota Press.
Ashplant, T.G., Dawson, G. and Roper, M. (eds) (2000) *The Politics of War Memory and Commemoration.* London: Routledge.
Ashworth, G.J. (1991) *War and the City.* London: Routledge.
Baillie, B. (2011a) The wounded church: War, destruction and reconstruction of Vukovar's Religious Heritage. PhD thesis, University of Cambridge.
Baillie, B. (2011b) Staking claim: Monuments and the making (and breaking?) of a border matrix in Vukovar. Paper presented at the conference 'Urban Conflict', Belfast
Bui, H.T., Jolliffe, L. and Nguyen, A.M. (2011) Heritage and aspects of nation: Vietnam's Ho Chi Minh Museum. In E. Frew and L. White (eds) *Tourism and National Identities. An International Perspective* (pp. 164–176). Abingdon: Routledge.
Carlyon, L. (2001) *Gallipoli.* New York: Bantam.
Doss, E. (2010) *Memorial Mania. Public Feeling in America.* Chicagom IL: University of Chicago Press.
Duijzings, G. (2007) Commemorating Srebrenica: Histories of violence and the politics of memory in Eastern Bosnia. In X. Bougarel (ed.) *The New Bosnian Mosaic. Identities, Memories and Moral Claims in a Post-war Society* (pp. 141–166). Farnham: Ashgate.
Graham, B., Ashworth, G.J. and Tunbridge, J.E. (2000) *A Geography of Heritage: Power, Culture and Economy.* London: Arnold/New York: Oxford University Press.
Hall, D.R. (2001) Tourism and development in communist and post-communist societies. In D. Harrison (ed.) *Tourism and the Less Developed World: Issues and Case Studies* (pp. 91–107), Wallingford: CAB International.
Inglis, K. (2005) *Sacred Places: War Memorial in Australian Landscape.* Carlton: Melbourne University Press.
Lowenthal, D. (1998) *The Heritage Crusade and the Spoils of History.* Cambridge: Cambridge University Press.
Makas, E. (2012) Museums and the history and identity of Sarajevo. Paper presented at the conference 'Cities and Societies in Comparative Perspectives', Prague.

Miller, P.B. (2006) Contested memories: The Bosnian genocide in Serb and Muslim minds. *Journal of Genocide Research* 8, 311–324.

Ministry of Defense of Croatia (2009) *Croatian Military Magazine*. Zagreb.

Naef, P. (2013) 'Souvenirs' from Vukovar: Tourism and memory within the Post-Yugoslav region. Via@ International Interdisciplinary Review of Tourism.

Naef, P. (2014) Guerre, tourisme et mémoire dans l'espace post-yougoslave: la construction de la 'ville-martyre'. PhD thesis, University of Geneva.

Nora, P. (1989) Between memory and history: Les lieux de mémoire. *Representations* 26, 7–25.

Pretes, M. (2003) Tourism and nationalism. *Annals of Tourism Research* 30, 125–142.

Rodriguez, M.C. (2014) Le 'tourisme des champs de bataille' au 20ème siècle. ['Battlefield tourism' in the 20th century.] Paper presented at the Conference 'Remembering in a Globalizing World: The Play and Interplay of Tourism, Memory and Place', Le Chambon sur Lignon, France.

Shumway, N. (1991) *The Invention of Argentina*. Berkeley, CA: University of California Press.

Smith, M. and Puczkó, L. (2011) Nationalism identity construction and tourism in Hungary. A multi-level approach. In E. Frew and L. White (eds) *Tourism and National Identities. An International Perspective* (pp. 39–51). Abingdon: Routledge.

Szilagyi, C. (2014) Representations of mass atrocities in imagined 'commemorative arenas'. A forensic reconstruction of the 1995 Srebrenica massacre in the archival space. *Versus – Quaderni di Studi Semiotici* 119, 71–91.

Tunbridge, J.E. and Ashworth, G.J. (1996) *Dissonant Heritage: The Management of the Past as a Resource in Conflict*. Hoboken, NJ: John Wiley and Sons.

Viejo-Rose, D. (2011) Memorial fictions: Intent, impact and the right to remember. *Memory Studies* 4, 465–480.

Vukovar Tourist Board (2006) *Vukovar*. Vukovar: Tourist Board.

Winter, C. (2011) Battlefield tourism and Australian national identity. Gallipoli and the Western front. In E. Frew and L. White (eds) *Tourism and National Identities. An International Perspective* (pp. 176–188). Abingdon: Routledge.

4 Away but Together: Diaspora Tourism and Narratives of Ukrainian Immigrants in the United States

Svitlana Iarmolenko, Deborah Kerstetter and Moji Shahvali

Introduction

In this chapter we demonstrate how 'narratives' reflecting nationalistic feelings of diaspora (individuals away from their original homeland) have the power to encourage diaspora tourism (migrants visiting their homeland). We begin by defining the concepts of 'nation' and 'nationalism', both of which are commonly understood by individuals yet have no agreed upon scientific definitions (Seton-Watson, 1977). Anderson (1983) suggested that nations be considered 'imagined political communities', while Gellner (1964: 169) posited that nationalism 'invents nations where they do not exist'. According to Pretes (2003: 128), the invention of nationalism occurs through 'guiding fictions, which are commonly held beliefs that shape people's attachment to the nation'. While guiding fictions or narratives may lead to feelings of nationalism (Macdonald, 2006), so does attachment to customs and traditions (Nairn, 1977) and a feeling of common identity (Pretes, 2003). Tourism promoters often use all three components of nationalism to attract tourists (Buzinde *et al.*, 2006; Pretes, 2003), but to date have given little attention to doing so with diasporas, that is, communities of nationals living abroad.

The act of travelling to the homeland or 'diaspora tourism' (also known as roots tourism, ethnic tourism, homeland tourism or legacy tourism) is broadly understood as an experience characterised by 'seriousness of purpose and emotional engagement' (Leite, 2005: 278), which has been shown to benefit immigrants in a number of ways (Basu, 2005). Diaspora tourism brings cultural and spiritual renewal to individuals (Pierre, 2009), connects diasporic individuals with political processes in their country of origin (Ostrowski, 1991), helps resolve a problematised sense of belonging in host and home countries (Basu, 2005), supports the diaspora communities' desire to maintain a distinct collective identity (Morgan *et al.*, 2003) and allows individuals to return to places associated with their own life history (Leite, 2005). Diaspora tourism (or 'homesick tourism') also allows tourists or the 'carriers of memory' to travel to their homeland 'for the purpose of verifying, solidifying and transferring memory and family history' (Marschall, 2014: 13) and bolstering their well-being (Van Oudenhoven & Ward, 2013). Despite these advantages, promoting diaspora tourism is a challenging process.

Morgan *et al.* (2003) insist that the most effective promotional approach with diasporas is to use narratives of homecoming, nationhood and searching for roots. Despite the emotionally laden connections immigrants have with their homeland, promoting diaspora tourism through formulaic advertisements is marginally effective. The same cannot be said of advertising that incorporates narratives or stories (Oatley & Gholamain, 1997). Scholars have found that narratives represent a 'fundamental mode of thinking' (Green, 2006: S163) that affects beliefs (Green & Brock, 2000), provides behavioural examples (Slater, 2002) and shapes individuals' cultural identities (Jacobs, 2002). Despite these findings, Dal Cin *et al.* (2004) argue that many challenges remain, including documenting what are the attributes of a 'quality' narrative.

Cultural appropriateness is an especially pertinent quality indicator of narratives, but difficult to attain with immigrant groups. For example, a carefully crafted national story may appeal to international tourists, yet feel inauthentic and be less persuasive to diaspora who have an emotional attachment to their home nation and a national myth of their own. Further, developing a hegemonic national narrative can be difficult, particularly for post-Soviet countries who must reconstruct a national identity after almost 70 years of nationalism-wiping efforts of the Communist party (Palmer, 2007).

According to Larkey and Hecht (2010), the process of creating culturally grounded narratives includes 'message development [that] enlists the experience of group members through the stories describing their social realities' (p. 117). While Hecht *et al.* (2003) have successfully applied this process to create a culturally grounded narrative to reduce Mexican American adolescents' substance use, it is unclear how culturally grounded narratives are developed and whether they are more effective than didactic or expository text. Thus, for this study, we chose to use the culturally grounded narrative process to build a narrative that could be used to promote Ukraine as a destination for the Ukrainian diaspora's travel. The process involved obtaining a sample of Ukrainian immigrants in the US, interviewing them about their immigration experiences, process of adaptation and relationship with Ukraine, creating a culturally grounded narrative based on the results of the interviews and assessing the narrative's effectiveness against a factual didactic text about Ukraine with a follow-up survey. Ukraine was chosen because it has struggled to build a national identity and has one of the world's largest diasporas (Duvell & Lapshyna, 2015), which could potentially positively respond to travel promotion built from a culturally grounded narrative.

Results

The results of this study are presented in two sections. The first section focuses on the process associated with creating the culturally grounded narrative. The second section addresses findings associated with assessing the effectiveness of the constructed narrative.

Creating the culturally grounded narrative

In this section we focus on the results derived from interviewing Ukrainian immigrants about their immigration experiences, process of adaptation and relationship with Ukraine. We also show how the results that comprise the seven themes and supporting quotes were used to create a culturally grounded promotional narrative.

For many Ukrainians, immigrating to the US is a dream, but also stressful. For example, Ruslana was very excited to win a green card in the national lottery, but when the time came she was scared to leave:

> When I found out about winning, I wanted to go so bad … But then when everything was ready… I didn't want to go anymore. … I was crying, I guess I just didn't want to leave … it was hard to leave everyone behind.

Moreover, being scared and experiencing stress extended into the first years of Ukrainians living in the US:

> There was a lot of nostalgia for home … I wanted to go back home right away … [I was uncertain] because you don't know the language, you don't know where you are and how the system works in America. That was what worried me the most (Kateryna).

These mixed feelings were reflected in the first few paragraphs of the culturally grounded narrative.

Although every year many families wait for their turn to immigrate to the US, for one Ukrainian family the life of being immigrants in the US did not turn out to be what they had expected. Two years after the Kovalenko family immigrated, they still felt the stress of being foreigners. 'My entire family is suffering', said Petro Kovalenko, the father of the family. 'I can see my wife and children unhappy and it is breaking my heart. I am the head of this family, I feel responsible for ensuring my loved ones are doing well. I feel like I am failing'.

For most fourth-wave Ukrainians, including this study's respondents, post-independence economic and political hardships in the homeland pushed them to migrate (Bazynskyj, 2009). Solomija's husband was the first to migrate because in the US he could earn money for a decent living much more easily than he could in Ukraine. Lidiya came to the US because she did not want to be a burden on her family:

> The reason [for going to the US] was that I could not provide for myself in Ukraine, and I didn't want to ask anyone for money to live on. I felt sorry for my parents because I also have a younger sister who they needed to put through school … It wasn't because I really wanted to go to America; just at that time I thought of such a solution for the situation.

Thus, to make the narrative culturally appropriate to these experiences, the protagonist family in our constructed narrative also left Ukraine for economic reasons. The Kovalenko family moved from Ivano-Frankivsk to the US after Ukrainian independence in 1991. The new economic reality of Ukraine threatened the survival of contractor Petro and his wife Nadiya, a nurse.

For the majority of Ukrainian diaspora in the US, family reunion is the major reason for immigration (Wolowyna & Lopukh, 2014). Solomija immigrated after her 'husband [had] already been here for some time', and Sofia immigrated to join her brother who '[had] already lived here in New York for five years'. The culturally grounded narrative reflected respondents' experiences: 'Petro asked relatives in the US for reunion papers which would allow his family to immigrate'.

New immigrants find that co-nationals provide the most support and assistance during their initial stages of adaptation. Kateryna reflected on her sources of support: 'Only Ukrainians! For me at least, I don't know how it works for other people, but for me this was how it turned out to be. Only our people'. Alternatively, Ruslana made contact with Ukrainian immigrants to arrange for their help upon her arrival in the US: 'I didn't know [anybody in the US], but I met with people … from my village … who lived in New York'.

This reliance on and knowing how to get help from other Ukrainian immigrants was incorporated into the culturally grounded narrative by stating that 'the father of the Kovalenko family heard that there was a sizable Ukrainian community in Manhattan and they could count on help'.

As a labour diaspora, post-Soviet Ukrainians move to the US in search of a better life. Vitaliy admitted, 'Despite the fact that at first I had to do different work, this country gives people a chance. And because of that it is loved'. This excitement about new opportunities was reflected as follows in the narrative: 'With two children, Andriy and Natalia, we came to the US in search of a better life and opportunities our homeland could no longer provide. We were extremely excited and hopeful', said Nadiya.

New immigrants' excitement fades very soon, however, as they have difficulty adjusting. Two main issues raised by a number of interviewees were housing and difficulty finding a job: the 'first two months were very terrible because I could not find a job' (Lidiya). The difficulties of finding a job seem to mainly stem from language issues:

> And so I started going around looking for a job, but you know how it is when you do not know anyone. And I basically didn't know any language ... And I needed to work somewhere, so I started going everywhere and asking people, and was offering some caretaking and all, but it didn't fit me, or I didn't fit them. (Sofia)

Because of poor language skills and an inability to confirm their college degrees, many immigrants are forced to settle for casual jobs, which are likely to impose a social demotion:

> I came to America when I was 39... and at that time I could not go to college and take more credits and study so that I could legalise my education ... well I mean it is legal but to confirm my diploma of English teacher and get a teaching license, and all of that ... I had to pay a lot out of my own pocket. (Olena)

Since Olena could not confirm her diploma, she could no longer work as a college professor as she did in Ukraine. With tears in her eyes she recalled going from being a college professor in Ukraine to being a housekeeper in the US:

> I can tell you that I got settled right away as a housekeeper ... The first day when I came to work it was a terrible feeling. And [my employer], she looked at me and said, 'I cannot believe that such an educated person', I think my face just didn't look as a simple peasant ... She said, 'I cannot believe this, I am not even comfortable to hire you'.

Vitaliy, another interviewee who had a graduate degree and had held various city administration positions in Ukrainian intelligentsia, shared a similar story. Coming to the US he worked construction, carpentry and other casual jobs. Since these struggles seemed to be universal, they were reflected in the narrative as words from the female protagonist:

> We knew some Ukrainians here in New York who agreed to help us find jobs and housing. But without the knowledge of American building codes Petro cannot work as a contractor, and my level of English is not high enough to confirm my medical degree. Working in our professions is impossible. Although we are getting tremendous help from other Ukrainians here, it's hard. We both have to settle for odd jobs.

The transition is also very difficult for children. Olena remembers her son's difficulties with accessing education because of his language skills: 'It happened so that for my child he needed to pass Test of English as a Foreign Language (TOEFL) right away and was a few points short [the first time he took it]'.

As the issues of children' adjustment seem very salient for immigrants, it was necessary to include a paragraph on children in the culturally grounded narrative. The transition was tough not only for the adults. Andriy was struggling in catching up to the school program in English, and would often be bullied because of his poor language skills and cultural difference. 'The principal calls me to school all the time', says Nadiya. 'Andriy cannot stand being made fun of and gets into fights with other kids'. While little Natalia behaved well in the kindergarten, she also came home crying because other children could not understand her and would not play with her.

The accumulation of issues with jobs, the language, and children precipitates stress and sadness. Ruslana commented that she sees it in her fellow immigrants: 'we see each other here … somehow you can see it in the eyes, some kind of pain or something, some sadness'. These emotions affect the quality of life for Ukrainian immigrants who want to find a way to remember where they came from: 'The most important thing is for everyone to hold together, not forget about their country, where they came from, so that they knew they are Ukrainian and know their history, that they love Ukraine, and not forget it' (Lidiya).

These difficulties and finding ways to cope with immigration related stress were portrayed in the narrative:

> 'I had to do something for my family', Petro admitted. 'If only I could find a way to help them cope with this stress we have accumulated, I feel like we could continue working hard and eventually make a good life for ourselves here'. Petro said that a few other families recommended that he take his family for a trip back to Ukraine, that reconnecting with the homeland and relatives back home will help his wife and children. However, he wasn't sure if that is what they needed.

Many respondents suggested that going back to Ukraine has been helpful in coping with their immigration-related stress. Trips home and maintenance of Ukrainian traditions are the source of stability and continuity in Sofia's life:

> [My life] almost did not change [much]. I go to a Ukrainian church, my husband also is of Ukrainian origin. Although he was born here, he knows all the traditions, and we celebrate all Ukrainian holidays. Practically nothing changed. We keep in touch with Ukraine. Just recently we all went to Ukraine because I have my mother there. So nothing changed.

The act of going to Ukraine and reconnecting with family as a means of achieving a sense of continuity and stress relief was incorporated into the cultural narrative. Several months later, another Ukrainian family was traveling back to Ukraine for a two-week-long visit and invited the Kovalenkos with them, promising to even lend them some money for airfares. Everyone was excited about the opportunity and, in a week, the Kovalenko family was on the plane to Ukraine. In just a little over 10 days in Ivano-Frankivsk Petro could not recognise his family. Nadiya reconnected with her girlfriends from the hospital and even helped them out a few times. Petro could see how his wife's face lit up every time she got a chance to do what she loved most: help people. Petro's parents were spending lots of time with Andriy and Natalia, telling them bedtime stories and showing them how to tend to the garden. Grandpa was showing Andriy some of his woodcarving skills and little Natalia was getting her first lessons on Ukrainian embroidery from her grandma. Petro felt very happy himself.

As the act of going home brings about tremendous relief, immigrants desire to continue to visit Ukraine:

> I would go home every year and I kept thinking … I could not get used to this land, it is still strange to me, not native, not mine … I am pulled to go back to Ukraine again and again. (Andrij)

> I have this vision … if a person goes to college, it means she will stay here forever. And when I am asked if I plan to stay here forever or I plan to come back, I cannot reply. It is a very difficult question. I would like to build my future here, but I cannot be torn away from Ukraine. The best option that I would like would be living here but having an opportunity to go to Ukraine often, maybe once a year of once every two years. To have an opportunity to visit Ukraine all the time. (Ruslana)

These sentiments were represented in the culturally grounded narrative by the main protagonist, the father of the Kovalenko family:

> I could see how this trip gave my family exactly what it needed', Petro rejoiced. 'We reconnected with family, my children were reminded who

they are and where they come from. We all came back much happier and ready to tackle any challenge. I now know why my friends were suggesting this trip. I have decided that, whatever the cost, we will try to go back to Ukraine every few years now.

In summary, we created a culturally grounded promotional narrative by building on the themes and quotes derived through interviews with Ukrainian immigrants. In the following section we discuss how we assessed the narratives' effectiveness.

Narrative assessment

Two texts were incorporated into an online survey administered to 56 Ukrainian immigrants. One was the culturally grounded narrative presented here and the other, which served as a control condition, was a neutral/factual text describing the geography of Ukraine. This text focused on the different geographic regions of Ukraine, the importance of its geopolitical location, the length of its borders with its neighbours and unique geographic areas such as rivers, lakes, mountains, plains and steppes. It, however, did not contain any characters or emotional tone.

As a result of random distribution, 27 respondents (48%) read the narrative and 29 respondents (52%) read the factual text. After being exposed to one of the two treatments, respondents were asked to rate the text they read using narrative assessment measures: how credible, informative, compelling, and interesting they found the text, and how much they agreed that it promoted travel to Ukraine. Independent t-test analyses were used to compare mean ratings between the narrative and factual texts. The means and significance levels are presented in Table 4.1.

As seen in the table, the culturally grounded narrative received higher mean ratings than the factual text on all assessment measures. However,

Table 4.1 Narrative versus factual text assessment

Narrative assessment measure	Means	Significance (p)
The article I just read was credible	Factual text 2.28 Narrative 3.87	0.001
The article I just read was compelling	Factual text 3.42 Narrative 3.75	0.554
The article I just read was interesting	Factual text 3.12 Narrative 3.50	0.449
The article I just read was informative	Factual text 2.20 Narrative 3.38	0.012
After reading the article, I believe going to Ukraine is good for immigrants	Factual text 3.56 Narrative 4.08	0.372

only credibility and informativeness reached statistical significance. It is notable that the mean score on the statement, 'After reading the articles I believe going to Ukraine is good for immigrants', is higher for individuals who were exposed to the culturally grounded narrative.

Conclusions

National stories and nationalistic sentiments (i.e. narratives) are commonly used by the tourism industry to promote various types of travel. The degree to which such narratives encourage diaspora tourism amongst immigrants, particularly people from countries with long histories of oppression or difficulty building a national identity, has to date been unclear (Palmer, 2007). In this study we began by using a process outlined by Larkey and Hecht (2010) to create a culturally grounded narrative. Our resulting narrative reflected images and stories of immigration presented by one diaspora – Ukrainians living in the US. When compared with a neutral/factual text describing the geography of Ukraine, the narrative was deemed more interesting, credible and persuasive.

Our results are important for at least three reasons. First, documenting how to develop a culturally grounded narrative that informs a promotional campaign is of value to tourism practitioners who are tasked with appealing to and obtaining response behaviour from immigrants. Second, our results lend support to Morgan et al.'s (2003) research. They found that culturally grounded narratives are successful in affecting diaspora's travel behaviour. Third, we have provided baseline data for future research that could potentially link diaspora tourism with immigrants' well-being. As Macdonald (2006: 11) states, helping diaspora to connect to their national heritage through activities such as tourism can help them cope with immigration-related illnesses (e.g. depression, anxiety, addiction; Falicov, 2007) and promote psychological well-being (Iyer & Jetten, 2011).

It is prudent to note that promotion campaigns focused around culturally grounded narratives require just as much attention as tourism campaigns based on didactic or expository material, if not more, for several reasons. First, these narratives are based on immigrants' lived experiences, and as experiences of different immigrant waves vary (Iarmolenko & Kerstetter, 2015), these narratives will have to be adjusted as well to remain appealing with culturally relevant cues.

Second, as the history of the country itself evolves, the emotions and feelings of immigrants towards it will shift accordingly (Iarmolenko & Kerstetter, 2016) – and narratives ought to follow. In the example of Ukraine, the ebb and flow of immigrants' feelings went from hope during the Orange Revolution (Karatnycky, 2005) to disappointment with its outcomes, to renewed aspirations and outrage at the situation around Euromaidan (Diuk, 2014).

In conclusion, culturally grounded narratives provide an effective option for diaspora tourism promotion that is authentic, credible and persuasive. Using culturally grounded narratives provides tourism practitioners with expanded opportunities, while at the same time presenting them with a completely different set of challenges associated with immigrant characteristics and the home country environment.

References

Anderson, B. (1983) *Imagined Communities: Reflections on the Origin and Spread of Nationalism*. New York: Verso Books.

Basu, P. (2005) Roots-tourism as return movement: Semantics and the Scottish diaspora. In M. Harper (ed.) *Emigrant Homecomings: The Return Movement of Emigrants* (pp. 1600–2000). Manchester: Manchester University Press.

Bazynskyj, A. (2009) Learning how to be Ukrainian: Ukrainian schools in Toronto and the formation of identity. Unpublished Master's thesis, University of Toronto, Ontario.

Buzinde, C.N., Santos, C.A. and Smith, S.L. (2006) Ethnic representations: Destination imagery. *Annals of Tourism Research* 33 (3), 707–728.

Dal Cin, S., Zanna, M.P. and Fong, G.T. (2004) Narrative persuasion and overcoming resistance. In E.S. Knowles and J.A. Linn (eds) *Resistance and Persuasion* (pp. 175–191). Mahwah, NJ: Lawrence Erlbaum Associates.

Diuk, N. (2014) Euromaidan: Ukraine's self-organizing revolution. *World Affairs* 176 (6), 9–17.

Duvell, F. and Lapshyna, I. (2015) The EuroMaidan protests, corruption, and war in Ukraine: Migration trends and ambitions. The Migration Policy Institute. See http://www.migrationpolicy.org/article/euromaidan-protests-corruption-and-war-ukraine-migration-trends-and-ambitions (accessed 22 November 2014).

Falicov, C.J. (2007) Working with transnational immigrants: Expanding meanings of family, community, and culture. *Family Process* 46 (2), 157–171.

Gellner, E. (1964) *Thought and Change*. Oxford: Blackwell.

Green, M.C. (2006) Narratives and cancer communication. *Journal of Communication* 56 (s1), S163–S183.

Green, M.C. and Brock, T.C. (2000) The role of transportation in the persuasiveness of public narratives. *Journal of Personality and Social Psychology* 79 (5), 701–721.

Hecht, M.L., Marsiglia, F.F., Elek, E., Wagstaff, D.A., Kulis, S., Dustman, P. and Miller-Day, M. (2003) Culturally grounded substance use prevention: An evaluation of the keepin'it REAL curriculum. *Prevention Science* 4 (4), 233–248.

Iarmolenko, S. and Kerstetter, D. (2015) Potential predictors of diaspora tourism for Ukrainian immigrants in the USA. *World Leisure Journal*, 57 (3), 221–234.

Iarmolenko, S. and Kerstetter, D. (2016) Identity, adjustment, and transnational activity patterns of fourth-wave Ukrainian diaspora in the United States. *Tourism Culture and Communication*, 15 (3), 237–247.

Iyer, A. and Jetten, J. (2011) What's left behind: Identity continuity moderates the effect of nostalgia on well-being and life choices. *Journal of Personality and Social Psychology* 101 (1), 94–108.

Jacobs, R.N. (2002) The narrative integration of personal and collective identity in social movements. In M.C. Green, J.J. Strange and T.C. Brock (eds) *Narrative Impact: Social and Cognitive Foundations* (pp. 205–228). New York: Taylor and Francis.

Karatnycky, A. (2005) Ukraine's orange revolution. *Foreign Affairs* 84 (2), 35–52.

Larkey, L.K. and Hecht, M. (2010) A model of effects of narrative as culture-centric health promotion. *Journal of Health Communication* 15 (2), 114–135.

Leite, N. (2005) Travels to an ancestral past: On diasporic tourism, embodied memory, and identity. *ANTROPOlogicas*, *9*, 273–302.

Macdonald, S. (2006) Undesirable heritage: Fascist material culture and historical consciousness in Nuremberg. *International Journal of Heritage Studies* 12 (1), 9–28.

Marschall, S. (2014) 'Homesick tourism': Memory, identity and (be)longing. *Current Issues in Tourism*, http://dx.doi.org/10.1080/13683500.2014.920773

Morgan, N., Pritchard, A. and Pride, R. (2003) Marketing to the Welsh diaspora: The appeal to hiraeth and homecoming. *Journal of Vacation Marketing* 9 (1), 69–80.

Nairn, T. (1977) *The Break-up of Britain: Crisis and Neo-Nationalism*. London: New Left Books.

Oatley, K. and Gholamain, M. (1997) Emotions and identification: Connections between readers and fiction. In M. Hjort and S. Laver (eds) *Emotion and the Arts* (pp. 263–281). New York: Oxford University Press.

Ostrowski, S. (1991) Ethnic tourism – focus on Poland. *Tourism Management* 12 (2), 125–130.

Palmer, N. (2007) Ethnic equality, national identity and selective cultural representation in tourism promotion: Kyrgyzstan, Central Asia. *Journal of Sustainable Tourism* 15 (6), 645–662.

Pierre, J. (2009) Beyond heritage tourism race and the politics of African diasporic interactions. *Social Text* 27 (98), 59–81.

Pretes, M. (2003) Tourism and nationalism. *Annals of Tourism Research* 30 (1), 125–142.

Seton-Watson, H. (1977) *Nations and States: An Enquiry into the Origins of Nations and the Politics of Nationalism*. London: Taylor and Francis.

Slater, M.D. (2002) Entertainment education and the persuasive impact of narratives. In M.C. Green, J.J. Strange and T.C. Brock (eds) *Narrative Impact: Social and Cognitive Foundations* (pp. 157–181). Mahwah, NJ: Lawrence Erlbaum.

Van Oudenhoven, J.P. and Ward, C. (2013) Fading majority cultures: The implications of transnationalism and demographic changes for immigrant acculturation. *Journal of Community and Applied Social Psychology* 23 (2), 81–97.

Wolowyna, O. and Lopukh, V. (2014) Center for Demographic and Socio-economic Research of Ukrainians in the US. Shevchenko Scientific Society, Inc. See http://www.inform-decisions.com/stat/ (accessed 28 April 2014).

5   Travelling to the Past: Xi'an and the Tang Imperial City

Yujie Zhu and Yang Yang

Introduction

Xi'an, an inland city in northwestern China and Tang Dynasty capital, holds a special place in the history of Chinese nation-building. The Tang is seen as an archetype of the Chinese empire owing to the state's competitiveness in economic and military power. Chang'an, as Xi'an was known then, is seen as a metropolis and home to global trade and cultural exchange. This historic image of a prosperous imperial capital on the Silk Road has become a convenient resource for the local government to boost its economy within the context of inter-city domestic competition. The current urban plan in Xi'an intends to restore the past of Chang'an as an emerging metropolis. In examining this Tang-themed development plan, this chapter focuses on Chinese nationalism in the context of cultural heritage and tourism development. We wish to explore how the Chinese state adapts heritage discourse to fulfil goals of nation-building and economic development. Ensuing questions include how local industry utilises the branding of heritage tourism and produces commodities to satisfy the imaginaries of modern consumers and how nationalism is performed and experienced by tourists.

First, we discuss the concept of nationalism and the Chinese discourse of cultural heritage. Second, we illustrate how the Xi'an local government uses the 'Tang Imperial City Plan' to produce new urban spaces for heritage tourism purposes. Third, we examine how nationalism is realised through practices that affect the actual feeling of tourists. We conclude the chapter by discussing the interplay between nationalism and heritage practices in Xi'an.

Instead of directly applying the Western discourse of nationalism in a Chinese setting, this study aims to investigate China and its modern nationalism in the context of cultural and economic globalisation. To avoid the dichotomies of East–West or China–the rest, this study combines three different approaches: a review of the traditional and modern nationalism; a discursive analysis of nationalism and cultural heritage; and an ethnographic observation of recent heritage tourism in Xi'an.

Revisiting Nationalism

The many aspects of nationalism have been debated extensively in the academic world. Different from the notion of 'state', where the focus is on political governance, nationalism refers to national identity and a unified community. Benedict Anderson's (1983) concept of the 'imagined community' successfully explained why people form social bonds without knowing each other. In this sense, nation construction is a process of imagining and transforming ideas into national coherence. Anderson's term is helpful to explain how identities in a nation-state are framed in relation to domestic and foreign policy. However, Herzfeld's (2015) intellectual review of nationalism illustrates that we need to adjust the use of this term in contemporary social and cultural contexts.

Formerly achieved through kinship or race, nation-building is now realised by governmental use of political power (Geertz, 1990). In this era of economic and cultural globalisation, the discussion of nationalism has been further enhanced by new research on practices such as transnational exchange, capitalist economy, diaspora and ethnic solidarity. These new research trends do not indicate the death of nation-states or nationalism, but rather indicate a continuous investigation of this dynamic and ever-changing phenomenon. Instead of solely emphasising the importance of national ideologies and bureaucratic politics, nationalism can now refer to the processes of ethnic management, cultural diplomacy and economic development (Hutchinson & Smith, 1994).

Recent scholarship has extended the discussion of nationalism as a strategy of governance in the context of economic globalisation (Volcic & Andrejevic, 2011; White, 2009). For instance, Seo (2008) analysed the cultural industry in China through the connections between commercial nationalism and markets. She argued that markets play a significant role in the production of political discourse in Chinese society. Similarly, Volcic (2008) discussed the concept of commercial nationalism by considering cultural regionalism and local nationalism in the Balkan region.

This chapter is concerned with Chinese nationalism in the context of cultural heritage practices. Since the 19th century, cultural heritage has been discursively framed as an 'invented tradition' to reinforce national consciousness or collective memory (Salazar & Zhu, 2015). Different cultural practices have been employed by nations as forms of governance to create a sense of longevity or authenticity. Along with the emergence of a unified Europe and the wave of decolonisation after the Second World War, nationalism and internationalism have become increasingly interrelated. In this context, to achieve a better diplomatic strategy in contemporary political and economic relations, nation-states often pursue a language of 'shared heritage' to create historical and cultural commonality (Winter, 2014). The tourism industry, a by-product of cultural heritage, not only attract tourists dollars, but also enhances the profile of the national imaginary amongst international visitors (Timothy & Boyd, 2006). These practices acknowledge local values and cultural memory while allowing local communities to connect with the wider world.

As seen in Xi'an, we argue that the realisation of nationalism can be imagined and practiced. One can perform the nation through celebrating national events, performing historic stories and conducting religious rituals. These mediated performances are important for the social, cultural and political coherence of the nation. They not only represent the symbolic nature of the state, but also have social, cultural and economic consequences. These practices boost the local economy, affect the actual feeling of people and revitalise social memories into everyday life.

To echo the theme of the book, we further argue that commercial nationalism can be achieved by individuals through their performance and generation of diverse meanings in the tourism space (Edensor, 2001). Heritage is not only a powerful tool for authorities, but also 'mediated by our bodies in an animation of space that combines feelings, imagination and sensuous and expressive qualities' (Crouch, 2002). Rather than just from certified knowledge and expertise, 'nationalism' is experienced through one's emotional, affective and sensuous relatedness to a place.

Chinese Discourse of Cultural Heritage

Since the 20th century, China has gradually adopted Western notions of 'nation' (minzu) and 'state' (guojia) to revise its traditional world outlook, resulting in the rise of modern Chinese nationalism. Having founded the People's Republic of China, the Communist government promoted nationalism through its domestic and regional economic development and social alliances with other nations. It also integrated the Leninist–Stalinist political model for its own party-state system.

In recent decades, China has undergone profound political and socioeconomic transformations. The central state recognised the significant role of cultural conservation in building national identity and promoting Chinese civilisation (Oakes, 1993). Cultural heritage in China has also been recognised as an economic resource in the context of economic modernisation (Svensson, 2006). The ideological shift to cultural revitalisation has motivated China to join the United Nations Educational, Scientific and Cultural Organization's (UNESCO) Convention Concerning the Protection of the World Cultural and Natural Heritage in 1985.

Subsequently, the promotion and preservation of cultural heritage in China has occurred through a number of policies and practices at the national, provincial and local levels. Many other actors besides the state participate in these national and regional campaigns, including business operators, scholars, tourism investors and local community groups (Zhu & Li, 2013). Private collectors organise cultural museums to represent local living heritage. University scholars and academic institutes develop research projects to support local governments in the development and promotion of local culture. The growth of heritage tourism – targeting domestic and international tourists – has motivated the search for and consumption of living culture, especially in ethnic minority areas (Zhu, 2012).

In the context of China's transition to a commercialised consumer society, historic cities have become one of the focal points of heritage tourism. The heritage tourism industry in these sites has played a significant role in stimulating both the regional and national economies (Oakes, 1993). Many historical city centres are characterised by globalisation and modernity, where traditional cultures and urban forms are increasingly recognised, reconstructed and even reinvented. They have become the focus of a global 'tourist gaze' (Urry, 1990) and a stage for socio-cultural representation of hegemonic discourses of nationalism. Regional and local governments have increasingly utilised urban renewal of historic cities for the purposes of heritage revival, tradition reinvention and commercial exploitation.

Xi'an and its Tang Imperial City Plan

Located in the northwest of China, Xi'an is the capital city of Shaanxi province. Serving as an industrial, economic and educational hub of northwest China, the city dates back to the 11th century. Formerly called Daxing in the Sui Dynasty (581–605) and then Chang'an in the Tang Dynasty (618–904), Xi'an was the most populous and civilised urban centre in China's imperial times, dominated by a sophisticated secular culture, yet involved with the spirit of monastic religion (Xiong, 2000: 1). Along with the arrival of merchants, missionaries, travellers and pilgrims from all over China and Asia, the city also played host to a dynamic and thriving political, religious and business community. It was regarded as the eastern end of the Silk Road for cultural and business exchange among China and Central Asian countries. This legacy of political and cultural dominance places the city at the forefront of debates on cultural heritage in the evolution of China (Feighery, 2011).

In the early 21st century Xi'an responded to the national launch of the Western Development Programme that aims to restore economic balance between China's western and eastern regions. Seeking to move beyond the city's industrial image, local authorities have attempted to develop new urban regeneration programmes focused on reconstructing traditional cityscapes through heritage-related practices and wholesale redevelopment.

In response to national policies of promoting tourism as a pillar industry, Xi'an has capitalised on its historic heritage as cultural resources for tourism consumption. In 2011, 66.5 million international and domestic tourists visited Xi'an, creating 53 billion Yuan (US$8.2 billion) in tourism revenue – this accounted for 14% of local GDP (Xi'an Bureau of Statistics, 2012). It is not an exaggeration to say that the development of the city, in particular its modernisation and integration into global networks, relies heavily on heritage tourism.

In 2005, the Xi'an municipal government launched the Tang Imperial City Plan, with a total investment of 23 billion Yuan (approximately US$3.5 billion; Feighery, 2011). Policymakers are keen to transform the densely populated areas of Xi'an's inner city into a functioning replica of the Tang Imperial City by 2050.[1] This will require reconstruction of the old city in the architectural style of the Tang Dynasty to, it is endeavoured, revive the former glory of Xi'an as the ancient capital and the hearth of Chinese civilisation.

Tang Imperial City planning, as with heritage tourism projects in other cities or sites, is a state-led project. It is conducted by cooperation between the Xi'an Department of Urban Planning and the Provincial Bureau of Cultural Heritage, both which are directly supervised and financially supported by Xi'an Municipality. As illustrated by an interview with an official from the Provincial Planning Department, Tang Imperial City Planning is part of the City Master Plan. In China, such a master plan is more than just a blueprint; it guides urban development and channels the flow of capital and people (Zhang, 2006). The plan has three main aims: to promote and differentiate Xi'an as a economic and administrative centre in the northwest region; to develop the city into a new commercial centre by capitalising on tourism, cultural industry and real estate; and to highlight the heritage city with its rich historical traditions.

To achieve these goals, several pilot projects have adapted the theme of Tang culture in the process of the urban renewal of Xi'an. Some have utilised the history of the Tang Dynasty as a cultural resource to develop tourism, leisure and the real estate industries. Others aim to transform religious or ethnic areas into heritage tourism spaces. In the following section, four heritage spaces are introduced to present different themes of Chang'an as imagined in the Tang Dynasty: the city wall, entertainment parks, the market and its Muslim district.

Experiencing Nationalism

City Wall

Following the Tang Imperial Plan, the current city wall has become a significant landmark, clearly dividing the inner and outer parts of city.

Formerly used as a military defence system, a striking remainder from imperial China, the wall represents an important part of the heritage of the Xi'an. It suffered great damage during wars in the late Tang Dynasty. From the early Ming Dynasty, the wall was partially rebuilt to enlarge the imperial city from 9 to 11.5 km^2 after several restorations. Although the current wall is a combination of the remains of walls from the Tang and Ming dynasties, it is still officially considered to be the primary representation of the Tang imperial city. Several towers as components of the wall were restored and its outer canal was cleansed in 2014.

The city wall has become a tourist attraction for both domestic and international tourists. The City Wall Management Committee organised several cultural activities to celebrate its 2006 nomination for the UNESCO World Heritage List as the historical starting point of the ancient Silk Roads. A wall museum was opened to exhibit its history and showcase archaeological remains from different dynasties. Daily ritual performances are held at the wall's entrance, where alongside soldiers in Tang-themed attire, a 'senior official' chants greeting messages from 'the emperor' to welcome all the visitors who enter the imperial city.

Walking or riding a bike around the wall are the easiest ways for tourists to see the landscape of the inner city. Symbols and decor of the Tang Dynasty were purposely applied to windows and roofs to beautify buildings surrounding the city wall. Xiao Zhang, a graduate student from Xiamen University, was on vacation in Xi'an and told us that he walked on the wall almost every day during his two week stay. 'It is a great feeling', he said, 'When I touch the wall and look at the Xi'an city, I feel a connection with the past. I am a history lover, but never have such feelings when I read history books'.

Beginning in September 2015, a nightly hour-long music and dance performance at the main gate of the city wall show entitled 'Dreaming Chang'an' was performed. The dance and music tell the history of Chang'an, and its importance in trading with Persian and Arab merchants. After watching the show, many tourists and local residents felt that they were members of the royal family back in the Tang, watching exotic dances and appreciating the precious spices, jewellery and other products offered by diplomats as tributes to the state.

Tang theme parks

As a cosmopolitan city in the Tang Dynasty, life in Chang'an was culturally rich with much time for leisure. At this time cultural practices such as singing, dancing, painting and calligraphy are considered to have peaked. To visualise this sophisticated culture, the Xi'an government took advantage of the historical appeal of the Qujiang district to redevelop it as a traditional Tang Dynasty entertainment area. Located in the southern suburb of Xi'an, the

Qujiang district covers 47 square kilometres and combines residential zones with a range of cultural, tourism and leisure facilities (Jaivin, 2010). Various heritage theme parks have been established there based on existing archaeological sites or folkloristic stories.[2] These theme parks are similar to the 'pleasure gardens' of 19th century Europe that used theatrical stages and the natural landscape to cater for tourism, recreation and entertainment activities. The theme parks display the prosperous Tang culture, folklore stories and legends.

Cold Cave Heritage Park (Hanyao) is one of the parks and features the legendary late Tang love story of Wang Baochuan and Xue Pinggui. Wang defied her wealthy family to marry a beggar and then waited in a cold cave for 18 faithful years for his return from the army. The story has been played in traditional operas for hundreds of years as a Confucian teaching on female fidelity; now it has been transformed into a modern tale of romance and love. In the official document, the park is described as 'a happiness industry base integrating heritage conservation, tourist development and cultural industry cultivation'.

Since opening on 1 May 2010, the park has become a popular spot for individual and group weddings. In 2012, more than 50 couples participated in a collective marriage ceremony, wearing costumes replicated from Tang fashions, and had an 'emperor' as their chief witness. Participation in such Tang-themed wedding ceremonies shows how young urban middle class people aspire to differentiate themselves from others by choosing a historically themed ceremony. Specifically, they are enthusiastic about this newly invented 'Tang wedding'. The love theme park allows them to experience a sense of personal freedom and romantic love in ways that differ from regular Chinese wedding ceremonies, which emphasise family bonds and community relationships.

The Tang West Market

In recent years the official regime has recognised and promoted Xi'an as the critical terminus of the New Silk Road initiative. As a network of trade, the Silk Road has long witnessed the linking of China with countries as far away as the Mediterranean region, and has facilitated exchanges in business, religion, scientific knowledge and cultural practices. In June 2014, the World Heritage Committee approved the Silk Road's Chang'an-Tianshan Corridor, covering China, Kazakhstan and Kyrgyzstan as part of the transnational network.

Since the nomination, the Xi'an government has actively integrated the Silk Road discourse into its Tang Imperial City Planning. To revitalise the market of business and trade exchange 1300 years ago, a Tang West Market was newly built on the site of the western market of Chang'an during the Tang Dynasty. The Tang West Market is not merely a market; it is a multifunctional district of museums, antique shops, hotels, restaurants and highend residential developments.

A Silk Road exhibition was held in the Tang West Museum to illustrate the historical significance of the city within the context of the Silk Road. For tourists, visiting the Tang West Market allows them to experience the mundane everyday life in the Tang period. They wander around the museum after hearing a history professor from Shaanxi Normal University give an engaging lecture on the different kinds of trade happening in the market at that time. Then they proceed to the exhibition hall, posing for pictures next to replica shops and artefacts. In the souvenir section, they buy booklets of replica ancient coins to remember their trip. After touring the museum, tourists walk around the Tang-themed shopping mall to explore boutiques of international brands. As one tourist commented, 'shopping in such a market place made me feel like I had travelled back to the past'.

Muslim Quarter

As another important component of the Silk Road and Xi'an, Muslim culture as found in one neighbourhood has been promoted as an important tourism destination. Arriving from Central Asia, these Muslim merchants took a significant role in trading with Central Asia along the Silk Road. In Xi'an, Chinese Muslims (or Hui) are now the dominant ethnic minority. Xi'an's historic Muslim residential neighbourhood is known as the Muslim Quarter (Gillette, 2000). The Xi'an government recognises the livelihood of the Muslim Quarter and the architecture of its Ming-era Great Mosque as important heritage resources and plans to transform it into a heritage space as part of the Tang Imperial Plan.

Located west of the Bell Tower in the old downtown of Xi'an, the Muslim Quarter occupies about one square mile, and is home to 30,000 Hui Muslims, accounting for approximately 50% of the total Hui Muslim population in the city. It is densely packed with small shops, restaurants and residential buildings, and 12 mosques are located within 13 streets and alleys. As the earliest landmark of the Muslim Quarter, the Great Mosque was also included in the World Heritage nomination of the Silk Road.

In 2005, the urban planning office chose a street around the Great Mosque to represent the theme of Hui food, now known as 'Hui Food Street'. Cooks and waiters perform preparing and serving food along the neon-lit street, making it one of the most popular tourism attractions in Xi'an. It attracts both local residents and tourists for its distinctive urban landscape and culinary heritage. For many tourists, visiting mosques and experiencing the vibrancy of Muslim food is an essential component of a trip to Xi'an. Ms Qiu came from Beijing to Xi'an for holiday in the summer of 2014. Of her feeling during the visits to the Muslim Quarter, she said:

> I came here every night. In my opinion, this is the most important place in Xi'an. The taste of food makes me remember my experience in this

ancient city … Frankly speaking, I am not very impressed by architecture and monuments, but am obsessed with these delicious foods. I like every bite, and enjoy watching the making of the food. I took a lot of photos and videos of food. They (photos and videos) make me feel really connected to Xi'an.

Conclusion

The story of Xi'an contributes to the understanding of the interplay between cultural heritage, tourism and Chinese nationalism. First, redeveloping this historic Chinese city based on an image of the ancient imperial capital echoes the necessity of 'inventing traditions' to support the political discourse of a nation growing more powerful. The Tang Imperial City Plan is a constellation of governing strategies to produce new urban spaces within historical narratives in the flux of modernity. The related cultural projects endorse the official discourse of the New Silk Road, seeking to strengthen China's alliance with other countries through their common economic agendas. As a result, local and central governments have combined to orchestrate nationalism through commercialising heritage.

Second, Tang-themed urban renewal projects in Xi'an represent China's efforts to implement nationalism through defining and legitimising heritage consumption and commercialisation. This imaginary of Chinese nationalism, as Seo (2008) suggests, needs to be supported by the commercial market. The prosperity of the Tang Dynasty is now situated in the modern context of developing shopping malls and generating profits through real estate booms in cultural heritage districts. In this process, the Tang is more than just an imagination of a certain period – the invented past of the imperial capital is a vital resource for boosting the local economy.

We argue that nationalism is not an abstract ideology: it can be performed through embodied experience. It is an accumulative process and performative practices of creating, preserving and reinforcing the sense of originality, roots or authenticity. In the story of Xi'an, we have illustrated that nationalism is embedded in different forms of tourism consumption. Yet tourists are not passive recipients of the designed discourse. Their understanding of the glorious past of the Tang Dynasty varies from individual to individual, accepting or rejecting the multiple scripts offered by the local government. Their own interpretations of visits to Xi'an's rebuilt past offers a connection between individual desires and national imaginaries.

However, these heritage-based urban renewal projects are not always a win–win game. Profits have been shared between governments, planners, tourism operators and tourists. Heritage becomes a governmental strategy to interpret and justify commercial development based on a dominant view of history. Yet local residents are often the victims of such development in the form of social stratification and gentrification; there is a tension between hegemonic power and local voices, between economic capital and human rights. Who has the right to generate representations of the past? Who should be included in such projects? Future research on the commercialisation of heritage must take into account these added dynamics.

Notes

(1) During the Sui and early Tang dynasties, the Imperial City of Chang'an was south of the Palace City. It was an enclosed space and hosted the offices of main central governmental agencies.
(2) In China, heritage parks (sometimes also called theme parks) created to promote Chinese folk legends and ethnic culture are extremely popular. For instance, Splendid China in Shenzhen, which opened in 1989, presents national scenic attractions to express 'the cream of glorious culture and long history of the Chinese nation' (Stanley, 1998: 66–67; Nyíri, 2011: 15). Following the success of Splendid China, hundreds of similar theme parks were created throughout cities in China.

References

Anderson, B.R. (1983) *Imagined Communities: Reflections on the Origin and Spread of Nationalism*. London: Verso.
Crouch, D. (2002) Surrounded by place: Embodied encounters. In S. Coleman and M. Crang (eds) *Tourism: Between Place and Performance* (pp. 207–218). New York and Oxford: Berghahn.
Edensor, T. (2001) Performing tourism, staging tourism: (Re)producing tourist space and practice. *Tourist Studies* 1 (1), 59–81.
Feighery, W.G. (2011) Contested heritage in the ancient city of peace. *Historic Environment* 23 (1), 38–47.
Geertz, C. (1990) 'Popular art' and the Javanese tradition. *Indonesia* 77–94.
Gillette, M. (2000) *Between Mecca and Beijing: Modernization and Consumption among Urban Chinese Muslims*. Stanford, CA: Stanford University Press.
Herzfeld, M. (2015) States and nationalism. *Emerging Trends in the Social and Behavioral Sciences: An Interdisciplinary, Searchable, and Linkable Resource* 1–14.
Hutchinson, J. and Smith, A.D. (1994) *Nationalism*. Oxford: Oxford University Press.
Jaivin, L. (2010) Qujiang Loved up on history and culture. *China Heritage Quarterly* 24. See http://www.chinaheritagequarterly.org/articles.php?searchterm=024_qujiang.inc&issue=024 (accessed 15 May 2015).
Nyíri, P. (2011) *Scenic Spots: Chinese Tourism, the State, and Cultural Authority*. Seattle, WA: University of Washington Press.
Oakes, T. (1993) The cultural space of modernity: Ethnic tourism and place identity in China. *Environment and Planning C: Society and Space* 11 (1), 47–66.
Salazar, N. and Zhu, Y. (2015) Heritage and tourism. In L. Meskell (ed.) *Global Heritage: A Reader* (pp. 240–258). Hoboken, NJ: John Wiley and Sons.
Seo, J. (2008) Manufacturing nationalism in China: Political economy of 'Say No' businesses. See http://www.allacademic.com/meta/p251595_index.html (accessed 15 June 2010).
Stanley, N. (1998) *Being Ourselves for You: The Global Display of Cultures*. London: Middlesex University Press.
Svensson, M. (2006) *In the Ancestors' Shadow: Cultural Heritage Contestations in Chinese Villages*. Lund, Sweden: Centre for East and South-East Asian Studies, Lund University.

Timothy, D.J. and Boyd, S.W. (2006) Heritage tourism in the 21st century: Valued traditions and new perspectives. *Journal of Heritage Tourism* 1 (1), 1–16.

Urry, J. (1990) *The Tourist Gaze: Leisure and Travel in Contemporary Societies* (1st edn). London: Sage.

Volcic, Z. (2008) Former Yugoslavia on the World Wide Web commercialization and branding of nation-states. *International Communication Gazette* 70 (5), 395–413.

Volcic, Z. and Andrejevic, M. (2011) Nation branding in the era of commercial nationalism. *International Journal of Communication* 5 (21), 598–618.

White, L. (2009) The man from Snowy River: Australia's bush legend and commercial nationalism. *Tourism Review International* 13 (2), 139–146.

Winter, T. (2015) Heritage diplomacy. *International Journal of Heritage Studies* 21 (10), 997–1015.

Xi'an Bureau of Statistics (2012) *Xi'an Statistical Yearbook 2011*. Xi'an: Xi'an Bureau of Statistics.

Xiong, V. (2000) *Sui-Tang Chang'an (583–904): A Study in the Urban History of Medieval China*. Ann Arbor, MI: University of Michigan.

Zhang, L. (2006) Contesting spatial modernity in late-socialist China. *Current Anthropology* 47 (3), 461–484.

Zhu, Y. (2012) Performing heritage: Rethinking authenticity in tourism. *Annals of Tourism Research* 39 (3), 1495–1513.

Zhu, Y. and Li, N. (2013) Groping for stones to cross the river: Governing heritage in Emei. In T. Bluemenfield and H. Silverman (eds) *Cultural Heritage Politics in China* (pp. 51–71). New York: Springer.

6   A New Indian National Story

Maya Ranganathan

Introduction

This chapter explores the implications of the change in government in 2014 for the Indian national story. The 'imagined' and 'abstract' community of nation relies on its spaces, artefacts and monuments to understand and draw from the concepts of nationhood. These structures serve as reminders of the national vision to the people within and as representative of the nation to those without. In their elaboration of the ways in which national identities and tourism are interlinked, White and Frew (2011: 2) assert that, even in the age of globalisation, 'significance of national identity seems to strengthen rather than diminish'. They attribute its continued importance to the two elements of 'immortality' and the flexible nature of its ideology, which allows for different interpretations of it (White & Frew, 2011: 4). 'Commercial nationalism' directed by governments takes the form of celebration of cultural icons that create associations designed to invoke particular imagination of the nation. As Pretes (2003) argues, signifiers created and nurtured by the state attempt to define characteristics of nationhood to popularise a hegemonic narrative of the nation. It then follows that the state could potentially recast the national imagination by creating new signifiers.

The resounding victory of the Bharatiya Janata Party (BJP) in the 2014 national elections changed equations in Indian politics in no uncertain terms (Sardesai, 2015). In the context of this chapter, the party's professed ideology that has always been placed in opposition to that of the Indian National Congress ('Congress' henceforth) that has directed 'nation-making' is of utmost significance. Although the BJP rode to electoral victory on the plank of 'economic development', its emergence as the single largest party capable of forming the government on its own for the first time in three decades signals an increasing acceptance of its Hindu nationalist ideology. The evaluation of BJP's policy pronouncements and budgetary allocations that follows, considered in the context of the relationship between tourism and power, enables an understanding of the trajectory of the Indian national story (Coles & Church, 2007).

A Clash of Ideologies

The election landscape provides the background to the ideological conflicts in relation to nation-building. Notwithstanding the range of political parties in the poll arena, Indian national elections in the recent past have been bi-partisan contests between two coalitions led by seemingly polar opposites – the Indian National Congress and the BJP.[1] In the ideological spectrum, the Congress party is considered 'Centre-left' and the BJP as 'Centre-right'. The 'liberal nationalism' of the Congress has been directed by 'Nehruvian consensus', a policy of inclusiveness and state action that has directed nation-making since the country's independence in1947 (Congress, n.d.),[2] while the BJP's nationalism has been directed by 'Hindutva', a belief in the supremacy of Hindu thought and values as opposed to non-Hindu and Western thoughts and beliefs (BJP, n.d.(a)).

The core argument in this chapter is based on two premises. First is that a government led by a political party that enjoys a majority in Parliament allows for the creation of a national imagery based on its ideology. The availability of a strong state is a prerequisite to forging any identity. The redefinition of Indianness based on Hindu nationalist aspirations rests on 'the availability of a strong state as an instrument through which to forge that identity' (Khilnani, 1997: 190). The second premise is that the process of construction of national identity involves the creation of signifiers that reflect and reiterate the idea of the nation. The nation's spaces and monuments serve as a reminder of the national vision to visitors, who 'develop an appreciation of the destination by understanding it through the lens of national identity' (White & Frew, 2011: 1).

The victorious run of the Congress in the first five elections since Independence was broken by the Janata Dal alliance, a coalition of non-Congress governments, in 1977. The second non-Congress government in 1989 was headed by V.P. Singh, a former Congress partyman who on leaving the party formed the Jan Morcha, which came together with other non-Congress parties to form the Janata Dal. The two non-Congress governments were unable to run to the full five-year term, owing to rifts in the coalition. It is interesting to note that the parties that comprised the coalitions on both occasions were united not by ideology but solely by their opposition to the Congress. The BJP was formed around this time in April 1980. It traces its origin to the nationalist movement of the Rashtriya Swayamsevak Sangh (RSS), which is guided by the belief in primacy of Hindu thought and values as espoused by religious and spiritual leaders such as Swami Dayanand Saraswati, Swami Vivekananda, Lokmanya Tilak and Mahatma Gandhi besides Dr Hegdewar, who founded the RSS. The BJP also regards the Bharatiya Jana Sangh, formed by Shyamaprasad Mukherjee in 1951, as its predecessor (BJP, n.d.(a)).

The ideological affiliation of the BJP sets it apart from many of the other political parties. Its emergence as a viable alternative to the Congress was evident in 1989 when it did not form part of the Janata Dal government but extended support 'from outside' to the government on the strength of the 85 seats (of a total of 542) it won in Parliament. The growing popularity of the party has been traced to public discourse in the late 1980s and early 1990s shaped by both the growth in regional press and the serialised presentation of Hindu mythologies 'Ramayan' and 'Mahabharath' by the national tele-caster Doordarshan (Jeffrey, 2000; Rajagopal, 2001). This was followed by BJP's 'rath yatra' (a journey by chariot) in September 1990 from the temple town of Somnath to Ayodhya, the birthplace of the Hindu God Ram, believed to have been desecrated by the building of a mosque in the time of Mughal King Babar in 1527.[3] In 1991 the Indian economy was liberalised by a Congress government, an act that directly impacted upon the media land-scape in India. The opening of the skies and the mushrooming of private television channels changed political discourse in unforeseen ways in the years to come. A media-savvy BJP was quick to adopt the vibrant mediascape for its own ends (Thomas, 2010: 77). The acceptance of the 'soft Hindutva' institutionalised by the BJP has been attributed to the communalisation of the Indian polity by the later Congress governments, the expanding Hindu middle class, the continuing problem of separatism in Kashmir and the emer-gence of an assertive Islamic fundamentalism in South Asia (Hibbard, 2010: 149–175). While the BJP met with success in the different state elections, a majority in Parliament has eluded it, much as it has eluded the Congress since the late 1980s. It won 161 seats in Parliament in 1996 to head the third non-Congress government, but the government collapsed in a matter of 13 days owing to rifts in the coalition. The next BJP-led coalition government in 1998, formed on the strength of the party winning 182 seats, lasted a mere 13 months. In the elections held the following year, the BJP won the same number of seats and presided over a coalition of 20 regional parties under the banner of National Democratic Alliance (NDA). The NDA lasted a full term. It lost power to the Congress-led United Progressive Front in 2004 and 2009. The NDA that fought the elections under the BJP leadership in 2014 com-prised 30 regional parties. The alliance won a total of 338 of 543 seats. Significantly, the BJP emerged as the single largest party with 281 seats, rendering its alliance with other parties superfluous to run the government to provide the first strong government in three decades.

While there are many striking issues that set the 2014 national elections apart from the earlier ones, I draw attention to issues relating to narratives of the nation. The issues are sought to be understood by looking at two aspects: (a) the election manifesto of BJP which eventually emerged victorious; and (b) the performance and pronouncements of its prime ministerial candidate Narendra Modi, who had served for three successive terms from 2001 to 2014 as the chief minister of the state of Gujarat in western India. The BJP's pledge contained in its manifesto relates to economic development on the 'foundation of our culture' (BJP, n.d.(a)). While the manifesto focuses on different segments of the society, the preface outlines the primacy that India held in science as early as the 11th century, mentions the advanced civilisations that existed 'several thousand years' before the Christian era, and the peaceful co-existence of religions over centuries. The historical past and the Indian freedom struggle 'inspired by Tilak, Gandhi, Aurobindo, Patel, Bose and others' civilisational consciousness', provide indications of the 'foundation of culture' referred to earlier (BJP, n.d.(a)). The narrative of India's cultural and civilisational greatness includes Buddhist and Jain contributions while excluding Christian influences and remaining silent on the developments in the Mughal era. The BJP asserts that it will draw from 'India's world-view', which it claims is not in consonance with the 'institutional framework of administration created by the Britishers'. Interestingly, the vision resonates with 'identity tourism' – 'the notion that tourism and finding out about one's identity has broad appeal' (Frew & White, 2011: 6). The later parts of the preface are devoted to more recent history, particularly the failure of the previous Congress-led government to keep the spirit of India alive. Notwithstanding the well-known stand on the abrogation of Article 370 from the Indian Constitution that allows for special status to the state of Kashmir and the commitment to build a Ram temple in Ayodhya, particular provisions sought to be implemented for the welfare of different sections of people are inclusive.[4] The departure from the earlier philosophies that guided Indian nation-making is clearly flagged. The BJP identifies tourism as a key sector to ensure socio-economic progress through the creation of jobs, to further infrastructure development and to promote foreign exchange earnings, and regards it as one of the five ways to revive 'Brand India' (BJP, n.d.(a)).

The Modi Years

The announcement of the candidature of Narendra Modi for prime ministership in late 2013 has widely been read as indicative of the trajectory of the national narrative in the event of a BJP victory. Modi has been a controversial political figure owing to the communal riots that took place in 2002 in Godhra during his first tenure as a chief minister (Engineer, 2003; Jaffrolet, 2003; Varadarajan, 2003). Modi's subsequent electoral victories in Gujarat and the verdict of the Special Investigation Team of the Supreme Court have been cited as proof of exoneration of his government's role in fomenting the riots. However, political and public discourse ahead of the election focused on the nature of 'secularism' that will prevail under Modi's leadership. Secularism in India has been a highly contested concept with any interpretation of it having serious consequences for the syncretic view of India (Tejani, 2008: 11,251; Sil, 2014: 346–347). The 'positive secularism' of the BJP is distinguished from 'European secularism' that is independent of religion, by its belief that all religions must be treated as equal (Seshia, 1998: 1036–1050; Guha, 2007: 226–227, 644; Jaffrolet, 1996). In popular discourse, the secularism of congress is identified with privileges to the minorities while BJP defines it as treating all religions on a par. The emergence of Modi as a prime ministerial candidate brought attention to the events and issues in Gujarat during his three terms as chief minister, including the 'model of development' adopted in the state. The six 'transformational initiatives' that have changed Gujarat which formed the 'vision for India' focused on improving infrastructure for a faster growth of the economy (BJP, n.d.(b)). The merits of the model and the claims of the BJP have been debated (Hirway et al., 2014; Kalaiyarasan, 2014). It is worth noting that the commercial nation is guided by the neo-liberalist ideology of the West even as cultural nationalism draws from the Hindutva ideology expressed in terms antithetical to Western liberalism (Hewitt, 2008: 41). It has been followed by regular assertions that history has been distorted by Western and secular historians and calls to commemorate true patriots (Tiwari, 2014; Saikumar, 2015).

Around the one year anniversary of the BJP coming to power, party president Amit Shah clarified that the party did not have enough of a mandate in Parliament to repeal Article 370 of the Constitution or to introduce a uniform civil code in the country (Mathew, 2015). Home Minister Rajnath Singh had earlier stated the inability of the party to build a Ram temple in Ayodhya owing to the lack of a majority in the Rajya Sabha (Upper House) (Indian Express, 2015). The bicameral system requires legislation to be passed by both of the Houses. The BJP has a mere 45 members of the total 243 in the Rajya Sabha. Even as the core issues that significantly impact upon the national narrative have been stymied by Constitutional procedures, they have not hampered the creation of a new national imagination through other measures. In fact, Prime Minister Modi's foreign policy makes explicit 'nation-branding', that is, 'the co-ordinated government efforts to manage a country's image' (Risen cited in Volcic and Andrejevic, 2011: 598). Two allocations in the Central budget that allow for the creation of key archival imagery are taken up for consideration. The budget set aside a sum of Rs 2 billion (US$32 million) for a 182 metre-high statue of Vallabhbhai Patel, the first Home Minister of free India, in Prime Minister Modi's home state of Gujarat, and Rs 21 billion (US$334 million) for 'the National Ganga Plan', to clean the River Ganges (Indiabudget, 2015). Among the activities listed in the BJP manifesto to promote tourism are the creation of 50 affordable tourist circuits, aiming to promote tourism in the Himalayas and coastal regions, besides developing heritage sites, and improving infrastructure by modernising airports (Chitravanshi, 2014). Neither of the two allocations are categorised under 'tourism development'; however, they form a significant part of the cultural artefacts and national ceremonies that contribute to the imagination of the nation (O'Sullivan *et al.*, 1994: 196–197).

Creation of Key Archival Imagery

The monument to Patel called the 'statue of unity' currently in progress is to be spread over an area of 20,000 square metres. It will face the Narmada dam on the river island near Vadodara, in Gujarat. Surrounded by a man-made lake covering a 12 km area, it will be the world's tallest statue when completed, constructed with steel framing, reinforced cement concrete and a bronze coating (Statueofunity, n.d.). Although the project was announced in 2010, it received a boost in December 2013 (also the time when the BJP began its campaign for the national elections) when the Gujarat government headed by Narendra Modi established the Sardar Vallabhbhai Patel Rashtriya Ekta Trust. The iron needed for the statue and other structures is to be collected from farmers all over the country for which 36 offices have been set up. This signals efforts to enlist public support, which is also characteristic of nation-branding (Anholt, 2003). The majority of the cost of about US$470 million is to be raised from private contributions, with the Gujarat Government allocating Rs 1 billion in the budget for 2012–2013 and Rs 5 billion in the 2014–2015 budget. The Central government's budgetary allocation covers a significant portion of the cost.

Vallabhbhai Patel is one of the founding fathers of the Indian Republic. Son of a farmer, he was a lawyer who qualified in England and established a successful practice in Ahmedabad, the capital of the state of Gujarat. A devout Hindu, he joined the Indian National Congress that led the movement for freedom in India. A close associate of Mahatma Gandhi, he rose to become the first Home Minister and Deputy Prime Minister of free India. He is known as the 'Iron man of India' for his fearless and pragmatic approach to issues. He is credited with having united the more than 500 self-governing princely states released from British suzerainty by the Indian Independence Act 1947 and the British colonial provinces allocated to India to form the Union of India (Gandhi, 1990; Guha, 2007: 39–44). He is addressed as 'Sardar', meaning 'chief'. He died in 1950. In 1991, Patel was posthumously awarded the highest civilian honour, Bharat Ratna, and in 2014, his birthday on 31 October was declared as Rashtriya Ekta Diwas (National Unity Day). Announcing the Centre's budgetary allocation, Finance Minister Arun Jaitley said that Sardar Patel stood as the symbol of the unity of the country and that leaders like Patel have to be honoured (Ghosh, 2014).

The argument that the statue of unity could potentially lead to a new imagination of India relates directly to the ensuing tussle between the Congress and the BJP over the appropriation of Patel's legacy and the emerging reasons for the adoption of Patel as the icon of modern nationalism (Gandhi, 2014; Zee News, 2013; Chaturvedi, 2013; Timesnow, 2013; FBpolitics, 2013). While the extent of the allocation to and the execution of the ambitious project have been debated, few have questioned the honour accorded to the leader, whose contribution to the making of modern India is indisputable. However, the manner of celebration of Patel exemplifies Smith's (1991: 79) assertion that, 'chameleon-like', nationalism takes colour from the context. In October 2013, a little over a month after his announcement as the BJP's prime ministerial candidate, Modi presided over the ceremony of laying the foundation stone for the statue. At the ceremony he said, 'Every Indian regrets Sardar Patel did not become the first prime minister. Had he been the first prime minister, the country's fate and face would have been completely different' (Reuters, 2013). The statement, aimed at castigating the past governments for the trajectory in which they had placed the Indian nation, presupposes the possibility of a radically different and alternative way of nation-building. Clearly, the monument is aimed to invoke a certain 'spirit of the nation', a spirit embodied by Patel when placed in contrast to other leaders (Huang & Santos, 2011).

The then Prime Minister Manmohan Singh of the Congress party who attended the ceremony said, 'Sardar Patel was instrumental in building India as we know it today. He (Sardar) was associated with the same party I am associated with' (Pathak, 2013). The wrangle over Patel's legacy has brought to attention the perceived differences between Patel and Jawaharlal Nehru. The differences in their approaches to a number of issues, including 'the freedom movement, the Indian constitution, issues related to integration of the reluctant princely states, and matters relating to combating communal violence' have now become part of public discourse (Basu, 2014). The projection of Patel as an ideological rival to Nehru in the Congress party has been seldom supported by history, which has depicted Patel and Nehru as collaborators and colleagues with perhaps different approaches to nation-building (Hewitt, 2008: 41; Gandhi, 1990, 2008: 55; Guha, 2012). Thus, implicit in the celebration of an unsung national hero are ways of projecting an alternative worldview. The positioning of Patel as opposed to Nehru calls into question not merely the Congress's Nehruvian–Indira Gandhi socialism, statism and nationalisation but also the effects of it on the Indian national story, particularly post-Independence. Placed in the context of the political discourse before and after the 2014 elections of the need to eliminate the Nehru family-dominated Congress from Indian politics, the statue of unity evokes a nostalgia for the pragmatism of Patel that allowed for visions of 'an industrialised India in which vibrant capitalism would coexist with Hindu traditions' – an idea that is at the core of BJP's ideology (Basu,

2014). In the process, the towering statue of Sardar Patel potentially is the 'synecdoche' – a visual image that works with other kinds of representations – of the new Indian story (Laclau, 2005). It also becomes part of the nation-branding campaign that address a range of issues, besides promoting tourism (Volcic & Andrejevic, 2011: 599).

Similarly, the renewed efforts to clean up the River Ganges and the revamping of the National Ganga Plan assumes significance in the context of continuing political discourse and the imagery that it evokes. The Ganges (or Ganga) is a river rising in the western Himalayas in the north Indian state of Uttarakhand. The river flows 2525 km through the 1,086,000 square km Gangetic Plain of North India into Bangladesh, where it empties into the Bay of Bengal. Historically, it has served as the centres of many kingdoms including the Mauryan Empire (322–185 BCE) and the Mughal Empire (1526–1857). The British founded Kolkata on the banks of its tributary, the Hooghly River, in the late 17th century. Along the river today are 118 towns. However, the religious significance of the river for the Hindus far exceeds that of any other river in India (Eck, 1983; Jacobs, 2010: 37–39). The movement to cleanse the River Ganges of the pollutants caused by domestic usage like bathing, laundry and public defecation and the release of toxins by countless tanneries, chemical plants, textile mills, distilleries, slaughter houses and hospitals along it has been a long-pending concern that has engaged non-governmental organisations, religious and spiritual leaders (savegangamovement.org, n.d.; sankatmochanfoundationonline.org, n.d.). The Ganga Action Plan initiated by the government in 1986 failed, despite an expenditure of US$190 million, and had to be withdrawn in the year 2000 (Singh, 2006: 590–592; Pandey, 2012); Mission Clean Ganges was announced in 2009 when the National Ganga River Basin Authority (NGRBA) authority was established.

The BJP's government is now stepping up efforts to clean the river. However, the disassociation from the earlier efforts is quite stark for the project is now placed primarily within the framework of the cultural ethos of the nation. The cleaning up of the major river is now also an effort to restore the cultural greatness and purity of the nation, a revival of tradition. The cleaning of the Ganges with people's participation features in the BJP election manifesto under the heading 'cultural heritage' (BJP, n.d.(a)). Of particular significance is that one of the constituencies that Modi contested in the 2014 elections is the Hindu sacred city of Varanasi (known also as Benares or Kashi) on the banks of the Ganges (ECI, n.d.; narendramodi.in, n.d.). In his election campaign in the city, he referred to the river as a stream of Indian culture, berating the earlier governments for their failure to cleanse it (narendramodi.in, 2013). An integrated Ganga Development Project to be called 'Namami Gange' (loosely translated from Sanskrit as 'obeisance to Ganges') was set up in July 2014 to oversee the project of cleansing the river (cleangangafund.com, n.d.). However, since then, the Supreme Court has twice censured the government for the slow progress of the project (Hindustan Times, 2015; Vaidyanathan, 2014). The debate on the viability of the project notwithstanding, the efforts to develop the city into a heritage and tourist centre are evident (Jha, 2014; Ramachandran, 2014). However, since the 2014 elections, an abiding image that was telecast live by both private televisions and the Public Service Broadcaster Doordarshan was that of the prime minister-designate Modi participating in the 'Ganga aarti' in Varanasi to celebrate the party's victory (Dixit & AFP, 2014; NewsX, 2014).

The 'Ganga aarti' is a ceremony held at dusk in various places on the banks of the river presided over by Hindu priests and accompanied by chanting and offering of flowers and lamps to the river. The appeal for funds for the project from non-resident Indians and the discourse surrounding the river continuously invoke the river's significance in Hindu culture. Indeed, Varanasi, believed to be over 3000 years old, is a city of temples. However, it is also the home of the Alamgir mosque and is known as an ancient centre of learning. The city has been a symbol of spiritualism, philosophy and mysticism and has produced great saints – Gautama Buddha, Mahavira, Kabir, Tulsi Das, Shankaracharaya, Ramanuja and Patanjali. Interestingly, the Union Ministry of Tourism had planned to develop tourism circuits based on Buddhism, Hinduism, Sufism, Jainism, Sikhism and Christianity religious themes during the 12th five-year plan period (2012–2017). The State Tourism Ministry sought World Bank aid under a pro-poor tourism development programme to develop the Buddhist circuit (Singh, 2014). A pristine Ganges, if indeed it could be achieved by the BJP government, will form an essential part of a national imagery evoking strong associations with Hinduism. On the one hand, the river and the rituals associated with it work towards typifying the Oriental experience for tourists (Said, 1978; Urry, 2002); on the other, they become part of 'identity tourism' and national branding campaigns with significant potential to rewrite the national story.

In 2014, India registered a 10.2% increase over the previous year in the arrival of foreign tourists, a 9.7% annual growth rate in US dollar terms, ranked 41 in the world in tourist arrivals, and 15 in world tourism receipts (India Tourism Statistics, 2014). The statue of unity when completed will exceed by 100 feet China's Spring Temple Buddha, currently the world's tallest statue at 502 feet. The potential impact of the two projects on tourism is indeed significant. Of equal import is their impact on the national narrative, especially in the context of the broad spectrum of public discourse that has ensued since the BJP's electoral victory. To cite a few instances, in January 2015 a Hindu group was stopped from installing the statue of Nathuram Godse, the assassin of Mahatma Gandhi, in a temple in the town of Meerut (Raju & Sandeep, 2015). It was preceded by much discussion in the public space on the motives behind Godse's act and the desirability of secularism as propounded by Gandhi (Lakshmi, 2015). The celebration of the 125th birth anniversary of B.R. Ambedkar, the architect of the Indian Constitution, has been marked by a tussle for his legacy between the Congress and the BJP (PTI, 2015). The relevance of the concept of secularism to India was brought into public discourse by the RSS in September 2015 (Bharadwaj, 2015). In February 2016 the arrest of a group of university students on charges of being 'anti-national' reignited discourse on Indian nationalism (Iyengar, 2016). When placed within the framework of the continuing strain of political discourse that projects an ideological conflict, commercial nationalism, among other issues, flags the trajectory in nation-making.

Conclusion

The exploration of the impact of commercial nationalism on the national narrative has been sparked by a paradigm shift in Indian politics in 2014 caused by the BJP winning a decisive mandate for the first time for any political party in three decades, ending an era of coalition politics and the politics of compromise. The BJP victory in 2014 allows for a clear ideation of the nation. Considered in the context of the BJP's ideology, hitherto presented and understood in terms oppositional to the one that prevailed and guided nation-making since Independence, the BJP's term in power signals new directions in nation-building. Making no argument for or against the desirability or otherwise of a new narrative, the chapter has instead focused on its trajectory. The political and public discourse that has followed the BJP government's performance indicates a radical shift in nation-making, also supported by some of its initiatives. Two of them, the phenomenal investments made in the statue of unity and Namami Gange projects explored in the chapter, constitute at one level the national government's efforts to build the physical nation, but on another are policy initiatives aimed at directing the trajectory of the national narrative by providing a foundational history for the building of national identity. Placed in the context of globalisation and the hard sell of the nation that nation-states are forced to embark on, the projects flag the potential for the emergence of a new national story.

The construction of the tallest statue has been an exercise not merely in producing a spectacular monument to a national leader, but also in promoting as preferable one set of ideas and beliefs over another, calling into question the very foundations that have guided the making of independent India. Similarly, the cleaning up of the major River Ganges, a much-needed improvement to infrastructure that has been attempted by many governments in the past without much success, is now more than a renewed effort to improve infrastructure. Couched in the rhetoric of restoration of the cultural heritage of the nation, a clean Ganga will symbolise the return to the civilisational greatness that India once enjoyed. Together these attempts re-define Indianness. The selective evocation of imagery, drawing as it does from existing cultural tropes, creates associations with Hindu cultural consciousness distinct from the Western narrative that has defined the Indian nation. The BJP government's efforts form part of the many initiatives that may transform far more than the physical nation. They are perhaps the first few pages of a new national story with the cultural icons under construction potentially emerging as the synecdoche for Indian nationalism.

Notes

(1) India's political system is adapted from the British Westminster model of Parliamentary democracy. There are the upper and lower houses. Elections are held every five years to the Lok Sabha (lower house) in 543 seats with two seats reserved for special members appointed by the President. Early elections may be held if the party leading the government loses its majority in the House. The system followed to decide the winner is the first-past-the-post system. The Rajya Sabha (upper house) has 250 members elected for fixed six-year terms. One-third of the members stand for election every two years and are elected by state assemblies and territories with 12 members appointed by the President. The Rajya Sabha endorse existing laws but cannot enact new ones. It can never be dissolved.

(2) Jawaharlal Nehru was a leader of the Congress party and was the Prime Minister from Independence in 1947 until his death in 1964. The leadership of the Congress party has remained with his family. His daughter Indira Gandhi (not related to Mahatma Gandhi), her son Rajiv Gandhi, Rajiv's widow Sonia Gandhi and her son Rahul Gandhi headed the Congress party from 1959 until the present. Indira Gandhi was Prime Minister from 1966 to 1977 and from 1980 until her assassination in 1984. Her son Rajiv Gandhi was the Prime Minister from 1984 to 1989. The Congress party and policies have come to be identified with the Nehru–Gandhi family.

(3) The mosque was destroyed by a mob in 1992 in the presence of senior BJP leaders who were addressing a rally at the site of over 150,000 people.

(4) Article 370 of the Indian constitution grants special autonomous status to Jammu and Kashmir. It is contained in Part XXI of the Constitution, which relates to Temporary, Transitional and Special Provisions. See Constitution of India, http://164.100.47.134/intranet/CAI/E.pdf (accessed 2 June 2015).

References

Anholt, S. (2003) *Brand New Justice: The Upside of Global Branding*. Oxford: Butterworth-Heinemann.

BJP (n.d.(a)) Bharatiya Janata Party. See http://www.bjp.org/.

BJP (n.d.(b)) Modi's Gujarat model: The vision that awaits India. See http://www.bjp.org/images/pdf_2014/the_gujarat_model.pdf (accessed 26 May 2015).

Basu, S. (2014) Revisiting Nehru–Patel differences, *Swarajya*, 12 October. See http://swarajya-mag.com/politics/revisiting-nehru-patel-differences-alternate-perspectives/ (accessed 30 May 2015).

Bharadwaj, A. (2015) RSS: Secularism irrelevant in India, *Indian Express*, 20 September. See http://indianexpress.com/article/india/india-others/rss-secularism-irrelevant-in-india/ (accessed 20 September 2015).

Chaturvedi, P. (2013) What Modi wants you to believe and what Sardar Patel really said about RSS, *Tehelka.com blogs*, 14 June. See http://blog.tehelka.com/what-modi-wants-you-to-believe-and-what-sardar-patel-really-said-about-rss/ (accessed 31 May 2015).

Chitravanshi, R. (2014) BJP manifesto: Tourism awaits new lease of life, *Business Standard*, 20 May. See http://www.business-standard.com/article/economy-policy/bjp-manifesto-tourism-awaits-new-lease-of-life-114051900865_1.html (accessed 19 September 2015).

Cleangangafund.com, (n.d.) Clean Ganga Fund. See http://www.cleangangafund.com/ (accessed 2 June 2015).

Coles, T. and Church, A. (2007) Tourism, politics and forgotten entanglements of power. In *Tourism, Power and Space* (pp. 1–39). Abingdon: Routledge.

Congress (n.d.) www.inc.in/

Dixit, P. and AFP (2014) Varanasi: Modi thanks Maa Ganga, performs aarti. *Hindustan Times*, 18 May. See http://www.hindustantimes.com/state-of-the-states/varanasi-gets-ready-for-modi-visit-security-tightened/article1-1220175.aspx (accessed 2 June 2015).

Eck, D.L. (1982) *Benaras, City of Light*. New York: Columbia University Press.

ECI (n.d.) Election Commission of India, General Elections, 2016, 16th Lok Sabha elections, List of successful candidates. See http://eci.nic.in/eci_main/archiveofge2014/4%20-%20List%20of%20Successful%20Candidates.pdf (accessed 2 June 2015).

Engineer, A.A. (2003) *Gujarat Carnage*. Hyderabad: Orient Longman.

FPpolitics (2013) War over Sardar Patel: The BJP–Congress slug fest gets uglier. *F. Politics*, 29 October. See http://www.firstpost.com/politics/war-over-sardar-patel-the-bjp-congress-slug-fest-gets-uglier-1199811.html (accessed 31 May 2015).

Frew, E. and White, L. (2011) *Tourism and National Identity: An International Perspective*. Abingdon: Routledge.

Gandhi, J. (2014) Beyond appropriation. *The Hindu*, 17 November. See http://www.the-hindu.com/sunday-anchor/sunday-anchor-politics-over-historical-icons-jawaharlal-nehru-sardar-vallabhbhai-patel/article6603381.ece (accessed 1 June 2015).

Gandhi, K. (2008) Glimpses of the Congress Party. In K. Gandhi (ed.) *India Beyond Sixty* (pp. 1–81). New Delhi: Allied.

Gandhi, R. (1990) *Patel: A Life*. New Delhi: Navaj.

Ghosh, D. (2014) Budget 2014: Rs. 200 cr For Sardar Patel Statue vs Rs. 150 cr for Women's Safety. *NDTV.com*, 10 July. See http://www.ndtv.com/india-news/budget-2014-rs-200-cr-for-sardar-patel-statue-vs-rs-150-cr-for-womens-safety-586649 (accessed 30 May 2015).

Guha, R. (2007) *India after Gandhi*. London: Macmillan.

Guha, R. (2012) Indians, great, greater, greatest? *The Hindu*, 21 July. See http://www.thehindu.com/opinion/op-ed/indians-great-greater-greatest/article3662823.ece (accessed 30 May 2015).

Hewitt, V. (2008) *Political Mobilisation and Democracy in India: States of Emergency*. New York: Routledge.

Hibbard, S.W. (2010) *Religious Politics and Secular States: Egypt, India, and the United States*. Baltimore, MD: The John Hopkins University Press.

Hindustan Times (2015) Will you clean up Ganga in this term? SC to Centre. *Hindustan Times*, 15 January. See http://www.hindustantimes.com/india-news/will-you-clean-up-ganga-in-this-term-or-the-next-sc-to-centre/article1-1306795.aspx (accessed 2 June 2015).

Hirway, I., Shah, A. and Shah, G. (2014) *Growth or Development: Which way is Gujarat Going?* New Delhi: Oxford University Press.

Huang, W. and Santos, C.A. (2011) Tourism and national identity: The case of Washington DC. In E. Frew and L. White (eds) *Tourism and National Identity: An International Perspective* (pp. 13–24). Abingdon: Routledge.

Indiabudget (2015) Union Budget 2015–2016. See http://indiabudget.nic.in/ (accessed 30 May 2015).

Indian Express (2015) Rajnath on Ram temple: No majority in Rajya Sabha, Centre can't Pass Law. *Indian Express*, 11 May. See http://indianexpress.com/article/cities/lucknow/

with-no-majority-in-rajya-sabha-cant-pass-law-for-ram-temple-rajnath-singh/ (accessed 31 May 2015).

India Tourism Statistics (2014) See http://tourism.gov.in/writereaddata/CMSPagePicture/file/marketresearch/statisticalsurveys/India%20Tourism%20Statistics%20at%20a%20Glance%202014New.pdf (accessed 19 September 2015).

Iyengar, R. (2016) The arrest of a student leader in a top university reignites India's intolerance debate. *Time*, 15 February. See http://time.com/4224571/india-jnu-kanhaiya-kumar-arrest-protests-sedition/

Jacobs, S. (2010) *Hinduism Today: An Introduction*. New York: Continuum.

Jaffrelot, C. (1996) *The Hindu Nationalist Movement and Indian Politics*. London: Hurst/New Delhi: Penguin India.

Jaffrelot, C. (2003) Communal riots in Gujarat: The state at Risk? Working paper no. 17. Heidelberg Papers in South Asian and Comparative Politics, July. South Asia Institute, Department of Political Science, University of Heidelberg.

Jeffrey, R. (2000) *India's Newspaper Revolution: Capitalism, Politics and the Indian-language Press*. London: Palgrave Macmillan.

Jha, S. (2014) All eyes on Modi's Ganga project. *Business Standard*, 23 May. See http://www.ndtv.com/india-news/your-plan-will-take-200-years-to-clean-ganga-supreme-court-raps-centre-658781 (accessed 2 June 2015).

Kalaiyarasan, A. (2014) A comparison of developmental outcomes in Gujarat and Tamil Nadu. *Economic and Political Weekly* XLIX (15), 55–63.

Khilnani, S. (1997) *The Idea of India*. Bloomsbury: Hamish Hamilton.

Laclau, E. (2005) *On Populist Reason*. London: Verso.

Lakshmi, R. (2015) Why some Indians want to build a statue of Mahatma Gandhi's killer. *The Washington Post*, 30 January. See http://www.washingtonpost.com/blogs/worldviews/wp/2015/01/30/why-some-indians-want-to-build-a-statue-of-mahatma-gandhis-killer/ (accessed 10 June 2015).

Mathew, L. (2015) No mandate for Ram mandir, Article 370: Amit Shah. *Indian Express*, 27 May. See http://indianexpress.com/article/india/politics/no-mandate-for-temple-art-370-amit-shah/99/ (accessed 27 May 2015).

Narendramodi.in (n.d.) Varanasi constituency. See http://www.narendramodi.in/varanasi#vision_details (accessed 2 June 2015).

Narendramodi.in (2013) Complete speech: Shri Narendra Modi addressing Vijay Shankhnaad Rally in Varanasi, UP, 20 December. See http://www.narendramodi.in/complete-speech-shri-narendra-modi-addressing-vijay-shankhnaad-rally-in-varanasi-up (accessed 2 June 2015).

NewsX (2014) Narendra Modi attends Ganga aarti in Varanasi. See https://www.youtube.com/watch?v=OJ1FaCXv7OE (accessed 2 June 2015).

O'Sullivan, T., Hartley, J., Saunders, D., Montgomery, M. and Fiske, J. (1994) *Key Concepts in Communication and Cultural Studies* (2nd edn). London: Routledge.

Pandey, B. (2012) Ganga gapped. *Tehelka Magazine*, 28 July. See http://archive.tehelka.com/story_main53.asp?filename=Ne280712GANGA.asp (accessed 2 June 2015).

Pathak, M. (2013) Narendra Modi, Manmohan Singh spar over Sardar Patel. *Livemint*, 29 October. See http://www.livemint.com/Politics/hn0YBp0bYb8uMu1n9nTCxL/Modi-Manmohan-spar-over-Sardar-Patel.html (accessed 31 May 2015).

Pretes, M. (2003) Tourism and nationalism. *Annals of Tourism Research* 30 (1), 125–142.

PTI (2015) Government to observe Ambedkar's 125th birth anniversary in a big way. *Indian Express*, 30 May. See http://indianexpress.com/article/india/india-others/government-to-observe-ambedkars-125th-birth-anniversary-in-a-big-way/ (accessed 10 June 2015).

Rajagopal, A. (2001) *Politics of Television: Religious Nationalism and the Reshaping of the Indian Public*. Cambridge: Cambridge University Press.

Raju, S. and Sandeep. (2015) Group prevented from installing Nathuram Godse statue at Meerut temple. *Hindustan Times*, 31 January. See http://www.hindustantimes.com/india-news/group-prevented-from-installing-nathuram-godse-statue-at-meerut-temple/article1-1312209.aspx (accessed 10 June 2015).

Ramachandran, S. (2014) Cleaning up the Ganges. *The Diplomat*, 15 September. See http://thediplomat.com/2014/09/cleaning-up-the-ganges/ (accessed 2 June 2015).

Reuters (2013) Sardar Patel birth anniversary: Modi aims at history and Gandhis with world's tallest statue. *Indiatoday.in*, 31 October. See http://indiatoday.intoday.in/story/sardar-patel-birth-anniversary-modi-inaugurates-worlds-tallest-statue/1/321035.html (accessed 30 May 2015).

Said, E. (1978) *Orientalism*. London: Routledge and Kegan Paul.

Saikumar, R. (2015) The rise of the liberal-right intellectual. *The Hindu*, 24 February. See http://www.thehindu.com/opinion/op-ed/the-rise-of-the-liberalright-intellectual/article6925966.ece (accessed 1 June 2015).

Sankatmochanfoundationonline.org (n.d.) Pollution in Ganga and Ganga Action Plan Failures. See http://www.sankatmochanfoundationonline.org/PollutionofGanga.html (accessed 2 June 2015).

Sardesai, R. (2015) *2014: The Election that Changed India*. New Delhi: Penguin.

Savegangamovement.org (n.d) See http://www.savegangamovement.org/index.php?option=com_content&task=view&id=25&Itemid=40 (accessed 2 June 2015).

Seshia, S. (1998) Divide and rule in Indian Party Politics: The rise of the Bharatiya Janata Party. *Asian Survey* 38 (11), 1036–1050.

Sil, R. (2014). India. In J. Kopstein, M. Lichbach and S.E. Hanson (eds) *Comparative Politics: Interests, Identities, and Institutions in a Changing Global Order* (4th edn, pp. 339–389). New York: Cambridge University Press.

Singh, B. (2014) Now, charm of Varanasi attracts tourists from Pakistan and China. *Times of India*, 22 January. See http://timesofindia.indiatimes.com/city/varanasi/Now-charm-of-Varanasi-attracts-tourists-from-Pakistan-and-China/articleshow/29196441.cms (accessed 19 September 2015).

Singh, P. (2006) Bridging the Ganga Action Plan: Monitoring failure at Kanpur. *Economic and Political Weekly* 41 (7), 590–592.

Smith, A. (1991) *National Identity*. London: Penguin.

Statueofunity (n.d.) See http://www.statueofunity.in/ (accessed 30 May 2015).

Tejani, S. (2008) *Indian Secularism: A Social and Intellectual History*, 1890–1950. Bloomington, IN: Indiana University Press.

Timesnow (2013) Cong-BJP spar over Sardar Patel. *Timesnow.tv*. See http://www.timesnow.tv/Cong-BJP-spar-over-Sardar-Patel/videoshow/4440245.cms (accessed 31 May 2015).

Tiwari, P. (2014) In praise of Hemu: Medieval king reveals true intent of Hindutva history. *F.India*, 10 October. See http://www.firstpost.com/india/in-praise-of-hemu-medieval-king-reveals-true-intent-of-hindutva-history-1749171.html (accessed 1 June 2015).

Thomas, P.N. (2010) *Political Economy of Communications in India: The Good, Bad and Ugly*. New Delhi: Sage.

Urry, J. (2002) *The Tourist Gaze*. London: Sage.

Vaidyanathan, A. (2014) Your plan will take 200 years to clean Ganga: Supreme Court raps Centre, *NDTV.com*. See http://www.ndtv.com/india-news/your-plan-will-take-200-years-to-clean-ganga-supreme-court-raps-centre-658781 (accessed 2 June 2015).

Varadarajan, S. (2003) *Gujarat Riots, Making of a Tragedy*. New Delhi: Penguin Books.

Volcic, Z. and Andrejevic, M. (2011) Nation branding in the era of commercial nationalism. *International Journal of Communication*, 5, 598–618.

White, L. and Frew, E. (2011) Tourism and national identities: Connections and conceptualisations. In E. Frew and L. White (eds) *Tourism and National Identities: An International Perspective* (pp. 1–10). Oxon: Routledge.

Zee News (2013) Congress fine with Gandhi family statues, but not with Sardar Patel's: BJP. *Zee News*, 1 November. See http://zeenews.india.com/news/nation/congress-fine-with-gandhi-family-statues-but-not-with-sardar-patels-bjp_887416.html (accessed 30 May 2015).

7 The Silk Road, Identities and Commercial Nationalisms

Alan Clarke

Introduction

National identities and especially emerging national identities are seen as one of the crucial sites of contestation in current approaches to communication for social change and tourism development programmes. New developments reinforce and, at the same time, challenge the status of our sense of national identity in an era which has been characterised in this book by the tensions between the globalisation of capitalism and the emergence of myriad resurgent nationalisms. The concept of Commercial Nationalism has appeared to add depth to critical interventions in the discussions of the fate of nationalism and national identity by exploring the relationship between state appropriation of marketing and branding strategies on the one hand, and, on the other, the commercial mobilisation of nationalist discourses. The complex concept seems particularly appropriate for the example elaborated here as it is potentially the critical 'test case' for these ideas as it only makes sense if the created identity operates not only with the complexity of the nation states but also within and around the transnationality of those states individually and collectively.

Silk Road Tourism

In 1994, 19 countries joined the United Nations World Tourism Organization (UNWTO) and the United Nations Educational, Scientific and Cultural Organization (UNESCO) in Samarkand, Uzbekistan, to launch the Samarkand Declaration. This was a milestone event for Silk Road tourism, with the Declaration calling for 'a peaceful and fruitful rebirth of these legendary routes as one of the world's richest cultural tourism destinations'. Twenty years later, an increasing number of stakeholders are working together to foster tourism development along the Silk Road. The results have been notable: transboundary tourism projects are growing, trade and consumer interest in the Silk Road continues to rise and the UNWTO Silk Road Programme already works with over 30 Member States. Member States participating in the UNWTO Silk Road Programme include: Albania, Armenia, Azerbaijan, Bangladesh, Bulgaria, China, Croatia, DPR Korea, Rep. Korea, Egypt, Georgia, Greece, Iran, Iraq, Israel, Italy, Indonesia, Japan, Kazakhstan, Kyrgyzstan, Mongolia, Pakistan, Russia, Saudi Arabia, San Marino, Syria, Tajikistan, Turkey, Turkmenistan, Ukraine and Uzbekistan.

The challenge for the Silk Road is complex. On the one hand, Marco Polo and the stories surrounding his travels and his commercial exploits are well known. It would not be known as the Silk Road otherwise. On the other hand, when questioned about the Road it becomes harder for people to specify where to locate it on a map and those readers with a keen eye will have noted the reference to routes in plural. Even the Silk Road Organisation (SRO) proposes two land routes and one maritime one. The project to relaunch the Silk Road has the task of repositioning the many claims and counterclaims for the route(s) as in the SRO attempts to promote a coherent brand to hold together disparate nations bridging Europe and Asia. There is much talk about the need to create a new narrative for the Silk Road and within that narrative will emerge the basis for new, emergent and resurgent commercial nationalisms.

Literature Contribution

As Jansen (2008: 122) points out: 'Branding not only explains nations to the world but also reinterprets national identity in market terms and provides new narratives for domestic consumption.' There are important political and cultural consequences to this reinterpretation which remain understudied at this point. Kaneva (2011) further notes that nation branding, 'is not a mere synonym for propaganda, nor are its suggested applications limited to influencing public opinion through advertising or public relations'. Despite nation branding's growing popularity, there is much disagreement about its meaning and scope (see, e.g. Dinnie, 2008; Fan, 2009). In light of this, our explorations should be particularly interested in developing a critique of nation branding because efforts to rethink nations as brands relate to theoretical debates central to critical scholarship of culture and communication. These debates include the problems of cultural imperialism and commodification (e.g. Mosco, 1996; Schiller, 1976, 1989), the perils of capitalist (neoliberal) globalisation (e.g. Beck, 2000; Sassen, 1998), the state of public spheres and civil society in a globalising world (e.g. Calabrese, 1999; Habermas, 2001) and the centrality of identities in contemporary experience (e.g. Castells, 1997; Hall & du Gay, 1996; Laclau, 1994). Critical theorisations of the transformation of space and place in postmodernity (e.g. Appadurai, 1996; Harvey, 1990, 2001;

Lefebvre, 1991) are also relevant and should be brought to bear in discussing the implications of nation branding. Finally, a growing body of recent critical work investigates brands and branding as distinctive phenomena of late capitalism that transcend the economic realm (e.g. Arvidsson, 2006; Einstein, 2007; Lury, 2004; Moor, 2007), but it mentions nation branding only in passing and does not consider the issues transnationally.

Benedict Anderson's (1991 (originally published 1983)) study helped to reconceptualise the way that nationalisms were viewed and deconstructed, particularly the notion of the 'imagined political communities'. This book suggested that the origins of imagined communities reflect the emergence and spread of different types of nationalisms. The argument is that these communities are imagined because, 'even the smallest nation will never know most of their fellow members, meet them or even hear about them, yet in the minds of each lives the image of their communion' (Anderson, 1991: 6). Anderson contends that official nationalism comes from the state and has as its primary feature a focus on serving the interests of the state first and foremost. This official nationalism is the 'willed merger of nation and dynastic empire' (Anderson, 1991: 86) – which we see explicitly throughout the Silk Road articulated at the transnational level.

The imagined community of the nation is maintained by cultural artefacts and a plethora of institutions such as literature, art, media and the education system, and a sense of nation is established and sustained 'by the quotidian rhythms of print and electronic media output, along with periodic national ceremonies' (O'Sullivan et al., 1994: 196–197). In further research (White, 2009) it has been noted that three forms of nationalism have been identified:

(1) Official nationalism uses civic, formal and ceremonial means. The deployment of anthems and flags gives power to this image.
(2) Popular nationalism (Ward, 1966) uses nationalist messages and images to inform discourses in popular cultural forms.
(3) Commercial nationalism refers to material, everyday nationalism harnessed to commercial interests. Commercial exploitation is through consumer-related use of these national symbols, icons and identities and this runs throughout the development of the Silk Road.

The complexity and diversity of the Silk Road was anticipated by Spillman (1997) who saw the positive resolution of this situation by arguing that complexity and diversity could themselves become an aspect of national identity and, as demonstrated here, transnational identity.

At this point, it is worth remembering that Aronczyk (2009) rightly points out that branding does not so much supersede pernicious and divisive forms of nationalism as replicate the claim to transcend and displace the political by transposing it into the register of the market. Therefore, if national identity is constituted in this paradigm as pre-political, the work of nation branding is presented as post-political – where the nation remains necessary not as a democratic resource for active participation or equal recognition, nor as a geopolitical force to mediate international conflict, but as an ensemble of non-threatening fragments of culture, history and geography determined by committee. This is the basis of the brand's rising popularity in foreign policy circles as a vehicle for public diplomacy (p. 294).

The Silk Road

Acclaimed and proclaimed as the 'greatest route in the history of mankind', the ancient Silk Road formed the first bridge between the East and the West and was an important vehicle for trade between the ancient empires of China, Central and Western Asia, the Indian sub-continent and Rome. As routes of integration, exchange and dialogue, the Silk Road contributed greatly to the common prosperity and development of humankind for almost two millennia.

With its richly diverse cultural heritage and its wealth of natural tourism attractions spanning thousands of kilometres of ancient lands, the Silk Road today offers visitors the opportunity to experience a unique network of destinations linked by a shared history. By venturing along the ancient Silk Road, tourists can walk in the footsteps of famed explorers such as Alexander the Great and Marco Polo. Studies in tourism, hospitality and events have considered the role of attractions and events in helping create a national identity. Pretes (2003) argues that a shared identity is often an official goal of countries comprising many different cultures where there exists a common urge to create a national identity to overcome diversity and difference within the nation-state. This is particularly pertinent when the analysis runs across competing and conflicting nationalist discourses, focused on the SRO, which is determined to see discourses of peace and harmony emerge as the countries demonstrate tolerance, peace and interdependence.

UNESCO experts and state parties have dedicated years of research to identifying and analysing the routes and corridors of the Silk Road. Through their findings, a vast array of ancient cities, caravanserais, mountain passes, forts and watchtowers, religious and archaeological sites have come to light. While there is significant potential for tourism development and local economic growth along the Silk Road, many of the route's cultural and natural sites are under threat, and significant investment and attention are required to ensure that they are safeguarded for the enjoyment of future generations. These plans, while constituted in the transnational context, will be the responsibility of individual nations, which may pose a threat to the transnational identity being built by the SRO.

As noted above, UNWTO's role in promoting the growth of Silk Road tourism dates back to 1994, when 19 countries called for the 'peaceful and fruitful re-birth of these legendary routes as one of the world's richest cultural tourism destinations'. Over the years, UNWTO has worked closely with key UN agencies such as UNESCO and United Nations Development Programme (UNDP) to advance sustainable development imperatives across the regions of the Silk Road.

It was in 2010 that UNWTO developed a specialised programme dedicated to advancing tourism along the Silk Road. The first Silk Road Action Plan 2010/2011 was launched at the 5th International Meeting on the Silk Road in Samarkand, Uzbekistan, where the three key focus areas were established as: (a) marketing and promotion; (b) capacity building and destination management; and (c) travel facilitation.

In 2013, following years of ground-breaking research by UNESCO, the International Council on Monuments and Sites (ICOMOS) and University College London on the sites and routes of the Silk Road, the UNESCO/ UNWTO Silk Road Heritage Corridors Tourism Strategy Project was launched as part of the transnational Silk Roads World Heritage Serial Nomination initiative.

Following extensive consultation with experts at a workshop in Almaty, Kazakhstan, in 2013, UNWTO and UNESCO launched a Roadmap for Development, a guideline document that set out the objectives and steps for maximising tourism development for the heritage corridors, while safeguarding the Silk Road's unique natural and cultural resources. With activities that witnessed an unprecedented level of collaboration between 15 countries, two World Heritage Nominations for the Silk Roads Heritage Corridors in Central Asia and China were submitted to UNESCO and the final evaluation of the nominations were completed in 2014. The nominations focus on four specific Silk Road Heritage Corridors: the first three crossing Kazakhstan, Kyrgyzstan and China, and the other between Tajikistan and Uzbekistan. What is known as the Silk Road's Chang'an-Tianshan Corridor was approved by the World Heritage Committee in June 2014 as Site No. 1442, consisting of 33 newly designated sites in China, Kazakhstan and Kyrgyzstan. The sites include capital cities and palace complexes of various empires and kingdoms, trading settlements, Buddhist cave temples, ancient paths, posthouses, mountain passes, beacon towers, sections of the Great Wall, fortifications, tombs and religious buildings. Collectively, the 33 sites cover an area of 164.7 square miles and have a buffer zone of 733.5 square miles.

The sites inscribed are categorised into four regions along the Silk Road by ICOMOS, which assessed eligibility for the World Heritage inscription.

(1) Central China – ancient imperial capitals in the Central and Guanzhong Plains of China:
     ○ Luoyang City of the Eastern Han to Northern Wei Dynasty, Luoyang, Henan Province;
     ○ Dingding Gate, Luoyang City of the Sui and Tang Dynasty, Luoyang, Henan Province;

- Longmen Grottoes (a pre-existing World Heritage Site), Luoyang, Henan Province;
- Hangu Pass, Lingbao, Henan Province;
- Shihao section of Xiaohan Route, Xin'an County, Henan Province;
- Weiyang Palace, Xi'an, Shaanxi Province;
- Daming Palace, Xi'an, Shaanxi Province;
- Giant Wild Goose Pagoda, Xi'an, Shaanxi Province;
- Small Wild Goose Pagoda, Xi'an, Shaanxi Province;
- Xingjiao Temple, Xi'an, Shaanxi Province;
- Bin County Cave Temple, Bin County, Shaanxi Province;
- Tomb of Zhang Qian, Chenggu County, Shaanxi Province;
- Maijishan Cave Temple Complex, Tianshui, Gansu Province.

(2) Hexi Corridor in Gansu Province, connecting China Proper and Xinjiang:
- Bingling Cave Temple Complex, Yongjing County, Linxia Hui Autonomous Prefecture, Gansu Province;
- Yumen Pass, Dunhuang, Gansu Province;
- Xuanquanzhi Posthouse, Dunhuang, Gansu Province;
- Mogao Caves (already inscribed on the World Heritage List), Dunhuang, Gansu Province;
- Suoyang City Ruins, Anxi, Gansu Province.

(3) North and South of Tianshan Mountains in the Xinjiang Uyghur Autonomous Region of China:
- Qocho (Gaochang) City Ruins, Turpan, Xinjiang Uyghur Autonomous Region;
- Yar City Site of Bashbaliq City (Jiaohe Ruins), Turpan, Xinjiang Uyghur Autonomous Region;
- Beshbalik City Ruins, Jimsar County, Xinjiang Uyghur Autonomous Region;
- Kizil Gaha Beacon Tower, Kuqa, Xinjiang Uyghur Autonomous Region;
- Kizil Caves, Kuqa, Xinjiang Uyghur Autonomous Region;
- Subash Buddhist Temple Ruins, Kuqa, Xinjiang Uyghur Autonomous Region.

(4) Zhetysu Region of the Ili and Talas Valleys of Kazakhstan and the Chuy Valley of Kyrgyzstan:
- Site of Kayalyk, Almaty Province, Kazakhstan;
- Karamergen, Almaty Province, Kazakhstan;
- Talgar, Almaty Province, Kazakhstan;
- Aktobe, Jambyl Province, Kazakhstan;
- Kulan, Jambyl Province, Kazakhstan;
- Akyrtas, Jambyl Province, Kazakhstan;
- Ornek, Jambyl Province, Kazakhstan;
- Kostobe, Jambyl Province, Kazakhstan;
- Suyab (Site of Ak-Beshim), Chuy Province, Kyrgyzstan;

- City of Balasagun (Site of Burana), Chuy Province, Kyrgyzstan;
- City of Nevaket (Site of Krasnaya Rechka), Chuy Province, Kyrgyzstan.

In 2012, UNWTO ran a very successful Ecole hôtelière de Lausanne (EHL)/ UNWTO Silk Road Strategy Challenge, where 200 final year students developed hospitality and marketing strategies for 10 Silk Road destinations. The students that developed the best strategy won a trip to the Altai region of Russia in 2013. Here they worked with local tourism authorities, private sector stakeholders and students in developing a hospitality management strategy for the region focused on health and wellness. The EHL graduates ran a series of interactive capacity-building workshops involving over 200 local groups.

In 2013, UNWTO also established a new partnership with the Council of Europe's Venice Office, Veneto Region of Italy and Marco Polo Systems. The VeRoTour project, a pilot maritime tourism initiative along the Venetian routes of the Silk Road, aims to develop transnational thematic tourism products and enhance competitiveness and sustainability along the western link of the Silk Road. The final stages of the VeRoTour project were implemented over the course of 2014.

UNWTO has also worked closely with educational institutions to engage young students and young professionals in Silk Road tourism initiatives. UNWTO works with Member States to enable local students to volunteer at its meetings, allowing them to gain knowledge on the issues surrounding sustainable tourism development.

Furthermore, in 2013, UNWTO launched its first Silk Road Action Plan Survey, which enabled Member States to give their feedback about activities and priorities for the future. The results of this open consultation survey were integrated into the current edition of the SRO Action Plan.

Key stakeholders of the Silk Road

The SRO have stressed that input, endorsement and engagement from a variety of stakeholders are essential to ensuring the success of the Silk Road Action Plan. They identify four themes and list the stakeholders deemed necessary for the successful delivery of the activities. Four key stakeholder groups are responsible for managing and implementing the main activities outlined in the Silk Road Action Plan.

(1) UNWTO:
- leads and drives the Silk Road Programme;
- provides a collaborative platform for building alliances;
- coordinates logistics of major events;
- communicates on progress;

- ○   seeks and manages donor funding/sponsorship.
(2)   UN Agencies:
- ○   provide expertise and input;
- ○   galvanise support;
- ○   promote the activities in the context of the UN Millennium Development Goals;
- ○   include for example the institutions UNESCO, UNDP, the United Nations Conference on Trade and Development (UNCTAD), the Food and Agriculture Organization of the United Nations.
(3)   Silk Road Task Force:
- ○   determines key strategies and actions;
- ○   endorses and drives implementation;
- ○   encourages sharing and exchange of best practices;
- ○   includes, for example, the bodies the national tourism organisation, private sector stakeholders and finance/investment.
(4)   Silk Road member states:
- ○   Ensure representation and involvement in the Silk Road Task Force;
- ○   actively participate in all meetings and events;
- ○   promote collaboration and cooperation among Silk Road member states.

What these groupings of stakeholders represent is the submergence of individualist and individual national identities beneath the mixture of the transnational agencies and collective meeting of the nation states. The transnational stakeholders elaborate discourses that are linked by the emblematic images, constituting a nexus among and around the locations. That the discourses are organised by nation states and transnational agencies leaves little room for the emergence of the traditional diaspora of stakeholders from the tourism literature. Individual entrepreneurs, for instance, are covered within the notion of the representation of the nation state.

Marketing and promoting the Silk Road

The stakeholders are responsible for constructing a unique network of destinations linked by a common cultural heritage. The Silk Road presents significant opportunities for collaborative marketing and promotional initiatives. Over the years, UNWTO has collaborated with major international travel fairs on numerous promotional activities to highlight the tourism potential of the Silk Road. The Internationale Tourismus-Börse Berlin has become the established meeting place for the Silk Road ministers, as they convene annually to address key challenges and opportunities for cooperation. Traditional marketing has been applied alongside increasing levels of activity utilising the social media activity, with Silk Road events being held on an annual basis within the context of the World Travel Market's Social

Media Mart. Bloggers have competed to create innovative Silk Road blogs, and the winners have been sent across the Silk Road to promote its multiple attractions.

UNWTO recognises the importance of market intelligence as key to developing effective marketing and promotion campaigns. Market research conducted in 2011 showed the prominence of the Silk Road as the world's most discussed travel route online – from a total of 300,000 blogs and social media sites reviewed, 26.5% of all discussions focused on the Silk Road.

To raise the profile of the Silk Road on the international stage, UNWTO has invited major institutions to its meetings, such as UNESCO, the World Bank, UNCTAD, the Association of Southeast Asian Nations, ICOMOS, the Pacific Asia Travel Association and the Council of Europe. The aim of this multisectorial approach is to tackle important issues and explore opportunities arising from global collaboration.

Outcomes

This chapter's unique contribution is to consider an emerging formation characterised by the transnational developments alongside as well as along the route: the focus has to be on the ways in which the Silk Road's nation states have come increasingly to rely on commercial techniques for questions of self-promotion, diplomacy and internal national mobilisation. The concerns of this emerging transnationalism focus on the developments in which new commercial media facilitate the mobilisation of configurations of these nationalisms and the transnational identity of the Route for the purpose of selling, gaining ratings and otherwise profiting.

Nation branding campaigns are enlisted by the state to address a whole range of issues related to public diplomacy and economic development. As political scientist Peter Van Ham (2001a: 1) puts it, 'most states still see branding as a long-term, cumulative effort that will influence foreign investment decisions and the state's market capitalization'. In an era of economic globalisation, in which international relations remain caught up in networks of interdependence and economic competition, Van Ham argues that: 'To do their jobs well in the future, politicians will have to train themselves in brand asset management. Their tasks will include finding a brand niche for their state, engaging in competitive marketing, assuring customer satisfaction, and most of all, creating brand loyalty' (Van Ham, 2001a: 1). Framed in these terms (Van Ham, 2001a, 2001b), branding and commercial competition become the continuation of warfare or, in this context, as the discourses bring these peoples together, we should view it as the continuation of peace.

The identities drawn upon are many and varied, often conflicting and rarely consistent. It is recognised that the route is about more than trade, although the trade was and continues to be a significant referent. The cultural and heritage exchanges that were promoted by, along and alongside the trade are more significant in looking at the identities to be observed along the route.

The next part of the chapter will examine the attempts to bring established identities together and forge a further dynamic identity for the route. The idea of routing through competing and disparate heritages raises issues of peace, tolerance and understanding. There are also some who question the authenticity of any/all claims for the route as Marco Polo is said to have written that he has only shared less than half of his stories from the journeys. Identities have been constructed, deconstructed and nations changed over time. The challenge now being addressed can be seen as reconstructing national and transnational identities to realise a huge commercial project in the 21st century from the basis of the 12th and 13th centuries.

Analysis

Nation branding is decidedly not post-political insofar as it opens up new spaces for the commercial exploitation of the political – for the use of nationalism to sell a range of cultural products and to build brand loyalty. In this regard, it fits neatly into the constellation of what recent literature on globalisation has described as commercial nationalism – the phenomenon whereby commercial institutions take on an increasingly important role in framing issues of national identity and promulgating branded forms of nationalisms and nationalist brand identities. The literature on commercial nationalism recognises the historical relationship between commercialism, capitalism and the nation state, but emphasises how recent transformations including economic globalisation, the decline of public service, state-supported broadcasting in the neoliberal era (especially in the post-socialist nations of Eastern and Central Europe, but also in other regions, including Asia and Western Europe) and the forms of competition associated with the 'enterprise state' re-contextualise the relationship between the national and commercial.

In the attempt to reinvent 'the state as a quasi-"enterprise-association"' (Cerny, 1997: 260), the metaphors of politics as marketing and 'brand community' as polity are, in a sense, realised – at least in theory. Aronczyk (2008: 54) notes that Anholt and other branding consultants advise nations to align their foreign and domestic policies with a well-researched set of national images, much as a successful marketing campaign requires a company to 'live the brand': 'The need to inspire such allegiance and affiliation in the brand identity reveals a critical dimension of the practice: as a form of communication, the media of the message are effectively the citizens themselves.' This formulation echoes the commercial logic of Web 2.0, and of the interactive economy more generally – the use of strategies for mobilising the population as a means of lateral and participatory, rather than 'top-down' and one-way, message transmission. If, in other words, nation branding relies on private 'expert' consultants, it does so in order to develop strategies for offloading the work of message circulation onto the populace.

Conclusion

Nation branding and national imagery can be explored using a range of methodologies and here it brings discourse analysis into play. The focus of this chapter is on how particular narratives are woven to tell, re-tell (and sell) a transnational story. By deconstructing the nationalist discourses, it becomes possible to see the Silk Road as a bridge from the legendary past to the commercial present. The Silk Road is wrapped in and portrays messages of peace and economic prosperity. The discourses rearticulate the ancient into the postmodern. The vision for tourism is capable of delivering a wonderful set of touristic experiences, but it is also expected to embody strong statements of nationalism and the transnationalism of the route.

We are witnessing a rekindling of the narratives of Marco Polo and Alexander the Great in order to calm discourses of conflict across a region beset by turmoils, insurrections and disagreements through the use of commercial transnationalism. There is selection, promotion and repression of images, icons and ideologies in order to place a new conceptualisation over older established national discourses. The commercial nationalism is not innocent as the Silk Road develops trade and commerce, as well as cultural and heritage exchanges. However these exchanges are deemed to be positive and the halo of this legitimacy cloaks the new Silk Road and protects it from the dangers of ancient conflicts.

References

Anderson, B. (1991) *Reflections on the Origins and Spread of Nationalism*. London: Verso.

Appadurai, A. (1996) *Modernity at Large*. Minneapolis, MN: University of Minnesota Press.

Aronczyk, M. (2008) 'Living the brand': Nationality, globality and identity strategies of nation branding consultants. *International Journal of Communication* 2, 41–65.

Aronczyk, M. (2009) How to do things with brands: Uses of national identity. *Canadian Journal of Communication* 34 (2), 291–296.

Arvidsson, A. (2006) *Brands: Meaning and Value in Media Culture*. New York: Routledge.

Beck, U. (2000) *What is Globalization?* Cambridge: Polity Press.

Calabrese, A. (1999) Communication and the end of sovereignty? *Info* 1 (4), 313–326.

Castells, M. (1997) *The Power of Identity*. Malden, MA: Blackwell.

Cerny, P.G. (1997) Paradoxes of the competition state: The dynamics of political globalization. *Government and Opposition* 32 (2), 251 – 274.

Dinnie, K. (2008) *Nation Branding: Concepts, Issues, Practice*. Oxford: Butterworth-Heinemann.

Einstein, M. (2007) *Brands of Faith: Marketing Religion in a Commercial Age*. New York: Routledge.

Fan, Y. (2009) Branding the nation: Towards a better understanding. Brunel Business School Research Papers. See http://bura.brunel.ac.uk/handle/2438/3496 (accessed 30 March 2010).

Habermas, J. (2001) *The Postnational Constellation: Political Essays*. Boston, MA: MIT Press.

Hall, S. and du Gay, P. (eds) (1996) *Questions of Cultural Identity*. Thousand Oaks, CA: Sage.

Harvey, D. (1990) *The Condition of Postmodernity: An Inquiry into the Origins of Cultural Change*. Cambridge, MA: Blackwell.

Harvey, D. (2001) *Spaces of Capital: Towards a Critical Geography*. New York: Routledge.

Jansen, S.C. (2008) Designer nations: Neo-liberal nation branding – Brand Estonia. *Social Identities* 14 (1), 121–142.

Kaneva, N. (2011) Nation branding: Toward an agenda for critical research. International *Journal of Communication* 5, 117–141.

Laclau, E. (ed.) (1994) *The Making of Political Identities*. London: Verso.

Lefebvre, H. (1991) *The Production of Space*. Cambridge, MA: Blackwell.

Lury, C. (2004) *Brands: The Logos of the Global Economy*. London, Taylor & Francis: Front Cover.

Moor, L. (2007) *The Rise of Brands*. Oxford: Berg.

Mosco, V. (1996) *The Political Economy of Communication: Rethinking and Renewal*. Thousand Oaks, CA: Sage.

O'Sullivan, T., Hartley, J., Saunders, D., Montgomery, M. and Fiske, J. (eds) (1994) *Key Concepts in Communication and Cultural Studies*. London: Routledge.

Pretes, M. (2003) Tourism and nationalism. *Annals of Tourism Research* 30 (1), 125–142.

Sassen, S. (1998) *Globalization and its Discontents: Essays on the New Mobility of People and Money*. New York: New Press.

Schiller, H. (1976) *Communication and Cultural Domination*. White Plains, NY: Sharpe.

Spillman, L. (1997) *Nation and Commemoration: Creating National Identities in the United States and Australia*. Cambridge: Cambridge University Press.

Van Ham, P. (2001a) *European Integration and the Postmodern Condition: Governance, Democracy, Identity*. New York: Routledge.

Van Ham, P. (2001b) The rise of the brand state: The postmodern politics of image and reputation. *Foreign Affairs* 8 (5), 2–6.

Ward, R. (1966) *The Australian Legend*. Oxford: Oxford University Press.

White, L. (2009) Foster's Lager: From local beer to global icon. *Marketing Intelligence and Planning* 27 (2), 177–190.

Part 2

Tourism Branding and Promotion

8   100% Pure Neoliberalism: Brand New Zealand, New Thinking, New Stories, Inc.

C. Michael Hall

Introduction

Since its launch in 1999, the New Zealand 100% Pure tourism campaign has generally been portrayed as an extremely successful tourism branding campaign that has reinforced the country's 'clean and green' positioning (e.g. Morgan *et al.*, 2002, 2003; Morgan & Pritchard, 2005, 2006; Tourism New Zealand, 2009), and which has influenced other countries' tourism and national branding strategies (e.g. Hall, 2007a; Hudson & Ritchie, 2009; Lee, 2009; Viosca *et al.*, 2006). Nevertheless, the representation of New Zealand's national branding strategies, as with much destination management and branding in general (Blain *et al.*, 2005), has generally failed to provide an appreciation of the broader implications of the strategy, as well as the political context within which place and destination brands and branding strategies are developed and implemented (Graan, 2013; Kania-Lundholm, 2014; Kemming & Humborg, 2010; Mayes, 2008; Ooi, 2008). In other words, place brands are usually presented as being an apolitical or neutral marketing tool that is focused on external markets rather than having emerged from a highly political context of domestic or internal competing interests and values. Indeed, Varga (2013: 825) suggests, 'Nation Branding is essentially an inner-oriented, cultural–political measure that targets the citizens of the national state, characterized by conservative, transformative and transferring political agendas'.

In the case of New Zealand's national branding strategy, what is usually not appreciated, especially in the tourism context, is that the 100% Pure campaign was originally only one element of a national branding strategy that sought to portray New Zealand as a highly innovative and entrepreneurial country in order to encourage foreign investment and exports (Hall, 2009a, 2010; Ministry of Economic Development, 2005, 2006). So strong was the tourism brand component that it overwhelmed other elements in the national brand and substantially influenced its development trajectory. However, this was not just the result of consumer preference and market forces, but was also a function of changes in government emphases in national brand development and governance. This chapter therefore examines the interelationships between the tourism and non-tourism components of national branding in New Zealand and the evolution of New Zealand's branding as part of the strategies of state-supported neoliberalism.

Place Branding and Competition

Nation branding is an essential element of contemporary place competition. Place branding, often referred to as place marketing and place imaging and reimaging (Hall, 1997; Kavaratzis, 2005; Skinner, 2008), is regarded as an important component in the attraction and retention of mobile capital, firms, people (including skilled and unskilled workers, domestic and international migrants, and domestic and international tourists), and in the promotion and sales of locally produced goods and services (e.g. Andersson, 2014; Anholt, 2007, 2010; Hall, 1997; Kotler et al., 1993; Kotler & Gertner, 2002; Pike, 2009, 2013). Tourism destination branding, although clearly important in its own right with respect to tourism promotion, is a subset of a wider range of place branding strategies and literatures as well as having its own specific literature (Ashworth & Kavaratzis, 2010; Gnoth, 2002; Hudson & Ritchie, 2009). Although the economic and social value of place competitive strategies, such as place branding, is often highly contested, many policy makers remain enthusiastic about the place competitive discourse and the opportunity to become 'winning' places (e.g. Bristow, 2005; Hall, 2007b; Malecki, 2004; Minford, 2006) with strong national brands (Anholt, 2010).

Place branding is undertaken via a mix of material and intangible means. Material strategies include such mechanisms as flagship projects or signature developments, often as part of broader planning strategies or redevelopment projects. Although these tend to be based more on a regional and urban scale (e.g. Kavaratzis, 2005), material strategies are also enabled on a national basis, for example, via the hosting of international sporting events such as World Cup football, cricket or rugby, which are based in several cities and centres, and which are used for national promotion (Van Der Merwe, 2007). Intangible strategies include the use of advertising, slogans, media placement and the development of new place myths (Anholt, 2007; Hall, 2014, 2015). Such strategies reflect greater focus on the constructed advantages between regions which emphasises the significance of symbolic and creative capital (Cooke & Leydesdorff, 2006). However, a major problem from a national branding perspective is how to create a sense of the whole when there are cities, regions and businesses within a country that are seeking to promote themselves internationally in order to attract capital and people.

The fact that place branding occurs at multiple levels and from multiple locations within a country or collection of countries can create significant issues for the governance and management of place brand architecture. Place brands can be formal (registered brands, trademarks) or informal (inferred) (overall image), with the formal and informal dimensions informing and influencing each other over time. Informal place brands are often developed over many years of media activity, advertising and social encounters with place that lead to the development of the stereotypes that represent a location (Blaikie, 2010; Busby & Meethan, 2008; Lukinbeal, 2005; Smyth, 2002). However, such inferred place brands can be extremely powerful and hard to shift in the minds of consumers and target audiences.

Figure 8.1 indicates the brand architecture of place brands, that is, the multiple spatial scales at which place branding occurs. A key issue in many countries seeking to successfully articulate a national brand is the degree of coordination between the different brand policy actors who operate on different scales (Ashworth & Kavaratzis, 2010; Pasquinelli, 2013). In Australia this was tackled in a tourism context via a formal agreement between brand actors (tourism marketing organisations) at the state and national levels (Hall, 2007a). However, effective national brand policies not only require coordination between place branding strategies and brand actors at different spatial scales but also on the same scale. Therefore from a national brand perspective there should also be a consistency of message between sectoral

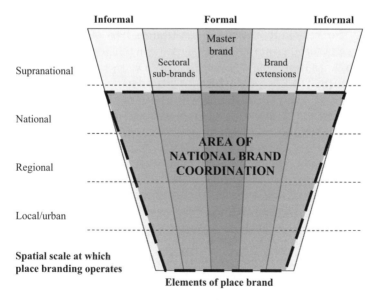

Figure 8.1 Brand architecture issues of place branding

sub-brands, for example, tourism, export, education and health, as well as other public and private brand extensions such as mega-events and national sports teams, in order to provide an effective 'umbrella' brand for an entire country or supranational jurisdiction (Dooley & Bowie, 2005; Hall, 2009b). Such issues are highly significant as they raise questions as to not only the extent to which tourism place brands actually create effective synergies with national umbrella brands as well as the branding strategies of other sectors, an issue which has been little studied in the tourism branding literature, but also how such coordination is undertaken. And it is to these questions in the New Zealand context that we will now turn.

The Development of 'Brand New Zealand'

New Zealand has a long history of formal and informal branding. Although the informal portrayal of a New Zealand identity extends to 17th and 18th century European mercantile exploration, which portrayed a Romantic interpretation of the South Pacific and its peoples (Hall, 2009b), New Zealand's colonial governments were early exponents of formal place branding in order to try and attract capital and migrants and, from the 1870s on, tourists (Dürr, 2007). According to Dürr (2007), not only was New Zealand's natural scenery advertised as attractive and distinct, but also colonial society. Throughout the 19th century the predominant promotional slogan for New Zealand was 'Scenic Wonderland' (Bell, 2008) with many of the natural attractions used in contemporary promotion of the country already utilised in Victoria era promotions. The early environmental and agrarian focus of New Zealand promotion was only further reinforced by the creation in 1901 of the Department of Tourist and Health Resorts, as well as subsequent incarnations of the organisation, such as the Department of Tourist and Publicity that operated in various forms from 1930 to 1990, and which integrated national promotion for tourism, migration and economic development purposes (McClure, 2004).

In the 1980s, the brand image of New Zealand was often regarded as consisting of little more than '70 million sheep and 3 million people' (Lodge, 2002). However, at the start of the 1990s, there was renewed government interest in national promotion, particularly as New Zealand faced an economic downturn in its traditional primary export sectors (Lodge, 2002). Government and private sector restructuring, corporatisation of government agencies and the development of a more commercial approach by government bodies also contributed to a greater interest in international branding of New Zealand products and sectors.

In response, the then New Zealand Market Development Board attempted to promote New Zealand by advertising in the European market as well as initiating national marketing innovations such as the so-called Dallas experiment (Lodge, 2002). The experiment involved saturating the city of Dallas in

Texas with New Zealand promotions, events and trade fairs in order to promote New Zealand agricultural products. Although the campaign increased exports for a year, it had no long-term effects on recognition of the New Zealand brand as the levels of awareness and purchase returned to the same levels as they had been before the experiment started (Lodge, 2002; Dinnie, 2008). At the same time as the Market Development Board sought to promote New Zealand produce, so the New Zealand Tourism Board and the national carrier, Air New Zealand, tried to promote the country as the 'environmental destination of the 1990s' (Kotler *et al.*, 1993) in order to take advantage of the growth of interest in nature-based tourism as well as to further build its image.

However, there was a realisation that the promotions of different national organisations created inconsistent images and there needed to be greater coordination in national branding. Building on its now well established internationally inferred brand of rural and green, New Zealand initially tried to promote itself as 'the orchard of the Pacific' (Lodge, 2002), which was attractive to the domestic market as well as prospective buyers (Dinnie, 2008). However, this branding campaign was regarded as not providing a consistent image of New Zealand that was applicable to all business sectors and in 1995 a new brand was launched, 'The New Zealand Way'.

The New Zealand Way

The New Zealand Way Limited (TNZWL) was a joint venture, set up in 1995 by the New Zealand Tourism Board (the government corporate body responsible for international tourism marketing and promotion now referred to as Tourism New Zealand) and Trade New Zealand (the government's international trade promotion agency now part of New Zealand Trade and Enterprise) to restore the fragmented image of New Zealand in global markets (Kent & Walker, 2000). TNZWL adopted six 'brand values' for the country's repositioning: environmental responsibility; achievement; cultural diversity; integrity; innovation; and quality (Kent & Walker, 2000). In late 1999, TNZWL registered the fern as a trademark so as to give New Zealand an official national icon (Florek & Insch, 2008), although the fern had been part of New Zealand tourism and product promotion for many years, dating back to the Victorian era. This approach to branding New Zealand was developed because:

> New Zealand is not top of mind internationally and whilst generally positive images exist they lack clarity and consistency. Research showed that while New Zealand was generally regarded as a distant and friendly country, with a strong 'clean and green' association, this was usually a vague understanding and did not translate into competitive advantage. In some developing markets, customers had little or no perception of New Zealand at all (New Zealand Way, 1998, in Hall & Mitchell, 2002).

TNZWL utilised a range of events, advertising, promotional activities and imaginative public relations exercises developed around themes such as 'Fresh The New Zealand Way', 'Taste The New Zealand Way' (both associated with food and wine) and 'Experience The New Zealand Way' (associated with tourism activities). In 1998, TNZWL's 170 brand partners jointly accounted for 20% of New Zealand's foreign exchange earnings and represented the top 20% of New Zealand companies (Hall & Mitchell, 2002).

100% Pure

Although arguably successful from a national perspective, TNZWL did not succeed in promoting New Zealand as strongly as the tourism industry desired (Morgan et al., 2002, 2003; Tourism New Zealand, 2009). In late 1998/early 1999, following a reorganisation of tourism at the national government level, including the replacement of the New Zealand Tourism Board by an even more market and commercially driven entity called Tourism New Zealand (Hall & Kearsley, 2001), it was decided to develop a global marketing campaign in order to brand New Zealand as a tourism destination in a consistent fashion in selected target markets. Such a decision was driven not only by industry and stakeholder frustration with previous highly fragmented marketing efforts (Tourism New Zealand, 2009), but also by the desire to gain a better return on government expenditures on tourism promotion and marketing.

In July 1999, Tourism New Zealand launched the 100% Pure campaign in order to reposition New Zealand as a tourism destination. This campaign focused solely on the tourism sector and was intended as a base to double New Zealand's foreign exchange by 2005 (Morgan et al., 2002). It used 'Landscape' as the brand essence and portrayed New Zealand as a young, beautiful and clean country (Morgan et al., 2002). The tagline of the campaign, '100% Pure' was copyrighted by Tourism New Zealand in its major markets: New Zealand, Australia, the European Union, the United States, Japan, Singapore, Taiwan, China, India, Thailand, Korea and Hong Kong (Mitchell, 2008). This campaign turned out to be one of the most successful international country-level promotional efforts of its time and has led to its recognition as an extremely powerful travel destination brand (Mitchell, 2008; New Zealand New Thinking, 2007; Tourism New Zealand, 2009), which is arguably seen by many consumers and stakeholders as the embodiment of 'Brand New Zealand'.

New Zealand New Thinking and Brand New Zealand

Although the 100% Pure campaign was driving an increase in international tourist visitation to New Zealand and greater destination awareness, the new Labour Government which came into power in 1999 was also seeking to promote other industry sectors internationally as well as develop a more innovative knowledge-based economy. On 12 February 2002, the then Prime Minister Helen Clark released a policy framework for economic transformation entitled

Growing an Innovative New Zealand (Clark, 2002). This 'Growth and Innovation Framework' (GIF) was designed to pursue long-term sustainable economic growth. The GIF strategy indicated that the national government should concentrate policies and resources in four areas (Clark, 2002).

- enhancing the existing innovation framework;
- developing, attracting and retaining people with exceptional skills and talents who are able to innovate and so contribute to increasing overall productivity;
- increasing global connectedness to overcome the tyranny of distance;
- focusing innovation initiatives in areas where their impact will be maximised.

A key role in the GIF for increasing global connectedness was to 'support initiatives to brand New Zealand as being technologically advanced, creative and successful and to present that consistently across sectors' (Clark, 2002: 7). According to Clark, 'We need to develop and promote a contemporary and future-focused Brand NZ, which projects New Zealand as a great place to invest in, live in, and visit' (Clark, 2002: 48).

Significantly, with respect to the relationship between destination and national branding of New Zealand, the GIF noted that tourism images and promotion may be at cross-purposes with the images desired by other sectors (Hall, 2009). For example, Clark (2002: 48) emphasised that 'Offshore perceptions of New Zealand are outdated. While there is some awareness internationally of our "clean green image", from a tourism point of view there is too little awareness of New Zealand as an innovative country at the leading edge of knowledge'. Similarly, the report noted that 'the requirements for marketing ICT are very different to those associated with primary products or tourism' (Clark, 2002: 61) and that, while previous international marketing and publicity 'has been successful in attracting tourism, it does not necessarily encourage entrepreneurial migrants' (Clark, 2002: 43). Such sentiments reflected a concern from the government department responsible for economic development that 'too close a relationship between the nation brand and the tourism brand, particularly for those tourism brands relying heavily upon rural or traditional imagery, can actually be regarded as detrimental for the country as a whole' (Ministry of Economic Development, 2006: 19). As the Ministry of Economic Development (2005: 19) also noted:

Overseas perceptions of NZ have too often stereotyped us around our picturesque landscape and related 'clean green' image. Although these perceptions have value (e.g. for tourism), we need other perceptions that better recognise NZ as a good place to do business and to do business with. This includes ensuring that NZers are recognised for their creativity, innovation and proficiencies in the use of technologies.

Concurrently with the development of the GIF, the TNZWL was revised to form Brand New Zealand (Brand NZ), which became the new trading name of TNZWL in 2002. This change was part of the broader goal to create greater international awareness of New Zealand as an innovative country. According to Prime Minister Clark (2002: 48):

> One of the reasons why the image of New Zealand internationally is not strong is that we have not presented a consistent brand image across our various sectors. This must change. To that end government, through Industry New Zealand, Trade New Zealand, and Tourism New Zealand is working with the private sector to develop a Brand New Zealand programme. The aim is to reposition the brand and develop a joint management structure so that government, industry and business can all utilise the same brand.

The objective of Brand NZ is 'to enhance New Zealand's national brand to better differentiate New Zealand internationally; support key sectors; and, enhance New Zealand's established/emerging areas of comparative advantage' (Ministry of Economic Development, 2006: 3). Tourism was not an area explicitly identified as being of comparative advantage (Hall, 2009a). The policy rationale for the Brand NZ programme was the need to actively manage the perception of New Zealand internationally, especially in what were regarded as the economically key biotechnology, creative industry and information and communications technology sectors, noting that, while the inferred 'clean and green' New Zealand brand 'may work well for major export sectors such as tourism and primary products, it is potentially irrelevant or an impediment to credibility in others, as it may be associated with a lack of technological sophistication' (Ministry of Economic Development, 2006: 10).

Brand NZ was intended to provide coordination and facilitation of New Zealand marketing and promotion related to trade and investment and to secure leverage from other public and/or private sector activities around the 'New Zealand New Thinking' theme. The Brand NZ Programme did not emphasise national branding mechanisms such as 'country of origin' or 'Made in New Zealand' but instead focused on consistency of marketing messages with respect to trade, investment and migration (Ministry of Economic Development, 2006). According to New Zealand Trade and Enterprise (NZTE) (2009) the fern mark that is the core brand icon of Brand NZ was created to build New Zealand's business reputation in key international markets and, by using the Fern Mark, NZTE, Tourism New Zealand and New Zealand businesses can tell a consistent story about New Zealand and increase international connections.

Figure 8.2 indicates the brand and governance relationships of Brand NZ. The Brand NZ Fern Mark is regarded as the umbrella brand under which are the 100% Pure New Zealand and the New Zealand New Thinking brands.

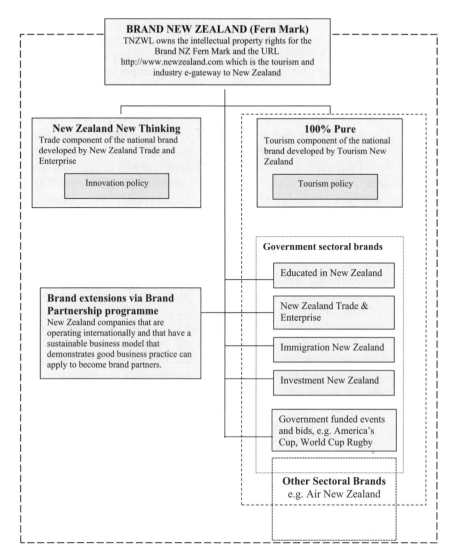

Figure 8.2 Governance and branding relationships of Brand New Zealand in the 2000s

The relationship is not only brand based but also one of governance and inter-agency coordination as Brand NZ is jointly owned by Tourism New Zealand and NZTE, while each agency is responsible for its own brand campaign. The New Zealand New Thinking programme aimed to improve Brand NZ by adding creativity, innovation and technological advancement to the brand values of Brand NZ and create a 'clean, green and smart' image (Ministry of Economic Development, 2006; New Zealand New Thinking, 2007) according to New Zealand New Thinking.

'100% Pure' is the Tourism New Zealand positioning of our national brand. 'New Zealand New Thinking' is the trade-related component. The two are complementary in building an overall brand personality of 'clean, green, smart, innovative, and creative [which is] especially important for the range of industries and businesses in New Zealand that are not operating in spheres where clean and green is relevant' (New Zealand New Thinking, 2009).

Under the umbrella of the fern mark, 'New Zealand New Thinking' was registered in 2004 (Florek & Insch, 2008). Five brand messages were developed for the 'New Zealand New Thinking' proposition. The messages consisted of: new Pacific nation; entrepreneurial spirit; globally connected; space and openness; and resourceful (Ministry of Economic Development, 2006). These messages not only differ from the brand values of TNZWL in 1995 but are also different from those of 100% Pure (see Tables 8.1 and 8.2). The target audience has also been expanded under 'New Zealand New Thinking'.

The difference in target audience, brand proposition and goals clearly has major implications for the expressed goal of creating synergies between New Zealand New Thinking and 100% Pure as part of the positioning and reinforcement of Brand NZ as something broader than just 'clean and green'. This is particularly the case if government is consciously trying to reposition or extend a national brand so as to try and benefit a wider range of industries as well as use notions of constructed advantage to benefit both brand and innovation strategies. Furthermore, it raises fundamental questions as to the successful integration of tourism and non-tourism place brands under the umbrella national brand and the goal of being perceived as 'clean, green and smart', especially as the government's own research highlighted major issues with how New Zealand was perceived internationally.

Brand NZ research conducted in 2004 indicated that for domestic consumers innovation ranked last at 3% as a differentiating factor for New Zealand in international markets, although 39% of those surveyed believed that New Zealand was viewed as innovative. Two-thirds of New Zealand business survey respondents would have liked the rest of the world to see New Zealanders as inventive or innovative but instead believed that overseas perceptions of New Zealand as a country are instead dominated by clean and green (77%), a great place to visit (66%) and a producer of rural products (60%). Similarly, although offshore businesses regarded New Zealand business people as entrepreneurial (22% of respondents), they believed that as a country New Zealand is 'naturally beautiful' (80%) and clean and green (64%) but not technologically advanced (6%) (Ministry of Economic Development, 2006). These findings were reinforced in a series of international surveys with respect to perceptions of New Zealand undertaken by NZTE over 2006–2008 that, with the exception of Australia, mirror the Ministry of Economic Development (2006) findings (see Table 8.3).

Nation branding is a slow process with no guarantee of long-term success. The desire of governments to reorient national place brands, even if

Table 8.1 Changes in New Zealand national brand attributes

Government	Label	Attributes and brand events
National (1990–1999)		
1995	The New Zealand Way	'Brand values': environmental responsibility; achievement; cultural diversity; integrity; innovation; and quality.
1999		100% Pure launched by Tourism New Zealand in July 1999.
Labour (1999–2008)		
2000		New Zealand New Thinking proposition of 'clean, green and smart' with 'brand messages' of: New Pacific nation; Entrepreneurial spirit; Globally connected; Resourceful; and Space and openness.
2002	Brand New Zealand	The New Zealand Way retitled as Brand New Zealand.
National (2008 – present)		
2012	New Zealand Story	'Core values': Kaitiaki – Care of people and place; Integrity – Trust, honesty, humility and reciprocal respect; Resourcefulness – fresh, outward-looking way of thinking. The Story is then told through a framework of 'three chapters': Open Spaces, Open Hearts and Open Minds.
2014–2016		National flag selection process and referendum.

based on empirical data, often does not easily match the realities of inferred brands and changes in politics and public administration. The results of NZTE research only served to highlight not only the strength of the country's inferred brand but also the success of a sectoral-brand '100% Pure' which is much more closely aligned with the inferred brand than the brand proposition and values that Brand NZ had sought to advance with respect to being innovative and creative. A change in government only served to reinforce the position of 100% Pure with the new Prime Minister, John Key, also the minister of tourism, raising the prospect of 100% Pure expanding to become a 'master brand' for the whole country. According to Key, '100% Pure forms a big part of our brand marketing for New Zealand Inc. ... We think it's a foundation brand to carry on into the future. We can use that to

Table 8.2 Comparison of New Zealand New Thinking and 100% Pure

	New Zealand New Thinking	100% Pure
Target audience	• The New Zealand public (initial primary target) • Offshore purchasers of New Zealand goods and services • Foreign investors • Potential migrants • Public and private sector business partners • Tourists and tourism marketers	• 'The Interactive Traveller' – regular international travellers who consume a wide range of tourism products and services. They are travellers who seek out new experiences that involve engagement and interaction.
Proposition	The brand messages underlying the New Zealand New Thinking proposition of 'clean, green and smart' are: *New Pacific nation* – a young nation with a stimulating and sophisticated lifestyle, shaped by its history, cultural mix and unique Pacific heritage *Entrepreneurial spirit* – a nation of innovators and entrepreneurs who dare to do things differently and have a desire to break new ground – an independent spirit that celebrates fresh, creative and unconventional thinking *Globally connected* – place in the world shapes perspective – successful New Zealand businesses recognise their fit in international markets and the value they can best contribute *Resourceful* – a resourceful nation with a history of rising to the challenge – modern businesses have transformed this resourcefulness into commercial innovation *Space and openness* – in both physical landscape and state of mind; room to think – freedom of expression, creativity and clarity	The purity of New Zealand is revitalising As based upon what are identified as New Zealand's unique attributes: authenticity (as umbrella concept for all attributes), pristine, isolated, (positive, genuine, uncorrupted, fresh, vital, raw, mythic, scenic, natural, fresh. Extension of brand proposition in 2007 to include notion of 'The Youngest Country'. The initial 100% Pure tagline has developed into an entire branding proposition that also conveys the more ephemeral concept of '100% Pure New Zealand-ness' in whichever situation it is placed. This is particularly favourable to agricultural sector exports.

Source: M&C Saatchi (2000), Ministry of Economic Development (2006), Ministry of Tourism *et al.* (2007), Tourism New Zealand (2009) and Hall (2010).

leverage not just our tourism activities but also our trade promotion and general promotion of New Zealand' (BusinessDay, 2009), although he did add that he thought that the logo may need some change such as inclusion of the silver fern (which is currently the master brand). As the Tourism

Table 8.3 Overview of main findings of NZTE studies of overseas perceptions of New Zealand (2006–2008)

Market (date of study)	Core findings	
	Perception of country	Perception of business
Australia (2007)	An extension of their domestic market	Business acumen is seen as 'pretty sharp'
China and Japan (2007)	A nice place to visit	Business acumen is low
India (2008)	Good ethics but no business appetite	Business appetite is low in New Zealand
Korea (2008)	Pure and friendly but too boring and relaxed	Business acumen is low in New Zealand
UK (2006)	A distant affection for something familiar/clean and green	Business acumen is low
US (2006)	An expectation of something different/clean and green	Business acumen is low

Source: New Zealand Trade and Enterprise (2006, 2007a, b, 2008a, b).

Industry Association chief executive Tim Cossar said, the 100% Pure brand was already representing the wider country: 'By default, we have curated it in some ways into a national brand' (BusinessDay, 2009).

New Zealand Story

In 2012 a new brand initiative developed out of the National Party government's business growth agenda which had a target of raising exports to 40% of Gross Domestic Product by 2025. Entitled the New Zealand Story (NZS) the project aimed to create 'One story that is a foundation for New Zealand's story for global audiences to support export earnings growth' and 'A communication toolkit of assets to assist businesses in telling the New Zealand story' (Smith, 2014: 1.1.1, 1.1.2). The mandate of NZS is to 'promote & protect New Zealand's brand' with the NZS Group ensuring 'a co-ordinated private public sector approach to the development of the overarching New Zealand Story' and being responsible for:

- articulation of a New Zealand Story to international stakeholders which enhance our international competitiveness;
- protection of the New Zealand brand mark (Fern Mark) and brand assets; and
- alignment of storytelling and brand protection across various sectors within New Zealand (Smith, 2014: 1.2).

According to the Director of NZS, Rebecca Smith, NZS is needed 'because people respond to the brand identity of a nation in the same way they respond to commercial brands like Nike, Apple or BMW. And like those other valuable global brands – our country's reputation can give us a significant competitive advantage' (Smith, 2015).

If we are to compete on a world stage and give our exporters an extra edge in trade discussions, we need to expand our New Zealand story.

What is Our New Zealand Story?

Right now, when people think of New Zealand, they think of wide, open spaces and breathtaking scenery. That is no surprise given the longstanding success of our 100% Pure New Zealand tourism campaign and the global impact of movies like *Lord of the Rings*. It makes a great story for tourism. Yet New Zealand is more than a film set. Our people are innovative thinkers who work well with others. We create brilliant products and deliver outstanding service. These are the stories we need to be telling (Smith, 2015).

The New Zealand Story Group is accommodated within the NZTE, comprising a Director and three staff, and is governed by the New Zealand Story Group Advisory Board (the Board) with representatives from NZTE, Tourism New Zealand, Ministry of Primary Industries, Education New Zealand (responsible for exporting and promoting New Zealand educational services internationally), Te Puni Kokiri (the lead agency responsible for Maori affairs), the Ministry of Foreign Affairs and Trade and three private sector members. According to Smith (2014) 'the New Zealand brand is deficient in three key areas which appear to impact upon our trade success':

- *Vibrancy* – we are seen as a beautiful agrarian country lacking vibrant cities or a rich diverse culture. This dominant view leads others to perceive us as unsophisticated or unable to deliver advanced, innovative solutions.
- *Science and technology* – although we have developed some world first solutions, scientific breakthroughs and innovations, we are not known for this. Alongside a perceived lack of sophistication, and a reputation for not being business savvy, our internationalising businesses have to work harder to make it into the buyers' consideration set.
- *Export goods and services* – we are respected as a provider of food to many nations; however, our portfolio of goods and services beyond this is not obvious. (Smith, 2014: 2.1)

In order to achieve a change, New Zealand Story 'must therefore work with partners to dial up factors that will contribute to a shift in perception'. Tasks include 'Recalibrate the New Zealand Story telling beyond open spaces to showcase a story that reflects our open minds and resourceful approach' and 'Continue to incorporate more imagery and resources that reflect our urban landscape, our innovations, know-how and our sectors' (Smith, 2014: 2.2). The New Zealand Story website (http://www.nzstory.govt.nz) provides a range of resources with respect to the chapters of the New Zealand Story, Open Spaces, Open Hearts and Open Minds, which are used to provide a framework for businesses to craft and communicate their own unique NZ Story. The tool kit includes professional quality images, infographics, videos, presentation templates, cases studies and event templates and resources available for free. The infographics serve to substantiate claims about New Zealand which may be especially valuable given criticisms of the 'clean and green' label and the gap with respect to the reality of the New Zealand environment (e.g. Bell, 2008; Grinlinton, 2009; Hall & Stoffels, 2006; Paterson & McDonald, 2004; Smith & Rodger, 2009). Other elements of NZS include branding public diplomacy and ensuring that the New Zealand government has a consistent approach in all its 'visual language' (Smith, 2014).

One possible element of the visual language that might be changed is the New Zealand Flag, which was subject to referenda in 2015 and 2016. The Prime Minister, John Key, has been a major proponent for a flag change (Moir, 2015), so as to ensure that it is more distinguishable internationally and has stated his preference for a silver fern design. A private sector member of the NZS group, Julie Christie, is also a member of the Flag Consideration Panel. Of the four final shortlisted flag designs, three of them are variations of the silver fern design with the fourth option being a koru, or unfurling fern frond (Hunt, 2015a). Hunt (2015b) suggests that 'A new flag for New Zealand is about a new brand, but what exactly that might be … no one seems to know or even care', and goes on to quote Jono Aidney, an advertising executive, on the government's process (see also http://pantograph-punch.com/post/so-you-want-to-rebrand-nz):

> The question we probably need to ask is 'why does New Zealand exist'? … Is our purpose unfettered economic progress? Is it to be an ethical voice on the world stage? A place where every child gets a fair start? Guardians of nature? Nature's pimps? If we can work out what our collective 'purpose' is, we'll have a chance of turning that idea into a flag. (Jono Aidney in Hunt, 2015b)

Indeed, such was the level of public dislike for the four shortlisted flag designs that, following a social media campaign and a petition to Parliament, the New Zealand Green Party successfully managed to add a fifth design, 'First to the Light', better known as 'red peak', into the flag referendum process in September 2015 (Vance, 2015).

Conclusions

New Zealand has long had an inferred brand based on agrarian and natural landscapes that are embodied in the concept of 'clean and green'. This image has been of great economic value to the agricultural and tourism sectors. The role of 'clean and green' in New Zealand's international image was further enhanced by the 100% Pure campaign of Tourism New Zealand, which has been in place since 1999 and which, to many people both in New Zealand and overseas, is New Zealand's international place brand. However, since the mid-1990s successive governments and their agencies, particularly the Ministry of Economic Development (now Ministry of Business, Innovation and Employment) and NZTE, have sought to extend the place branding of New Zealand under the concept of Brand NZ so as to try and portray the country as being innovative, entrepreneurial and creative – what has been referred to as 'clean, green and smart' (Ministry of Economic Development, 2006). The problem is that, while this may be believed by the domestic market and to an extent in New Zealand's closest market, Australia, the rest of the world does not perceive it and instead sees New Zealand in the terms reinforced by 100% Pure – clean and green and a nice place to visit but not smart (Hall, 2010). This situation also reflects a little-examined issue in destination marketing that what may be good for branding in tourism terms may have significant negative impact on the brand perceptions of other sectors.

Changing an inferred, and to a significant extent from a tourism and agricultural perspective, formal national brand takes a long time. Successive governments have been keen to place their own mark on how New Zealand is branded, yet their approaches tend to be variations on the same theme. What has not been questioned by government is that the country does need a formal national brand. As Lewis (2011: 280) commented, 'Economic nationalism, which reduces national identity building ... is deeply embedded. It is cultivated by popular media, industry actors, education curricula, science funding, and even domestic art, as well as national development agencies'. Indeed, an increasingly vital element of promoting New Zealand is the role of New Zealand Inc./NZ Inc., which is referred to in many government reports. For example, the 2013/2014 Annual report of NZTE notes under 'Our purpose': 'We work with international investors to identify business opportunities in New Zealand, focused on target industries and regions that need capital and connections to grow, and, alongside our NZ Inc. partners (within government and the business community), to build credibility in our national brand' (New Zealand Trade and Enterprise, 2014: 4).

The notion of NZ Inc. embraces not just a 'whole of government' approach to branding, but also refers to the inclusion of corporate partners in the development of branding policies and strategies. Such is the extent of NZ Inc. thinking that it reflects an approach where the country is run like a business with the prime minister as its chief executive and the voters as the profit-maximising stock and shareholders looking for the best possible return from the national enterprise. In order to achieve this, the John Key-led National Party's neoliberal economic model is highly centralised and interventionist with 'one people united under a single business plan' (McCrone, 2012; see also Amore and Hall (2016) on the Christchurch rebuild), to which can be added, brand, with businesses using the images and by-lines of the New Zealand Story (as interpreted by NZ Inc.). The NZ Inc. model is therefore one of state intervention to maximise economic growth accompanied by its framing in terms of national wellbeing and presented as a 'necessity' rather than ideology. Brand NZ, and branding New Zealand, is therefore about more than brand awareness, value adding and linking firms to markets; it 'is a calculated and calculating entanglement of territory, imaginary, measurement, technology, practice and identity building' and 'is far from politically, culturally, socially or economically innocent' (Lewis, 2011: 282, 283).

Nevertheless, a country is more than a brand. With respect to the flag debate for example, Morgan (2015) comments,

> To begin with the Prime Minister just wants a logo – he is a child of the corporate world and as he keeps telling us brand is everything. ... To reduce the national flag to a brand has to be the most banal, vacuous attempt by Corporate NZ to take over our identity. It shows no respect for who we are, what our national identity is, it's crass commercialisation, nothing more. He even has the gall to boast of the 'billions' we'll make if we Coca-Colarise ourselves.

Lyon (2015) suggests that, with respect to the significance attached to image by the Key government, 'We are living in an age of spin. The Roman leaders gave their people bread and circuses. Sadly, we no longer get the bread'. One of the major issues with branding is that, ultimately, the brand values need to be based on reality for them to be perceived as authentic and sustainable in the long term. Here, Brand NZ may be undercut by criticisms of the country's environmental record while the images portrayed have to be inclusive of and believable for the local population, this latter point becoming increasingly problematic given widespread child poverty and a growing gap between rich and poor. 'Brand NZ is about succeeding in the global, not about local aspirations or any challenge to the global that it is performing' (Lewis, 2011: 284). Even Kotler *et al.* (1993), who provide the standard case text for place marketing, acknowledged that 'the escalating competition ... for business attraction has the marks of a zero-sum game or worse, a negative-sum game, in that the winner ultimately becomes the loser' (Kotler *et al.*, 1993: 15).

The commercial nationalism of Brand NZ is therefore part of the wider neoliberal project in which places are competing for capital and people. The (narrowly framed) success of businesses, economies and brands is now a form of sport in which you can see your team's performance in the latest league table. The rules of the game are also changing so that a free trade agenda is pursued that deepen the effects of globalisation still further as the result of investment, labour and trade flows while simultaneously there is increased deregulation and privatisation. In order to train for the competition, businesses are encouraged to be team players and engage in the story, and the education system, including universities, encourages students to develop enterprise and cultural competencies to make them more 'resilient' and 'competitive' for the future. Nation branding is not a neutral tool but a reflection of a set of assumptions about the way the world does and should run. In the New Zealand case, the country's formal branding process is part of a wider neoliberal discourse of competitiveness and a dominant stakeholder belief system that reinforces the commercial imaginaries of national branding. However, not everyone is a member of NZ Inc., and the costs of competition and what success actually means needs a far more rigorous and critical examination (Hall, 2007b), even if the country's inferred brand can be shifted. The central problem is not only what and how places win but also why they lose, as in any competition not everyone can be a winner.

References

Amore, A. and Hall, C.M. (2016) Regeneration is the focus now: Anchor projects and delivering a new CBD for Christchurch. In C.M. Hall, S. Malinen, R. Vosslamber and R. Wordsworth (eds) *Business and Post-disaster Management: Business, Organisational and Consumer Resilience and the Christchurch Earthquakes*. Abingdon: Routledge.

Andersson, I. (2014) Placing place branding: An analysis of an emerging research field in human geography. *Danish Journal of Geography* 114 (2), 143–155.

Anholt, S. (2007) *Competitive Identity: The New Brand Management for Nations, Cities and Regions*. London: Palgrave Macmillan.

Anholt, S. (2010) *Places: Identity, image and reputation*. Basingstoke: Palgrave Macmillan.

Ashworth, G. and Kavaratzis, M. (eds) (2010) *Towards Effective Place Brand Management. Branding European Cities and Regions*. Cheltenham: Edward Elgar.

Bell, C. (2008) 100% PURE New Zealand: Branding for back-packers. *Journal of Vacation Marketing* 14, 345–355.

Blaikie, A. (2010) Imagining the face of a nation: Scotland, modernity and the places of memory. *Memory Studies* 4, 416–431.

Blain, C., Levy, S. and Ritchie, J.R.B. (2005) Destination branding: Insights and practices from destination management organizations. *Journal of Travel Research* 43, 328–338.

Bristow, G. (2005) 'Everyone's a winner': Problematising the discourse of regional competitiveness. *Journal of Economic Geography* 5, 285–304.

Busby, G. and Meethan, K. (2008). Cultural capital in Cornwall: Heritage and the visitor. *Cornish Studies* 16 (1), 146–166.

BusinessDay (2009) Key seeks expansion of 100% Pure. *BusinessDay*, 31 July. See http://www.stuff.co.nz/business/industries/2705859/Key-seeks-expansion-of-100-Pure

Clark, H. (2002) *Growing an Innovative New Zealand*. Wellington: Office of the Prime Minister.

Cooke, P. and Leydesdorff, L. (2006) Regional development in the knowledge-based economy: The construction of advantage. *Journal of Technology Transfer* 31, 5–15.

Dinnie, K. (2008) *Nation Branding: Concepts, Issues, Practice*. Oxford: Butterworth-Heinemann.

Dooley, G. and Bowie, D. (2005) Place brand architecture: Strategic management of the brand portfolio. *Place Branding* 1, 402–419.

Dürr, E. (2007) Representing purity: National branding, nature, and identity in New Zealand. Paper presented at *Transformations '07: Composing the Nation: Ideas, Peoples, Histories, Languages, Cultures, Economies, the Congress of Te Whāinga Aronui/The Council for the Humanities*, Victoria University of Wellington, Wellington, 27–28 August.

Florek, M. and Insch, A. (2008) The trademark protection of country brands: Insights from New Zealand. *Journal of Place Management and Development* 1 (3), 292–306.

Gnoth, J. (2002) Leveraging export brands through a tourism destination brand. *Journal of Brand Management* 9, 262–280.

Graan, A. (2013) Counterfeiting the nation? Skopje 2014 and the politics of nation branding in Macedonia. *Cultural Anthropology* 28 (1), 161–179.

Grinlinton, D. (2009) *Clean Green New Zealand – Reality or Myth?* Washington DC: Georgetown University, Centre for Australian and New Zealand Studies.

Hall, C.M. (1997) Geography, marketing and the selling of places. *Journal of Travel and Tourism Marketing* 6 (3/4), 61–84.

Hall, C.M. (2007a) *Introduction to Tourism in Australia: Development, Issues and Change* (5th edn). Frenchs Forest: Pearson Education Australia.

Hall, C.M. (2007b) Tourism and regional competitiveness. In J. Tribe (ed.) *Advances in Tourism Research: New Directions, Challenges and Applications* (pp. 217–230). Oxford: Elsevier.

Hall, C.M. (2009a) Innovation and tourism policy in Australia and New Zealand: Never the twain shall meet? *Journal of Policy Research in Tourism, Leisure and Events* 1 (1), 2–18.

Hall, C.M. (2009b) Heritage tourism in the Pacific: Modernity, myth, and identity. In D. Timothy and G. Nyaupane (eds) *Cultural Heritage and Tourism in the Developing World* (pp. 108–125). London: Routledge.

Hall, C.M. (2010) Tourism destination branding and its affects on national branding strategies: Brand New Zealand, clean and green but is it smart? *European Journal of Tourism and Hospitality Research* 1 (1), 68–89.

Hall, C.M. (2014) Will climate change kill Santa Claus?: Climate change and high-latitude Christmas place branding. *Scandinavian Journal of Hospitality and Tourism* 14, 23–40.

Hall, C.M. (2015) Polar gateway cities: Issues and challenges. *Polar Journal*; doi: 10.1080/2154896X.2015.1080511

Hall, C.M. and Kearsley, G.W. (2001) *Tourism in New Zealand: An Introduction*. Melbourne: Oxford University Press.

Hall, C.M. and Mitchell, R. (2002) The changing nature of the relationship between cuisine and tourism in Australia and New Zealand: From fusion cuisine to food networks. In A. Hjalager and G. Richards (eds) *Tourism and Gastronomy* (pp. 186–206). London: Routledge.

Hall, C.M. and Stoffels, M. (2006) Lake tourism in New Zealand: Sustainable management issues. In C.M. Hall and T. Härkönen (eds) *Lake Tourism: An Integrated Approach to Lacustrine Tourism Systems* (pp. 182–206). Clevedon: Channel View Publications.

Hudson, S. and Ritchie, J.R.B. (2009) Branding a memorable destination experience. The case of 'Brand Canada'. *International Journal of Tourism Research* 11 (2), 217–228.

Hunt, E. (2015a) New Zealand's new flag: Final four designs announced. *The Guardian*, 1 September.

Hunt, E. (2015b) New Zealand's prime minister John Key wants a new flag. Does anybody else? *The Guardian*, 11 August.

Kania-Lundholm, M. (2014) Nation in market times: Connecting the national and the commercial. A research overview. *Sociology Compass* 8, 603–613.

Kavaratzis, M. (2005) Place branding: A review of trends and conceptual models. *The Marketing Review* 5 (4), 329–342.

Kemming, J. and Humborg, C. (2010) Democracy and nation brand (ing): Friends or foes? *Place Branding and Public Diplomacy* 6 (3), 183–197.

Kent, H.A. and Walker, R.H. (2000) Place of origin branding: Towards reconciling the requirements and purposes of destination marketing and export marketing. In *ANZMAC 2000 Visionary Marketing for the 21st Century: Facing the Challenge* (pp. 653–657). Brisbane, Queensland: Griffith University.

Kotler, P. and Gertner, D. (2002) Country as brand, product, and beyond: A place marketing and brand management perspective. *Journal of Brand Management* 9 (4–5), 249–261.

Kotler, P., Haider, D.H. and Rein, I. (1993) *Marketing Places: Attracting Investment, Industry and Tourism to Cities, States and Nations.* New York: Free Press.

Lee, J. (2009, August 27) Resist taglines and slicks ads for 'brand Australia': Experts. *Sydney Morning Herald.* See http://www.smh.com.au/travel/travel-news/resist-taglines-and-slicks-ads-for-brand-australia-experts-20090827-f0l2.html

Lewis, N. (2011) Packaging political projects in geographical imaginaries: The rise of nation branding. In A. Pike (ed.) *Brands and Branding Geographies* (pp. 264–288). Cheltenham: Edward Elgar.

Lodge, C. (2002) Success and failure: The brand stories of two countries. *Journal of Brand Management* 9 (4), 372–384.

Lukinbeal, C. (2005) Cinematic landscapes. *Journal of Cultural Geography* 23 (1), 3–22.

Lyon, P. (2015) Nothing but spin coming from our Government. *New Zealand Herald,* 31 August.

M&CSaatchi (2000) Building a multifunctional tourism brand, unpublished powerpoint presentation, October.

Malecki, E.J. (2004) Jockeying for position: What it means and why it matters to regional development policy when places compete. *Regional Studies* 38, 1101–1120.

Mayes, R. (2008) A place in the sun: The politics of place, identity and branding. *Place Branding and Public Diplomacy* 4 (2), 124–135.

McClure, M. (2004) *The Wonder Country: Making New Zealand Tourism.* Auckland: Auckland University Press.

McCrone, J. (2012) The business of NZ Inc. *The Press,* 8 September.

Minford, P. (2006) Competitiveness in a globalised world: A commentary. *Journal of International Business Studies* 37, 176–178.

Ministry of Economic Development (2005) *Review of Economic, Industry and Regional Development Policies and Programmes.* Wellington: Ministry of Economic Development.

Ministry of Economic Development (2006) *Evaluation of Brand New Zealand.* Wellington: Ministry of Economic Development.

Ministry of Tourism, Tourism New Zealand and Tourism Industry Association New Zealand (2007) *New Zealand Tourism Strategy 2015.* Wellington: Ministry of Tourism, Tourism New Zealand and Tourism Industry Association New Zealand.

Mitchell, R. (2008) International business, intellectual property and the misappropriation of place. In T. Coles and C.M. Hall (eds) *International Business and Tourism* (pp. 201–219). London: Routledge.

Moir, J. (2015) John Key lists his reasons for a new flag video. *Stuff,* 20 August.

Morgan, N. and Pritchard, A. (2005) (PR)omoting place: The role of PR in building New Zealand's destination brand relationships. *Journal of Hospitality Marketing and Management* 12, 157–176.

Morgan, G. (2015) The New Zealand flag should be more than a brand. *Dominion Post,* 17 August.

Morgan, N. and Pritchard, A. (2006) Promoting niche tourism destination brands: Case studies of New Zealand and Wales. *Journal of Promotion Management* 12, 17–33.

Morgan, N., Pritchard, A. and Piggott, R. (2002) New Zealand, 100% Pure. The creation of a powerful niche destination brand. *Journal of Brand Management* 9, 335–354.

Morgan, N., Pritchard, A. and Piggott, R. (2003) Destination branding and the role of the stakeholders: The case of New Zealand. *Journal of Vacation Marketing* 9 (3), 285–299.

New Zealand New Thinking (2007) *FAQ*. See http://www.newzealandthinking.com/faq (accessed 1 April 2007).

New Zealand New Thinking (2009) *FAQ*. See http://www.newzealandthinking.com/faq#question1 (accessed 1 April 2009).

New Zealand Trade and Enterprise (2006) *Perceptions of New Zealand Overseas Research in the UK and US, 2006*. Wellington: New Zealand Trade and Enterprise.

New Zealand Trade and Enterprise (2007a) *Perceptions of New Zealand Overseas Research in Australia, 2007*. Wellington: New Zealand Trade and Enterprise.

New Zealand Trade and Enterprise (2007b) *Perceptions of New Zealand Overseas Research in Shanghai and Tokyo, 2007*. Wellington: New Zealand Trade and Enterprise.

New Zealand Trade and Enterprise (2008a) *Perceptions of New Zealand Overseas Research in India, 2008*. Wellington: New Zealand Trade and Enterprise.

New Zealand Trade and Enterprise (2008b) *Perceptions of New Zealand Overseas Research in South Korea, 2008*. Wellington: New Zealand Trade and Enterprise.

New Zealand Trade and Enterprise (2014) *Annual Report 2013/2014*. Wellington: New Zealand Trade and Enterprise.

New Zealand Way (1998) New Zealand Way. See http://www.nzway.co.nz/Media/discover_nzway.html (accessed 1 April 2008).

Ooi, C.S. (2008) Reimagining Singapore as a creative nation: The politics of place branding. *Place Branding and Public Diplomacy* 4 (4), 287–302.

Pasquinelli, C. (2013) Competition, cooperation and co-opetition: Unfolding the process of inter-territorial branding. *Urban Research and Practice* 6 (1), 1–18.

Paterson, M. and McDonald, G. (2004) *How Clean and Green is New Zealand Tourism?* Lincoln, New Zealand: Manaaki Whenua Press.

Pike, A. (2009) Geographies of brands and branding. *Progress in Human Geography* 33, 619–645.

Pike, A. (2013) Economic geographies of brands and branding. *Economic Geography* 89 (4), 317–339.

Skinner, H. (2008) The emergence and development of place marketing's confused identity. *Journal of Marketing Management* 24, 915–928.

Smith, I. and Rodger, C. (2009) Carbon emission offsets for aviation-generated emissions due to international travel to and from New Zealand. *Energy Policy* 37, 3438–3447.

Smith, R. (2014) *New Zealand Story. Briefing for the Incoming Ministers.* Auckland: New Zealand Story.

Smith, R. (2015) Blog. Why do we need a New Zealand Story. See http://www.nzstory.govt.nz/blog/why-do-we-need-a-new-zealand-story (accessed 1 September 2015).

Smyth, W. (2002) A plurality of Irelands: Regions, societies and mentalities. In B. Graham (ed.) *In Search of Ireland: A Cultural Geography* (pp. 19–43). London: Routledge.

Tourism New Zealand (2009) *Pure As: Celebrating 10 Years of 100% Pure New Zealand. 100% Pure New Zealand 10 Years Young*. Wellington, New Zealand: Tourism New Zealand.

Vance, A. (2015) Flag debate: Red Peak to be included on ballot. *Stuff*, 23 September. See http://www.stuff.co.nz/national/politics/72334191/Flag-debate-Red-Peak-to-be-included-on-ballot

Van Der Merwe, J. (2007) Political analysis of South Africa's hosting of the rugby and cricket World Cups: Lessons for the 2010 Football World Cup and beyond? *Politikon* 34 (1), 67–81.

Varga, S. (2013) The politics of nation branding: Collective identity and public sphere in the neoliberal state. *Philosophy and Social Criticism* 39, 825–845.

Viosca, R.C. Jr, Bergiel, B. and Balsmeier, P. (2006) Country equity South Africa, a case in point. *Journal of Promotion Management* 12 (1), 85–95.

9 National Identity in Africa's Tourism Industry

Kelly Phelan

Introduction

Although Africa is the second most populous continent (Population Reference Bureau, 2014), it is not considered part of the Western world. No African countries are considered advanced economies by the International Monetary Fund (2012) and only five are categorised as having high human development by the United Nations Human Development Index (United Nations Development Programme, 2014). As such, Africa is often overlooked and widely misunderstood by outsiders. A continent composed of more than 50 countries, Africa is frequently viewed as a cohesive unit. This generalisation could not be further from the truth.

Similar to the plight of Asian citizens, who are at times mistaken for the wrong ethnicity by foreigners, Sub-Saharan Africans are often considered homogenous. More than 2000 different native languages are spoken throughout the continent (UNESCO, 2010), Nigeria alone has more than 400 ethnic groups (Salawu, 2010) and scientific evidence has shown Africans that are more diverse genetically than the rest of the worldwide population (Achenbach, 2009). Suffice to say, homogeneity is largely absent in Africa.

African nations are composed of wide varieties of tribes and ethnic groups, each with their own distinct language, culture, history and identity. At times it has been challenging for countries to create a sense of national identity owing to such diversity. Some nations, such as South Africa, have made concerted efforts to not only unite citizens from assorted backgrounds, but also foster a sense of national pride and belonging around those differences. Brand South Africa not only promoted the country for business and tourism purposes (Brand South Africa, n.d.), but assisted in developing a sense of community among its citizens which was further solidified as a result of the 2010 World Cup.

In contrast, some West African nations have struggled to generate national identities that support the historic attractions that draw tourists (Phelan, 2015b). While heritage tourists coming to visit slave tourism sites anticipate a connection with locals through their shared history, many locals fail to acknowledge any association.

In recent years, Kenya has manufactured its own sense of national identity primarily for tourism purposes. Since the election of US President Barack Obama, Kenyans have promoted tourism as an opportunity for visitors to experience the hospitality of 'Obama's people'. This has in turn led many cosmopolitan Kenyans to develop a new sense of identity and national story.

Forging a Legacy for the Rainbow Nation through Sport

When Nelson Mandela was released from Robben Island in 1990, it marked a turning point in South Africa's long established apartheid legacy. The negotiations to end apartheid that took place over the next four years reshaped South Africa's government and society, but also re-established South Africa from a branding perspective.

Nation branding is practised in an effort to increase a country's image and familiarity internationally, particularly for the purposes of increasing commerce, developing business and promoting tourism (Dinnie, 2008). However, nation branding extends beyond typical destination branding in that locals are highly involved; citizens are expected to 'live the brand' (Aronczyk, 2008). As such, nation branding can also be harnessed as a means of promoting national identity (Aronczyk, 2008).

The rebranding of South Africa which occurred as apartheid drew to a close involved outward symbolism, such as the creation of a new flag and national anthem. Yet the rebranding efforts went further, striving to transform the national mindset from one of division and distrust into a unified and cohesive community. As one example, to demonstrate its appreciation for diversity, South Africa has 11 official state languages, more than any other nation in the world (Government of South Africa, 1996).

A phrase first coined by Nobel Peace Prize winner, Archbishop Desmond Tutu, and later used by President Nelson Mandela, the 'Rainbow Nation' has become an integral part of South Africa's national identity. Used to describe the multiculturalism of South Africa, 'rainbowism' is prominently promoted in government, business and tourism. Tourism officials even developed the 'rainbow route', a tourism initiative between inland destinations and Zululand on the coast as a way to showcase South Africa's various native communities (South African Tourism, 2015).

The tourism sector was particularly keen to capitalise on South Africa's 'rainbow' legacy. Similar to other developing countries, tourism was viewed as a means of potential economic growth for South Africa (Phelan, 2015a). Excitement surrounding the end of apartheid, the governmental reorganisation and Nelson Mandela's election resulted in a 22.3% increase in international arrivals in 1995 (Cornelissen, 2005). This momentum continued for several more years, leading to international tourism arrivals averaging near 10% annually, compared with the average 3% worldwide growth, until 2000 (Cornelissen, 2005).

Despite deliberate rebranding efforts, the 'Mandela syndrome' that catapulted South Africa onto the world stage had lost considerable traction by the 2000s (Cornelissen, 2005). Coupled with a steep rise in the frequency of violent crime and political unrest, South Africa saw its international arrivals figures stall and begin to decrease (Ferreira & Harmse, 2000). Violence and crime against international tourists became so serious that, when Cape Town bid for the 2004 Olympics it lost to Athens, in part owing to the International Olympic Committee's concerns regarding whether the safety of athletes and spectators could be ensured (Ferreira & Harmse, 2000).

In 2002, Brand South Africa, a subsidiary of the International Marketing Council of South Africa (IMC), was established 'to help create a positive and compelling brand image for South Africa' (Brand South Africa, n.d.). At its inception, many felt that South Africa was sending mixed and inconsistent messages to the rest of the world. While the concept of a Rainbow Nation was appealing to foreigners, many questioned its authenticity. As politicians claimed credit for a peaceful, post-apartheid transition, many locals felt that the so-called 'multicultural unity' was fictitious (Habib, 1997). Brand South Africa was launched in part to remedy these inaccuracies. In addition to marketing South Africa for business and tourism purposes, the IMC Board Chairman stated that '[Brand South Africa] strives to contribute to national economic growth by ensuring that South Africans buy into, and, live the brand promise made in the country's marketing campaigns' (Brand South Africa, 2010).

In order to succeed in generating international investment and promote tourism, Brand South Africa acknowledged the need to 'build and sustain national pride and patriotism through encouraging active citizenship' (Brand South Africa, 2014). To achieve this objective, Brand South Africa began by articulating nine national brand values: ubuntu, innovation, sustainability, possibility, diversity, competitiveness, realness, determination and humility. Ubuntu is a South African philosophy that emphasises human kindness (Battle, 1997). It is often explained as humanity towards others or the universal bond that connects all humanity (Battle, 1997).

To encourage South Africans to adopt and actively demonstrate these national brand values, Brand South Africa created a nationwide campaign called 'Play Your Part' (Play Your Part, n.d.). Play Your Part was marketed as a means of 'encouraging all South Africans to contribute to positive change.' Citizens were urged to become brand ambassadors by participating in programmes intended to lead to socio-economic growth within South Africa. Community development initiatives, volunteerism, after-school sports clubs, libraries, recycling programmes, and health education are some of the many projects that grew out of the Play Your Part initiative (Play Your Part, n.d.).

The establishment of national brand values and the Play Your Part campaign proved particularly valuable when South Africa decided to bid for the 2010 FIFA World Cup. While national identity was beginning to strengthen owing to Brand South Africa and Play Your Part, nothing solidified a sense of community in South Africa quite like hosting the World Cup. Radiating pride from being selected as the first African nation to ever host the event, South Africans united in an effort to show the world they truly could function as a Rainbow Nation. Despite strained race relations and differing views regarding the decision to host the event, across the nation all agreed that the legacy of the World Cup would be South Africa's place in history, if nothing else (South African Government News Agency, 2010).

As the month-long event drew to a close, South African President Jacob Zuma stated, 'The explosion of national pride and unity that has been displayed by all South Africans is an invaluable benefit of the tournament' (South African Government News Agency, 2010). Just a few months prior, many had questioned whether locals could find common ground. As *The Times*, one of South Africa's leading newspapers, reported,

> The tournament could not have come at a better time. Just a few months ago, due mainly to disturbing political developments, our very existence as a unified and non-racial nation was being questioned. Large numbers of people appeared to be retreating to their racial laagers and tribal comfort zones. But with the World Cup came the outpouring of South African patriotism in ways we have never seen before. The national flag was everywhere, and the national soccer team enjoyed support from South Africans across past racial lines. (The Times, 2010)

The Times went on to encourage South Africans to harness this new-found common ground, 'This is a spirit we should not lose now that the tournament has ended. Let us build on what we achieved in the past month to make our country better' (The Times, 2010).

The excitement which surrounded the 2010 World Cup was the ultimate nation-branding experiment. It took a very diverse country and helped that diversity to become the major aspect in South Africa's national identity. Headlines from journalists covering the event called attention to the success of the Rainbow Nation ideal: 'South Africa's Rainbow Nation happily seems to be colour blind' (Chiles, 2010) and 'Another Rainbow Nation miracle'

(Smith, 2010). However, ultimately, South Africans were seen around the world as more than just citizens of the Rainbow Nation.

As the first World Cup host in Africa, South Africa held the honour, and burden, of representing a continent. This expectation is atypical of most tourism attractions and events. Brazil was the first South American country to host the Olympics in 2016, but there has been little emphasis placed on the country as a representative of the greater continent. However, given the world's tendency to view Africa as a collective entity, the 2010 World Cup was often considered by the media as an African endeavour. This only further strengthened national pride and social cohesion (Sullivan, 2014). South Africans wanted to be recognised for their connection to their country, but they understood the importance of representing their neighbours throughout the continent.

Often referred to as the African World Cup, the 2010 event was seen globally as an enterprise that represented the continent, and South Africans were proud to fill that role. As President Zuma stated,

> We have witnessed the explosion of national pride across all races and cultures. One thing is certain; Africa will never be the same again. The world's view of this continent has been changed. When they think about Africa, they now see competent people capable of getting things done. (Federation Internationale de Football Association, 2010)

Ultimately, the 2010 World Cup helped South Africa solidify its reputation as a Rainbow Nation. While efforts had been made prior to the event to transform a diverse population into a unified community, the World Cup provided the impetus to develop a strong sense of national pride and identity. In addition, by being seen by outsiders as representatives of the African continent as a whole, South Africans developed a heightened sense of national pride, and helped to increase the sense of community felt amongst Africa's many nations.

Rejecting Identity in West Africa's Slave Tourism Destinations

While South Africa attempted to foster unity through Brand South Africa and references to the Rainbow Nation, ultimately it was a mega-event in the form of the 2010 FIFA World Cup that helped create a sense of pride, community and national identity. This differs significantly from other African nations which have attempted to ignore or rewrite their national history and identity.

For roughly three centuries, from the middle of the 16th until the late 19th century, the trans-Atlantic slave trade flourished (Akyeampong, 2000).

However, this did not mark the end of emigration out of Africa. Starting in the 1950s, when many African colonies were granted independence, those with financial means often left for Western nations (Omeje, 2007). When the colonial rulers exited Africa, many social systems, such as healthcare and education, collapsed because the resources which were previously funnelled into the continent from the colonial entities were no longer provided and no self-sustaining state leadership was established that could replace them (Englebert, 2000). This led to political and economic instability, which in turn produced heavy-handed dictatorships, civil wars and other tragedies, such as genocide and the spread of infectious diseases (Omeje, 2007). These circumstances further prompted Africans to seek educational and career opportunities abroad (Omeje, 2007).

These African immigrants, and their subsequent offspring, have become known as the African diaspora (Omeje, 2007). In some cases, African diaspora members are far removed from their roots as a result of their ancestors having been taken as slaves many generations ago. In other instances, diaspora individuals left of their own accord, perhaps quite recently. Regardless, the ties these individuals and families have to the continent often entice them to pursue tourism there. Unfortunately, their desires to visit the Motherland and reconnect with their distant relations are often left unfulfilled.

Many West African nations which participated in the slave trade have historic remnants left behind from that era. Extending from Senegal in the north to Angola in the south, more than a dozen countries served as supply centres for the trans-Atlantic trade. With the heightened interest in slave history and locations from African Americans, several of those countries have attempted to capitalise on tourism opportunities. Senegal and Ghana have been particularly successful in attracting international visitors to slave tourism destinations.

The Cape Coast Castle and Elmina Castle in Ghana and Goree Island in Senegal are some of the most highly marketed and visited slave tourism destinations in Africa. These locations were designated as United Nations Educational, Scientific and Cultural Organization (UNESCO) World Heritage Sites in the late 1970s (Tillet, 2009). These World Heritage Site designations, along with the creation of 'The Slave Route Project' in 1994 (UNESCO, 2015), prompted a new appreciation and interest in attractions associated with the slave trade.

Hundreds of thousands of African diaspora return annually to Africa as tourists (Polgreen, 2005). Many choose their itineraries specifically because they long to visit historic slave destinations and connect with locals. Goree Island is perhaps the most well-known slave destination in the world, hosting approximately a quarter of a million tourists annually (Murphy, 2004). Many well-known celebrities and political figures have visited the 'House of Slaves' and stood at the 'Door of No Return' through which slaves allegedly departed the facility to board ships bound for the Americas (Nakamura, 2013).

While the locals appreciate the business generated from these tourists, they fail to recognise their own personal connection to the slave trade history in their regions. This is particularly disappointing for the African-American tourists as they are often in search of greater meaning and human connection during these trips.

In Ghana, the locals refer to tourists as 'obrun' which means 'white man' (Bruner, 1996). The term is used widely to describe any outsider or foreigner regardless of skin colour. Asians, Arabs, Europeans, Americans and African-Americans are all referred to as 'obruni' when in Ghana. Hearing this term is particularly discouraging to African Americans who see themselves as black and often feel more closely connected to their African heritage than to their white neighbours back home. They frequently envision a trip to Africa as returning to the Motherland, but instead feel rebuffed when they are labelled obruni (Bruner, 1996).

Despite the rich history and the utilisation of slave landmarks for tourism purposes, the locals have elected to distance themselves from the national identity that foreign tourists expect them to exhibit (Keren, 2009). Rather than acknowledging their connection to the slave trade, locals view it as a piece of history that belongs to 'outsiders'. This disassociation has proven detrimental and in some cases caused resentment on the part of African-American tourists (Keren, 2009).

In an effort to make slave tourism visitors, and African Americans in particular, feel more welcome and connected to local communities, some regions have attempted to train the local community to be more receptive (Polgreen, 2005). For instance, Ghana launched massive advertising campaigns that encouraged locals to utilise the saying, akwaaba anyemi which translates as 'welcome, brother or sister' and cease the use of obruni (Polgreen, 2005).

Slave and diaspora tourism are both subcategorisations of heritage tourism which by definition is visitation to sites that authentically represent stories and people of the past (Lowenthal, 1979; Timothy, 1997). Tourists to heritage sites are motivated to visit those locations based upon their own heritage or ancestral history (Lowenthal, 1979; Timothy, 1997). The difficulty in West African countries with slave tourism attractions is that the locals consider African Americans and slave heritage completely separate from their own. The national identity in these regions fails to represent the existing heritage. Despite efforts from tourism planners, this discrepancy continues, which leaves tourists disappointed with the experience.

Manufacturing a National Identity: How a Kenyan Became President of the United States

Unlike South Africa, whose national identity was solidified by a mega-event, or West Africa, where locals shun a centuries-old national identity,

Kenya has taken a new approach to national identity as it relates to tourism: it has artificially manufactured a new one.

Barack Obama first visited Kenya in 1987, prior to entering graduate school and long before he had any hope of running for public office (Liang, 2015). During that first visit, he met distant family members, but his trip was nothing of note as he was not yet a public figure. Obama mentioned his visit to Kenya, and his father's village of Nyang'oma Kogelo in his memoir, *Dreams from my Father*, which was published in 1995 (Obama, 1995). However, the book, and Obama's connection to the country, did not achieve international recognition until 2006 when he was a US Senator and beginning his presidential bid (Yusuf, 2015). Obama's victory in late 2008 forever changed Kenya's tourism industry and its national identity.

While Barack Obama is not a Kenyan citizen, his connection to the country through his late father has been consistently mentioned in the media and heralded by locals in the country. To many he is Kenyan and it is not uncommon for American tourists to hear residents refer to, 'the Kenyan who became President of the United States' (Ikonya, 2008). In short, Kenyans are happy to claim Obama as one of their own (Carotenuto & Luongo, 2009), which is a significant contrast to the way West Africans distance themselves from African American tourists. The pride Kenyans hold regarding Barack Obama's success has led to a reframing of the country's national identity.

During the days and weeks surrounding the 2008 presidential election, a sense of 'Obamamia' spread throughout Kenya (Van Bemmel, 2013). Following his victory, even before he took office, the Kenyan government anticipated an increased interest in domestic and international tourism to destinations associated with the newly elected president. To encourage tourism to these locations, preparations were made to allow greater access and comfortable amenities for potential visitors. Most notably, the day following Obama's win, vehicles from the national electric company arrived in his ancestral village of Kogelo and connected it to the power grid for the first time in its history (Van Bemmel, 2013).

Between 2007 and 2008, revenue earned from tourism, Kenya's second largest industry, dropped by 50% (Jordan, 2009). International arrivals and tourism earnings declined owing to increased violent crime and terrorist attacks, which in turn prompted travel advisories and cancelled travel plans from citizens of many Western countries (Jordan, 2009). After Obama's election, locals mobilised to welcome visitors to 'Obama's Kenya'. Aspiring entrepreneurs began marketing everything from t-shirts to umbrellas, and even more unique Obama paraphernalia such as mobile phone ringtones compiled from parts of his inauguration speech (Chandler, 2015).

Obama souvenirs were just the tip of the iceberg. Fortunately for the locals, more permanent infrastructure arose from interest in the region. At the time of Obama's election, his father's village, where his step-grandmother still lives, was connected to surrounding areas by only a single dirt road.

Since then a paved highway has been laid, and a conference centre hotel and the Barack H. Obama Recreation Center and Restaurant have been constructed (Hammer, 2012). These facilities have been utilised by tour companies bringing visitors interested seeing Obama's village and hoping to interact with his relatives (Hammer, 2012).

While on the surface it may appear that Kenya is exploiting the earning potential of Obama's name, in truth, it is national pride and a sense of common identity that fuel these ventures. As with most African countries, Kenya is composed of multiple tribes. Obama is from a minority tribe, called the Luo, which is often discriminated against by the dominant, ruling ethic groups (Carotenuto & Luongo, 2009). Despite the lower social standing which the Luo typically maintain, Obama's Kenyan heritage has managed to serve as a uniting factor amongst different ethnicities. Rather than dismiss his Luo roots, Kenyans have bonded together and created a new sense of national identity resulting from Obama's ties to the nation as a whole.

Conclusion

National identity is often difficult to articulate. In Africa, it is even more so. Much of the outside world views Africa as one cohesive entity. It is common among Africans to remind tourists that 'Africa is a continent, not a country' (Kayser-Bril, 2014; Phelan, 2013). Yet even within those separate countries, national identity is not a simple philosophy to define as the diversity of its citizens is so great. With each country boasting its own national identity, and often multiple identities within its borders, the difference is evident in the way various nations promote their tourism industry.

Some nations, such as South Africa, have attempted to convert their challenging history and different backgrounds into a new national identity. Initially, the experiment was questionable. Foreigners questioned the authenticity of the Rainbow Nation until the unified South African fans at the 2010 World Cup proved that they were indeed a cohesive community.

African nations with ties to the former trans-Atlantic slave trade have an established history which tourists expect to shape their national identity. Instead, the citizenry have decided to ignore that past. The refusal to demonstrate a national identity that reflects historical accounts has proven to be disappointing to African American tourists, as they long to reconnect with distant relatives.

One of the most intriguing examples of national identity is Kenya's connection to Barack Obama. Although Obama has never lived in Kenya, and has only visited a few times, Kenya claims him as one of their own. Kenyans have invented a new national identity around his familial connection to the country, overlooking differences in beliefs and tribal lineage.

National identity plays an important role in the tourism experience. It assists tourists with making sense of the community and locals with whom they interact. It serves as a guide for branding a destination, both domestically and internationally, and it contributes to international relations and the national consciousness. National identity in Africa is a perplexing concept, but it is particularly valuable in aiding foreign tourists in comprehending the cultural variations in such a vast continent.

References

Achenbach, B. (2009) Study finds Africans more genetically diverse than other populations. *The Washington Post*, 1 May. See http://www.washingtonpost.com/wp-dyn/content/article/2009/04/30/AR2009043002485.html (accessed 21 June 2015).

Akyeampong, E. (2000) Africans in the diaspora: The diaspora and Africa. *African Affairs* 99 (395), 183–215.

Aronczyk, M. (2008) 'Living the brand': Nationality, globality and the identity strategies of nation branding consultants. *International Journal of Communication* 2, 41–65.

Battle, M.J. (1997) *Reconciliation: The Ubuntu Theology of Desmond Tutu*. Cleveland, OH: The Pilgrim Press.

Brand South Africa (n.d.) Who we are. See http://www.brandsouthafrica.com/who-we-are (accessed 21 June 2015).

Brand South Africa (2010) IMC appoints new CEO. Press release, 10 March. See http://www.brandsouthafrica.com/press-room/389-imc-appoints-new-ceo (accessed 20 June 2015).

Brand South Africa (2014) Brand South Africa: Annual report 2013–2014. See http://www.brandsouthafrica.com/images/pdfs/Annual_Report_2014.pdf

Bruner, E.M. (1996) Tourism in Ghana: The representation of slavery and the return of the black diaspora. *American Anthropologist* 98 (2), 290–304.

Carotenuto, M. and Luongo, K. (2009) Dala or diaspora? Obama and the Luo community of Kenya. *African Affairs* 108 (431), 197–219.

Chandler, A. (2015) Obama's Kenya visit sets off a turf war over grass. *The Atlantic*, 23 July. See http://www.theatlantic.com/international/archive/2015/07/president-obama-africa-kenya/399500/ (accessed 23 June 2015).

Chiles, A. (2010) World Cup 2010: South Africa's Rainbow Nation happily seems to be colour blind. *The Telegraph*, 19 June. See http://www.telegraph.co.uk/sport/football/teams/south-africa/7838553/World-Cup-2010-South-Africas-Rainbow-Nation-happily-seems-to-be-colour-blind.html (accessed 25 June 2015).

Cornelissen, S. (2005) Producing and imaging 'place' and 'people': The political economy of South African international tourism representation. *Review of International Political Economy* 12 (4), 674–699.

Dinne, K. (2008) *Nation Branding: Concepts, Issues, Practice*. Oxford: Elsevier.

Englebert, P. (2000) Pre-colonial institutions, post-colonial states, and economic development in tropical Africa. *Political Research Quarterly* 53 (1), 7–36.

Federation Internationale de Football Association (2010) South Africa wins hearts. 2010 FIFA World Cup South Africa, 12 July. See http://www.fifa.com/worldcup/news/y=2010/m=7/news=south-africa-wins-hearts-1273210.html (accessed 25 June 2015).

Ferreira, S. and Harmse, A. (2000) Crime and tourism in South Africa: International tourists' perception and risk. *South African Geographical Journal* 82 (2), 80–85.

Government of South Africa (1996) Constitution of the Republic of South Africa. See http://www.gov.za/documents/constitution/chapter-1-founding-provisions#5

Habib, A. (1997) South Africa – The Rainbow Nation and prospects for consolidating democracy. *African Journal of Political Science* 2 (2), 15–37.

Hammer, J. (2012) A journey to Obama's Kenya. *Smithsonian Magazine*, May. See http://www.smithsonianmag.com/travel/a-journey-to-obamas-kenya-62249625/?page=1 (accessed 25 June 2015).

Ikonya, P. (2008) *The Kenyan Boy who Became President of America*. Nairobi: Media Horizons Network.

International Monetary Fund (2012) World economic outlook: Growth resuming, dangers remain. See http://www.imf.org/external/pubs/ft/weo/2012/01/pdf/text.pdf

Jordan, T. (2009) Out of Africa. *Meanjin Quarterly* 68 (2), 28–33.

Kayser-Bril, N. (2014) Africa is not a country. *The Guardian*, 25 January. See http://www.theguardian.com/world/2014/jan/24/africa-clinton (accessed 25 June 2015).

Keren, E. (2009) The transatlantic slave trade in Ghanaian academic historiography: History, memory, and power. *The William and Mary Quarterly* 66 (4), 975–1000.

Liang, A. (2015) Barack Obama in Kenya: How this trip compares to his 1987 visit. *The Telegraph*, 24 July. See http://www.telegraph.co.uk/news/worldnews/africaandindianocean/kenya/11761025/Barack-Obama-in-Kenya-how-this-trip-compares-to-his-1987-visit.html (accessed July 29 2015).

Lowenthal, D. (1979) Environmental perception: Preserving the past. *Progress in Human Geography* 3 (4), 549–559.

Murphy, J. (2004) Powerful symbol, weak in facts. *The Baltimore Sun*, 30 June. See http://www.baltimoresun.com/news/bal-slavery0630,0,7878935.story (accessed 25 July 2015).

Nakamura, D. (2013) Obamas visit Door of No Return, where slaves once left Africa. *The Washington Post*, 27 June. See http://www.washingtonpost.com/news/post-politics/wp/2013/06/27/obamas-visit-door-of-no-return-where-slaves-once-left-africa/ (accessed 26 July 2015).

Obama, B. (1995) *Dreams from my Father: A Story of Race and Inheritance*. New York: Random House.

Omeje, K. (2007) The diaspora and domestic insurgencies in Africa. *African Sociological Review* 11 (2), 94–107.

Play Your Part (n.d.) *About Play your Part*. See http://www.playyourpart.co.za/about-us (accessed 22 June 2015).

Phelan, K.V. (2013) African views on Mandela vary by country. *The Baltimore Sun*, 11 December. See http://articles.baltimoresun.com/2013-12-11/news/bs-ed-africa-20131211_1_nelson-mandela-botswana-batswana (accessed June 28 2015).

Phelan, K.V. (2015a) Elephants, orphans and HIV/AIDS: Examining the voluntourist experience in Botswana. *Worldwide Hospitality and Tourism Themes* 7 (2), 127– 140.

Phelan, K.V. (2015b) Staged authenticity and identity conflicts: Cultural tourism in Africa. In G.R. Ricci (eds) *Travel, Tourism and Identity* (pp. 163–174). London: Transaction.

Polgreen, L. (2005) Ghana's uneasy embrace of slavery's diaspora. *The New York Times*, 27 December. See http://www.nytimes.com/2005/12/27/international/africa/27ghana.html?pagewanted=all&_r=0 (accessed 27 June 2015).

Population Reference Bureau (2014) 2014 World population data sheet. See http://www.prb.org/pdf14/2014-world-population-data-sheet_eng.pdf

Salawu, B. (2010) Ethno-religious conflicts in Nigeria: Causal analysis and proposals for new management strategies. *European Journal of Social Sciences* 13 (3), 345–353.

Smith, D. (2010) World Cup 2010: Sceptics drowned out by another rainbow nation miracle. *The Guardian*, 11 July. See http://www.theguardian.com/football/2010/jul/11/world-cup-2010-south-africa-success (accessed 29 June 2015).

South African Government News Agency (2010) World Cup instilled national pride-Zuma. South African Government News Agency, 10 July. See http://www.sanews.gov.za/south-africa/world-cup-instilled-national-pride-zuma (accessed 30 June 2015).

South African Tourism (2015) KwaZulu–Natal Zululand. See http://www.southafrica.
net/za/en/articles/entry/article-southafrica.net-kwazulu-natal-zululand (accessed 21
June 201).

Sullivan, G.B. (2014) *Understanding Collective Pride and Group Identity: New Directions in
Emotion Theory, Research and Practice*. New York: Routledge.

Tillet, S. (2009) In the shadow of the castle: (Trans)nationalism, African American tourism, and Goree Island. *Research in African Literatures* 40 (4), 122–141.

The Times (2010) World Cup success shows that SA can tackle its challenges. *The Times*
newspaper, 11 July. See http://www.timeslive.co.za/opinion/editorials/2010/07/11/
world-cup-success-shows-that-sa-can-tackle-its-challenges (accessed 29 June 2015).

Timothy, D.J. (1997) Tourism and the personal heritage experience. *Annals of Tourism
Research* 24 (3), 751–754.

UNDP (2014) Human development index and its components. United Nations
Development Programme. See https://data.undp.org/dataset/Table-1-Human-
Development-Index-and-its-components/myer-egms?

UNESCO (2010) Why and how Africa should invest in African languages and multilingual education: An evidence- and practice-based policy advocacy brief. United
Nations Educational, Scientific and Cultural Organisation. See http://unesdoc.
unesco.org/images/0018/001886/188642e.pdf

UNESCO (2015) The slave route. United Nations Educational, Scientific and Cultural
Organisation. See http://www.unesco.org/new/en/culture/themes/dialogue/the-
slave-route/ (accessed 24 June 2015).

Van Bemmel, K. (2013) Obama made in Kenya: Appropriating the American dream in
Kogelo. *Africa Today* 59 (4), 68–90.

Yusuf, M. (2015) Kogelo, Kenya, residents hope for visit from Obama. *Voice of America*, 25
July. See http://www.voanews.com/content/kogelo-kenya-residents-hope-for-visit-
from-obama/2872093.html (accessed 29 July 2015).

10 Branding a Nation-state after Half a Century of Independence: The Case of Malta

Marie Avellino Stewart and George Cassar

Introduction

In the centre of the Mediterranean Sea, at the crossroads of three continents – Europe to the north, Africa to the south and Asia to the east – lies a small archipelago called Malta. The islands are vested with a long and variegated history, the signs and residues of which permeate to this day the physical landscape as well as the social texture. Malta's cultural heritage is marked by the legacies of the many and successive occupations and dominations that have controlled the Maltese for centuries.

The tourists who visit the islands today can get a glimpse of the vestiges of the presence of Phoenicians, Carthaginians and Romans (Bonanno, 2005) as well as those of the Byzantine, Arab and Aragonese occupations (Dalli, 2006). They can have a fuller and five-dimensional experience of Malta's megalithic period, which goes back to around 5000 BC (Trump, 2002), as well as of the magnificence of the Baroque phase that flourished during the rule of the Order of St John between 1530 and 1798 (Hughes & Thake, 2003). The touristic experience can be enhanced by an introduction to the turmoil and heroism dominating the two-year interlude (1798–1800) of subjugation by the forces of Revolutionary France (Testa, 1997). One further phase is the British colonial period (1800–1964) during which Maltese society came face-to-face with the Anglo-Saxon mentality, culture and authority. Malta was turned into a fortress-colony in the service of the Crown and an important naval station of the British Empire and the mighty, omnipresent Royal Navy (Mallia-Milanes, 1988).

Exposing the Cleavage

The last 200 years or so of Malta's history have been inescapably steeped in the colonial ups and downs of dominator and dominated. The mix of feelings for and against, emanating from the colonial vestiges, have undoubtedly been an intrinsic part of the life of Malta and the Maltese. To compound this mix of stances and loyalties, the Maltese islands have also, from antiquity, been overshadowed by a third culture, that of neighbouring Italy. Italian culture has created a strong link between the locals of both nations leading to the islands being considered a sort of appendix – real, perceived or desired – of Italy. This has permeated the social texture of the Maltese landscape at various levels and has persisted to this day. The upper social divisions, and more so the educated and influential middle-classes, established their mark of distinction through speaking the Italian language, by following the art and culture scene of their geographic neighbours and by evoking affinities, including the judicial system, which they considered inviolable and worth defending to the last against what was perceived to be British invasive colonial arrogance aimed at destroying their 'national' identity. The common people, on the other hand, thought in more utilitarian and functional ways as they deduced that their best means of survival lay in getting closer to the providers of their employment and that meant that the English ways and language would necessarily have to be learnt and adopted. Many, for example, sought employment with the armed services stationed in their fortress-colony, which they saw as a secure and stable way to make a living (Frendo, 2012).

These circumstances led to a dichotomy which to an extent was carried on in the ways of the locals beyond 1964, the year political independence was achieved. Post-colonial Malta can be described as a dialectic of perceptions and realties. Questions revolving around who the Maltese are, and what they would wish others to think of them, have at times created animated interactions amongst the locals at the social and political levels. The contrasts and contentions have emerged in matters such as first names, food, language, education, music and sports, but also in discourse about national identity, political independence and other themes (Mizzi, 1995). The ever-growing and expanding tourism and hospitality industry is indeed an area that has triggered and stimulated discussion on what type of branding and which image the Maltese want/need to present to foreigners visiting Malta.

Such a discussion is based on the socio-historical and anthropological aspects of how the Maltese islands continuously negotiate their identity sourced principally from the legacy of their British and Italian influences. Many foreign elements have become indigenised and are now entrenched through a natural or a conscious process into what is taken to be the Maltese national identity. Some are tempted to call it an 'elusive' national identity; others feel more patriotically convinced and declare it to be their authentic heritage (Cortis, 1989; Gambin, 2004; Schiavone, 1994).

The Road to a Malta Brand

In the post-colonial context, Malta continues to use a frame of reference underpinned by the cultures that once dominated every aspect of its everyday social, economic, political and cultural life. It uses this reference when portraying its national brand, which is called 'product Malta' in the Maltese tourism context. It uses and adapts representations of Anglo-Italian influence to project a modern image. However, such an image is strengthened by 7000 years of rich and multicultural heritage.

In a highly competitive tourism market, islands such as Malta have to find that element that distinguishes themselves from other comparable destinations. Whereas similar and competing Mediterranean and other destinations may have chosen to market themselves primarily as Sun, Sand and Sea destinations, and ignore their cultural heritage (Cameron & Gatewood, 2008), the Maltese islands soon realised that this would not be the best way forward. The narrow 3Ss marketing strategy would bring in mass tourism in the high season, with its negative impact and tarnished image of crowded beaches and jam-packed entertainment venues, but would leave the islanders facing unemployment with accommodation under occupied during the low and shoulder seasons.

Prior to the run-up to Malta's political independence, the Malta Government Tourism Board was set up in 1958 with the main objective of promoting Malta to the rest of the world (Pollacco, 2003). The islands were practically an unknown entity beyond the circumscribed world of those who had regular access to them – that is, the British and allied forces personnel and members of their families. Even at that early phase the tourism board was sensitive to ensure that the low season would also be supported through some form of marketing campaign. However, funds were limited and arrivals amounted to just 38,400 people, which in foreign exchange meant around £1.5 million. The government introduced a programme for capital spending on improving access to beaches, promotion and advertising. A grants programme was also implemented in order to encourage the building of new hotels. Although this was costly, it was very successful and by 1969 Malta had 101 hotels with over 186,000 tourists visiting the island and leaving over £10.8 million in earnings in the Maltese coffers (Mangion, n.d.).

In 1967, the Robens Report, which was the document of the Joint Mission for Malta, emphasised the importance of 'planning and skilful management to ensure that the uniqueness of the island was sustained' (Joint Mission for Malta, 1967). This was to include the development of various types of accommodation to suit different sectors of the market and to expand Malta's promotional efforts to the whole of Europe as opposed to just the British market. It also stressed the importance of Malta's historical and architectural attractions (Boissevain, 1979). Indeed the Maltese government of the 1960s led by the Nationalist Party, after achieving independence, embarked on a long-term plan for the island's tourism industry and thus considered the prospect of launching a local airline by the name of Air Melita (Flightglobal, n.d.), an idea which, however, for the time being remained just a pipedream.

By 1971 Malta had experienced a change to its political administration. The Labour Party in government decided to end British military presence on the island (as this had continued also after 1964) and talks were taken up to bring this objective to its finality. On 31 March 1979, the last British soldier vacated the once highly important and strategic island-fortress. No more funds could thus be expected for the lease of the base and new financial sources had to be generated for the development of Malta's industrial infrastructure as tourism was considered to be too vulnerable as a source of national income (Mizzi, 1995).

One past idea which now became a reality was the creation of a national air carrier. Going by the name of Air Malta, the airline was set up in 1974 with the aim of reducing the dependency on foreign carriers. With Malta controlling its own airline, discounted rates could thus be established to attract more tourists and boost the occupancy rate of the island's hotels, strengthening the industry and in turn triggering the need for more hotels and other self-catering establishments (Briguglio & Vella, 1995; Pantzar & Panyik, 2014). By becoming a low-cost tourist destination, Malta would thus see a revival of the boom which it had experienced in the late 1960s. The cue was at once taken up by the local entrepreneurs and apartments previously belonging to the British Services where converted into tourist self-catering accommodation. In the 1970s, places which up until then were more or less remote and desolate areas, such as Buġibba, or scantily populated drowsy villages, such as St Paul's Bay, experienced a phenomenal sprawl of tourism-oriented buildings which by 1981 had increased the accommodation potential to 29,000 beds (Mangion, n.d.).

As the 1980s rolled in, the situation of Maltese incoming tourism stood at 730,000. The worrying element here was that 77% of the tourists were British, which meant that the destination promotion was focused on the mass market from a single source. One could conclude that Malta had been unsuccessful in its diversification attempt (Oglethorpe, 1984), if any had really been intended at all. What had been undeniably intended was to 'focus on more attractive pricing, better publicity and higher levels of investment in the infrastructure' (Pantzar & Panyik, 2014: 339). The failure was even more pronounced as demand continued to rise, which led to an increase in price, while quality began to fall and Malta experienced massive infrastructural problems. Malta also struck a poor image on the overseas market, which axed arrival numbers to 480,000 and a 44% drop in income accentuated by an international recession (Mangion, n.d.).

At this point Malta's situation and its image needed a boost. In 1987, with a change in government, the newly elected Nationalist Party took this to task. It contracted UK advertising agency Horwath and Horwath Ltd to draw up a Tourism Master Plan, the result of which introduced a focus on market diversification, quality improvement and the development of heritage and cultural tourism (Horwath & Horwath, 1989). The new administration also embarked on a major road construction project, easing congestion in main urban areas, and set in motion the construction of a new international airport terminal to accommodate the increase in tourist numbers. Many recreational areas sprang up in beachfront towns such as Marsascala, St Julians and Sliema. The 1990s saw an overall increase in demand, leading to a rise in employment and accommodation opportunities. Since the strategy was to move away from mass tourism and focus more on higher-quality tourists, there was investment in four and five star hotels (Boissevain & Serracino-Inglott, 1997). Positive results in tourist response showed that the marketing and branding strategies which had now been adopted and adapted to the highly competitive globalised tourism market had been well thought out and adequately managed – so much so that the one million mark in incoming tourism was reached in 1992 and numbers continued to move towards the two million mark over the years (Pantzar & Panyik, 2014). By 2014, Malta had notched numbers in the region of 1.7 million, with the British and Italian source markets placed respectively first and second (Malta Tourism Authority, 2015: 6).

As Malta entered the third millennium it came up with the concept that the islands should have a brand. In 2005, the Malta Tourism Authority (MTA) embarked on appropriate research in an effort to identify the main criteria that influenced foreign air travellers to choose Malta as their destination. Once these criteria and their supporting values were identified, they would be tested out on the tourists visiting Malta from the main geographical source markets (UK, Germany, Italy and France) and on the Maltese population. This exercise revealed two significant results. Firstly, Malta's identified core values already featured very strongly in the perceptions of travellers in the main markets. Secondly, there was a strong relationship between the views of potential travellers and those who had already visited Malta. The study recommended that 'Brand Malta' should be built on the core values of Heritage, Diversity and Hospitality, with the accompanying vision statement 'Enriching your life' (Pantzar, 2009). More specifically, Malta's 'distinct heritage based on a long historical tradition', its 'impressive diversity, with hundreds of leisure options a maximum of only 30 minutes away from any one point', and moreover the Maltese 'warm hospitality "straight from the heart"' were to be the distinctive elements for the brand (Timesofmalta.com, 2005).

The results of this exercise were released to the general public by the MTA in 2005. While these may have been received with a measure of optimism by the tourism operators and by the general public, the campaign nevertheless had its setbacks. The implementation of the branding roadmap which the MTA claimed it had, was met with lukewarm reactions verging on disappointment, claiming it was simply a waste of money (Pace, 2006). Hoteliers thought that the targets were nowhere in sight (Massa, 2006). Locals also objected to being told by the National Authority that they would need to conform or modify their own attitudes to fit in with the national brand being proposed by the MTA, especially as this was being expected of them without any real effort to bring the infrastructure up to scratch (Zammit Tabona, 2006; Schembri Wismayer, 2006). This meant that branding continued to be more centrally managed through the official channels for the national effort while other entities pretty much followed their own initiatives and perceptions as to how Malta was to be presented to their guests. Yet an effort to integrate all the stakeholders involved at all levels has continued (Micallef, 2014).

Images of Malta for Foreigners: Enticement and Imagination

With Malta having been more or less just a fortress colony for so long, up until the 1950s prospective tourists were bound to dismiss the island as a fortified rock and not much more. This meant that any touristic image – if one could speak of such – was that of a destination bristling with military installations and with servicemen running around its streets. This was not far from the truth. Yet as Malta progressed towards its political independence, the new administrators, who were now Maltese, had to recreate an island and produce a desirable destination for any who cared to enquire about this island in the middle of the Mediterranean Sea. What independent Malta undeniably possessed were long months of sun and a blue, relatively clean, sea. Furthermore, it had 6000 years of culture and history which, if exploited and presented well, would be enviably enticing. Otherwise, it had few hotels, fewer beach facilities, restaurants and water sports amenities, scarce night life and was surely no inspiring tourism playground (Mirabelli, 1992).

Malta's political freedom meant that now it needed to show who and what it was. The new nation had to create a brand by means of which it could introduce itself into the world of the tourist. Guidebooks and official literature at different times have illustrated, as they continue to do to this day, the images that independent Malta has wished to put forward. The images of Malta and its people have emerged thorough the discourse that guidebooks and official literature have presented to prospective tourists. This chapter takes travel discourse to mean 'a social practice, which constitutes and conditions in its representation of power structures' (Simmons, 2014: 43; see also Foucault, 1972; Wodak, 1996).

While the British base was still active, albeit Malta was politically independent, the link with the UK and its people was certainly still very strong. Malta thus wanted to entice the British tourist to visit the ex-colony. It needed to remind such visitors that in Malta they would feel in a familiar environment, yet they were bound to have an interesting experience. One such book that brought Malta to the British audience was *Malta: a Handbook to the Island*. The discourse in this 1965 publication was based on the element of privilege through a message intertwined in the narrative that Malta was the right choice for the right visitors – in this case the British ex-Service personnel. Naturally, the image projected was that Malta was a fitting place to visit for those who had served on the island during the Second World War and now wished to bring their relatives to see the war-scarred island where they had risked their lives. It was also floated that those who had now retired from the Services would find Malta an ideal place to resettle. The winter season was much milder than that in the UK and that was more and more beneficial the older one got. Besides, as prices in Malta were more reasonable than those charged in Italy, northern France and Spain, one's pension and savings purchasing power was stronger. To top all these advantages, the island used the British pound sterling for its currency (O'Callaghan, c. 1965).

Forty years later, after the new millennium, the discourse had changed. Now, it was not the British tourist that had to be convinced to come – that had been achieved to perfection in the immediate post-independence decades. The island now sought the attention of the other Europeans and those beyond. What Malta needed to emphasise was its assets, which went beyond the natural benefits derived from the sun and the sea. It was the cultural heritage that needed to be stressed as the tourist had become more discerning. Many more travellers went to places for an experience that touched the person and the emotions, and satisfied deeper curiosities. The new Malta was important to the self-education of the visitor – it was an open history book, a timeline in the streets and a depository of civilisation. The *DK Eyewitness Top 10 Travel Guide* described and branded Malta as a destination thus:

> The tiny Maltese archipelago, floating on the cusp of Europe and Africa, has been coveted and invaded throughout its history. The Knights of St John (later of Malta) bequeathed palaces, fortresses and the glorious golden capital Valletta, while the British left red telephone boxes, iced buns and a predilection for tea.

It was the islands' earliest settlers who left the most spectacular legacy: the extraordinary megalithic temples, unparalleled elsewhere in the world.

Malta, the largest island, has the most cosmopolitan resorts and the edge in cultural treasures, while sleepy Gozo and tiny Comino offer unspoilt countryside and a gentler pace (Gallagher, 2007: 6).

The MTA takes care of marketing and spreading Brand Malta all over the globe. Its remit is to find those characteristics that create the tourist experience and accentuate them. In Italy, the second largest market for the Maltese tourism industry, Malta in 2015 is described as: 'più paesaggio da scoprire; più cultura da conoscere; più ricordi' [more scenery to discover; more culture to experience; more memories] (Focus Storia, 2015). Malta's dilemma with regard to Italy is a tangible reality. How can it inspire Italian tourists to visit a place that has for centuries been perceived by those who have heard about Malta to be almost a 'little Italy'? The branding strategy that has been adopted in the case of Italy, therefore, is that of focusing on the differences rather than trying to compete on the similarities (Department of Information – Malta, 2007). Historically, up until the 16th century, Malta was linked to Sicily in much of what it did and was. Only after the Order of St John took over the government of the Maltese islands did things begin to take a different direction. This Order (known today as the Sovereign Military Order of Malta) was basically a conglomeration of Europeans deriving from many parts of the continent and with territorial possessions spread all over Europe. The Order of Knights introduced into Malta all that was European. Then when the islands were taken over by the British, the locals were inculcated with all that was essentially English. This is the image of difference that needed to be projected to the Italians, who would then be tempted to travel to tiny Malta, being there in two hours, enjoying a destination well equipped for a business travel vacation with excellent conference and incentive facilities, but also offering whatever the tourist required (Department of Information – Malta, 2007).

Malta has come a long way from describing itself as the 'British Riviera in the Mediterranean' in the pre-World War Two years (Pollacco, 2003). Through a process of image selection and refinement, changing circumstances and new realities, the contemporary brand that Malta has adopted touches on many and varied aspects. The *Lonely Planet Malta & Gozo* publication probably just about says it all. Malta is eclectic, with its 'mysterious prehistoric temples' and 'magnificent' buildings in the baroque style, it is adorned with 'celebratory feasts of rabbit [Malta's traditional dish] to festas of noisy fireworks'. Malta was now a celebration of diversity, appealing to a wide audience from the region and afar:

> Malta is a microcosm of the Mediterranean, a sponge that has absorbed different dollops of character from its neighbours and conquerors: listen to the local language to hear the Arabic influences; sample the Sicilian-inspired cuisine on its menus; and look out for the legacies of 150 years of British rule.

To drive the point home the authors stress; 'be in no doubt – Malta is not just a notional outpost of Italy or a relic of colonial Britain. The diminutive island nation has a quirky character all of its own'. The island is still 'a beach-holiday destination' which justifies the title, but it is also a cultural treasure trove of ancient temples, renaissance fortifications and museums 'dedicated to tales of WWII heroism'. Add to all of this the 'warm, friendly locals, character-filled villages, scenic landscape, decent nightlife and first-class diving opportunities and you've got a pocket-rocket destination offering drawcards out of all proportion to its size'. Malta joined the European Union in 2004. It is also part of the Eurozone, a decision that has attracted much foreign investment, and the EU funds have helped it to upgrade its infrastructure, roads and communications and pump money into new heritage projects. On top of all this, Malta is served by budget airlines, which makes it affordable and reachable by many, many more (Wilson & Bain, 2010: 11). The small, compact, complete island in the idyllic blue Mediterranean is blessed with a mild climate, bursting with culture and effortlessly accessible from anywhere in the world.

Conclusion

The image of Malta has undoubtedly progressed from that of an ex-British colony generally popular only with the few thousands that visited in the 1950s and 1960s coming from the mother country, to one where the British legacy, though still visible and to some extent tangible, has been largely relegated to the history books. Or has it?

While hospitality is a Maltese trait and welcoming foreigners is traditionally a local quality, this may also be one form of neo-colonial attitude. Many still consider the British as a 'special' group of visitors; having English as an official language along with Maltese, strengthens this feeling further. More than a century and a half under British domination has left its mark on the Maltese, and the around 30% of its tourism market still deriving from the UK emphasises even more the importance of the British presence and its prevailing influence among a people.

Arguably the vestiges of Imperialism still linger on in Maltese contemporary travel narratives and they do not appear to bother many locals too much. It may take many decades yet before we see this neo-colonial reality subsiding and tapering off. The Maltese are still, in many ways, quite 'British' or 'colonial'.

This does not, of course, discount the fact that 21st century Malta is a cosmopolitan, free, highly engaging and modern destination, where an effort is exerted – consciously or unconsciously – to relegate the shackles of a colonial past to oblivion, but without missing the chance to extract from it what it can offer towards a stronger and more enticing tourism product. The archipelago is now part of the EU and as such has to abide by the laws and regulations of this powerful and significant regional union of independent states. Some have argued that this too is a form of neo-colonialism, but many say that, on the contrary, it has enhanced its image within the world. How much one or the other viewpoint is correct needs to be researched further. The perception of the locals has still to be investigated.

Malta is at a point where, while it looks forward to further development, it wants to make sure that it does not leave the safety zone. Small islands tend to do this, naturally. One thing is however certain. Today's Malta is being branded as a welcoming destination for whoever wishes to join its people in an experience of relaxation, culture, good cuisine and an exciting stay.

References

Boissevain, J. (1979) The impact of tourism on a dependent island: Gozo, Malta. *Annals of Tourism Research* 6 (1), 76–90.

Boissevain, J. and Serracino-Inglott, P. (1997) Tourism in Malta. In E.B. De Kadt (ed.) *Tourism: Passport to Development?* (pp. 265–284). Oxford: Oxford University Press.

Bonanno, A. (2005) *Malta – Phoenician, Punic and Roman*. Malta: Midsea Books.

Briguglio, L. and Vella, L. (1995) The competitiveness of the Maltese Islands in Mediterranean international tourism. In M. Conlin and T. Baum (eds) *Island Tourism: Management, Principles and Practices* (pp. 133–147). Chichester: John Wiley and Sons.

Cameron, C.M. and Gatewood, J.B. (2008) Beyond sun, sand and sea: The emergent tourism programme in the Turks and Caicos Islands. *Journal of Heritage Tourism* 3 (1), 55–73.

Cortis, T. (1989) *Kungress Nazzjonali: L-Identità Kulturali ta' Malta*. Malta: Dipartiment ta' l-Informazzjoni.

Dalli, C. (2006) *Malta – The Medieval Millenium*. Malta: Midsea Books.

Department of Information – Malta (2007) L'Onorevole Censu Galea – Ministro Della Competittività e Comunicazione: 'Pubblicizzare Malta in Italia', press release, no. 0220A, 20 February 2007. See http://www.doi-archived.gov.mt/EN/press_releases/2007/02/pr0220A.asp (accessed 10 August 2015).

Flightglobal (n.d.) May start for Air Melita? *Flight International*, 27 March 1969, p. 147.

Focus Storia (2015). Malta is more, advert, January 2015, outside back cover.

Foucault, M. (1972) *The Archaeology of Knowledge*, transl. S. Smith. London: Tavistock.

Frendo, H. (2012) *Europe and Empire: Culture, Politics and Identity in Malta and the Mediterranean*. Malta: Midsea Books.

Gallagher, M.A. (2007) *DK Eyewitness Top 10 Travel Guide: Malta & Gozo*. London: Dorling Kindersley.

Gambin, K. (ed.) (2004) *The Development of Malta from an Island People to an Island Nation*. Malta: Heritage Malta.

Horwath and Horwath (1989) *Maltese Islands Tourism Development Plan*. London: Horwath and Horwath.

Hughes, Q. and Thake, C. (2003) *Malta – The Baroque Island*. Malta: Midsea Books.

Joint Mission for Malta (1967) *Report 18th July 1967*. Malta: Department of Information.

Mallia-Milanes, V. (ed.) (1988) *The British Colonial Experience 1800–1964: The Impact on Maltese Society*. Malta: Mireva.

Malta Tourism Authority (2015) *Tourism in Malta – Edition 2015*. Malta: MTA.

Mangion, M.L. (n.d.) Tourism development in Malta. See http://www.mta.com.mt/index.pl/tourism_development_in_malta (accessed 20 August 2008).

Massa, A. (2006) Branding roadmap on track, insists MTA chairman. *timesofmalta.com*, 24 June 2006. See http://www.timesofmalta.com/articles/view/20060624/local/branding-roadmap-on-track-insists-mta-chairman.49814 (accessed 11 August 2015).

Micallef, G. (2014) *Tourism Product of the Maltese Islands – An Analysis ... A Proposal*. Malta: MTA.

Mirabelli, T. (ed.) (1992) *25 Years on but who's Counting? The Story of the Association of Travel Agents in Malta*. Malta: Association of Travel Agents –Malta.

Mizzi, E. (1995) *Malta in the Making 1962–1987: An Eyewitness Account*. Malta: the author.

O'Callaghan, S. (c. 1965) *Malta – A Handbook to the Island* (2nd edn). Nairobi: Palmerston Press.

Oglethorpe, M.K. (1984) Tourism in Malta: A crisis of dependence. *Leisure Studies* 3, 147–161.

Pace, P. (2006) Brand Malta a waste of money (1). *timesofmalta.com*, 11 August 2006. See http://www.timesofmalta.com/articles/view/20060811/letters/brand-malta-a-waste-of-money-1.44901 (accessed 11 August 2015).

Pantzar, H. (2009) Is internal branding useful? A case study of the internal branding of Malta. Unpublished MA European Tourism Management dissertation, Bournemouth University, UK and FH Heilbronn, Germany.

Pantzar, H. and Panyik, E. (2014) Tourism in Malta: From the Knights of St John's to an independent state. In C. Costa, E. Panyik and D. Buhalis (eds) *European Tourism Planning and Organisation Systems: The EU Member States* (pp. 335–351). Bristol: Channel View Publications.

Pollacco, C. (2003) *An Outline of the Socio-economic Development in Post-war Malta*. Malta: Mireva.

Schembri Wismayer, M. (2006) Brand Malta a waste of money (2). *timesofmalta.com*, 11 August 2006. See http://www.timesofmalta.com/articles/view/20060811/letters/brand-malta-a-waste-of-money-2.44900 (accessed 11 August 2015).

Schiavone, M.J. (1994) *Kungress dwar l-Identità Maltija 8–9 ta' April, 1994*. Malta: PIN.

Simmons B.A. (2014) Saying the same old things. In M. Hall and H. Tucker (eds) *Tourism and Postcolonialism: Contested Discourses, Identities and Representations* (pp. 43–56). New York: Routledge.

Testa, C. (1997) *The French in Malta 1798–1800*. Malta: Midsea Books.

Timesofmalta.com (2005) 'Brand Malta' presented to tourism industry, 14 July 2005. See http://www.timesofmalta.com/articles/view/20060714/local/brand-malta-presented-to-tourism-industry.47757 (accessed 8 August 2015).

Trump, D.H. (2002) *Malta – Prehistory and Temples*. Malta: Midsea Books.

Wilson N. and Bain, C.J. (2010) *Lonely Planet Malta & Gozo*. London: Lonely Planet.

Wodak, R. (1996) *Disorders of Discourse*. London: Longman.

Zammit Tabona, K. (2006) Branded! Who? Me? *timesofmalta.com*, 8 August 2006. See http://www.timesofmalta.com/articles/view/20060808/opinion/branded-who-me.45142 (accessed 11 August 2015).

11 Who Owns 'Brand Estonia'? The Role of Residents and the Diaspora

Brent McKenzie

Introduction

'E-Stonia', 'Welcome to ESTonia', 'Estonia. Positively Transforming', 'Estonia. Positively Surprising' – these are a few of the examples of marketing slogans that have been used to describe and brand the smallest, and most northern, of the three Baltic countries, the Republic of Estonia (Latvia and Lithuania being the other two). As a country forcibly incorporated into the Soviet Union in 1944, Estonia has engaged in numerous campaigns to both define and market its nation since its return to independence in 1991.

One result of the forced annexation of Estonia into the Soviet Union was the creation of a worldwide Estonian diaspora. The role of a diaspora has been shown to have an impact on the maintenance and proliferation of a country and its cultural identifiers and often serves as the leading voice to their local communities in terms of communication and education about their ancestral country (Conway & Timms, 2010). What has been less studied are the similarities and differences in ethnic identities between ethnic residents (those who reside in the titular nation of the culture) and their diaspora (those who reside outside of the titular nation of the culture, but self-identify with that culture) and their impact on the brand development of the country. Thus, the aim of this chapter is to advance the literature on resident and diaspora ethnic identity, and its impact on the shaping and development of a country brand.

Research Literature

The study of culture, generally defined as a complex construct based on similarities in beliefs, values, customs, laws and morals (Tylor, 1871), represents a significant realm for study, across a number of fields of interest. The

development of ways in which to measure culture has been the focus of numerous research studies over the last half century. From the seminal work of Geerte Hofstede (1980, 2001), who developed a cultural framework to compare and contrast national cultures, to individual measures of culture across different countries by Shalom Schwartz (1992), the use of culture to compare and contrast people and countries continues to grow.

In terms of the application of culture, its use extends to research in diverse fields of enquiry such as individual and group behaviour (Shechtman et al., 2003), personality (Cheung, 2011) and concepts of power (Torelli & Shavitt, 2010). The field of business and management research has benefitted from extensive exploration of the impact of culture from a number of perspectives. These include international marketing research (Steenkamp, 2001; Yaprak, 2008), marketing strategy (Laroche, 2009, 2011), tourism (Brown & Cave, 2010) and consumer behaviour (Engelen & Brettel, 2011).

The related, but more inclusive, concept of ethnicity is most often defined from a social perspective for those that share characteristics of culture, religious, language and other identifiable variables. Additional definitions of ethnicity include, from a social psychology perspective, ethnicity relating to cultural values, attitudes and behaviours, which are the result of the member's group, and their experiences with that group (Phinney, 1996), while ethnicity has also been viewed as a social construct in relation to lived experiences and historical occurrences (Fearon, 2003). This latter definition is measured and perpetuated through self-identification of individuals into categories of people as contained in governmental forms such as a census (Longstreet, 1983). This political definition of ethnicity has both supporters and critics, but has become of greater interest in the later 20th and early 21st centuries with the rise/return of a number of nation states.

As in the case of culture, ethnicity has been used to help better understand a number of activities and behaviours. From the effect of ethnicity on group behaviour (Etlyn & Briner, 2007), and comparisons between different ethnic groups (Dewberry, 2001), previous research has shown that ethnicity can also be used to actively engage in marketing and business activities to better define a firm within the minds of that group. There has been less research on the role of ethnicity and branding, but one study examined the impact of ethnicity on brand recall (Mckelvie & Macgregor, 1996), while another looked at a consumer's ethnicity as it relates to perceptions of US brands (Dimofte et al., 2010).

Although there is strong support for the idea that both culture and ethnicity play a key part in the shaping of an individual's identity, there is equal support that the environment of an individual also impacts their sense of being and belonging (Dowley & Silver, 2000). One such influence is the country in which one lives. An individual's country of residence leads to the third construct of interest, that of national identity. National identity, as the word 'identity' implies, serves as a self-defined label. There are generally two schools of thought with respect to national identity. The first is a 'strict' definition emanating from the works of Weber (Roth & Wittich, 1978) and Connor (1994). As discussed by Dahbour (2002), the strict definition of national identity does not occur until an ethnic group self identifies with a nation. The second school of thought provides a 'loose' definition of national identity. Building on the work of Poole (1999), national identity is a personal belief of an identity that has a political and moral composition (Dahbour, 2002).

As noted by Keillor and Hult (1999), the construct of national identity has been defined by a limited number of variables, but those variables allow for a greater understanding of different cultures. One stream of literature that centres on national identity, from a diaspora perspective, particularly from a political standpoint, is that of long-distance nationalism. As defined by Anderson (1992), long-distance nationalism studies how migrant groups have a greater orientation to their country of origin, rather than their country of residence. Long-distance nationalism has been used as a framework to study a number of different diaspora groups such as Serbians in the UK (Pryke, 2003), Turks in Germany (Østergaard-Nielsen, 2003) and Sri Lankans in Canada (Thiranagama, 2014). Thus, the aim of this chapter is not to debate the merits of one definition versus another, or one research framework from another, but as will be discussed, what the implications are of the role of national identity in terms of resident versus diaspora communities.

It is suggested that one limitation in the extant literature has been that the traits and characteristics of national identity have most often been measured and applied based on the national identity items evaluated solely by the residents of the country of interest (Sinnott, 2006). In contrast, the study of national identity within the diaspora community in terms of their country of heritage has also been examined, most often from the perspective of the degree of acculturation to the country in which they reside (Silbereisen, 2008). What is less clear is what the similarities or differences are in national identity between the two groups, and from the perspective of this chapter, what may be the impact of these similarities and differences on issues such as brand development.

Twentieth-century Diaspora and Home Country Branding

The examination of ethnic groups and their impact on in-country activities is plentiful (Rosenthal & Bogner, 2009; Isurin, 2011; Collyer, 2013). Where the literature appears to be silent is on the comparison of the identifiers of national identity between residents and their diaspora, and how those differences may have an effect on behaviour. This inquiry is of particular interest for diaspora communities that were the result of economic and political difficulties in the past, but whose membership can now travel freely to their ancestral nations (Ali & Holden, 2011).

The number of people that fall within this category of diaspora has grown substantially in the second half of the 20th century and the early 21st century. Members in this group include those fleeing the Communist regimes in Central and Eastern Europe and the Soviet Union after the Second World War, those fleeing from Southeast Asia for similar reasons in the 1970s and 1980s and more recent examples such as those seeking safe haven from ongoing ethnic and religious conflict in the Middle East and parts of Africa. Although these groups are not homogeneous in nature, they nonetheless share a home national identity that they took to their new country of residence.

Arguably, the most notable of these groups are the diaspora from the former Communist regions of Central and Eastern Europe, and the Soviet Union (Hall, 1990). The largest diaspora groups of these countries were established outside their homelands in the years prior to, and the early years of, the Communist era (~1914–1925 from the Soviet Union, and ~1940–1945 from the Soviet Union and Central and Eastern Europe). The major ethnic groups from these countries established communities of noticeable size, not out of desire to immigrate, but rather because they did not, or could not, return to their homelands (Anonymous, 1992). Examples include the Polish communities in the United States (Mach, 1993) and Baltic communities in Canada (Dreifeld, 1988).

With the end of Communism in Central and Eastern Europe in 1989 and the Soviet Union in 1991, these diaspora could now freely return to visit or move to the country of their birth or heritage. Conversely, those relatives of the diaspora could now travel to these diaspora communities, resulting in shared experiences (Anonymous, 1992).

Estonian Identity and Culture

As noted, following the end of the Second World War, the growth of Communism and the Cold War, and its subsequent end in the late 20th century, the study of ethnic identity has received a great deal of attention. The mass movement of ethnically identifiable groups both voluntarily and forced, particularly to the West, has resulted in numerous examples where non-trivial numbers of diaspora have settled in countries and cities with different ethnic identities. One such group is the Estonian diaspora in Canada (Aun, 1985; Dreifield, 1988).

The first Estonian Republic was established in the aftermath of the First World War and the subsequent Russian Revolution (for most of the 19th and early 20th centuries, Estonia was subsumed within the Russian Empire).

Estonia was then occupied by the Soviet Union in 1940, then by Nazi Germany until 1944, and then back into the Soviet Union until Estonian re-independence was achieved in August of 1991 (Plakans, 2011). During the Soviet period, thousands of ethnic Estonians fled to neighbouring Sweden, and eventually to North America. One of the largest groups of Estonian diaspora would emigrate to Canada, and more specifically, Canada's largest city, Toronto (Aun, 1985).

The Estonian diaspora in Toronto, as did other similar groups, created their own ethnic network in terms of businesses, including retailing (Veidenbaum, 1975; Lillakas, 1985). There were Estonian shops and bakeries that advertised in the local Estonian newspaper, *Eesti Elu* (*Estonian Life*). For the next 40 years, the Estonian diaspora in Canada, as part of the larger group of those who identified with Estonian culture outside of Estonia, struggled to maintain their Estonian identity (Kopvillem, 2004). Thus, for this reason, Canada was selected as the country in which to study the impact of that diaspora on nation branding and national imagery, as there are approximately 24,000 Canadians that identify themselves as of Estonian heritage (The Canadian Encyclopedia, n.d.).

With the re-establishment of the Estonian Republic in 1991, the Estonian diaspora could now more readily travel to Estonia, and many of those who were first- or second-generation members of the first Republic returned to Estonia, in many instances to claim ancestral homes or other types of property, or at minimum to vote in Estonian elections (Verdery, 1998). What many found was that a half-century of Soviet and the Communist political, economic and social systems had caused a deep chasm between the Estonian residents and the diaspora. What remained though, particularly two key areas of ethnic identity, was the Estonian language and other cultural identifies such as the role of the arts, like singing, particularly choirs (Ojamaa, 2011). The continuous seeking out and consumption of key Estonian foods such as dark rye bread strengthened these ties, and other foodstuffs associated with key Estonian events such as Christmas and weddings persisted (Karner, 2005).

Who and what defines Estonia and Estonian identity?

One result of this new openness to travel and direct communication between the resident and diaspora Estonians was a question of who 'better' represented Estonian identity. Many from the diaspora viewed their vision of Estonian identity as the truest form as they had maintained the links directly to the first Estonian Republic, and in fact should be credited with maintaining a continued lifeline for Estonian culture. Not surprisingly, the residents of Estonia, most of whom appreciated the fact that they could better connect with Estonians from around the world, saw a greater need to establish a distinct vision and brand for Estonia (Kopvillem, 2004).

Brand Estonia

The aforementioned Estonian, language and other cultural identifiers (Raun, 2002) were not enough for the residents of Estonia, particularly in terms of seeking outside recognition and attraction for investment. Thus since 1991, numerous efforts in Estonia have been made to brand the country (Jansen, 2008). However, what role does, and should, the diaspora play in the development and shaping of the national or ethnic identity of the Estonian brand? In order to seek this answer, primary data was collected from two groups of Estonians.

Research Study

The data that was collected came by way of a two-sample survey collection. One sample was of Estonian residents, and the other from those that identify as Estonian-Canadians. The participants in the survey were contacted by way of snowball sampling through contacts that had been previously established by the author through family, friends and numerous trips to Estonia since 1998. Snowball sampling for this type of research is a preferred method for ensuring that only participants who have the required experiences for the focus of the study, in this case self identification as Estonian or Estonian-Canadians, are selected (Cleveland et al. 2011). It was determined that the best way to collect this comparative information was to utilise existing scale items that focused on ethnicity and national identity. With respect to ethnic identity, the questions were drawn from the Multigroup Ethnic Identity Measure scale items developed by Phinney (1992), while the national identity questions were drawn from the National Identity scale developed by Keillor et al. (1996). In order to better match the Estonian-Canadian sample in terms of their ties to Estonia, the Estonian-Canadians were those, based on their age, who would have had experiences of Estonia that were shaped during the Soviet period, as well as subsequent to Estonia's re-independence in 1991 (i.e. older than 40 years of age).

Included were Ethnic Identity items (EI) and National Identity (NI) items (see Appendix 1). The first seven questions (six EI and one NI) were yes/no questions, while the remaining 15 used a nine-point Likert scale, from 'strongly agree' (score of 1) to 'strongly disagree' (score of 9). There were also three open-ended questions included in the survey. The first asked the respondents to include words that they felt best described Estonia as a country, while the second question asked the same thing but as it pertains to Estonian culture. The final question allowed for additional insight about Estonia and Estonian culture, as the participant saw fit.

For the Estonian version of the survey, the author worked with a colleague located in Estonia, and through translation, back-translation and a further review of the survey by an additional Estonian speaker, it was determined that there were no issues in terms of item clarity and understanding. The physical survey instrument was developed using Qualtrics software. An email invitation was sent to potential participates. Those email recipients were also asked to forward the survey link to those that may also be interested in participating in the study. The result was a total of 31 usable surveys from Estonian residents and 37 from the Estonian-Canadians.

Survey findings and discussion

As expected, there were a number of items that indicated no statistical differences between the two groups, but there were four items that did show statistically different findings. These were 'I understand about my Estonian culture' ($p = 0.07$), 'I am clear as to what it means to be Estonian' ($p = 0.04$), 'One must be able to speak Estonian to be Estonian' ($p = 0.09$) and 'It is always best to purchase Estonian-made products if available' ($p = 0.01$). Additionally, even for those items that did not have statistical differences in the means, there were some interesting findings in terms of the directions of the ratings.

For both the Estonian and Estonian-Canadian sample, the statement 'If a person learns to speak Estonian, they can be considered Estonian' ($\pi = 5.54$ and 5.43 respectively) was the one ranked the highest, or closest to the 'do not agree' rating, but still fell within the 'neutral' rating. In contrast, for the Estonian-Canadian sample, the highest 'strongly agree' item was 'Estonians are proud of their heritage' ($\pi = 1.63$), while it was 'I feel strongly about being Estonian' ($\pi = 2.29$) for the Estonian sample.

For the qualitative, culturally related, open-ended questions (see Appendix 2), Word clouds were created (Puretskiy et al., 2010). Word clouds (also known as Tag clouds) are a helpful qualitative research technique to help visualise data (Fingal, 2008; McNaught & Lam, 2010). The first word cloud, for the words that define Estonia as a country, is shown in Figure 11.1. The word 'Small' is the most prominent, while the terms 'hostage', 'calm' and 'pride' are also quite pronounced. In Figure 11.2, which asked about Estonian Culture, the words 'song', 'festival' and 'hostage' dominate, with secondary leading words such as 'folk', 'traditions' and 'language'.

For the Estonian-Canadian word clouds, there were similarities for defining Estonia as a country, 'small', 'proud' and 'innovative', with 'stubborn', 'language' and 'resilient' being the next most prominent (Figure 11.3). For words that define Estonian culture, 'music', 'language', 'proud' and 'rich' were the most prevalent (Figure 11.4).

The final 'other' word clouds, also provided some interesting themes (Figures 11.5 and 11.6). The main terms of 'Estonian' and 'History' remained, but additional inclusions of specific Estonians was interesting. For the Canadian respondents, the responses were much more verbose (i.e. the average Canadian comment included twice as many words as the average

Estonian comment) in comparison to the Estonian responses, and included terms such as 'Soviet', and 'Russian', additional references to other countries and no inclusions of specific Estonians.

Implications of the findings

So what is the impact, or relevance of these findings on country branding in general, and Brand Estonia specifically? Although the majority of the items were not directly related to the Estonian branding, the item 'It is always best to purchase Estonian-made products if available' can have an impact on how certain products are marketed to residents and diaspora. For instance, Estonian products can benefit from being labelled as 'Made in Estonia' for the diaspora market, while there may be greater benefit of being labelled as 'Made in the EU' versus 'Made in Estonia' for the resident market. The related question of 'Estonians are proud of their heritage' can also allow businesses to either play up or down this connection depending on the market.

Of the four statistically different items, three were related to ethnic identity and one to national identity. This result may not be surprising given that the Canadian-Estonian sample was drawn from those who had resided outside of Estonia for many, if not all, of their lives. Nonetheless, one telling finding was that the item 'I understand about my Estonian culture' indicated that Estonian-Canadians view Estonian culture as something they have to work at maintaining in comparison to Estonian residents.

Conclusions

One of the expected results found in the survey data was a great degree of similarity in terms of ethnic versus national identity measures of residents and diaspora. There was an expectation that the differences in terms of the findings from the survey data would provide greater understanding of the Estonian nation brand, and by extension could be useful to both domestic governmental agencies and tourism firms that wish to attract investment and tourists. Research directed at the study of tourism intentions and practices of diaspora Estonians, or other diaspora populations, can help to address a stated lack of inclusion of research on consumer culture beyond the dominant domestic population (Kalmus et al., 2009). There was also the hope to provide insights into how the ethnicity, country of residence and country of origin of a defined group of people can be used for comparisons in terms of non-culture-related activities.

Although this chapter only examined a small sample of Estonian residents and Estonian diaspora in one country, Canada, future research of this nature could examine other areas of interest such as quantitatively measuring the similarities and differences of the Estonian brand image between

Estonians and Estonian-Canadians. It is expected that the findings of this type of study will specifically provide greater insights as to what role diaspora play in shaping the brand image of Estonia.

Similar research is also encouraged in other countries with large 'forced' diaspora, diaspora that can now return to their heritage homeland if they so desire. The insights gained can also be of interest to other country brand development programmes that have a strong diaspora community. The findings will also help to advance knowledge on nation branding and national imagery in terms of the types of tools and measurement instruments that should be used in this field of study.

Appendix 1: Ethnic Identity and National Identity Questions

Section 1a – Estonian identity (yes/no responses)

(1) I participate in activities that are considered Estonian.
(2) In the last 6 months I have listened to Estonian music.
(3) In the last 6 months I have eaten Estonian food.
(4) In the last 6 months I have read an Estonian book.
(5) In the last 6 months I have watched an Estonian television show or movie.
(6) I have attended event(s) in the last 6 months to learn more about Estonia.
(7) I purchase Estonian-made products if available.

Section 1b – Estonian identity ('strongly agree' – score of 1 – to 'strongly disagree – score of 9)

(1) I understand about my Estonian culture.
(2) I feel strongly about being Estonian.
(3) I am clear as to what it means to be Estonian.
(4) One must be able to speak Estonian to be Estonian.
(5) If a person learns to speak Estonian, they can be considered Estonian.
(6) It is important to learn about famous Estonians of the past.
(7) It is important to learn about famous Estonians of today.
(8) The way to preserve the Estonian culture is to study Estonian history.
(9) Estonia has a strong historical heritage.
(10) Estonians possess certain cultural attributes that others do not have.
(11) Estonians believe they have a common history.
(12) Estonians are proud of their heritage.
(13) Estonians must engage in activities that are considered Estonian.
(14) I am clear about Estonian culture.
(15) It is always best to purchase Estonian-made products if available.

Appendix 2: Word Clouds

Section 2 – Estonian culture

advanced black bread calm clean compact costumes country dogmatic education estonian folk forest free go-ahead green heavy history hostage independent innovaatiline innovative internet irreverent kama language living midsummer milk national nature newer northern opportunity patient people pre-continued pride proud revolution sauna sausage size skype small stubborn sydamlik talent technology warm

Figure 11.1 List up to five words that best define Estonia: Estonian residents

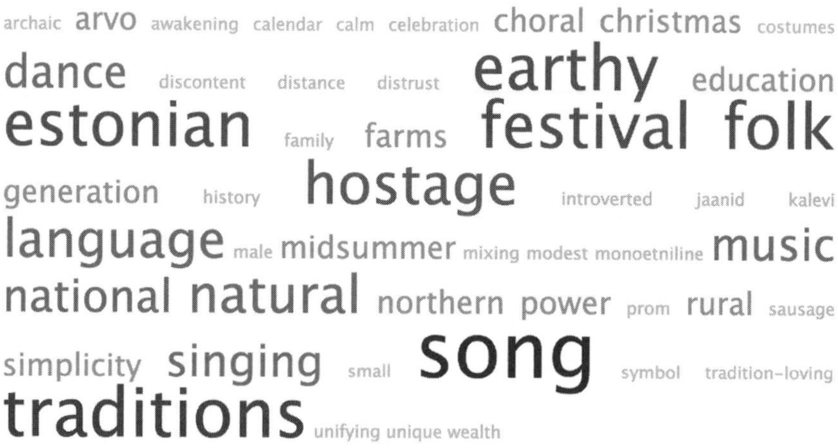

archaic arvo awakening calendar calm celebration choral christmas costumes dance discontent distance distrust earthy education estonian family farms festival folk generation history hostage introverted jaanid kalevi language male midsummer mixing modest monoetniline music national natural northern power prom rural sausage simplicity singing small song symbol tradition-loving traditions unifying unique wealth

Figure 11.2 List up to five words that best define Estonian culture: Estonian residents

advanced baltic closeness cosmopolitan country culturally date educated european evolving forested future-oriented geographical green gulf hard hard-working history homogeneous independent innovative insecure interested inviting isolated language location music nordic perseverant professionals proud resilient rich rural sea singers small song soul strong stubborn survivor tech threatened unique vibrant viking white work

Figure 11.3 List up to five words that best define Estonia: Estonian-Canadian residents

accessible art artistic background belong bright choral colourful community confident critical dance diverse eager estonian european festival finno-ugric folk food fun government history influence intellectual land language literate literature marketable mixed multifaceted music others passionate patriotic proud provincial rich rooted self singing social song soul unique versatile vibrant viking west

Figure 11.4 List up to five words that best define Estonian culture: Estonian-Canadian residents

ability access activities adamson-erik adaptation alive appeal appreciate art arvo believing country culture different estonia estonian etc events food form german going heritage history identity important influence kalevipoja keep literature lots marble modest music national nature people poor power rapid rocks seasonal slavs small storm talent traditions traversed understand weather

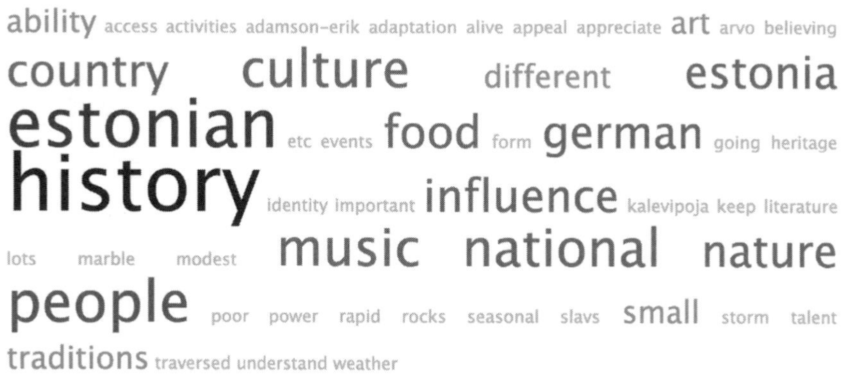

Figure 11.5 Additional things you think would help others to better understand Estonia and Estonian culture: Estonian residents

Figure 11.6 Additional things you think would help others to better understand Estonia and Estonian culture: Estonian-Canadian residents

References

Ali, N. and Holden, A. (2011) Tourism's role in the national identity formulation of the United Kingdom's Pakistani diaspora. In E. Frew and L. White (eds) *Tourism and National Identity: An International Perspective*. New York: Routledge.

Anderson, B. (1992) *Long-distance Nationalism: World Capitalism and the Rise of Identity Politics*. Amsterdam: Center for Asian Studies.

Anonymous (1992) The homecoming. *The Economist*, 26 December, pp. 73–76.

Aun, K. (1985) *The Political Refugees: A History of Estonians in Canada*. Ottawa: McClelland and Stewart.

Brown, K.G. and Cave, J. (2010) Island tourism: Marketing culture and heritage – editorial introduction to the special issue. *International Journal of Culture, Tourism and Hospitality Research* 4 (2), 87–95.

The Canadian Encyclopedia (n.d.) Estonians. See www.canadianencyclopedia.ca (accessed 2 April 2015).

Cheung, F. (2011) Toward a new approach to the study of personality in culture. *The American Psychologist* 66 (7), 593–603.

Cleveland, M., Laroche, M. and Papadopoulos, N. (2011) Ethnic identity's relationship to materialism and consumer ethnocentrism: Contrasting consumers in developed and emerging economies. *Journal of Global Academy of Marketing Science* 21 (2), 55–71.

Collyer, M. (2013) *Emigration Nations: Policies and Ideologies of Emigrant Engagement*. New York: Palgrave Macmillan.

Connor, W. (1994) *Ethnonationalism: The Quest for Understanding*. Princeton, NJ: Princeton University Press.

Conway, D. and Timms, B.F. (2010) Re-branding alternative tourism in the Caribbean: The case for 'slow tourism. *Tourism and Hospitality Research* 10 (4), 329–344.

Dahbour, O. (2002) National identity: An argument for the strict definition. *Public Affairs Quarterly* 16 (1), 17–37.

Dewberry, C. (2001) Performance disparities between whites and ethnic minorities: Real differences or assessment bias? *Journal of Occupational and Organizational Psychology* 74 (5), 659–673.

Dimofte, C., Johansson, J. and Bagozzi, R. (2010) Global brands in the United States: How consumer ethnicity mediates the global brand effect. *Journal of International Marketing* 18 (3), 81–106.

Dowley, K. and Silver, B. (2000) Subnational and national loyalty: Cross-national comparisons. *International Journal of Public Opinion Research* 12 (4), 357–371.

Dreifeld, J. (1988) The political refugees: A history of the Estonians in Canada. *Canadian Historical Review* 69 (3), 409–410.

Engelen, A. and Brettel, M. (2011) Assessing cross-cultural marketing research and theory. *Journal of Business Research* 64 (5), 516–523.

Etlyn, J. and Briner, R.B. (2007) Ethnicity and behavior in organizations: A review of British research. *Journal of Occupational and Organizational Psychology* 80 (3), 437–457.

Fearon, D. (2003) Ethnic and cultural diversity by country. *Journal of Economic Growth* 8, 195–222.

Fingal, D. (2008) Tools that create buzz: Words in a cloud. *Learning and Leading with Technology* November, 23.

Hall, S. (1990) Cultural identity and diaspora. In J. Rutherford (ed.) *Identity: Community, Culture, Difference.* London: Lawrence and Wishart.

Hofstede, G.H. (1980) *Culture's Consequences: International Differences in Work-related Values.* Newbury Park, CA: Sage.

Hofstede, G.H. (2001) *Culture's Consequences: Comparing Values, Behaviors, Institutions and Organizations Across Nations.* Thousand Oaks, CA: Sage.

Isurin, L. (2011) *Russian Diaspora Culture, Identity, and Language Change.* New York: De Gruyter Mouton.

Jansen, S. (2008) Neo-liberal nation branding – Brand Estonia. *Social Identities* 14 (1), 121–142.

Kalmas, V., Keller, M. and Kiisel, M. (2009) Emerging consumer types in a transition culture: Consumption patterns of generational and ethnic groups in Estonia. *Journal of Baltic Studies* 40 (1), 53–74.

Karner, K.A. (2005) *Estonian Tastes and Traditions.* New York: Hippocrene Books.

Keillor, B. and Hult, G.T.M. (1999) A five-country study of national identity: Implications for international marketing research and practice. *International Marketing Review* 16 (1), 65–84.

Keillor, B., Parker, R. and Schaefer, A. (1996) Influences on adolescent brand preferences in the United States and Mexico. *Journal of Advertising Research* 36, 47–56.

Kopvillem, P. (2004) A place in the heart: We learned about the lost Estonia. But what to do once it's found? *Maclean's* 117 (19), 40.

Laroche, M. (2009) Impact of culture on marketing strategy: Introduction to the special issue. *Journal of Business Research* 62 (10), 921–923.

Laroche, M. (2011) Globalization, culture, and marketing strategy: Introduction to the special issue. *Journal of Business Research* 64 (9), 931–933.

Lillakas, V. (1985) *Eestlased Kanadas II (Estonians in Canada, Volume 2).* Toronto: Oma Press.

Longstreet, W.S. (1983) Needed: The rational definition of ethnicity. *Contemporary Education* 54 (2), 74–78.

Mach, Z. (1993) *Symbols, Conflict and Identity: Essays in Political Anthropology.* New York: SUNY Press.

Mckelvie, S.J. and Macgregor, R.M. (1996) Effects of interactive pictures and ethnicity on recall of brand names. *Canadian Journal of Administrative Sciences* 13 (1), 33–45.

McNaught, C. and Lam, P. (2010) Using Wordle as a supplementary research tool. *The Qualitative Report* 15 (3), 630–643.

Ojamaa, T. (2011) *60 aastat eesti koorilaulu multikultuurses Torontos [60 Years of Estonian Choral Singing in Multicultural Toronto].* Tartu: Eesti Kirjandusmuuseumi Teaduskirjastus.

Østergaard-Nielsen, E. (2003) *Transnational Politics: Turks and Kurds in Germany.* London: Routledge.

Phinney, J.S. (1992) The Multigroup ethnic identity measure: A new scale for use with diverse groups. *Journal of Adolescent Research* 7, 156–176.

Phinney, J.S. (1996) When we talk about American ethnic groups, what do we mean? *American Psychologist* 51 (9), 918–927.

Plakans, A. (2011) *A Concise History of the Baltic States.* Cambridge: Cambridge University Press.

Poole, R. (1999) *Nation and Identity.* London: Routledge.

Pryke, S. (2003) British Serbs and long-distance nationalism. *Ethnic and Racial Studies* 26 (1), 152–172.

Puretskiy, A.A., Shutt, G.L. and Berry, M.W. (2010) Surveys of texts visualization techniques. In M.W. Berry and J. Kogan (eds) *Text Mining: Applications and Theory.* Chichester: John Wiley and Sons.

Raun, T. (2002) *Estonia and the Estonians.* Stanford, CA: Hoover Institutional Press.

Rosenthal, G. and Bogner, A. (2009) *Ethnicity, Belonging and Biography: Ethnographical and Biographical Perspectives.* Piscataway, NJ: Mu"nster.

Roth, G. and Wittich, C. (1978) *Max Weber, Economy and Society: An Outline of Interpretive Sociology* (Vol. 1). Berkeley, CA: University of California Press.

Schwartz, S.H. (1992) Universals in the content and structure of values: Theoretical advances and empirical tests in 20 countries. In M.P. Zanna (ed.) *Advances in Experimental Social Psychology* (Vol. 25, pp. 1–65). San Diego, CA: Academic Press.

Shechtman, Z., Hiradin, A. and Zina, S. (2003) The impact of culture on group behavior: A comparison of three ethnic groups. *Journal of Counseling and Development* 81 (2), 208–216.

Silbereisen, R.K. (2008) New research on acculturation among diaspora migrants. *International Journal of Psychology* 43 (1), 2–5.

Sinnott, R. (2006) An evaluation of the measurement of national, subnational and supranational identity in crossnational surveys. *International Journal of Public Opinion Research* 18 (2), 211–223.

Steenkamp, J. (2001) The role of national culture in international marketing research. *International Marketing Review* 18 (1), 30–44.

Thiranagama, S. (2014) Making Tigers from Tamils: Long-distance nationalism and Sri Lankan Tamils in Toronto. *American Anthropologist* 116 (2), 265–278.

Torelli, C.J. and Shavitt, S.K. (2010) Culture and concepts of power. *Journal of Personality and Social Psychology* 99 (4), 703–723.

Tylor, E. (1871) *The Origins of Culture.* Primitive Culture (Vol. 1, reprint, originally published 1958). New York: Harper and Row.

Veidenbaum, S. (1975) Eestlased Kanadas pärast Teist Maailmasõda [Estonians in Canada after the Second World War]. In A. Kurlent (exec. ed.) *Eestlased Kanadas I.* Estonians in Canada (Vol. 1). Toronto: Oma Press.

Verdery, K. (1998) Transnationalism, nationalism, citizenship, and property: Eastern Europe since 1989. *American Ethnologist* 25 (2), 291–306.

Yaprak, A. (2008) Culture study in international marketing: A critical review and suggestions for future research. *International Marketing Review* 25 (2), 215–229.

12 When the Incredible Got Lost in Controversies: Selling Tourism in India

Sagar Singh

Introduction

The Hindu-oriented political party that came into power in India in May 2014 also brought with it the baggage of 'restoring India's lost glory' and economic development. As the author writes, discussion continues on the Internet through Indian news websites like Yahoo! News India, MSN News India and on Facebook about how soon (and whether) 'the good days' can return. In June 2015, the government simplified the in-bound tourism process by allowing e-Visas for tourists from a good number of countries. The visit to China by current Prime Minister Narendra Modi, one of the rarest events in Indian politics, the picking up of the 'Atithi Devo Bhavah' ('the guest is a god') and the Incredible India campaign for the last 10 years, have created the impression that commercialising the national image through advertisements has power enough to change the course of tourism, inbound as well as domestic. It is also thought that impinging consumers with messages that extol the virtues of the nation will bring about change for the better. Sadly, this does not seem true since crimes against tourists, although they are met with flashing 'breaking news' minutes of a hungry media and decried by all 'right-minded' Indians, have not come to an end.

It seems, therefore, true that commercial advertisements compete as well with social advertising as 'feel good' messages on Facebook compete with the sting of posts that bring attention to negatives: both survive and people do not seem to change. The main purpose of this chapter is to analyse whether commercial nationalism does any good to the tourism process: if it does not, what needs to be done, where might weaknesses lie and how can these weaknesses be overcome? The chapter will look at different types of commercialisation and tourism: whether the heritage be natural, mainstream cultural (in the broadest sense), or spiritual and religious (as something that is described not by culture alone). Cases will be taken from each of these areas.

What also needs emphasis is that commercial nationalism is not of any one type of phenomenon but is a product of the modern state: what has been called 'propaganda' in the past and is the by-product of the 'new industrial state' (Galbraith, 1967) and commercial interests in marketing the benefits of the state against its detractors. Thus, while it is maintained that similarities and differences exist between 'official nationalism' (that generated by government departments through public events and advertising campaigns) and 'commercial nationalism – the brand of nationalism generated by private organisations' ... 'understanding the complex relationships and interconnections ... between these two discourses of nationalism is a subject worthy of analysis' (White, 2009). This chapter examines how official nationalism can be both helpful and detrimental, and how commercial nationalism 'hijacks' the official nationalism to suit its ends.

However, official nationalism should not be viewed as a product of what is called 'populist policies' or even of 'the neo-liberal state' since it is used for marketing communist or socialist policies just as much as it is used by conservatives, and seems, at its basic level, to be an attempt to allow market forces to deal with all those disgruntled elements that refuse to be dominated by any particular sort of government. It also seems to be an ideal-typical construct through which the modern nation-state can be analysed. Thus, it is both a reality 'out there' and a thought-process that allows us to understand how the state functions. In taking such a view, this chapter suggests that Marxian dialectical historical materialism can be seen in light of the changed circumstances of the world as pregnant with 'idealism' combined with 'materialism'. In the process, it should be a reminder to those of a Marxian view that human society functions in more complex ways than such historicism would or could provide for.

The image makeover of Russia through the annexation of Crimea in 2014 was designed to attract international tourists and earn money, as well as to send a signal to patriotic Russians that 'all is well'. Similarly, the dismantling of the embargo on tourists to Cuba (from the United States) in 2015 was another image makeover for both nations. Clearly, then, the world today is governed more than ever before by nation-state image makeovers designed to attract tourists.

The purpose of this chapter is to show how this has, and has not, worked for India, and how official nationalism is being utilised by the current regime in this country by the intense image-building by Prime Minister Narendra Modi, who has visited more than 20 nations in the first year of the National Democratic Alliance government. The rise of the 'Atithi Devo Bhavah' campaign, and moves to improve both inbound and domestic tourism through better administration and policies, seen in respect of the

Incredible India campaign, which has been in existence for over a decade (mostly under the previous Indian Congress-dominated United Progressive Alliance government), are cases in point that will illustrate how such nationalism works with respect to tourism. This chapter will be divided into three parts: brief case studies in the realms of the various spheres of heritage, where the failures and inadequacies of official nationalism and selling tourism will become apparent. It will also show, among other things, how commercial nationalism in this context is a case of hitching on to the official bandwagon.

Natural Heritage and Tourism: The Valley of Flowers National Park

The Valley of Flowers case calls to attention how official nationalism in India benefited by bringing an example of outstanding natural heritage within the ambit of a system of world conservation – and how it failed, for want of a policy and action on conservation that transcends state barriers. It also shows how the nation-state has failed in important matters like the interplay of heritage conservation, tourism policy, tourism administration and commercial interests – a sad instance of how nationalism that is dependent on free reign of commercial interests, or commercialism, can become subservient to rightful official nationalism that extols and builds on what truly belongs to the nation (and the world) and can be commercialised in a limited and controlled way, while promoting scientific research and development, including on climate change, ecology, and alternative medicine.

The Valley of Flowers, located in the Chamoli district of the mountainous Uttarakhand state, was designated a national park in 1982 and became a World Heritage Site in 1988. First 'discovered' by British mountaineer and botanist Frank S. Smythe in 1931 (Smythe, 1938), it came to the attention of tourists after the 1970s but became really popular in a limited way in the 1990s. While the peak tourist season lasts for only three months, from July to September, peak visitation never crossed the 9000-mark in any recent year (Gusain, 2015), which is just as well for the extremely fragile ecosystem that is perhaps one of the best examples of the ecological succession of plants anywhere in the world.

With over 500 species of flowering and medicinal plants, it is also home to some rare mountain fauna, such as the colourful Monal pheasant, which is the national bird of Nepal and is endangered in certain areas of India, as mentioned by the International Union for Conservation of Nature and Natural Resources (IUCN, also known as the World Conservation Union). Five species found in the Valley are new to the world (Kala, 2004). The Valley is also home to the Brahma Kamal, whose value as an alternative general anesthetic can be put at millions of dollars (Singh, 2015), while the exponential existence value cum productive use value of the Valley and its resources through analysis of how it can help in adapting to climate change (in places with a similar climate and/or for growing medicinal plants) is beyond calculation at present (Singh, 2016).

In view of these facts, which though not precisely formulated by previous researchers can very well be presumed by the many botanical expeditions that have been carried out in the area, a policy and action plan for conservation should have been in place. On the contrary, all that the Uttarakhand state administration did was help increase visitation of tourists to the area, while curbing visits by local people, who have been associated with it for hundreds of years. Even descriptions of the Valley and its attendant flora and fauna, its history and location on the internet (including Wikipedia) are inadequate or simply wrong: for instance, the growing presence of a certain weed is reported to be recent, whereas this researcher was able to find mention of the same weed in the first detailed account of the Valley (Smythe, 1938).

Moreover, no attempt has been made to scientifically estimate the tourism carrying capacity of the Valley, although an ad hoc number of 60 persons per day was chosen around the same time that it was made a national park in 1982 (Kaur, 1985). However, those who have studied the Valley (Kaur, 1985) and know its importance owing to their being native to the region, such as O.P. Kandari (personal communication, January 2015), stress that even the limit of 60 visitors per day is too high. Environmental journalists concur (Down To Earth, 2013) with such an opinion. Yet even this limit may be crossed on many days since there is no system of regulating tourists on an even diurnal basis, the permit being given on an arbitrary first-come-first-served basis on the spot. A check-post on the way in, just one kilometre from the Valley, with a lone guard, is all the protection that the Valley has to prevent over-exploitation and disruption of this extremely fragile ecosystem. Even a visitor orientation centre is missing from Ghangaria, the point where the track to the Valley diverges from the common path to it and the Sikh shrine of Hemkund Sahib, with just an inadequate 'interpretation centre'.

To top it all, there is no regulation of or interaction with the tour operators who bring trekking parties to the Valley; lastly, the visitor fee of Rs 150 per Indian national and Rs 600 per foreign tourist (valid for three days, instead of the logical one day, given the small size of the park and limitations on visiting hours) is woefully inadequate to fund conservation in the Valley. Clearly, the state of Uttarakhand is all out to only exploit the Valley for raking in as much money as quickly as possible, instead of ensuring a fair, steady and conservation-orientated supply of income from this unique place. This becomes even more apparent from the Master Plan for Tourism developed by the Government of Uttarakhand (2008) in conjunction with the Government of India, United Nations Development Programme (UNDP) and United Nations World Tourism Organization (UNWTO) in 2007. Table 12.1

Table 12.1 Tourist visits in Uttarakhand as a percentage of total tourist arrivals

	India (mean)		Uttarakhand (mean)		Percentage share (%)	
Year	Domestic	Foreign	Domestic	Foreign	Domestic	Foreign
2001	234.20	5.42	10.37	0.055	4.43	1.01
2002	269.60	5.16	11.37	0.056	4.22	1.09
2003	309.04	6.71	12.58	0.063	4.07	0.95
2004	366.22	8.30	13.34	0.075	3.64	0.90
2005	390.47	9.94	15.92	0.093	4.08	0.93
2006	461.16	11.40	18.99	0.096	4.12	0.84

Source: Uttarakhand Tourism Development Master Plan 2007–2022, Vol. 3, Appendix 2, Table 3.

shows how grossly the tourism statistics are used in the Appendix to the Master Plan, and how an effort is being made, despite all indications to the contrary, by Uttarakhand's failing ecological system and dwindling forests to somehow maximise tourism, especially by attracting international tourists, whose arrivals are said to be declining. Thus, for instance, the table shows 2006 international 'tourist visits' to be 11.4 million and therefore Uttarakhand's percentage share of foreign tourist arrivals 'declined'. The actual UNTWO figure for India in 2006 (cited by Stark Tourism Associates, 2015a) is 4.45 million foreign tourists, with the six million mark being crossed for the first time only in 2011. Thus, statistics are abused to make a case for promotion.

In the same plan, visitation to the Valley of Flowers is said to be '5', with no mention of whether this is in hundreds or thousands (it certainly cannot be units!). The excessive exploitation of natural resources, dynamite blasting for making roads, pollution and deforestation finally led to a devastating flood in Uttarakhand in 2013 that killed thousands and left many more thousands homeless. The exact cause was not known, but what is certain is that more than one cloudburst occurred, possibly from the seeding of clouds by large particles of carbon that were released from over-pollution by motor vehicles in the fragile mountain air. A similar cloudburst occurred in 2014, but was limited in area, and sudden, heavy downpours have happened in 2015. The 2013 flood devastated a large portion of the road leading to Badrinath, which is the same route as for the Valley of Flowers and Hemkund road-head, Govindghat. Even the track from Govindghat to Ghangaria was washed away in places, along with footbridges along the route, closing all visitation to the Valley for nearly two years.

In 2013 there were 484 visitors to the Valley, after which it was closed owing to the flood. In October 2014 the park opened only for 15 days and there were just 181 visitors, attributed largely to lack of advertising and/or damage to the route. In contrast, 8,577 visitors enjoyed the beauty of the

Valley of Flowers in 2009; in 2010 5,118 visitors arrived, rising in 2011 to 6,855; and in 2012 there were 7,665 visitors (Gusain, 2015). Considering that the park authorities had put an estimated upper limit of visitors at 60 per day, this translates to 6,300 visitors over the 3.5 months of the season in which flowers bloom in the Valley. Clearly, the upper limit has been exceeded many times in recent years. While tourism to this mountain state is picking up in 2015, the problem of over-visitation to areas like the Valley of Flowers is likely to come up again, and lack of foresight in managing a national and international treasure shows the lack of administrative abilities not only of the state government, but also of the central government, which changed only in 2014. Thus, no limitation is put on the number of times private tour operators can bring tourists to the Valley, or how many tourists they bring; these tour operators advertise the Valley freely on websites, including on Tripadvisor.in, as one of the world's (and India's) most unique valleys, thus cashing in on an image that official nationalism has spread. Clearly, official and commercial nationalism are both acting to the detriment of the heritage, with no solution in sight.

Even the idea of making tourism an item in the 'concurrent list' of administrative matters (currently tourism is on the state list, hence the union government cannot trespass on state management), currently being reviewed, alone, will not help. What is required is a national conservation body and laws that govern national heritage use by tourists and techniques for preservation. Special techniques for preservation are being taken up with the Taj Mahal in Agra, but it is only possible since the National Archeological Survey of India is employed; no such organisation exists for natural heritage sites. On the positive side, the Hindu heritage that the Valley presents (since it is connected to the legend of Lord Rama and a Hanuman temple exists in the vicinity) may be a reason for the current Hindu-orientated government to earmark it for action. Yet even the present regime is not keen on promoting the Hindu agenda, but, along with new policies and frameworks for tourism and an emphasis on economic development, may help bring the plight of this unique heritage under the purview of a national body for the promotion of tourism.

A key point that needs to be made here is the total lack of foresight on the part of the then (admittedly Indian National Congress-dominated) government that did not see fit to bid for a separate international natural heritage status for the Valley, and included it with Nanda Devi National Park and biosphere reserve (which does not actually completely abut the Valley of Flowers, and where tourism has been almost completely stopped), making administration and policy measures difficult for this world heritage area. Lastly, the value of this unique area was lost on the world largely because the government did not see a dovetailing of conservation measures and tourism revenue from this site: it can be said that commercial nationalism may have 'sold' this area better, while ensuring funds for continued conservation, if it had been put to use in a strategic way, and had been tempered with rationalism for long-lasting gains, rather than short-term gain of just 'a world heritage attraction'. As it currently exists, the Valley is open to all of the problems and pitfalls of tourism development but none of its advantages in helping conservation, when allowed in a regulated way (Singh, 2015, 2016).

Cultural Heritage: Indian Values, the Middle Class and Tourism

Many tourist places that are being 'sold' to foreign tourists are dependent both in imagery and factually on a stable, value-abiding, educated Indian middle class, which is variously estimated to be close to 350 million. These are the chief constituents of 'the other' that a foreign tourist meets face to face in tourist cities that are inundated with Indian tourists just as much as international ones. Many of those, especially the relatively more affluent ones who constitute a lesser proportion, who stay in lower star hotels and upmarket budget accommodation not only share many restaurants with these foreign tourists, but are also on the lookout for the same sort of sights, entertainment, transport and adventures, but who are also seen often as 'guiding' the foreigner – whether directly or through websites such as Indian TripAdvisor. Back in the 1960s, 1970s and early 1980s, this image – often of a reticent, reserved, humorous and yet culturally bound middle class Indian man (or woman) – was the basis of films such as *The Householder, The Party, Heat and Dust* and even the science fiction movie *Close Encounters of the Third Kind*, which had scenes apparently shot in Dharamshala in the mountain state of Himachal Pradesh.

The same hill town was in the news in 2015 for a sexual atrocity against a young female said to have been politically motivated; a bus mishap in which the vehicle fell into a deep ravine, killing most of those on board and last but not the least, the ever-present benevolent leader of the Tibetans in exile, the Dalai Lama. Advertisements, even as this chapter is being written, proclaim the exoticness of a rainy season stay in Triund, a trek from Upper Dharamshala, while a recent Facebook post of a friend shows how crowded the road to Upper Dharamshala has become, with traffic jams common. The fact is, India does not seem to need inbound tourism much, and its strong middle class-dominated domestic tourism does not need commercial nationalism to keep the industry healthy. Yet it is this class that helps keep tourism alive and ready for the eventual foreign tourist. It is also this class that, once the mainstay of values, has on the one hand helped keep the tourism experience friendly, and which now, for all its ills – like binge drinking and partying until the small hours in big cities and tourist areas like Goa – is both an attraction for foreign tourists on the lookout for 'the smiling native' and the nemesis for those who follow its precepts without due caution, as the case of increasing numbers in crimes in the largely tourist-friendly Goa shows.

According to observers and critics of Goa tourism, such as Holden (1984) and Noronha (2005), even without the tourist culture that arose from the partying hippies of the 1970s and 1980s in Goa, the Indian middle class tourist follows the Western, who follows the Indian – and all of these follow not what the brochures tell, but whatever gossip says is becoming of that particular tourist place. Doctoral research by Chauhan (2009) and this author's observations in 1998 and in later years, show that the presence in large numbers of Israeli tourists in Himachal, many of whom do not mind taking hallucinogens that are easily available, say, in Triund or old Manali, has nothing to do with commercial nationalism. However, such tourist cultures have developed in Manali and Goa and are consumed by upper or upper middle class 'deviant' Indians as much as foreigners, and sub-national commercial cultures do nothing to stop it. In Goa, casinos and energy- and water-hungry five-star hotels are emerging not as a result of government laxity, but to attract the affluent Briton as much as the Russian (TNN, 2012a, 2012b). While the previous chief minister of Goa flatly denied the presence of a 'Russian or Israeli or German' mafia (TNN, 2013), a crime culture seems to accompany the use of hard drinks (laced with drugs or not), attributed promiscuity of foreign tourists, increasing land ownership by foreigners – such as Russians (and the British) in Goa, and the fact that, in spite of vendors of food and their criticised lack of cleanliness, the beaches are more or less 'clean' (MSN News, 2012).

Even though many middle class Indian and foreign tourists find Goan beaches dirty, promotion through advertorial imagery won Goa the Pacific Asia Tourism Writers Association award for 'Best Beaches' in April 2013 at the ITB Berlin travel mart (Indiainfoline, 2013). Thus, official nationalism has, in conjunction with a more Western, world-oriented middle class and commercial nationalism extolled the cleanness of Goa, downplayed the crimes against tourists as well as nationals and promoted popular tourist cultures such as those that include cheap food and drink, reasonably cheap accommodation (when condominiums on a shared basis are considered), sun, sand, sea and sex, with popular music festivals like Sunburn Goa thrown into the bargain. Lately, yet another music event has been added to the list in Goa, and marketing through Facebook has taken the place of plain Internet advertising. In other words, the 'hip and upmarket' Goan experience is even now being advocated through the use of web marketing along with British tour operators' attempts to provide 'upmarket products to Britons' visiting Goa. Also, a solution to the problem of seasonality of tourism in Goa (the much advertised but repeatedly failing 'Goa in the Rains' campaign) has been found. TripAdvisor comment threads in 2013 indicated that the as-yet relatively neglected south Goa has won over the crowded north in terms of reasonable rates. However, tourist trips to south Goa from Panjim to visit the churches and monuments (another cultural world heritage complex), rather than actual stays, are more commonplace.

All this tourism promotion, however, has failed to bring to the notice of both foreign tourists and Indians the scarcity of potable water for tourists as well as locals. Many former Goan tourism experts/native commentators seem to have given up (Noronha, 2005). Meanwhile, even food supplies, along with bottled water, often have to be imported from the neighbouring states of Maharashtra and Karnataka, and the 'annexation of Goa', as leakage of tourism income continues, is complete, going by 'dependency theory', seen in a regional context. In this case, official and commercial nationalism had once again played up commercial aspects of tourism, with little gained in terms of conservation of heritage. However, what seems to be a product of Hindu 'hardline' thinking, but can rightfully be considered an 'alternative viewpoint', has been justified by some: floats brought out during the original three-day (now extended to five-day) Goa Carnival would represent the Hindu majority culture just as much as the minority (but often wrongly thought 'dominant') Christian culture.

At the time of writing, much is being made of the killing of Cecil the Lion by an American tourist in an African country, with frequent Facebook posts and online signature campaigns to end such slaughter, as well as to somehow stop airlines operating in these countries from carrying carcasses. Recently, the environment magazine *Down To Earth* (2015) has quoted IUCN as saying that the majority of tigers left in the world are in India (where, incidentally, a few years ago, an international tourist entered a tiger reserve without seeking permission from the authorities, was attacked by some miscreants, and brought attention to the misbehaviour of tourists that often leads to crimes against them). Between 2013 and 2015, at least five cases of molestation, rape or murder of foreign tourists have been reported by the media, with tourists from such diverse backgrounds as the UK, Australia, Austria, Germany and Japan, making it clear that no one nationality is to blame for any 'misbehaviour' that may be said to have precipitated the action, as some Indian television channels claim. Yet such misadventures originated in such seemingly safe places as the posh town of Chandigarh in Punjab and the largely rural Datia in Madhya Pradesh (in the latter, the tourist couple had set up camp in the wilderness known to be prone to marauders, without asking people/authorities about how 'safe' such an action could be). In 2014, a Facebook post reported that the number of rapes in India is not higher than in developed countries like the United States. A *Wall Street Journal* blog corroborated this fact even as early as 2013 (Wright, 2013), although these are per capita figures (and, in any case, not defensible). In fact, in the former a greater emphasis by the media in recent reportage has highlighted cases so that the authorities may take action. After coming to power, the Modi government instituted tourist police in such hitherto neglected places as Varanasi (Benares/Banaras) and stepped up their vigil in Goa, which was among the top four destinations for foreign tourists successively in 2012 and 2013, along with Delhi, Mumbai and Bengaluru (Bangalore) (Stark Associates, 2015b).

Wrong reporting like that done by Indian websites like HolidayIQ.com can mislead people. For instance, discussion by the author with locals and tourists revealed that Bengaluru is among the safest cities in India and is tourist-friendly as well (save for the manners of some auto-rickshaw drivers), but was put as among the 20 places in India that are not tourist friendly by this website. Strangely, Agra, Trivandrum (Thiruvananthapuram) and Srinagar (Jammu and Kashmir) were classed by the same website as the '20 most livable non-metro cities' in India on the basis of culture, and yet these three were also classified as among the '20 most tourist *unfriendly*' places. While Agra, on the basis of three visits by the author over the years, can certainly not be classified a very tourist friendly city – and fell from rank 8 to 9 of the top 10 foreign tourist destinations in India (Stark Tourism Associates, 2015b) and Srinagar may be classed as sometimes Indian tourist unfriendly (discussion with tourists over the years), the latter is quite foreign tourist friendly, and Trivandrum in Kerala is actually very tourist friendly.

The question then arises: what have the Rs 200 crore (roughly US$30.3 million at average 2015 rates) spent on the Incredible India campaign over the last decade (Economic Times, 2015a) achieved? Not much, going by the share of world international tourists received by India in this period. However, if the data is analysed for percentage increase in such tourists, the result is not bad: arrivals rose from 3.46 million in 2003 to 6.97 million in 2013, an increase of nearly 100% (Stark Tourism Associates, 2015a), and after the formation of the new government, with its focus on economic development and improving the image of India abroad, there was a 7.1% increase in international tourists (the highest in all these years, save the boost given by Delhi's hosting of the Commonwealth Games) to 7.46 million arrivals in 2014 (Business Standard, 2015). It seems then that official nationalism, and its dovetailing with commercial nationalism, was better understood by the image makeover and tourist and tourism friendly policy that the Modi regime achieved in one year.

Spiritual Heritage and Tourism in India

In 2015, India celebrated International Yoga Day on June 21, and in 2016 yoga was declared an 'intangible world heritage' by the United Nations Educational, Scientific and Cultural Organization. While Yoga Week has been celebrated every year in February since the early 1990s, with special events in Rishikesh in Uttarakhand, the value of yoga (understood as postures and exercises) versus its value as a spiritual philosophy for India as a whole came in for much discussion in 2015. Debates on television emphasised that, although yoga can be adjusted to any religion, it should not be foisted upon others, as the National Democratic Alliance government apparently tried to do. However, it had been claimed, and even established, by yoga gurus such as Swami Rama of the Himalayas, who lived later in life in the US and founded the Himalayan International Institute of Yoga Science and Philosophy, Pennsylvania, that yoga adjusts well to even Christianity (Arya, 1978). The most vociferous protest was lodged by some Muslims on television debates and in newspapers regarding the universality of yoga and its relevance for Islam, even as MSN News India reported how yoga was being practised in some places in Pakistan, which usually maintains that it is a strictly Islamic state.

While it is too early to assess what impact this will have on foreign tourist arrivals and experiences in India, what is certain is that inbound tourism, and even domestic tourism, has received a fillip. However, no research has been done on 'spirituality-and-yoga tourism marketing', the only PhD work on marketing of spirituality for tourism having being done, as far as is known, by a student from Pakistan, studying at Charles Darwin University in Australia (Haq, 2011). The only point that needs emphasis in this area is that yoga philosophy emphasises what people in the West have started calling 'slow food', which from the spiritual point of view is necessarily completely vegetarian (or even vegan, except for intake of milk), balanced in proteins and carbohydrates, and organic (Singh, 2012). Therefore, any marketing of yoga spirituality for tourism shall have to emphasise this aspect of living and how it dovetails with the philosophy of slowness that is typically Indian (and yogic, to boot), if a genuine experience has to be supplied to tourists. Commercialisation of this aspect is evident in the food business started by a yoga guru in India; commercial nationalism in this respect has gained many adherents and the positive side is that, even though a limited number of people stand to gain from this, it has brought attention to India, and within India, regarding sources of organic and wholesome food. Future marketing campaigns should find a foothold in this aspect of spirituality that is typically Indian.

Conclusion

In July 2015, the Government of India decided that it will come up with a national policy on tourism and make tourism an item in the concurrent list of administrative tasks, as against the state list, which hampers proper management. It has also decided to set up a national tourism advisory board, a national tourism authority and an inter-ministerial coordination committee on tourism (Businessworld, 2015). This, combined with the easing of visa rules and e-visas for more than 110 countries (TNN, 2015), is likely to boost tourism substantially. A recent government move to make spending on corporate social responsibility compulsory for large corporates (Economic Times, 2015b) may lead to more equitable tourism, given the August 2015 takeover of Kuoni Travels India by Thomas Cook India, which makes it fall within its ambit, along with other major tour operators. It has been shown in this chapter that officially supported commercial nationalism is not necessarily a sad story of selling tourism, but, when regulated and policed, is a viable means of earning income. Needed, however, is foresight on how to circumvent a kind of tourism that is deleterious and not sustainable in the medium term, both for the natural environment and for cultural and spiritual heritage. As the debate on spirituality and tourism shows, the essence should not be misinterpreted and laid open to commercial interests to cash in on without reference to a strategy that can sustain it.

It is apparent from this chapter that many of the advantages of commercial nationalism, supported by official nationalism and used as a ploy for tourism marketing, are lost when basic issues that affect the tourist-receiving population have not been sorted out or at least brought to a point where they can be reasonably managed. These include social happenings and situations like crime and rape, affordable housing (slum tourism in Indian cities like Mumbai has become quite popular and has been decried by nationalists as well as newspapers as 'indecent'), offending sexuality versus social norms, drug abuse and cleanliness. Much of the money spent on tourism marketing such as on the Incredible India campaign and through such nationalism as recalls India's ancient roots, going back more than 7,000 years to the Indus Valley/Harappan Civilisation, as well as values and knowledge symbolised by ancient universities like Nalanda in modern day Bihar, which was in existence even before the Buddha (before 680 BCE) and would now have been 3,000 years old (and has been recently reinstituted) comes to nought because of problems of social anomie outlined in this chapter. It can be concluded, therefore, that rhetoric fails where efficient administration and inculcation of values can bring better results in the medium to long term. At the same time, exhortations to value cultures as ancient as India's cannot be said to be out of place: every long journey begins with a small step.

References

Arya, U. (1978) Introduction. In O'Brien, J. (author) *Yoga and Christianity*. Honesdale, PA: Himalayan International Institute of Yoga Science and Philosophy.

Business Standard (2015) Foreign tourist arrivals to India rises 7.1% to 74.62 lakhs in 2014. See http://www.business-standard.com (accessed 7 February 2015).

Businessworld (2015) National tourism policy on the anvil: But is the industry ready for it? See www.new.businessworld.in/economic-policy-opinion-column-anvil-industry-ready-it#sthash.MCLcKzd64.dpbs (accessed 31 July 2015).

Chauhan, P. (2009) The problem of tourism growth management in the Himalayas: The case of Manali in the Kullu Valley. PhD thesis, Himachal Pradesh University, Shimla, India.

Down To Earth (2013) Tourism in Uttarakhand needs regulation. *Down To Earth*. See http://www.downtoearth.org.in/news (accessed 26 June 2015).

Down To Earth (2015) Only 3000 tigers left in the world, says IUCN. *Down To Earth*. Posted on www.facebook.com (accessed 3 August 2015).

Economic Times (2015a) Government spent Rs 200 crore on Incredible India campaign. *Economic Times*, 21 July 2015, p. 5.

Economic Times (2015b) CSR spend may grow over 4 times to $ 2.5 bn: Study. *Economic Times*. See www.economictimes.indiatimes.comon (accessed 15 February 2015).

Galbraith, J.K. (1967) *The New Industrial State*. London: Hamish Hamilton.

Government of Uttarakhand (2008) *Uttarakhand Tourism Master Plan 2007–22*. Dehradun, India: Uttarakhand Tourism Board/Govt of India/UNDP/UNWTO.

Gusain, R. (2015) Valley of Flowers in Uttarakhand set to reopen with new trekking route after damage wrought by 2013 floods. *Daily Mail Online*. See http://www.dailymail.co.uk/india (accessed 22 May 2015).

Haq, M.F. (2011) Marketing spirituality: A tourism perspective. PhD thesis. Charles Darwin University, Palmerston, Australia.

Holden, P. (1984) *Third World People and Tourism*. Bangkok: Ecumenical Coalition of Third World People.

Indiainfoline (2013) Goa tourism creates history at ITB Berlin. See www.indiainfoline.com/markets/news/goa-tourism-creates-history (accessed 20 April 2013).

Kala, C.P. (2004) *The Valley of Flowers: Myth and Reality*. Delhi: International Book House.

Kaur, J. (1985) *Himalayan Pilgrimages and the New Tourism*. New Delhi: Himalayan Books.

MSN News (2012) Goa tourism policy may lose its 'fun'. See news.in.msn.com/business/articles.aspx?cp-documentid=250062595 (accessed 20 April 2013).

Noronha, F. (2005) North Goa feels the tourist pinch. See www.peopleandplanet.net/?id=28011&section=47&topic=27 (accessed 20 April 2013).

Singh, S. (2012) Slow tourism and Indian culture: Philosophical and practical aspects. In S. Fullagar, K. Markwell and E. Wilson (eds) *Slow Tourism: Experiences and Mobilities* (pp. 214–226). Bristol: Channel View Publications.

Singh, S. (2015) The problem of assessing heritage value of the Valley of Flowers, India, and suggestions for a new form of ecotourism. *Tourism Spectrum* 1 (2), 31–37.

Singh, S. (2016) Devising an electronically-supported heritage conservation method for the Valley of Flowers in the Indian Himalayas. *Journal of Heritage Tourism* 11 (4), 411–419.

Smythe, F.S. (1938) *The Valley of Flowers*. London: Hodder and Stoughton.

Stark Tourism Associates (2015a) India's share of international tourist arrivals, 1997–2013. See www.starktourism.com/india_tourism.html (accessed 7 August 2015).

Stark Tourism Associates (2015b) Top Indian destinations, 2012–13. See www.starktourism.com/india_tourism.html (accessed 7 August 2015).

TNN (Times News Network) (2012a) More Russians than Britons in Goa. See articles.timesofindia.indiatimes.com>collection (accessed 12 January 2013).

TNN (2012b) 12 more five-star hotels eye Goa's tourism pie. See http://timesofindia.indiatimes.com/city/goa/12-more-five-star-hotels-eye-Goas-tourism-pie/articleshow/17148920.cms (accessed 14 August 2016).

TNN (2013) Drug mafia and police killed Scarlett: Mother. *The Times of India*, Lucknow, 28 February, p. 6.

TNN (2015) I-Day gift: E-tourist visa for 36 more countries. *The Times of India*, New Delhi, 11 August, p. 19.

White, L. (2009) Foster's lager: From local beer to global icon. *Marketing Intelligence and Planning* 27 (2), 177–190.

Wright, T. (2013) Are women safer in India or the US? See blogs.wsj.com/indiarealtime/2013/01/02/are-women-safer-in-india-or-the-u-s/ (accessed 27 August 2015).

13 From Risky Reality to Magical Realism: Narratives of Colombianness in Tourism Promotion

Juan Sanin

Introduction

In the last decade, nation branding initiatives and tourism campaigns have reinvented imaginaries of Colombianness by creating a series of commercial narratives that have been successfully 'sold' to local and foreign audiences. Internally, these campaigns have attempted to invent a collective national identity, beyond the regional diversity that characterises the country's population, and around a series of consumer-friendly and stereotypical attributes such as 'passion' and 'magic'. As in other countries, this new identity has been utilised by state agencies and private companies to mobilise Colombian citizens in favour of political, economic and cultural agendas (Sanín, 2015a). Externally, these campaigns have been used to change the ways in which the country is perceived around the world. It is well known that the main objective of nation branding is to position specific countries in the global market (Kaneva, 2011), a context where – as nation branding consultants argue – nations around the world become products on a supermarket shelf where they compete with each other to sell exports and attract tourists and investors (Anholt, 2002a, 2002b). In the case of tourism promotion, the process of branding the nation focuses on the construction of commercial narratives around specific aspects of a national culture that might become attractive to international travellers. In the specific case of Colombian tourism campaigns, these narratives have attempted to invent a new sense of Colombianness by representing the country as a magical place.

This chapter analyses the construction of commercial narratives for tourism promotion in Colombia by analysing the tourism campaigns used in the last decade to sell the nation as a tourist destination. It focuses on two tourism campaigns implemented by the Colombian government. The first campaign is 'Colombia: the only risk is wanting to stay', an initiative introduced in 2007 by Alvaro Uribe's government as part of the country brand 'Colombia is Passion'. The second is 'Colombia is magical realism', a campaign introduced in 2013 by Juan Manuel Santos' government as part of a new country brand called 'The answer is Colombia'.

In analysing these campaigns, this chapter builds on the notion of commercial nationalism. In the literature on cultural and media studies, the concept of commercial nationalism has been widely used to explain the use of nationalistic motifs by commercial entities as a strategy for increasing profits by appealing to national audiences (James, 1983; White, 2009a, 2009b). Recently, some scholars examining the phenomenon of nation branding have examined a different feature of commercial nationalism, involving the incorporation of marketing techniques by governments as a strategy for advancing their nationalistic agendas in the 'free market'. This twofold perspective is defined by Volčič and Andrejevic (2011: 613) as the 'double logic of commercial nationalism': 'On the one hand, commercial entities sell nationalism as a means of winning ratings and profits, while on the other, the state markets itself as a brand'. This double move is important because it takes the study of commercial nationalism beyond the corporate realm and brings the apparatus of the state into the discussion of nationalism and consumer culture.

Building on this understanding of commercial nationalism, this chapter analyses commercial narratives of Colombianness, with a focus on three interrelated phenomena associated with tourism promotion. The first phenomenon is the use of branding and marketing techniques as part of the state machinery of nation-making. In the Colombian case, this is manifested in the use of tourism campaigns to advance government policies, and in the subsequent interpretation of their success as an indicator of successful governance. The second phenomenon involves the combination of commercial and nationalistic motifs in the symbolic register used to represent the nation. This combination is evident in the commercialisation of Colombian geography, history and society through narratives that reinvent them as 'magical' in order to make them attractive for foreign consumption. The third phenomenon is related to the mediation of nation-ness through consumption practices. This is visible in the transformation of national culture into a series of commercial experiences that locals and tourists are invited to consume in order to have the experience of Colombianness. These three points reveal a shift in the construction of national identities, and explain some of the processes behind the commercial reinvention of Colombia into a 'magical' place.

This chapter involves three sections. The first section explains the history of this phenomenon by examining the internal politics of Colombia in the 1990s, a moment when the bad reputation of the country in the world made difficult the entrance of its economy into the global markets opened up by the rise of neoliberalism. This background is crucial for understanding the moment when the Colombian government, entrepreneurs and private companies decided to adopt marketing techniques to invent a new commercial image for the country. The second section of this chapter focuses on the tourism campaigns run by the Colombian government in the last decade, a period of time during which the governments of Alvaro Uribe and Juan Manuel Santos have implemented extensive promotional strategies to integrate the nation into the global market and sell Colombia as a tourist destination. The third section discusses the commercial narratives created by these initiatives and explains how both campaigns have been relatively successful in selling Colombia to the world, despite continuous internal problems and contradictions between the narratives presented in these campaigns and 'real' life in Colombia.

Background

The narratives used to sell Colombia to the world are being presented as new and spontaneous. As in other countries, Colombian nation-branding campaigns have been presented to the public as innovative initiatives led by the population. Similarly, tourism campaigns have been presented as advocacy projects that give locals the opportunity to show the best of their country and invite international visitors. These types of narratives, representative of the nation-branding paradigm, are populist strategies utilised by government agencies, private companies and tourism operators to mobilise citizens, and 'put them to work' in favour of their interests (Volčič & Andrejevic, 2011). In the particular case of Colombia, the apparent novelty and spontaneity of nation branding and tourism narratives elide what is, in fact, a long history of these campaigns. This history extends back to the 1990s and earlier, and is characterised by strategic attempts to sell Colombia in the global market.

In the 1990s, Colombia went through one of the most disastrous periods in the country's history. Decades of political corruption, social inequalities and the 'easy money' culture of drug dealing had degenerated into a complex internal conflict that involved drug cartels, guerrilla armies, paramilitary groups and the state. This conflict transformed cities and rural areas into battlefields where car bombs, massacres, shootings and kidnappings became part of everyday life. As a result of this situation, it was common to see in the media a series of narratives describing Colombia as one of the most dangerous places in the world.

In the late 1970s, when Colombian drug cartels started to control the drug market in the United States, Colombia became the topic of media coverage. For instance, the cover of *Time* magazine published in January 1979 depicted a marijuana leaf, a small plane and a boat, with the title 'The Colombian Connection', 'billions in pot & coke'. The cover story reported the consolidation of a 'billion dollar network' based in Colombia devoted to smuggling drugs into the US (Time, 1979). Although the report was labelled by local media as 'bad press', similar reports started to appear in local newspapers (Camacho, 1981). In the 1980s, the Colombian government tried to curtail drug smugglers, and in response the 'Medellin Cartel' declared war against the state and its institutions. This confrontation transformed cities such as Medellin, Bogota and Cali into battlefields. During the decade, this conflict worsened to the extent that in 1988, *Time* declared Medellin the most dangerous city in the world (Borrell, 1988).

As a result of this situation, governments around the world started to publish travel warnings advising their citizens against visiting the country. In the late 1980s, the State Department of the US started to publish these travel warnings. In one example, the White House warned that the Colombian government's 'massive crackdown on drug traffickers' would have negative consequences for the internal stability of the country. As a result, Americans were advised to postpone all trips – for recreational or business purposes – to the South American nation (The Day, 1989). A decade later, Colombia had been declared off-limits by the State Department. Travel warnings advised forgoing unnecessary travel to Colombia and pointed out different risks to which local and foreign citizens would be exposed. The warnings explained that the internal conflict had gone beyond remote and rural areas, and 'violence by narcotics-traffickers, guerrillas, paramilitary groups and other criminal elements' were affecting all parts of Colombia (Herald Tribune, 1999).

These narratives frustrated attempts to implement neoliberal agendas in the country, and in particular, plans to 'sell' Colombia as a tourist attraction. In the mid-1990s, when the government of Cesar Gaviria attempted to integrate the national economy into the global market, it became apparent that the negative reputation of the country was a significant obstacle. *The Monitor Report*, a study commissioned by the government, suggested that, in order to open the national economy, Colombia needed to change how it was perceived around the world (Porter, 1994). Since then, successive governments have tried to develop marketing strategies to create a new image. However, owing to the internal political situation and the continued negative reputation of the country, these initiatives have been understood to be a waste of money (Revista Dinero, 2005). The situation started to change in 2002, when Alvaro Uribe became president. Uribe was a politician whose stances were characterised by aggressive security policies and a populist discourse. In his presidential campaign, Uribe used the motto 'firm hands, big heart', thereby promising an end to the internal conflicts, and new prosperity for the population. After two years, Uribe's controversial policies started to show positive results in terms of internal security and economic growth.

The apparent success of Uribe's policies facilitated the emergence of an optimal environment for creating a series of new narratives for the country.

His populist discourse transformed him into a form of national idol. His aggressive security policies gave the middle and upper classes a sense of confidence, and his economic agenda allowed corporations to exploit national culture, heritage and resources. This combination of policies initiated a commercial revival of national identity, a sort of re-Colombianisation in which governmental organisations, private companies, the media and citizens shaped a new understanding of Colombianness. This was most evident and most easily exercised in the marketplace (Sanín, 2010a, 2010b), where new commercial narratives of Colombianness emerged as part of this commercial revival.

Colombian Tourism Campaigns: From Risk to Magical Realism

Between 2005 and 2015, the Colombian government implemented two nation-branding initiatives, each of them including a particular strategy for tourism promotion. In 2005, the country launched its first country brand, 'Colombia is passion'. In 2007, as part of this initiative, the government presented 'Colombia: the only risk is wanting to stay', a tourism campaign aimed at attracting international tourists. Seven years later, 'Colombia is passion' was replaced with a new country brand, 'The answer is Colombia', and in 2013 a new tourism campaign, 'Colombia is Magical Realism', was presented to international audiences. Each of these tourism campaigns has been framed within the broader context of the national brand, but has operated independently in terms of promotion.

'Colombia: the only risk is wanting to stay' was launched in November 2007 during the 17th World Tourism Organization General Assembly, hosted in Cartagena, Colombia. Government officials and celebrities were involved in the presentation of the campaign, which is a common manifestation of commercial nationalism. The campaign began with a speech in which the Colombian Minister for Commerce, Industry and Tourism celebrated the improvements achieved by the country in terms of security, economy and quality of life. Colombian celebrity and Grammy winner Fonseca then performed a concert for tourism delegates and journalists from 150 nations (Revista Dinero, 2007). The campaign was part of 'Colombia is passion', the 2005 nation branding initiative implemented by Alvaro Uribe's government in order to change the image of the country and gain acceptance in the global market.

The campaign strategy, created by a local branch of the multinational agency BBDO, included the publication of testimonials of foreigners who had migrated to Colombia. The main features of the campaign were nine commercials in which migrants described their experiences living in the country. The intention of these commercials was to de-emphasise risk – commonly associated with travelling to Colombia – in favour of opportunity, in order to attract international travellers. This strategy was clearly visible in the commercials, most of which promoted cities and regions cited in the travel warnings published by foreign governments advising citizens of the potential dangers of visiting Colombia.

According to Proexport, the organisation in charge of Colombian tourism promotion, the inclusion of foreigners' testimonials was intended to gain more credibility for the campaign. If the commercials had featured locals, they argued, no one would have believed the message (Revista Dinero, 2007). The videos starred Daniel Fliori, an Italian living in San Andrés isle; Johan Ilsen, a Belgian who decided to stay in Santa Marta after travelling the world; Salvo Basile, an Italian actor who has been living in Cartagena since 1968; Mele Valeria Walter, an Argentinian who had married a Colombian and lived in Medellin; Simone Gonzalez, a Brazilian who had married a Colombian and lived in Bogota; Leann Bravo, an American married to a Colombian who lived in Cali; Heike Van Gils, a Dutch woman and biology student who lived in Amazonas; Russell Coleman, a British man who managed a travel agency in the so-called 'Café Triangle' (departments of Caldas, Risaralda and Quindío); and Shaun Clohesy, an Australian in search of adventure who lived in Santander. The purpose of including these nine testimonials was to convince tourists that Colombia is not dangerous, despite travel warnings stating the opposite.

The nine commercials were part of a broader 'aggressive' strategy, as described by the Government. It included participation in international fairs; invitation of entrepreneurs, journalists and bloggers to visit Colombia; a web portal and social networking sites; and the broadcasting of these and other promotional pieces on television channels such as CNN, Fox and National Geographic (Revista Dinero, 2009a, 2009b).

By 2010, when Uribe's time in government was coming to an end, the campaign was considered a huge success. His aggressive security policies had been relatively successful in recovering control over territories and roads previously controlled by the insurgency, and this facilitated an increase in foreign tourists. The number of international visitors had more than doubled; Colombia had been included in more than 400 travel brochures, and some countries had eased their travel warnings. Tourism had become the third most important export sector, and Colombia was entering the global market (Buitrago & Santamaria, 2010; Santamaria, 2010).

At the end of 2010, Juan Manuel Santos – Uribe's pupil and previously Minister for Defence – became president. Despite having inherited Uribe's government, Santos' security and economic policies were very different. In 2012, his government initiated peace talks with the Fuerzas Armadas Revolucionarias de Colombia (FARC) – the most powerful guerrilla organisation in the country – and jettisoned the 'Democratic Security' policy he had enacted as Minister for Defence. The same year, the government replaced 'Colombia is Passion' with the new country brand, 'The answer is Colombia' (Revista Dinero, 2012), and the next year a new tourism campaign, 'Colombia is magical realism', was launched (El Espectador, 2013). The new campaign was created by the agency McCann Erickson, and was ostensibly based on a new concept in order to present the country from a new perspective. According to Proexport, the contemporary situation of the country had changed, and the previous country brand and its respective tourism campaign were no longer able to represent the country. While the campaign 'Colombia: the only risk is wanting to stay' tried to convince tourists that the country was not dangerous, the new campaign merely tried to persuade them to visit Colombia (Uribe, 2013).

The persuasion strategy was influenced by the work of Colombian Nobel Prize winner Gabriel Garcia Marquez, one of the central figures of the magical realism genre in the late 20th century. The campaign cited the notion of magical realism to create a narrative, by which travel experiences in Colombia are understood to be not only unique, but magical. This narrative was developed through four television commercials presenting couples who had travelled to different regions. It also included a series of online videos and other promotional pieces based on testimonials of the four couples and other foreign travellers. As in the previous campaign, these promotional pieces were part of an aggressive strategy that continued to include participation in international exhibitions; invitations to entrepreneurs, journalists and bloggers; and the broadcasting of commercials on international television channels. In addition, 'Colombia is magical realism' included a series of multisensorial strategies such as printed advertisements with coffee aromas, and Colombian foods tastings in airports and fairs (El Espectador, 2013; El Tiempo, 2014b).

By 2015, two years after 'Colombia is magical realism' was launched, the campaign was considered a success. For instance, in 2014 the country was visited by 4,192,742 international tourists, far exceeding government expectations (Ministerio de Comercio, 2015; Revista Dinero, 2015). Moreover, one of the television commercials was awarded a prize by the World Tourism Organization, during its 21st General Assembly held in Medellín in 2015 (El Tiempo, 2015). This prize, which constitutes one of the most recent recognitions of the campaign, was considered by the Colombian media to be the result of the combined efforts of government organisations and private companies to change the international image of the country.

Colombia's Tourism Narratives and Commercial Nationalism

Tourism narratives and governance

A main characteristic of commercial nationalism is the adoption of marketing techniques as part of the state's machineries of nation-making. This integration is evident when governments create official organisations in charge of advancing economic, political and cultural agendas through nation branding and tourism campaigns. Additionally, it is also seen when promotional and commercial indicators related to these campaigns are used to demonstrate successful governance in terms of policies and popularity. This dimension of commercial nationalism is visible in different initiatives implemented by the Colombian government in order to advance its agendas. In the particular case of Colombian tourism promotion, the combination of marketing campaigns has become part of the complex machineries of nation-making. Of particular interest in this phenomenon is that the policies linked to tourism campaigns are not only economic, but also related to internal security. Since the main problem for the Colombian tourism industry is an internal political conflict characterised by delinquency and insurgent activity across the national territory, tourism campaigns have been linked to and are supported by government policies to alleviate the situation.

The 'Colombia: the only risk is wanting to stay' campaign was, since its introduction and during all the years it operated, associated with the 'Democratic Security' policy. This was one of the first policies implemented by then President Alvaro Uribe, and became the centrepiece of his two consecutive governments. The objective of the policy was to recover, reinforce and guarantee security across all national territory, by implementing a series of strategies for strengthening government authority (Presidencia de la Republica, 2003). Strategies included the militarisation of urban and rural areas, relentless bombings and attacks upon insurgent camps, and in some cases the involvement of civilians in the conflict. These military procedures quickly began to achieve the security outcomes wanted by the government, and this result increased the acceptance of this military approach among the population.

When 'Colombia: the only risk is wanting to stay' was launched, it was directly related to and presented as part of the Democratic Security policy. The campaign was aimed at not only attracting international tourists, but also at demonstrating to the world the important security advances of the country (Revista Dinero, 2007). These connections between tourism promotion and government policies became common in the following years, in which advancements in tourism or security were presented as complementing each other, and in particular, as proof of increasing levels of successful governance (Revista Dinero, 2010). In 2010, when Uribe's term in government was coming to an end, Juan Manuel Santos gave a speech highlighting the progress of Colombia's tourism industry, in which he promised to triple the number of visitors to Colombia in the next four years. In his opinion, these tourism achievements were the result of the Democratic Security policy, and he emphasised the need to continue consolidating the policy in order to meet his promise (Presidencia de la Republica, 2010). However, when 'Colombia is magical realism' was then launched, the policies associated with the campaign had changed. President Santos not only dissolved the policy, but also began peace talks with the FARC, something which would have been unthinkable during Uribe's government. Subsequently, the new campaign started to be associated with the apparent state of safety and tranquillity achieved through the peace process. Since then, associations between peace talks and 'Colombia is magical realism' have become common in local media, and it is expected that, once the military conflict has been resolved through political agreements, Colombia will become a prominent world tourism destination.

Since both campaigns have been aligned with policies, their commercial achievements have been interpreted as indicators of government success. This is evidenced in media reports about increases in international visitors; broadcasting commercials and programmes about Colombia on foreign television channels; the inclusion of Colombia in international tourist guides; and social media statistics. These indicators are considered to be not only the result of marketing strategies, but also demonstrations of improvements in internal security (El Tiempo, 2014a). This situation has created a form of media populism (Sanín, 2015b), in which tourism promotion is not solely about attracting international visitors, but also involves the creation of a platform for improving popular opinion about governance on the basis of statistics, ratings, Facebook likes and tweets.

Despite improvements in the tourism industry, the successes of the policies associated with each campaign remain debatable, especially regarding internal security. The Democratic Security policy has been criticised and condemned for its excessive use of violence, not only against the insurgency, but also against civilians. In 2008, it was revealed that, in military actions implemented as part of this policy, members of the Colombian army murdered innocent civilians and reported them as insurgents killed during combat. It is now calculated that more than 3,000 innocent civilians were murdered by the Colombian army during the years that policy operated (Kraul, 2012). In addition, peace talks between the government and the FARC have not resolved the conflict. Even during periods of ceasefire, the peace process has included ongoing insurgent actions against civilians, members of the army and police. Moreover, the peace talks and their potential for the future stability of the country have been strongly criticised by sectors of the public and international organisations for allowing impunity for serious crimes (El Tiempo, 2014c).

Colombia the magical country

Another prominent characteristic of commercial nationalism is the commercialisation of the main elements of national identity – community, territory and past (Smith, 1991) – in order to make these elements attractive for local and foreign consumption. In the case of Colombia's tourism promotion, this commercialisation process has involved the manipulation of ideas associated with national society, geography and history using marketing techniques. This is evident in the subsequent reinvention of Colombian national identity through commercial narratives presenting Colombia as a magical country. Although 'Colombia: the only risk is wanting to stay' and 'Colombia is magical realism' built on different concepts and have been associated with different approaches to the internal conflict, there is a clear continuity in these narratives. In this regard, both campaigns have worked towards the reinvention of Colombia as a magical country. During the introduction of the first tourism campaign, Colombia was described as a magical and mysterious place. This narrative was subsequently reinforced throughout the years it operated and was consolidated in the campaign 'Colombia is magical realism'.

The introductory video of 'Colombia: the only risk is wanting to stay' used a poetic register that described the country through a fictional narrative:

> There is a place where people believed impossible wasn't a word. A place where the river wanted to be an ocean, and the ocean … joined the waterfall, the mountain, the snow peak, and even another ocean. A place where the past lives harmoniously with the future, and the word infinite is written in the colours of the beach, the mountains, the jungle and the sky. A place that challenges the imagination every single day. A place called Colombia …

The video concluded: 'you would realise that Colombia is not what you thought it was. A place where you will be surprised every day in a different way, where reality can be magical, where happiness is just around the corner'.

This lyrical register was characteristic of the nine promotional pieces in which migrants described their life in Colombia as not only safe, but magical. According to the commercials, in Amazonas there are 'trees that are too big to fit in the imagination'; Cartagena's 'walled city is … mysterious, magical, surrealistic, full of stories' and people 'live like in a movie'; San Andrés is a place 'where angels go on vacation'; Santa Marta's 'Parque Tayrona is hallucinating'; Santander is 'full of small mysteries'; 'The Café Triangle goes beyond the imagination'; and in Cali 'heaven has a subsidiary, where every place is a miracle'.

Although the campaign 'Colombia: the only risk is wanting to stay' was superseded because it was not able to represent the country anymore, the same narratives continued and were reinforced in 'Colombia is magical realism'. The online video that introduced the campaign to Colombians explained: 'We offer a diverse country, where you can live unique experiences as taken from a fiction novel; where reality is strengthened by the imagination and the magic'. A similar narrative was presented in the scripts of four television commercials, in which international visitors were invited to: 'Be enchanted by magical places, where taste and aroma reveal their secrets. And the exquisite pleasures of the Colombian coffee region await you'; to 'discover a magical city that inspired a Nobel Prize novelist'; and to 'discover a place where colours come to life, covering every street, every house, every space'. In addition to the magical connotations of the language, each of these commercials contained psychedelic and surrealist imagery.

For almost 10 years these two campaigns and their commercial narratives attempted to transform the image of Colombia in the world by depicting the country as a place beyond reality and as defying instrumental rationality. This apparently magical place, however, is probably unknown and strange for most Colombians, for whom the experience of living in Colombia is very different. Both campaigns and their foundational narratives were based on foreign perspectives and tailored for foreign audiences. Both campaigns were based on market research conducted in various countries, in which thousands of foreigners were surveyed about their expectations in relation to Colombia. Additionally, all the promotional materials star foreign actors with unique life experiences. Many of the promotional materials for the campaign 'Colombia: the only risk is wanting to stay' are based on the experiences of people who have travelled the world for business or adventure, most of them men. Other promotional material depicts the experiences of women who have emigrated to Colombia for reasons of romantic relationships or motherhood commitments. The commercials within 'Colombia is magical realism' are also based on foreign perspectives, and more precisely, on the experiences of couples who have visited specific places in Colombia. The advertisements demonstrate that the individual experiences of each person had influenced their perception of the country, and may not be representative of life in Colombia more broadly.

The experience of Colombianness

Studies on nation branding have argued that this marketing paradigm commoditises the nation by arbitrarily selecting and packaging features of national identity that might prove attractive for specific audiences, and selling these features in different forms (Aronczyk, 2007, 2013). This is indeed the case for the Colombian campaigns. The narratives of the campaigns 'Colombia: the only risk is wanting to stay' and 'Colombia is magical realism' have transformed Colombianness into a commercial experience, a form of immaterial commodity that is accessible for tourists through specific consumption rituals. These experiences have been created by strategically selecting specific features of Colombian national identity that have proven to be attractive for international publics. Once selected, these experiences have then been rearranged into fictional narratives that have redefined national history, geography and society.

The transformation of Colombianness into a commercial experience began with the first campaign. In the nine promotional videos of 'Colombia: the only risk is wanting to stay', different cities and regions were redefined according to the migrants' perspectives and were packaged as life experiences ready to be consumed by others. The same process can be seen in the touristic guides published as part of this campaign. In one of these guides, regions and places of national territory are represented using titles based on specific attractions. According to the titles: Amazonas is 'a heaven of nature and culture'; Cali is 'the salsa destination'; Cartagena is 'Colombia's destination for a history, culture, beach and sun'; Medellin is 'mountains of flowers and a modern city'; San Andrés is the 'ocean of seven colours and amazing corals'; and Santander is 'a modern destination for both adventure and colonial communities' (Proexport, 2011).

These titles work as slogans that frame each place around geographical, historical and social features, and redefine them as a series of consumption rituals that must be performed. It is as if each place had a hidden essence that visitors could uncover by eating a particular dish, photographing a landscape, visiting a cathedral, talking with a local or dancing salsa. The advertising suggests that all of these performances make it possible for tourists to have the experience of Colombianness.

In the case of 'Colombia is magical realism', the conversion of Colombianness into commercial experiences is also visible. In addition to the four television commercials, the campaign includes a series of online videos, in which tourists give testimonials of their experiences in various destinations. These experiences, however, are far from being authentic or spontaneous, because each of them was created according to the expectations of specific audiences. As part of the campaign, the Colombian government conducted market research to identify the expectations of diverse market segments, and the results informed the creation of these promotional materials (Uribe, 2013).

For instance, market research revealed that British, German and French tourists are interested in visiting places where they can watch birds and whales. Consequently, the campaign includes two testimonial videos presenting these activities as magical moments. In two of them, British and German tourists describe their experiences watching birds and whales, with one tourist describing his visit to Colombia as 'walking through a natural history collection'. The same research revealed that Argentinian tourists seek locales with sunshine and beaches. For them, there is a testimonial video of an Argentinian couple who are convinced, having visited San Andrés, that 'Neptuno, god of the seas lives in the isle'. Market research also suggested that, because Japanese tourists are icon seekers, they might be interested in Colombia's main cultural icon: coffee. Strategically, the television commercial about the coffee cultural landscape stars a Japanese couple, and in one of the testimonials Yuko Yoko Yama describes how she learnt to grow coffee as part of her experience in the coffee region. Narratives of Colombia as a magical country might appear unrealistic for locals, and the experiences presented in both campaigns are perhaps unknown for Colombian citizens.

Conclusion

This chapter has examined the narratives of Colombianness created in the last decade through tourism promotion. The Colombian case demonstrates how commercial technologies of nation branding are utilised to reinvent the image of countries whose economies have been affected by their negative international reputations. 'Colombia: the only risk is wanting to stay' and 'Colombia is magical realism' are clear examples of this process in the context of the tourism industry. Both campaigns have attempted to replace narratives found in the media and travel warnings representing Colombia as a dangerous country with a series of new images and stories according to which Colombia is not just safe, but also magical. Although these narratives build upon 'real' features of Colombia's national culture, they are constructed using a fictional tone that overlooks Colombian history and politics to emphasise the aesthetics of the country.

Although these new narratives have emerged from the tourism industry, their objective is not as simple as attracting tourists and increasing profits. Apart from their economic objectives, the campaigns have worked as a platform for advancing political agendas. As the chapter has shown, both campaigns have been utilised by two different governments to advance policies aimed at managing Colombia's internal conflict. 'Colombia: the only risk is wanting to stay' was used by Alvaro Uribe's government to promote the notorious Democratic Security policy, and 'Colombia is magical realism' has been used by Juan Manuel Santos as a positive background to present the peace talks between his government and the FARC. Subsequently, media reports about the commercial success of these campaigns have been interpreted and presented to the public as validation of these policies. Interestingly, these associations between tourism promotion and security policies suggests that – at least in Colombia – marketing and branding are being used as tools for governance.

Seen from the perspective of commercial nationalism, the narratives developed in the last decade to sell Colombia as a tourist destination make evident a series of interrelated shifts in the construction of the nation. These shifts start with the adoption of commercial technologies as part of the machineries of nation-making. This use of marketing techniques demonstrates the collaboration between governmental organisations and multinational advertising agencies to create commercial narratives aimed at selling the nation. As a result of this collaboration, the symbolic repertoire used to represent Colombian national identity has been transformed. The narratives presented by official maps and history museums are being replaced with tourist guides and television commercials presenting Colombia as a magical place. As part of this process, Colombianness is being transformed into a commercial experience. Everyday routines and picturesque scenes representative of Colombian ways of life are being transformed into immaterial commodities that must be consumed in order to uncover the hidden essence of the country.

However, the narratives of Colombianness created through tourism promotion do not correspond to the internal political situation and domestic perceptions of the country. What 'Colombia: the only risk is wanting to stay' and 'Colombia is magical realism' have created is a new version of Colombianness for foreign consumption. Local citizens exposed to these narratives, as I am, might perceive Colombia to be a foreign country, vastly different from the place where they spend their everyday lives. As a result, in order to have the experience of Colombianness offered in these narratives, local citizens might find themselves having to behave as foreigners in their own land.

References

Anholt, S. (2002a) Foreword. *Journal of Brand Management* 9 (4/5), 229–239.

Anholt, S. (2002b) Nation branding: A continuing theme. *Journal of Brand Management* 10 (1), 59–60.

Aronczyk, M. (2007) New and improved nations. Branding national identity. In C.J. Calhoun and R. Sennet (eds) *Practicing Culture*. New York: Routledge.

Aronczyk, M. (2013) *Branding the Nation: The Global Business of National Identity*. London: Oxford University Press.

Borrell, J. (1988) Colombia the most dangerous city. Welcome to Medellin, coke capital of the world. *Time Magazine*, 21 March, p. 131.

Buitrago, A. and Santamaria, R. (2010) OMT pone de nuevo a Colombia en el radar del turismo internacional. *El Tiempo*, 20 February. See http://www.eltiempo.com/archivo/documento/MAM-3326456

Camacho, A. (1981) *Droga, Corrupcion y Poder: Marihuana y Cocaina en la Sociedad Colombiana*. Colombia: Universidad del Valle.

El Espectador (2013) Nace campaña 'Colombia, el realismo mágico'. *El Espectador*, 10 April. See http://www.elespectador.com/noticias/politica/nace-campana-colombia-el-realismo-magico-articulo-415086 (accessed 25 October 2015).

El Tiempo (2014a) Campaña 'Colombia es realismo mágico', con alto impacto en el exterior. *El Tiempo*, 7 May. See http://www.eltiempo.com/archivo/documento/CMS-13949901 (accessed 25 October 2015).

El Tiempo (2014b) Colombia llegará con su 'realismo mágico' a España. *El Tiempo*, 16 January. See http://www.eltiempo.com/archivo/documento/CMS-13368918 (accessed 25 October 2015).

El Tiempo (2014c) Dura advertencia de la Corte Penal Internacional a Colombia. *El Tiempo*, 2 December. See http://www.eltiempo.com/politica/justicia/dura-advertencia-de-la-corte-penal-internacional-a-colombia/14920616 (accessed 25 October 2015).

El Tiempo (2015) El video 'Colombia es realismo mágico' ganó Premio de la OMT. *El Tiempo*, 16 September. See http://www.eltiempo.com/economia/sectores/colombia-es-realismo-magico-gano-premio-de-la-omt/16376030 (accessed 25 October 2015).

Herald Tribune (1999) Two countries put off limits. *Herald Tribune*, 24 April.

James, P. (1983) Australia in the corporate image: A new nationalism. *Arena* 63, 65–106.

Kaneva, N. (2011) Nation branding: Toward an agenda for critical research. *International Journal of Communication* 5, 117–141.

Kraul, C. (2012) In Colombia, 6 sentenced in 'false positives' death scheme. *Los Angeles Times*, 14 June. See http://articles.latimes.com/2012/jun/14/world/la-fg-colombia-false-positives-20120614 (accessed 25 October 2015).

Ministerio de Comercio, Industria y Turismo (2015) *Colombia superó la meta de 4 millones de turistas extranjeros en 2014*. See http://www.mincit.gov.co/publicaciones.php?id=32586 (accessed 25 October 2015).

Porter, M. (1994) *Informe Monitor*. Colombia: Presidencia de la Republica. See www.camaramed.org.co/docs/01informe_monitor_colombia.doc (accessed 25 October 2015).

Presidencia de la Republica (2003) *Política de Defensa y Seguridad Democrática*. Colombia: Presidencia de la Republica.

Presidencia de la Republica (2010) Palabras del Presidente Juan Manuel Santos en el Día Internacional del Turismo Colombia: Presidencia de la Republica. See http://wsp.presidencia.gov.co/Prensa/2010/Septiembre/Paginas/20100927_04.aspx (accessed 25 October 2015).

Proexport (2011) *Colombia. El Riesgo es que te quieras quedar*. Colombia: Ministerio de Industria, Comercio y Turismo.

Revista Dinero (2005) El corazon no es suficiente. *Revista Dinero*, 16 September. See http://www.dinero.com/agenda-publica/edicion-impresa/articulo/el-corazon-suficiente/29735 (accessed 25 October 2015).

Revista Dinero (2007) Colombia: El riesgo es que te quieras quedar. *Revista Dinero*, 27 November. See http://www.dinero.com/actualidad/noticias/articulo/colombia-riesgo-quieras-quedar/54915 (accessed 25 October 2015).

Revista Dinero (2009a) Colombia registra incremento de viajeros. *Revista Dinero*, 15 May. See http://www.dinero.com/negocios/articulo/colombia-registra-incremento-visitantes-extranjeros/78128 (accessed 25 October 2015).

Revista Dinero (2009b) Colombia, el riesgo es que te quieras quedar ahora en Fox y Natgeo. *Revista Dinero*, 13 August. See http://www.dinero.com/actualidad/noticias/articulo/colombia-riesgo-quieras-quedar-ahora-fox-natgeo/81848 (accessed 25 October 2015).

Revista Dinero (2010) Colombia vuelve al mapa del turismo mundial. *Revista Dinero*, 19 February. See http://www.dinero.com/edicion-impresa/negocios/articulo/colombia-vuelve-mapa-del-turismo-mundial/91272 (accessed 25 October 2015).

Revista Dinero (2012) Marca pais: Esta es la nueva image. *Dinero*, 7 September. See http://www.dinero.com/empresas/articulo/marca-pais-esta-nueva-imagen/159252 (accessed 25 October 2015).

Revista Dinero (2015) Colombia turística, a tono con tendencia mundial. *Revista Dinero*, 27 September. See http://www.dinero.com/pais/articulo/balance-campana-colombia-realismo-magico-procolombia/213949 (accessed 25 October 2015).

Sanín, J.D. (2010a) Libertad, Pasión y Orden. Reconfiguración de la simbología nacional a través del Mercado. In G. Vanegas (ed.) *Preámbulo: Ejemplos empíricos de identidad nacional de baja intensidad en Cundinamarca y Boyacá* (pp. 103–150). Bogotá: Ministerio de Cultura, Presidencia de la República.

Sanín, J.D. (2010b) Made in Colombia. La construccion de la colombianidad a través del mercado. *Revista Colombiana de Antropología* 46 (1), 27–61.

Sanín, J.D. (2015a) Colombia was Passion: Commercial nationalism and the reinvention of Colombianness. In Z. Volčič and M. Andrejevic (eds) *Commercial Nationalism. Selling the Nation and Nationalizing the Sell*. Basingstoke: Palgrave.

Sanín, J.D. (2015b) There's nothing like Australia: From social advocacy to social media populism. *Platform: Journal of Media and Communication* 7 (1), 23–31.

Santamaria, R. (2010) Positivo balance de la campaña el riesgo es que te quieras quedar. *El Tiempo*, 3 January. See http://www.eltiempo.com/archivo/documento/MAM-3781657 (accessed 25 October 2015).

Smith, A.D. (1991) *National Identity*. Reno, NV: University of Nevada Press.

The Day (1989) Colombian travel warning issued. *The Day*, 28 August.

Time (1979) The Colombian connection. How a billion-dollar network smuggles pot and coke into the U.S. *Time*, 29 January, p. 113.

Uribe, J. (2013) Así nació la idea de unir turismo y realismo mágico. *El Tiempo*, 14 April. See http://www.eltiempo.com/archivo/documento/CMS-12740926 (accessed 25 October 2015).

Volčič, Z. and Andrejevic, M. (2011) Nation branding in the era of commercial nationalism. *International Journal of Communication* 5, 598–618.

White, L. (2009a) Foster's lager: From local beer to global icon. *Marketing Intelligence and Planning* 27 (2), 177–190.

White, L. (2009b) The Man from Snowy River: Australia's bush legend and commercial nationalism. *Tourism Review International* 13, 139–146.

Part 3

Festivals, Events and National Identity

14 'Imagine Ben Hur in Formula One': An Analysis of the National Gallop in Hungary

Tamara Rátz and Anna Irimiás

Introduction

The National Gallop is a horse race held in Budapest, Hungary that was created in 2008 with the aim of reviving the country's ancient horse riding traditions in the form of a modern, urban cultural event. As White (2011) has pointed out, horses are powerful symbols of freedom and independence, concepts strongly related also to the tourism and leisure industries, and are widely used in tourism marketing by several countries. As the chapter will demonstrate, horses have played an important role both in Hungarian history and in the nation's tourist image: historically, Hungarians were renowned for their equestrian expertise, traditional horsemanship skills are regularly exhibited in the programme of organised tours to rural areas and the country offers favourable conditions for equine tourism. However, the use of horse-riding heritage in national identity building has been an ambiguous issue for decades. From the 19th century, the stereotypical image of Hungarians, especially in the German-speaking world, included gallant hussars and brave rural horsemen who were able to perform amazing tricks with their horses (Watzatka, 2014). This imagery was very actively used both in tourist product development and in national marketing until the 1990s; since then it has been perceived as partly outdated, but also partly inescapable, an essential characteristic of being Hungarian and a unique heritage resource in the centre of Europe (Jenes, 2009). Owing to the circumstances of its creation, the National Gallop was seen – especially in the first years of its existence – as a highly controversial event. On the one hand, it was the celebration of national horsemanship traditions, and on the other hand, the commercialised reinterpretation of national heritage was celebrated. In this chapter, after explaining the significance of horsemanship and horses in

Hungarian national identity, we make an attempt to analyse the character-istics and the perceptions of the event and its transformation between 2008 and 2015.

National Identity, Commercial Nationalism and Tourism

The notions of tourism and national identity are interrelated in many ways: the development of heritage attraction can contribute to the creation and maintenance of national identity (Butler *et al.*, 2014), and visiting such sites may affect tourists' national sentiments (Edensor, 1997). Tourism can play a significant role in the process of identity building, representing one possible way in which a country can project a particular self-image (Light, 2001). Consequently, tourism has considerable ideological importance for the former socialist states of Central and Eastern Europe that are seeking to affirm distinctly post-socialist identities. In the process of constructing a new post-socialist identity, both domestically and internationally, reaching back to ancient traditions is one possible and, for traditionalist social groups, highly attractive alternative. However, the creation of a national brand that provides narratives for international and domestic consumption and reflects the coun-try's history, culture and ethnicity without falling into the trap of chauvin-ism is a major challenge, as demonstrated by Volcic and Andrejevic (2011).

Official nationalism, that is, the promotion of a sense of national identity by using national themes, symbols and discourses, both internally and exter-nally, has served as a means of furthering national interests and promoting a sense of loyalty and belonging throughout the history of the nation-state. However, partly as a consequence of economic globalisation, private compa-nies have also started to discover the market advantages of building brands based on national messages, resulting in the concept of commercial national-ism. Commercial nationalism, as defined by White (2009a: 178), is 'a con-tinuation and extension of the overall theme, style and symbols of official nationalism as generated by the nation-state'. The messages conveyed by official and commercial nationalism may be slightly different in terms of their visual or textual representation, but are not contradictory, since it is in the interests of the private companies to draw on the patterns established by official bodies or depicted in popular stories (White, 2009b).

Cultural events, festivals and hallmark sports events can contribute to the reinvention of national identity, and can promote the culture-led regen-eration of urban places when rooted in unique, place-based factors (Della Lucia & Franch, 2014). Such events may be developed as representatives of *a priori* existing ideas of a nation, but may also become sites of the performa-tive construction of the concept. Although the organisers of events with a deliberately national identity-strengthening objective often need to face the criticism of inauthenticity, as Graml (2004) demonstrated in his analysis of Salzburg's *The Sound of Music* heritage, in the context of cultural globalisation, supposedly inauthentic practices can authenticate experiences of identity and belonging.

The Role of Horses and Horse Riding in Hungarian National Identity

The historical homeland of Hungarians is the Carpathian Basin. The conquest of the Carpathian Basin by the wandering Magyar tribes, a Finno-Ugrian nomadic pastoral people expert in horse breeding, dates back to the closing years of the 9th century (Sugar *et al.*, 1994). The legendary conquest on horseback of the fertile lands of the Carpathian Basin originated the myth of the seven founding tribes led by Árpád, the predecessor of the only Hungarian royal dynasty (the House of Árpád ruled the country until 1301). Today, the tribal chiefs are represented in monumental equestrian statues in the centre of Heroes' Square, the emblematic site of the National Gallop, in Budapest. Although the nomadic tribes settled down in the region, Hungarian warriors continued their military attacks and booty-producing raids into the Carolingian and Byzantine empires (Makkai, 1994). Their military technique, based on fast-moving light cavalry that could shoot arrows while riding their horses backwards, was unknown in the West and resulted in many victories in the battlefield. As an early medieval prayer said: 'Our Lord, save us from the arrows of the Hungarians!' (Makkai, 1994: 14). The raids finally came to an end in 955 when the Hungarian army suffered a devastating defeat by the Germans led by Otto I near Augsburg. The Battle of Lechfeld, as it was called throughout the Middle Ages, was considered an epoch-making event in Central Europe because it reinforced the Holy Roman Empire and convinced the semi-nomadic Hungarian tribes to definitely settle down and convert to Christianity. The conquest's history imbued with legendary warriors holds a crucial position in the development of Hungarian national identity (Türk, 2012). At the increasingly frequent battle re-enactments this military style has been revoked and, among traditionalist groups, archery on horseback has become both a popular sports activity and a tourist attraction (Povedák, 2014). Hungarian consciousness rooted in the myth of free and independent warriors was evoked several centuries later in the Reform Age when the country was still under the domination of the Habsburg Empire (Mikos, 2006).

The Reform Age (1825–1848) was one of the most vibrant and progressive periods of Hungarian history. Count István Széchenyi (1791–1860), remembered as 'the Greatest Hungarian' for his outstanding achievements in modernising the country, was the emblematic figure of that era (Kovács Kiss, 1992). Count Széchenyi was a wealthy nobleman who travelled widely around Europe, especially to France and England, where he encountered progressive ideas. He returned to Hungary eager to change the conservative and feudalistic country into a modern and culturally leading state. His great accomplishments, besides the foundation of the Hungarian Academy of Sciences and the initiation of the first permanent stone bridge over the river Danube (today called Széchenyi Chain Bridge in his honour), included the introduction of the modern English practices of horse-racing and horse-breeding, summarising his views on the subject in his pamphlet *On Horses* (Széchenyi, 1828). His ideas quickly became popular among the aristocracy, and led to such achievements as the victory of the stallion Kisbér at the Epsom Derby in 1876 and the breeding of the undefeatable mare Kincsem, a legendary phenomenon in Hungarian equine history. Maintaining a stunning record, Kincsem was the winner of 54 races between 1876 and 1879, making her the most successful thoroughbred race horse ever (Justice, 2012). Her legendary status, and the place of horses in Hungarian national identity in general, is illustrated by the fact that a movie currently being shot depicting Kincsem's life has received a 2.2 billion HUF (7 million euro) grant from the Hungarian National Film Fund, making it the most expensive Hungarian film production ever (Varga, 2015). The National Equestrian Programme, aiming to revive traditional Hungarian horsemanship, is also named after her (KIM, 2012).

Tourism promotional materials repeatedly affirm that 'Hungarians are equestrian people' (HNTO, 2015), although the estimates suggest that only about 5% of the population ride more or less regularly (Czauner, 2009; there is no reliable data available on the number of riders). The gallop and trot speed races at the Kincsem Park racetrack are generally followed by a small group of passionate fans. However, equestrian programmes showing the performances of skilled herdsmen at the Hortobágy *puszta*, a United Nations Educational, Scientific and Cultural Organization World Heritage site, and at farms located closer to the country's major tourist destinations, Budapest or Lake Balaton, have been popular among tourists for presenting a fairly romanticised image of pastoral life (Béki et al., 2013), and the country provides ideal terrain for long, uninterrupted trail rides.

The significance of horses and horse riding in Hungarian historic identity formation is also reflected by the figure of the gallant hussar (light cavalryman), a central icon in the nation's cultural memory. The first written testimonies of hussars date back to 1481 when King Matthias Corvinus, in his correspondence with the King of Naples, mentioned them, 'equites levis armaturae, quos husarones apellamus' ('the light cavalry called hussars'; Nagy, 2004). Hussars were fighting against the Ottoman Empire in the 16th century, in the Napoleonic wars (1803–1815), in the Hungarian revolution and war of independence (1848–1849), but also in the American Civil War (1861–1865) and the two World Wars (1914–1918, 1939–1945). The hussars' fame was rooted in the idea of extremely brave and fast soldiers with noble sentiments and high moral standards. Hussars, in addition, were distinguished from the other cavalry troops by their colourful uniform, richly decorated with braid and gold trim, and for the hussar shako with golden chains and braiding. At the National Gallop, every rider wears a historically authentic gold-braided hussar uniform provided by the organisers, in order to reflect the traditionalist aspect of the event (personal interview, 2015).

The myth of the gallant hussars deeply influenced both Hungarian folk and high cultures (Gráfik, 2004). Hussars are protagonists of many children's tales and legends, and hussar-shaped gingerbread is still sold at traditional fairs. The most famous Hungarian poet, Sándor Petőfi, dedicated his classic epic poem to a hussar ('János vitéz' – 'John the Valiant'), later adapted to the stage as a musical play with a strong nationalist undercurrent: both versions are still highly popular today. Emblematic figures in Hungarian history are often portrayed by artists on horseback in hussar uniform. Even in chess the knight in Hungarian is called 'hussar'. Thus it may be concluded that the hussars, in several ways, have been embedded in the formation of Hungarian cultural heritage and have contributed to the imaginative construction of national identity.

Currently, the country's equestrian heritage is manifested in various ways: while horse riding as an outdoor leisure activity and betting at the races have no hidden cultural meaning, many forms of traditional horsemanship, such as mounted archery, (quasi-)authentic re-enactments of military tournaments and long-distance horseback expeditions, belong exclusively to the cultural terrain of the nationalist–conservative circles. From a tourism point of view, the range of services offered to visitors in Hungary includes riding lessons, therapeutic riding, cross-country tours, harness racing, horse carriage tours, driving lessons and horse shows (Michalkó, 2002).

Methodology

In order to analyse the perceived image of the National Gallop as well as the event's transformation between 2008 and 2015, qualitative research methods were used: interviews with the organisers and thematic analysis of the event's media coverage. Altogether 163 news items were examined, collected from the following types of printed and online media sources: two tabloids (11 items), two conservative daily and weekly newspapers (101), two liberal daily and weekly newspapers (20) and two trade magazines (31). Within the first three categories, the media sources with the highest readership were selected (based on the data of the Hungarian Audit Bureau of Circulation), while in the last group the country's two established tourism trade magazines and their online versions were analysed. Although the same number of publications was selected for examination in the tabloid, conservative and liberal categories, the disproportionately high ratio of conservative news items is striking. This might be explained by the emotional state of confusion experienced among the nationalist–conservative circles during the first years of the Gallop's history, and the consequently increased frequency of the topic's media coverage.

The NVivo programme was used to perform an inductive or data-driven thematic analysis of the collected news items. The process involved the following phases: familiarisation with the collected data; generation of initial codes; a search for themes among codes; review of themes; definition and naming themes; and a search for structures between the themes. Conceptual mapping was used to provide an overview of the major themes that helped us understand the perception of the event by different audiences (Grbich, 2013).

The Creation, Features and Evolution of the National Gallop

The National Gallop was first organised in 2008, with the clear aim of establishing a new tradition of celebrating Hungarian horsemanship and instilling pride among residents in a well-known theme of Hungarian culture. The event was designed to honour the glorious aspects of Hungarian history related to horses and horse riders, using the stylised figure of a galloping hussar as its logo. By design, the National Gallop is a three day festival with themed horse races, award ceremonies and various entertainment programmes held in Heroes' Square, one of the best known and most spectacular locations in Budapest. The event was described throughout as 'Ben Hur meets Formula 1' (National Gallop, 2011), 'the grandest of festivals on the grandest of scales … a monumental reinvention of history and tradition' (National Gallop, 2014) or, in the words of Vilmos Lázár, President of National Gallop and President of Hungarian Equestrian Federation, 'the equestrian celebration of our national holidays that brings together not only generations, but the whole country and nation' (National Gallop, 2015a). Based on these narratives, it should have gained immediate popularity among the Hungarian society's traditionalist circles, since it clearly intended to highlight national symbols and values and convey them to wide audiences.

However, the event was proposed by Péter Geszti, a former rapper, musician, X Factor jury member, copywriter and all-round media personality: someone who seemed to represent everything that was urban, multicultural and trendy, and who embodied the exact opposite of the values assumed by the conservative crowd. Initially, both the idea of organising a historic horse race right in the centre of Budapest as well his personal involvement raised doubts, among liberals and conservatives alike, about the real intention behind the festival, the meaning of the event, and its possible quality and authenticity. Although Geszti's earlier 'bridge-building' projects also demonstrated that he was unwilling to accept the 'warlike ideology that divided the world between left-wing and right-wing' (Trencsényi, 2014) in Hungarian cultural politics, and he repeatedly claimed that the Gallop was to be a politically neutral celebration of the nation's equestrian heritage, the traditionalist circles' preconceptions remained strong during the first few years of the event. Only when the world champion horse carriage drivers (Vilmos and Zoltán Lázár) took over ownership of the festival in 2011, did the original reluctance start to disappear, owing to the new owners' well recognised equestrian expertise and established social position in conservative circles.

The selection of Heroes' Square as the event's location was equally welcomed and opposed by the public. The square is rich in historic symbolism and encapsulates the essence of Hungarian identity, from the larger-than-life central sculpture group of the conquering Magyar chieftains on horseback through the obelisk topped by Archangel Gabriel (who offered the crown to the first Hungarian king, St Stephen, in his dream) to the pantheon of kings and revolutionary leaders in the background with allegorical sculptures of War and Peace driving horse-carriages, and the memorial of the unknown soldier. According to the website of the event, Heroes' Square is:

> the inspiration for the National Gallop, when this stunning symbol of the nation is transformed into a racetrack and modern-day heroes on horseback will gallop around it, grandstands will encircle it, and the crowds will encounter and enjoy every aspect of Hungarian history around the square and on impressive Andrássy Avenue. (National Gallop, 2015b)

Also from a promotional point of view, the visually stunning Heroes' Square was an optimal location for an event that aimed to attract both large numbers of spectators and major media interest, as illustrated by the dramatic photos taken during the festival. However, organising the race in an urban setting – and not even in any urban setting, but right in the centre of the notoriously liberal capital city – was seen as the appropriation of traditional heritage values by many conservatives, while the place's status as a highly popular tourist attraction raised concerns about the commercialisation of Hungarian culture. Furthermore, the square in its original form was unsuitable for the race, so it had to be significantly transformed by constructing a racetrack with 6,200 square metres of special equine-friendly sand to provide a safe environment for horses and riders. Despite the professional design of the track, several accidents of horses and riders have happened during the history of the festival, each time resulting in additional security measures.

The National Gallop is based on three pillars: the horses, the riders and the participating settlements. In accordance with its goal to become a celebration of Hungarian horsemanship, the organisers have encouraged from the beginning the involvement of settlements located within the wider Hungarian cultural community in the Carpathian Basin, outside the country's political borders, which led to the organisation of local Gallops in Romania (from 2011), Serbia (from 2013) and Slovakia (2015). In 2015, 72 riders representing Hungarian towns and villages entered the race in Budapest, with almost 300 competitors riding in the 18 qualifying races held in Hungary and in the neighbouring countries. Since the first event held in 2008, the National Gallop has been organised annually around a specific theme created in cooperation with experts from different fields, although the hussar motive remains a central element each year; for example, in 2014 the First World War was commemorated in collaboration with the Museum of Military History, but the festival honoured the memory of sergeant László Skultéty (1738–1831), the longest serving hussar in Hungarian military history. Although the Gallop does not have a permanent organising body, owners Vilmos and Zoltán Lázár coordinate the programme and exercise professional control over the various elements. In order to ensure that all participants have equal chances, only non-professional riders of Hungarian origin can enter the race, and certain horse breeds (Argentine polo ponies, Akhal-Teke, thoroughbreds, half-bred competition horses and those of unknown origin) have been excluded since 2011. The message conveyed by these rules recalls the fairytale character of the youngest son who, despite all odds, overcomes every obstacle: a classic figure commonly seen as a metaphor of being Hungarian, surviving for a thousand years in a small, isolated country, surrounded by alien nations (Fényes, 1842).

Besides the change of rules concerning participation, the programme of the National Gallop has also been modified and expanded throughout the history of the festival. Although a celebrity charity race, owing to its evident capacity to attract the media's attention, various spectacular activities have been added, such as mock battles on horseback, stunt performances, mounted archery, a ladies' race, show jumping, a foal championship, an international race with invited representatives of countries playing an important role in Hungary's foreign policy, and a chariot race. Since the existing race carriages were not suited for the Heroes' Square racetrack, a new type of chariot had to be built, a modern cross between the Scythian war wagons and the Roman race chariots, with a vintage look but the latest technology inside, bringing to the audience's mind both the contemporary Formula 1 Grand Prix and the classic chariot race of the *Ben Hur* movies (National Gallop, 2011).

The Perceived Image of the National Gallop as Reflected by its Media Coverage

The figures below represent the main themes identified in the narratives of the analysed news items concerning the National Gallop. We decided not to include a map for the tourism trade articles, since they tended to focus predominantly on the practical aspects of the event: the show elements, the schedule of the festival and its accessibility. Slightly surprisingly, there is very little information available about the role of the event in Hungarian tourism; according to Tapolcsányi and Tőzsér (2013), the number of spectators has been growing steadily and surpassed 200,000 by 2012, but it is only assumed that the majority are Hungarians and that the Gallop's impact on either incoming tourism or on Budapest's destination image has been rather limited.

Although several themes, such as the race, tradition or information, recur in all three categories (tabloid, liberal, conservative), their significance differs, and each category features certain distinctive themes as well. The main portrayal of the event follows a relatively homogenous pattern in all categories, evidently based on the initial description (with significantly different comments coming from the two sides of the political platform): according to this, the National Gallop is a monumental horse race, based on Hungarian traditions, with a historic atmosphere, a cultural event that preserves national heritage and creates new heritage at the same time. Neither the tabloids nor the trade press questioned the cultural value or the national identity-strengthening role of the festival, and although the liberal media discussed, to some extent, the political context in which the Gallop was created, major criticism only came from the conservative publications.

Besides providing information on the event's date, accessibility by various transportation means and admission, the analysed tabloids highlighted two key themes distinctive to this category: the celebrity world and the danger associated with the race (see Figure 14.1). Although the risks associated with the race and the accidents that happened during the years were mentioned in all three categories, the tabloids' treatment of danger and accidents was distinctive in their dramatic phrasing and their more elaborate discussion of the incidents. As for the theme of the celebrity world, Péter Geszti's original idea of including a charity race with celebrity riders as a public relations stunt to attract the media's attention to the newly established festival proved to be justified: both the results of the charity race and the participating riders' concurrent personal stories were reported each year. Moreover, the tabloids also covered the appearance of well-known media and business personalities among the audience, and paid special attention to their style (particularly the hats, since many celebrities found the Gallop an appropriate event to introduce one further tradition, that of the Royal Ascot dress code).

Although famous and popular riders were also mentioned in the liberal media (see Figure 14.2), discussion was mostly limited to their results achieved in the competition and the charities that they represented. The overall image represented by the analysed liberal media sources seems to reflect an effort to offer a relatively neutral, informative coverage of the National Gallop, focusing mainly on various aspects of the race and providing practical information on the activities and programmes of the festival, as well as its place and

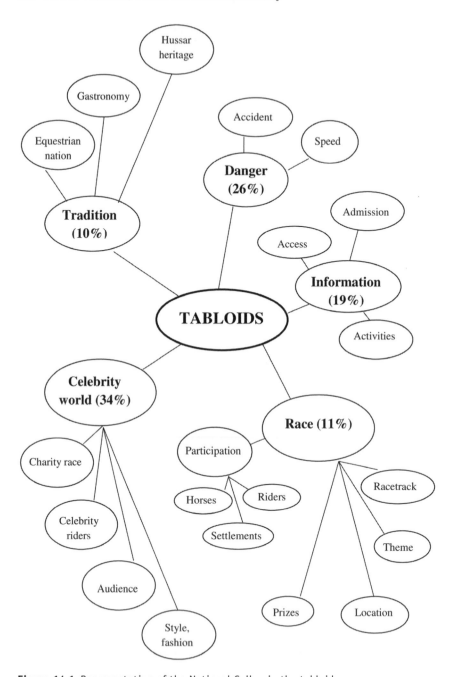

Figure 14.1 Representation of the National Gallop in the tabloids

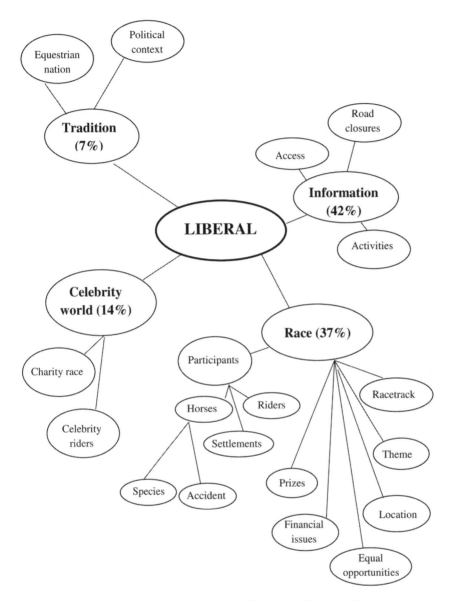

Figure 14.2 Representation of the National Gallop in the liberal media

schedule. The theme of tradition appeared mostly in association with the Gallop's description, highlighting its foundation on the consensual image of Hungarians as an equestrian nation, but also situating the idea in a political context and questioning, albeit moderately, its relevance in Budapest in 2015. Compared with the tabloids, a more professional approach is also demonstrated by the emergence of the themes of equal opportunities provided to the participants by the organisers, and that of horse breeds allowed to join the competition (since these Hungarian breeds, in case of good performance, may have increased value in the international market).

Owing to the tradition- and identity-related issues discussed earlier, the analysis of the conservative media sources (see Figure 14.3) resulted in the most interesting and complex overall picture, adding two completely new themes: judgement (almost exclusively from the 2008–2011 period, i.e. before the equestrian expert conservative Lázár brothers took over the festival) and equestrian life (especially in recent years). The initial idea of the Gallop was met mainly with rejection on the conservative side, their attitude often being based on prejudices.

In Hungary, the urban elite has perceived, for a long time, everything traditional and typically Hungarian as outdated and downright embarrassing, especially internationally. The traditions have become objects of derision, Hungarian customs were identified with provincialism and the use of national symbols was considered a revival of fascism. The conservative response to this attitude, not surprisingly, is defiant resistance, 'shooting arrows backwards' (Borókai, 2010).

However, from a traditionalist point of view, it was rather difficult to deliberately reject an event that was based on the exact values that the conservative circles claimed to revere and protect. This emotional and cognitive perplexity led to declarations such as:

> We know that on the so-called national side there are strong opinions according to which the liberal world's national tradition-related experiments can only be false and destructive (and the founder Péter Geszti is clearly pigeonholed as one of them), therefore should be rejected. However, we have seen that the National Gallop – although needing improvement – is a praiseworthy adaptation, a significant community organizing force, and a novel approach to the Hungarian hussar cavalry and traditions. (Borókai, 2010)

The negative attitudes and prejudices were often also modified by personal and family experiences and by the recognition that, unless traditionalists are also able to create a modern culture that reflects the spirit of the age yet remains uniquely Hungarian, the heritage values that they wish to preserve will be dissolved in a homogeneous global consumer society and young Hungarians will be completely alienated from tradition. Thus, it was gradually accepted that the National Gallop was an opportunity for traditionalists to reconsider their automatically negative, suspicious attitude to any initiative originated from the liberal platform of the Hungarian cultural scene and rethink their approach related to the optimal ways of heritage revival. The transition from downright rejection to approval and respect was not an easy one.

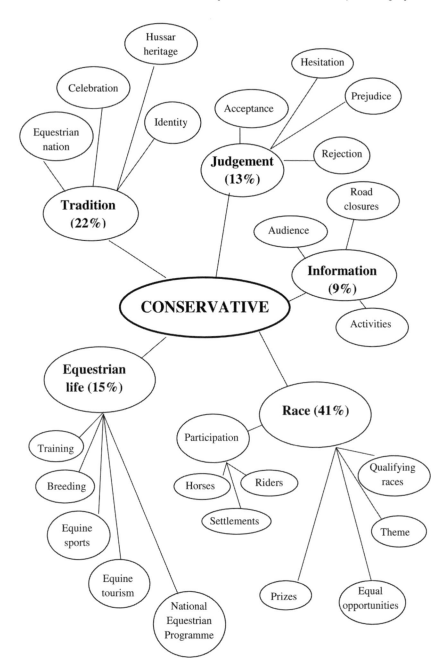

Figure 14.3 Representation of the National Gallop in the conservative media

The theme of equestrian life, particularly that of training and breeding, that is, the preparation for participation in the National Gallop and the associated potential benefits, appeared markedly in recent years, mainly owing to the ownership change and the consequently increasing involvement of professional equestrian associations and groups. Since the Hungarian equestrian community started to identify with Gallop as a celebration of their activities and traditions, its perception gradually changed, and it slowly gained acceptance as an 'outstanding national event' (KIM, 2012: 44).

Conclusions

The analysis of the National Gallop's media coverage confirmed that the narratives presented by the mass media may significantly affect an event's ability to contribute to national identity construction and reinforcement. In the case of the National Gallop, acknowledged national themes, symbols and narratives were successfully used in a commercial setting to create a festival that is able to attract large numbers of visitors. Although destination image development was also one of the key objectives of the event from the beginning, it cannot be ascertained whether it has helped international spectators develop a deeper understanding of Hungarian culture and national identity. However, the Gallop's significance has reached beyond the practical brand-enhancing and visitation-increasing objectives, by attempting to symbolically build a bridge over the political and cultural gap dividing liberals and conservatives in Hungary.

During its history, the image of the National Gallop portrayed by the media has undergone a major transformation. In the first stage of its development, a marked political division of opinions resulted in strong criticism expressed by the conservative side with regard to the practice of commercial nationalism reflected in the event, accusing the organisers of 'recycling' national symbols. In the second stage, owing to the gradually improving relationship between the Gallop and the Hungarian equestrian community, a professional discourse started to override the categorical criticism of the event, and first tolerance, then acceptance, replaced rejection. In the third stage, as the festival's popularity grew, a general consensus started to formulate about the National Gallop's status as a real celebration of Hungarian horsemanship and its ability to represent national identity values. From a practical point of view, it is also acknowledged by the equestrian community that the event has significantly contributed to the increasing popularity of horse riding and other equestrian activities, despite its urban location and initially artificial creation. For non-riders, however, the Gallop is one more spectacular leisure event organised in Budapest that may be worth a visit but, at the same time, is the reason for road closures and traffic jams every September.

Despite the organisers' clearly communicated objective to provide a platform for the competing settlements to present themselves to the wider public, this opportunity has largely remained unexploited by the participants. Although the event includes various ways to build connections with the visitors and among the participating towns and villages (e.g. exhibition pavilions set up along the Gallop Promenade, the mayor's breakfast as a networking tool or being featured in the festival's media campaign), most settlements lack the necessary expertise to gain significant exposure from these opportunities. Consequently, from a regional or local marketing point of view, the Gallop's impact on the competing communities' perceived destination image are rather moderate: mainly the winner's town or village benefits, for a short period, from the subsequent media coverage. Although the event certainly contributes to increasing local pride in the community and its equestrian customs, in order to become able to gain further advantage from participation in the Gallop, most settlements would require expert assistance in destination marketing and brand development.

Acknowledgement

The authors would like to express their sincere gratitude to Kitti Boros, MA student in Tourism Management, Kodolányi János University of Applied Sciences, Hungary, for her assistance in the data collection phase of the research.

References

Béki, P., Vágó, T. and Lasztovicza, D. (2013) The present of equine tourism in Hungary in reflection to an empirical research. *Applied Studies in Agribusiness and Commerce* 7 (1), 19–23.

Borókai, G. (2010) Dacos ellenállás helyett. *Heti Válasz*, 12 June 2010. See http://valasz.hu/publi/dacos-ellenallas-helyett-29957/ (accessed 13 May 2015).

Butler, G., Khoo-Lattimore, C. and Mura, P. (2014) Heritage tourism in Malaysia: Fostering a collective national identity in an ethnically diverse country. *Asia Pacific Journal of Tourism Research* 19 (2), 199–218.

Czauner, P. (2009) Nyeregbe, magyar! *Népszabadság Online*, 12 September 2009. See http://nol.hu/gazdasag/20090912-nyeregbe_magyar-349074 (accessed 1 October 2015).

Della Lucia, M. and Franch, M. (2014) Culture-led urban regeneration and brand building in Alpine Italian cities. In F. Go, A. Lemmetyinen and U. Hakala (eds) *Harnessing Place Branding through Cultural Entrepreneurship* (pp. 122–140). Basingstoke: Palgrave Macmillan.

Edensor, T. (1997) National identity and the politics of memory: Remembering Bruce and Wallace in symbolic space. *Environment and Planning D: Society and Space* 15 (2), 175–194.

Fényes, E. (1842) *Magyarország statistikája*. Pest: Trattner-Károlyi.

Gráfik, I. (2004) A huszár alakja a magyar népművészetben. In Gy. Csihák (ed.) *A magyar huszárság története. A lovasműveltség sajátosságai* (pp. 88–102). Budapest-Zurich: Zürichi Magyar Történelmi Egyesület és Heraldika Kiadó.

Graml, G. (2004) (Re)mapping the nation: Sound of Music tourism and national identity in Austria, ca 2000 CE. *Tourist Studies* 4 (1), 137–159.

Grbich, C. (2013) *Qualitative Data Analysis: An Introduction.* London: SAGE.

HNTO (2015) Pattanjunk nyeregbe – Lovaglás Magyarországon. *HNTO website.* See http://aktiv.itthon.hu/lovaglas (accessed 8 June 2015).

Jenes, B. (2009) A 'pusztaromantika' helye a magyar országimázsban. *Marketing & Menedzsment* 43 (2), 64–72.

Justice, C. (2012) *The Greatest Horse of All. A Controversy Examined.* Bloomington, IN: AuthorHouse.

KIM (2012) *Kincsem – Nemzeti Lovas Program, munkaanyag.* Budapest: Közigazgatási és Igazságügyi Minisztérium.

Kovács Kiss, Gy. (1992) 'A kiművelt emberfő programjához híven …' (Tallózás a születése 200. évfordulójára megjelent Széchenyi-irodalomból). *Erdélyi Múzeum* 54 (1–4), 168–171.

Light, D. (2001) 'Facing the future': Tourism and identity-building in post-socialist Romania. *Political Geography* 20, 1053–1074.

Makkai, L. (1994) The Hungarians' prehistory, their conquest of Hungary and their raids to the West to 955. In P. Sugar, P. Hanák and T. Frank (eds) *A History of Hungary* (pp. 8–15). Bloomington, IN: Indiana University Press.

Michalkó, G. (2002) Az aktív turizmus elméleti megközelítése. In L. Dávid (ed.) *Aktív turizmus* (pp. 5–16). Debrecen: Didakt Kiadó.

Mikos, É. (2006) 'Hármat üt Árpád vezér rettentő pajzsára'. A magyar honfoglalás szöveghagyományának megkonstruálása és popularizálása a XVIII–XIX. században. PhD thesis, University of Pécs.

Nagy, K. (2004) A magyar huszár születése, dicső harcai és történelmi jelentősége. In Gy. Csihák (ed.) *A magyar huszárság története. A lovasműveltség sajátosságai* (pp. 23–32). Budapest-Zurich: Zürichi Magyar Történelmi Egyesület és Heraldika Kiadó.

National Gallop (2011) Újdonság! Fogatvágta – Új sportág születik a Hősök terén! National Gallop website, 7 September 2011. See http://vagta.hu/news/421/ujdonsag!-fogatvagta---uj-sportag-szuletik-a-hosok-teren! (accessed 12 June 2015).

National Gallop (2014) What's the National Gallop? National Gallop website, 1 September 2014. See http://en.vagta.hu/news/656/what's-the-national-gallop? (accessed 12 June 2015).

National Gallop (2015a) Elnöki köszöntő. National Gallop website. See http://vagta.hu/menu/327/elnoki-koszonto (accessed 10 September 2015).

National Gallop (2015b) Heroes' Square. National Gallop website. See http://en.vagta.hu/menu/257/heroes-square (accessed 10 September 2015).

Povedák, I. (2014) MOGY. Egy neonacionalista fesztivál elemzése. In G. Barna and I. Kerekes (eds) *Vallás, egyén, társadalom* (pp. 123–143). Szeged: SZTE BTK Néprajzi és Kulturális Antropológiai Tanszék.

Sugar, P., Hanák, P. and Frank, T. (eds) (1994) *A History of Hungary.* Bloomington, IN: Indiana University Press.

Széchenyi, I. (1828) *Lovakrul.* Budapest: Petrózai Trattner J.M. and Károlyi I.

Tapolcsányi, B. and Tőzsér, A. (2013) A Nemzeti Vágta turisztikai jelentősége hazánkban. *Acta Carolus Robertus* 3 (2), 159–169.

Trencsényi, Z. (2014) Geszti Péter: Manapság minden fillér számít. *Népszabadság Online,* 9 September 2014. See http://nol.hu/kultura/az-arcmuvesz-1485063 (accessed 12 June 2015).

Türk, A. (2012) A korai magyar történet kutatásának új régészeti programja. *Magyar Régészet – Hungarian Archaeology* 1 (2), 1–6.

Varga, F. (2015) Ennyi pénzt még soha nem tettünk fel egy lóra. *Origo*, 24 October 2015. See http://www.origo.hu/filmklub/blog/riport/forgatas/20151016-kincsem-forga tasi-riport-herendi-gabor-nagy-ervin-petrik-andrea-andy-vajna-hutlassa-tamas.html (accessed 24 October 2015).

Volcic, Z. and Andrejevic, M. (2011) Nation branding in the era of commercial national- ism. *International Journal of Communication* 5, 598–618.

Watzatka, Á. (2014) Puszta, Husaren und Zigeunermusik – Franz Liszt und das Heimatbild von Nikolaus Lenau. *Studia Musicologica* 55 (1–2), 103–118.

White, L. (2009a) Foster's lager: From local beer to global icon. *Marketing Intelligence & Planning* 27 (2), 177–190.

White, L. (2009b) The Man from Snowy River: Australia's bush legend and commercial nationalism. *Tourism Review International* 13 (2), 139–146.

White, L. (2011) The role of horse in Australian tourism and national identity. In E. Frew and L. White (eds) *Tourism and National Identities. An International Perspective* (pp. 65–76). New York: Routledge.

15 Examining Cherry Blossom Celebrations in Japan and Around the World

Michael Basil

Introduction

This chapter proposes that an interesting effort at commercial nationalisation can be seen in the Japanese and foreign promotion of cherry blossom festivals, or 'Hanami'. Japan has a long history of cherry blossom celebrations. These blossoms are a sign of spring and historically signalled the start of the new year. However, cherry blossom festivals are now celebrated in other parts of the world. Why study holidays? There is growing acknowledgement of the importance of rituals and holidays in society. Marketing scholars have also begun to examine holiday rituals, largely with an interest in how celebrations are celebrated or undergo changes over time and in different incarnations. One example of these changes can be seen in the commercialisation of holidays (Schmidt, 1991). For example, many formerly religious holidays such as Christmas and Easter have morphed to become more focused on presents and chocolates than on historical religious significance. Many holidays have also undergone globalisation so that important holidays in the Western hemisphere, such as Christmas, are now celebrated in the Eastern hemisphere and non-Christian countries such as Japan, through the adaptation of only a few symbols, such as Santa Claus (Kimura & Belk, 2005). This chapter compares how cherry blossom festivals are celebrated in Japan with how they are celebrated in other parts of the world.

The roots of many seasonal celebrations may be based in natural animal behaviour. Biological research, for example, has demonstrated seasonal patterns of activity and food consumption for mammals such as squirrels (e.g. Short & Duke, 1971). Seasonality has been observed in human food consumption patterns (e.g. Larson, 1997). 'The seasons influence not only what consumers buy, but how they feel and think during different times of the year' (Waldrop & Mogelonsky, 1992: 14). Similar seasonality has been observed in the sexual behaviour of mammals and humans (Wellings, Macdowall, Catchpole & Goodrich, 1999). At its most poetic this seasonality can be observed in Alfred Tennyson's (1835) poem, 'Locksley Hall', 'In the Spring a young man's fancy lightly turns to thoughts of love'. At its most base, this seasonality may be seen in some of the rituals at spring break of alcohol and sex (Josiam et al., 1998; Maticka-Tyndale & Herold, 1997). Overall, these drives may explain the basis of many seasonal festivals around the world (Cross & Proctor, 2014).

Volcic and Andrejevic (2015) suggest that many countries have attempted to define or redefine their role in the world in an effort they term 'commercial nationalism'. To this end countries and entities within countries attempt to brand or self-brand their importance, often with an eye to their unique cultural heritage and contributions to the world. They suggest that an unintended consequence of these efforts may also be seen as one of the forces leading to globablisation.

White (2009) proposes that one example of an attempt at commercial nationalisation can be seen in Australian stories surrounding 'The Man from Snowy River'. Initially a Banjo Paterson poem of a typical Australian legend, this poem has since been commercialised into a novel, film and TV series. With regard to globalisation, the poem and its commercial offshoots also provided a theme for the Sydney 2000 Olympic Games welcome ceremony. A second example of commercial nationalisation can be seen in a Japanese attempt to promote the Takarazuka Revue's performances in Japan and in the United States during the postwar period (Park, 2015). Park argues that these efforts were built on the Japanese government's efforts to encourage domestic nationalistic pride. In terms of globalisation these performances were also used in an attempt to improve Japan's international position by illustrating a shared popular culture through international performances in the US.

Examining Celebrations Around the World

The ways in which holidays and other festivals are celebrated has begun to receive investigation by consumer researchers (e.g. Wallendorf & Arnould, 1991). Holiday rituals can be an important experience to consumers (e.g. Belk, 1993; Golby & Purdue, 1986; Wallendorf & Arnould, 1991). An important question is 'What purpose do they serve?' Etzoni and Bloom (2004) propose that holidays and related rituals provide an integrative function by providing a unifying narrative to a range of citizens. Kubal (2006) suggests that these rituals provide a thematic tradition along the line of Durkheim's totems that symbolise group identity. Research on holidays seems, at least at first glance, to support this assertion. Some research in this area has focused on the fall harvest festival of American Thanksgiving. Wallendorf and

Arnould (1991), for example, discovered a collective discourse of consumption around Thanksgiving that is in accord with the American (self) ideal of family and material abundance. From its foundation as an autumn harvest festival, the lack of a prescribed perspective has allowed Thanksgiving to acquire a negotiated and culturally constructed meaning.

Yet there are many reasons to doubt that holidays provide the monolithic symbols that Kubal proposes. The first way in which holidays and their celebrations may vary is through increasing commercialisation, often attributed to marketing (Duffy, 2008). In an examination of this phenomenon, Schmidt (1991) investigated several American holidays. He considered the historically important Christmas and Easter, a created Mother's Day holiday and failed attempts at creating a Candy Day and Friendship Day. Schmidt's conclusion was that, although many existing holidays have been altered through commercialisation, people have rejected some newly constructed holidays. Schmidt's (1995) more recent tome on the topic of the transformation of American holidays takes a less capitalistically hegemonic perspective; instead, Schmidt can be placed in the tradition of Mary Douglas, whose *The World of Goods* (2002) proposed that gifts and other commercial products are simply woven into the tapestry of celebratory rituals that are fundamental to celebrations (Heinze, 1996: 297). To Schmidt, holiday celebrations are not 'a tale of woeful secularization' because the sacred and the secular have been intertwined throughout their history and commercialisation is an inherent part of broadening the appeal of the holiday.

A second way that holidays may change is through their globalisation. Several theorists have proposed that holidays are being altered in how they are celebrated internationally (Kimura & Belk, 2005). As evidence, Kimura and Belk (2005) note the adoption of certain Christmas images in Japan, mainly in the form of secular symbols such as Santa Claus, sleighs and snowmen. This international adoption of Christmas symbols is evidence of globalisation.

Importantly, however, there is evidence of local adaptations of only some of those Christmas symbols, such as Christmas cake, and the creation of new ones such as Kentucky Fried Chicken and sake. The partial adoption and adaptation of Christmas in a local form can be seen as a form of 'glocalisation'. Glocalisation is a term sometimes attributed to Japanese management techniques where global companies adopt local adaptations (Peak, 1991; Quigley, 2002). As a result, glocalisation is sometimes explained as a hybrid between the local and global (Kraidy, 1999). According to this view, while globalisation is a homogenous compression of the world, glocalisation allows that to be unique and distinct. The idea of glocalisation can also be seen in Disneyland Paris, where the Disney theme park is slightly adapted for France (Matusitz, 2010). This concept of adaptation is also visible in the adoption and appropriation of the high school prom from the US into the UK (Tinson & Nutall, 2010). Other evidence of holiday modifications can be seen in in the adoption and adaptation of Valentine's Day in Japan, where some aspects of the holiday, such as the giving of chocolate, were adopted while other aspects, such as the gift giving aspect, were adapted so that women give the chocolate to men (Minowa *et al.*, 2011).

These lines of recent research appear to suggest that holidays and their celebrations are not monolithic but that the adaption of holidays can occur at a local level. This variability suggests that exploring how holiday celebrations and rituals are adopted and adapted is worthy of investigation (Tinson & Nutall, 2010). To this end, this study involved an analysis of holiday behaviours related to cherry blossom celebrations around the world to examine possible commercialisation and globalisation.

Method and Sources

This study involved an observational analysis of behaviours occurring at cherry blossom celebrations around the world. This research attempted to gain insights through exploration using a combination of methods. This approach arose from a desire to triangulate through a variety of observational methods that might provide insights into behaviours, including some that might be automatic and ritualised (Moisander *et al.*, 2009). To provide both insights into the behaviours themselves as well as self-reported interpretations of these behaviours, this study relies on a naturalistic observation of both verbal and visual self-reported activities that compare how this holiday is celebrated around the world.

This process involved four steps. First, published writing about this holiday provided a basic grounding in this celebration. This provided a background on the history and perspectives on its celebration. Next, an exploration of online postings including websites, blogs and photographs on the topic of cherry blossom festivals or 'Hanami' were used to select a sample of critical activities and people's thoughts about their activities. This analysis was used to find and frame prototypical representations of the holiday and associated consumption rituals. Consensus or convergence in this case involved achieving saturation after viewing at least 50 postings on the holiday with no new representations or rituals for the last 10 postings. This approach can be seen as applying a visual analysis similar to that of Worth and Adair (1972) and Wallendorf and Arnould (1991), who used asked people to turn cameras on their own celebrations; in this case, however, people did it of their own accord, often to share with family and friends. For the third step, data was collected via personal visits to Japan, Australia, Canada, and the US to observe and photograph cherry blossom celebrations. This involved a single two week visit to Japan for Hanami, while the observations of cherry blossom activities in other countries occurred over multiple celebrations while living in those countries. This method provided an observer's insights (Penaloza, 1998). Finally, these visual observations were then compared with a 'netnographic' study that examined how this holiday is celebrated in other locations as portrayed on the Internet (Kozinets, 2015).

Across these sources, a convergence on what constitutes the celebration of Hanami was found. The comparison of these verbal and visual narratives with direct observation required the research to focus on observable acts of real-world behaviours. Photographs were used to record these consumption practices (e.g. Belk *et al.*, 1989; Wallendorf & Arnould, 1991) so these behavioural patterns could be further studied. Therefore, this study constituted a combination of grounding, a netnographic analysis of online postings, visual observational research and a return to netnographic evidence to discover and understand ritualistic consumption behaviours associated with these different types of celebrations as they are celebrated around the globe.

Cherry Blossom Celebrations

Historically, observation and celebration of spring blossoms or 'sakura' in Japan can be traced as far back as [the equivalent of] 712 A.D. (Ohnuki-Tierney, 1998). The early focus was often on the plum blossom, carried over from China, but over time the cherry blossom and Hanami activities have developed as a national identity for Japan (Ohnuki-Tierney, 2002). As a result, cherry blossom viewing has been described as so central to Japan that it is seen as a 'total social phenomenon' (Ohnuki-Tierney, 1998: 213). Many aspects of the Japanese year begin with spring, including fiscal and school years (Brender, 2003). The old and emergent nature of Hanami identifies it as a celebration that plays out mostly as a non-religious event. There is usually no formal organisation of festivities, but the observation is typically based on individual initiative.

Cherry blossom viewing is focused on finding ways to capture the ephemeral aspects of the season through established sakura consumption activities (Kobayashi, 2002). A critical part of Hanami is the search for cherry blossoms. This hunt is partly temporal, in finding out when the cherry blossoms will be opening and peaking. Timing the blossoms' peak is a critical factor in the search, and online websites and news reports play an important role in this process. The search is also geographic, as the search for the best cherry blossoms takes on epic proportions in Japan (Noritake, 1992). Culturally, travel is important in Japan, likely a derivation of pilgrimages in both important religions, Buddhism and Shinto (Eiki, 1997), that can be traced back at least as far as the Heian era (794–864). These are not real pilgrimages; however, Hanami provides an easy and non-religious way for people to engage in a 'quasi-pilgrimage' (Roy, 2005: 121–129), which takes the form of travel to specific locations to observe and celebrate the cherry blossoms and the coming of spring. The historical importance of travel for Hanami can be observed through old postcards which were used by travellers to communicate with family and friends back home. Although there are some people who document travel along the 'sakura zensen' (sakura front), pursuing the warming weather to observe cherry blossoms open from the south to the north, contemporary Hanami quasi-pilgrimages more typically involve a simple sojourn to a sacred site such as a temple, a secular site such as a particular park known for its cherry blossoms, or reliving a recognisable ritual such as sipping sake in a local park with co-workers. This usually involves a visit to a sacred site such as a Buddhist temple or Shinto shrine.

Painting cherry blossoms is a ritual that dates back at least as far as the Edo Period (1603–1868) (Riko, 2005). A more contemporary version is photography. The consumption of sake is often an important part of Hanami (Ohnuki-Tierney, 1998) and some view its consumption as an act of kinship and hope for a bountiful crop of rice, which is planted in the spring (Ohnuki-Tierney, 1998). The role of sake can be seen in academic (Ohnuki-Tierney, 1998) and popular writing (Brender, 2003).

Analysis of Websites

Many websites or blogs are hosted on Japanese or North American sites. These are often built by people who are living in Japan temporarily (often employed as English teachers) or simply visitors to Japan. In both cases the primary motivation for these websites appears to be explaining the phenomenon and the beauty to friends and family back home. A second common motivation appears to be photographers sharing their images. A third common motivation is seen in websites built by Japanese tourism organisations.

An important aspect of the Japanese Hanami hunt involves capturing images of the fleeting cherry blossoms themselves in the form of painting or photographing the blossoms. In contemporary times, many of these websites or blogs record images of cherry blossoms. The importance of recording the cherry blossoms themselves was observed in all forms of data – blogs, websites, photography and my own observations. Almost every website or blog included at least one photograph of cherry blossoms, and for many this was the focus of the blog or website, especially on a photograph-sharing website such as flickr. In 2005, a search on flickr for 'cherry blossoms' turned up 700,000 'hits'.

Visiting specific temples and parks is often a part of the spring ritual, and is seen depicted in blogs, websites and photography. In their pursuit and celebration of cherry blossoms, people can be observed gathering together in public places to share the experience. Although some gatherings involve families, many of the public gatherings involve other groups such as schools and employers. Although the notion of gatherings is not mentioned in most academic writing about cherry blossom celebrations, descriptions and images of these gatherings were prevalent on blogs, websites and photographs, and in first-hand observation of cherry blossoms. So the 'gather together' aspect

seen in other holiday rituals can also be seen in Japanese Hanami celebrations, although the gatherings are generally less nuclear for Hanami than
they are for Thanksgiving or Christmas in North America.

An important consumption ritual of Hanami based on online reporting
and observation is the consumption of special foods such as seasonal 'Hanami
bentos'. Bentos are special lunch boxes, although they are not necessarily
limited to lunch. A celebration of the seasonal aspects of food can be seen in
much of Japanese food, especially that of 'highbrow' Kansai cuisine (from
the region around Kyoto), such as kaiseki. For Hanami, there are often special
seasonal additions. Hanami bentos will often focus on decorations such as
cherry-blossom-shaped vegetables or pink or light green dumplings. Even
deserts can be decorated with cherry blossom images.

The consumption of sake is often mentioned on websites. The importance of sake was observed in verbal form in blogs or websites but was less
likely to be seen in photographs. Other evidence of its importance can be
seen in specially decorated sake bottles and cups that are sold and reported
on people's blogs and websites. In addition, pink plum wine is growing in
popularity and is often promoted as a spring product in a newer consump-
tion-related homage to spring.

Observation

In the course of 12 days in Japan between 27 March and 7 April 2009,
I travelled to dozens of temples, shrines and parks in the Kansai region,
including Kyoto and Osaka, which had been identified as important locations for cherry blossom viewing and Hanami celebrations. The timing was
perfect because in this period the blossoms advanced from just opening to
reaching full bloom (as judged by japan-guide.com's 'Cherry blossom Report
2009'). Judging by the number of attendees and their activities, these were
indeed important sites for these activities.

One of the most common Hanami activities I observed was people taking
photographs of the blossoms and having one's picture taken in front of
cherry blossoms. A typical scene is shown in Figure 15.1. Judging from what
people were most likely do as soon as they arrived, and spend a good deal of time
on, photography appeared to be a critical focus for cherry blossom visitors. There
were a few instances of cherry blossoms being recorded through drawing, but
this was rare (only three times in the two weeks).

I often felt part of a pilgrimage in visiting these locations. This was
sometimes felt in travelling to these locations. I also felt this way walking
towards many of the temples and shrines where I had a feeling of being
swept up in a crowd going to those events, often in a sometimes hushed or
possibly giddy exhuberation that reminded me of walking into a sporting
event or musical performance. I would describe this as a feeling of a

Figure 15.1 Searching for and capturing the images of cherry blossoms

quasi-pilgrimage. I also received some special tickets that were printed for many sacred sites such as Kyoto's Kiyonomizudera temple to commemorate the visit, similar to how pilgrims collect stamps or other evidence of their pilgrimage. In general I felt that visits to temples and shrines tended to be quieter and more reflective than those in parks, which tended to be more social, louder and more likely to involve food purchases.

Group gatherings were frequently observed. There were several situations where people simply travelled to a temple, shrine or park, took a few photographs, ate a little food and moved on. I found this was more typical earlier in the day. In the later afternoon and evening, especially in parks, there was more evidence of group gatherings. As might be expected, family gatherings were more frequent on weekend afternoons, and work or school-based groups on weekdays and at night. These celebrations can be seen in Figure 15.2 (a family picnic in a park).

Many, if not most, participants in park Hanami festivities were consuming some form of food or drink. Bentos were readily observed, but other

Figure 15.2 Contemporary Hanami rituals

Figure 15.3 Special Hanami food decorated with images of cherry blossoms

foods that were found to be sold at these locations included squid on a stick, octopus balls and udon. Therefore the importance of food was observed in all forms of data – blogs, websites, photography and my own observations. An example is shown in Figure 15.3.

Drinking was also seen to be an important part of many celebrations. My own observations suggest a possible explanation for the lack of photographic images of sake for websites and blogs – that most of the sake drinking occurs after dark, which does not lend itself to photographs. Heavy drinking also may not lend itself to wanting or taking an immediate visual record, yet result in remembering it the following day as recorded on personal blogs. Attempts to tie plum wine to Hanami was seen in the use of labels making use of cherry blossom images, the seasonality of the promotion, and even in the form of displays that are used to associate plum wine with Hanami; however, I did not see any consumption of plum wine in practice.

Singing was sometimes associated with Hanami celebrations. This seemed to be uncommon in family-based activities, but often a part of a school or a company gathering. Singing may not be inherent to the Hanami celebrations, but rather a source of group identity in Japan (Head, 2004), or perhaps even as related to the importance of karaoke as general entertainment. That is, singing occurs, but may not be a critical aspect of Hanami celebrations themselves, especially for families.

Another insight from my observations is that commercialisation of Hanami is typically in terms of small-scale food enterprises at the cherry blossom events themselves, more likely in city-based locations such as Osaka's castle and not at most of the temples or shrines. I observed no sponsorships or branded ventures at any of the cherry blossom events. Instead, symbols and themes of cherry blossoms and Hanami pervade much Japanese marketing and advertising (Moeran & Skov, 1997), and this was definitely found near Hanami time. An example can be seen in Figure 15.4.

Figure 15.4 Commercialising the images of cherry blossoms

International Context

The celebration of cherry blossoms also occurs in other parts of the world, often as formal 'festivals'. In the US, the most famous cherry blossom festival is probably celebrated in Washington, DC. This is usually framed as a remembrance of a gift of cherry trees from Japan, with the 2012 celebration a commemoration of the 100th anniversary. Cherry blossom festivals are also celebrated in many US west coast cities including San Francisco, Seattle and Portland, and in Vancouver, Canada – each city having received a good number of Japanese immigrants. Other US cherry blossom festivals are celebrated in Honolulu, Los Angeles and two other locations in southern California, as well as Conyers and Macon, Georgia, New Jersey, Brooklyn, New York and Philadelphia. In the southern hemisphere, Australia, Brazil and Peru, countries with a large population of Japanese immigrants, all host cherry blossom celebrations, and evidence suggests that the festivals began after immigration. Sydney, Australia, despite limited Japanese immigration, also celebrates Hanami.

Through examining the websites, blogs and other descriptions of these celebrations, in all of these festivals, although the primary symbol of the celebration is the cherry blossom, the form of these celebrations is often modified in these international contexts. In overseas locations, the cherry blossom festivals often have less focus on cherry blossom themselves or their discovery and capture. In fact, I have even observed the San Francisco festival relying heavily on artificial cherry blossoms (although this did make it easier for participants to capture, store and transport than living cherry blossoms).

One important difference between these exported cherry blossom festivals is their organisation. Japanese Hanami observations are typically disorganised, individual and less formal. Foreign festivals, however, are typically more formal. The overseas celebrations and their dates of observance are normally arranged months in advance. An aspect of the formalisation can also be seen in the arranged activities. For example, the Washington, DC festival includes cultural performances, kite flying, fireworks and a parade, none of which are typically a part of Japanese Hanami celebrations.

In the UK, Alnwick Gardens in rural Northumberland purports to host the UK's first and only cherry blossom festival, including 'an origami workshop, a bonsai tree exhibition, Japanese calligraphy and afternoon parades'. One Hanami celebration in Cowra, Australia noted the cherry blossoms, Japanese garden tea ceremony, Ikebana (Japanese flower arranging), calligraphy or bonsai, martial art experts and Sumo wrestlers. Similar activities are promoted for the Dandenong Ranges Gardens near Melbourne:

> In September, the Cherry Tree Grove is in full bloom and is celebrated at the annual Hanami Festival. Hanami is the Japanese tradition of 'flower viewing' but mostly refers to the celebration and appreciation

of the sakura or cherry blossom – Japan's unofficial national flower. 'In keeping with tradition, visitors are treated to traditional Japanese flower arranging demonstrations, origami, ikebana and bonsai display, calligraphy demonstrations and tea making ceremonies.' (Beautiful Altona, 2015)

Similarly, in 2010, Tasmania's Emu Valley Rhododendron Garden promoted beautiful images of cherry blossoms among what appears to be Shinto shrines and offers the visitor the opportunity to 'Join in the celebrations and see Japanese artists and crafts during this weekend' (Emu Valley, 2010).

Perhaps the most non-traditional version of Hanami is Macon, Georgia, USA's festival. Here the activities include a formal ball, bed race, fashion show and tour of homes. These activities probably reflect more of Georgia's culture than that of Japanese cherry blossom festivities, and therefore demonstrate an example of its adaptation to local interests and culture.

Many of the consumption rituals, however, are similar across these various overseas locations. The general form of cherry blossom festivals still involves the consumption of food. The typical products associated with Hanami in Japan, however, such as Hanami bentos and sake, are not as central as they are in Japan, in fact they are downright rare. Instead, cherry blossom festivals are likely to include a wide variety of Japanese food such as sushi and yakitori, probably because of their broader familiarity and appeal to people outside of Japan.

One of the main differences between Japanese Hanami celebrations and the exported version is that the exported celebrations are often seen as a Japanese cultural event and therefore they put additional emphasis on Japanese culture. For example, many cherry blossom festivals outside of Japan include a demonstration of the traditional Japanese practice of calligraphy or drumming, neither of which is typical of Hanami celebrations in Japan.

A second difference that is observed with the celebration of Hanami overseas is the substantially different nature of travel. In Japan, figuring out the optimal timing for a specific location and a pilgrimage to the particular spot is all part of the 'search' process. For celebrations in other parts of the world, the date of the celebration and its location are dictated and getting to the Hanami festival is no different than going downtown to work or shop. As a result, the search is more about finding out about the celebration, adding it to your calendar and just getting there.

A minor difference that can be seen in the celebration of Hanami in different locations is not in form but in timing – the date of the celebration is altered depending on when the cherry blossoms occur. In the Northern Hemisphere this depends on the latitude and local climate, and is some time in March, April or May. In the Southern Hemisphere this also depends on the latitude and climate, but the reversal of the seasons means that this typically happens in September or October. Again, these dates are usually set in advance as part of a more formally organised celebration.

So, in sum, outside of Japan, Hanami is less focused on seeing actual cherry blossoms in the open air, searching for them, photographing them and eating a little food and drinking some sake. Instead these 'cherry blossom festivals' typically morph to a more formally organised and broader celebration of Japanese culture.

Conclusion

This study examined a seasonal celebration in the form of cherry blossom festivals. The historical roots of this celebration in Japan go back more than 1,000 years. Consistent with previous research in commercial nationalism, historical precedent and traditions have shaped this celebration. As observed in Japan there is a 'searching' theme to Hanami that involves seeking out the best cherry blossoms. There is often a desire to try to capture some aspects of those blossoms. The search and attempts to capture these elements may involve an effort to participate in the active construction of the celebration (Fine, 1997; Holbrook & Hirschman, 1982). The celebration also provides considerable opportunities for consumption in the form of food and ritual in the form of seasonal food, sake and celebrations, often under the trees. Although it is virtually impossible to know if the Japanese celebration has become more commercialised over time, it is apparent that a number of commercial activities such as the sale of food are sanctioned at these events, often in the form of commercial consumption. Cherry blossom images are also often used as themes in marketing and advertising.

Cherry blossom festivals are also celebrated in other cultural contexts. This exportation to other cultures is evidence of the globalisation of this celebration to other parts of the world, probably as a result of immigration. Despite the consistent theme of the cherry blossom, however, there are a number of significant modifications or interpretations of the celebration that suggest evidence of globalisation, but also glocalisation. Examining how the celebration changes in other cultures and climates demonstrates the extent to which the event is modified or 'glocalised' to each environment. First off, there is adaptation in the timing of the event. Second, there is a tendency to move the celebration inside, which is quite a modification from its Japanese roots. Third, another major modification of exported cherry blossom celebrations is that these festivals primarily become a celebration of Japanese culture using whichever Japanese foods, activities or symbols are important at that time and to that culture. So the celebration of Hanami seems to show significant modification to its staging overseas. Fourth, there is also evidence of a good many adaptations to these various overseas locations including celebrations of manga in Germany and home shows, bed races and a fashion show in Georgia. In sum, these international celebrations show evidence of globalisation through their worldwide celebration, but they also demonstrate glocalisation in the local adaptation and interpretation of the form of the celebration itself. Therefore, it is argued that Japanese cherry blossom festivals provide an interesting example of commercial nationalism.

References

Beautiful Altona (2015) See http://altonabeauty.blogspot.ca/2012_10_01_archive.html (accessed 12 August 2015).

Belk, R.W. (1993) Materialism and the making of the modern American Christmas. In D. Miller (ed.) *Unwrapping Christmas* (pp. 319–344). Oxford: Oxford University Press.

Belk, R.W., Wallendorf, M. and Sherry, J.F. (1989) The sacred and the profane in consumer behavior: Theodicy on the Odyssey. *Journal of Consumer Research* 16, 1–38.

Brender, A. (2003) Sake, students, and cherry blossoms: Japanese drinking rituals mark the cycle of the academic year. *The Chronicle of Higher Education* 49, 34.

Cross, G.S. and Proctor, R.N. (2014) *Packaged Pleasures: How Technology & Marketing Revolutionized Desire*. Chicago, IL: University of Chicago Press.

Douglas, M. (2002) *The World of Goods: Towards an Anthropology of Consumption* (Vol. 6). London: Psychology Press.

Duffy, B. (2008) Candy to network of fear: Marketing's influence on contemporary Halloween rituals. Paper presented to the International Communication Association.

Eiki, H. (1997) Pilgrimage and peregrination: Contextualizing the Saikoko Junrei and the Shikoku Henro. *Japanese Journal of Religious Studies* 24, 271–299.

Emu Valley (2010) See http://www.emuvalleyrhodo.com.au/index.html (accessed September 2010).

Etzioni, A. and Bloom, J. (2004) *We Are What We Celebrate: Understanding Holidays and Rituals*. New York: New York University Press.

Fine, B. (1997) Playing the consumption game. *Consumption, Markets, and Culture* 1, 7–29.

Golby, J.M. and Purdue, A.W. (1986) *The Making of the Modern Christmas*. Athens, GA: University of Georgia Press.

Head, J. (2004) Japanese revive company songs. BBC News. See http://news.bbc.co.uk/2/hi/asia-pacific/3725775.stm (accessed 11 July 2012).

Heinze, A.R. (1996) Sacrifestivals: On Christianity and mass consumption in America. Review of Consumer Rites: The Buying and Selling of American Holidays by Leigh Eric Schmidt. Review. *American History* 24, 668–675.

Holbrook, M.B. and Hirschman, E.C. (1982) The experiential aspects of consumption: Consumer fantasies, feelings, and fun. *Journal of Consumer Research* 9, 132–140.

Josiam, B.M., Hobson, J.S., Dietrich, U.C. and Smeaton, G. (1998) An analysis of the sexual, alcohol and drug related behavioural patterns of students on spring break. *Tourism Management* 19 (6), 501–513.

Kimura, J. and Belk, R.W. (2005) Christmas in Japan: Globalization versus localization. *Consumption, Markets and Culture* 8, 325–338.

Kobayashi, A. (2002) Cherry blossoms. In S. Buckley (ed.) *Encyclopedia of Contemporary Japanese Culture* (p. 63). London: Taylor and Francis.

Kozinets, R.V. (2015) Netnography. *The International Encyclopedia of Digital Communication and Society* (pp. 1–8). New York: John Wiley & Sons.

Kraidy, M.M. (1999) The global, the local, and the hybrid: A native ethnography of glocalization. *Critical Studies in Mass Communication* 16, 456–476.

Kubal, T. (2006) We are what we celebrate: Understanding holidays and rituals by Amitai Etzioni and Jared Bloom. *Contemporary Sociology* 35, 46–47.

Larson, R.B. (1997) Food consumption and seasonality. *Journal of Food Distribution Research* 28 (2), 36–44.

Maticka-Tyndale, E. and Herold, E.S. (1997) The scripting of sexual behavior: Canadian university students on spring break in Florida. *The Canadian Journal of Human Sexuality* 6, 317–328.

Matusitz, J. (2010) Disneyland Paris: A case analysis demonstrating how glocalization works. *Journal of Strategic Marketing* 18, 223–247.

Minowa, Y., Khomenko, O. and Belk, R.W. (2011) Social change and gendered gift giving rituals: A historical analysis of Valentine's Day in Japan. *Journal of Macromarketing* 31, 44–56.

Moeran, B. and Skov, L. (1997) Mount Fuji and the cherry blossoms: A view from afar. In P.J. Asquith and A. Kalland (eds) *Japanese Images of Nature: Cultural Perspectives* (pp. 181–205). Richmond: Curazon.

Moisander, J., Anu Valtonen, A. and Heidi Hirsto, H. (2009) Personal interviews in cultural consumer research – Post-structuralist challenges. *Consumption, Markets and Culture* 12, 329–348.

Noritake, K. (1992) The travel-loving tradition of the Japanese. *Japan Echo* 19, 66–71.

Ohnuki-Tierney, E. (1998) Cherry blossoms and their viewing: A window onto Japanese culture. In S. Linhart and S. Frühstück (eds) *The Culture of Japan As Seen Through Its Leisure* (pp. 213–236). Albany, NY: SUNY Press.

Ohnuki-Tierney, E. (2002) *Kamikaze, Cherry Blossoms, and Nationalism: The Militarization of Aesthetics in Japanese History*. Chicago, IL: University of Chicago Press.

Park, S.M. (2015) Staging Japan: The Takarazuka revue and cultural nationalism in the 1950s–60s. *Asian Studies Review* 39 (3), 357–374.

Peak, M.H. (1991) Developing an international style of management. *Management Review* 80 (2), 32–35.

Penaloza, L. (1998) Just doing it: A visual ethnographic study of spectacular consumption behavior at Nike Town. *Consumption, Markets & Culture* 2, 337–400.

Quigley, M. (2002) Glocalization versus globalization: The work of Nick Park and Peter Lord. *Animation Journal* 10, 85–94.

Riko, I. (2005) Edo-period painting and the language of flowers. *Japan Echo* 32 (5), 54–60.

Roy, C. (2005) *Traditional festivals: A Multicultural Encyclopedia*. Santa Barbara CA: ABC-CLIO.

Schmidt, L.E. (1991) The commercialization of the calendar: American holidays and the culture of consumption. *The Journal of American History* 78, 887–916.

Schmidt, L.E. (1995) *Consumer Rites: The Buying and Selling of American Holidays*. Princeton, NJ: Princeton University Press.

Short, H.L. and Duke, W.B. (1971) Seasonal food consumption and body weights of captive tree squirrels. *Journal of Wildlife Management* 35 (3), 435–439.

Tennyson, A. (1835) Locksley Hall. https://www.poetryfoundation.org/poems-and-poets/poems/detail/45362

Tinson, J. and Nutall, P. (2010) Exploring appropriation of global cultural trends. *Journal of Marketing Management* 26, 1074–1090.

Volcic, Z. and Andrejevic, M. (2015) *Commercial Nationalism: Selling the Nation and Nationalizing the Sell*. Basingstoke: Palgrave Macmillan.

Waldrop, J. and Mogelonsky, M.K. (1992) *The Seasons of Business: The Marketer's Guide to Consumer Behavior*. Ithaca, NY: American Demographics Books.

Wallendorf, M. and Arnould, E.J. (1991) 'We gather together': Consumption rituals of Thanksgiving Day. *Journal of Consumer Research* 18 (1), 13–31.

Wellings, K., Macdowall, W., Catchpole, M. and Goodrich, J. (1999) Seasonal variations in sexual activity and their implications for sexual health promotion. *Journal of the Royal Society of Medicine* 92, 60–64.

White, L. (2009) The Man from Snowy River: Australia's bush legend and commercial nationalism. *Tourism Review International* 13 (2), 139–146.

Worth, S. and Adair, J. (1972) *Through Navajo Eyes*. Bloomington, IN: Indiana University Press.

16 Canadian Nationalism and the Memory of the First World War in France and Belgium

Jean Martin and Pascale Marcotte

Introduction

Northern France and Belgian Western Flanders do not possess much natural attraction for tourism. The landscape is rather bland, the weather generally cool and wet, and apart from a fairly pleasant coastal strip, elegant and pleasurable retreats are hard to find. True, the local population is quite friendly and the architecture of old cities like Arras, Lille and Ypres is very interesting, but one usually needs other reasons to make a first visit to the area and find out about these treasures.[1] The main and almost unique attraction in this part of Europe are the numerous traces and vestiges of the First World War. The Nord-Pas-de-Calais and the Ypres Salient were the scene of hard and repeated fighting during the First World War, and the country is scattered with their relics. This is one of the rare places where the armies of France and Germany, but also of Belgium, Great Britain and its dominions fought and lost thousands of their men. The Commonwealth War Graves Commission (CWGC) maintains 851 cemeteries in the two French departments of Nord and Pas-de-Calais, and 196 more can be found in the Belgian province of West-Vlaanderen. Dozens of memorials and monuments scatter the landscape, and visitors travel in great number the short distance across the English Channel for a pilgrimage in this nearly British domain.

Canadians also fought with the British army in that same area, leaving more than 50,000 dead in the field. Nine Canadian or Newfoundland memorials were erected in northern France and four more in Belgium.[2] The following analysis is largely based on a series of visits and interviews the authors made in the area in 2013 and 2014.[3] It will demonstrate how, a century after the start of the First World War, the Canadian memory of the event in northern France and Belgium has remained decidedly nationalistic in its approach, in comparison with that of other participating nations. This will be done after a brief overview of the memorial landscape in the area and of the various initiatives to revitalise it on the eve of the centennial. The Canadian experience will subsequently be more specifically analysed, with a particular emphasis on the highly symbolic site of Vimy Ridge.

Elements of Memory

Coming from Paris, the visitor is quickly surrounded by signs of the First World War as he/she enters the department of the Somme, driving north towards Pas-de-Calais and Nord: white crosses in a relatively small number of French cemeteries and, soon afterwards, a host of CWGC burial grounds with sometimes just a few of their typical bullet-shaped headstones. Whereas the French buried large numbers of their dead in vast necropolises, the British preferred to establish sometimes very small cemeteries closer to where the soldiers fell. One can thus recognise the layout of the frontline through this string of miniature graveyards in farming fields; larger cemeteries can also be found in the rear area where regimental aid posts or casualty clearing stations used to be located. CWGC cemeteries all look very similar, with their closely mown lawn, their stone of remembrance and cross of sacrifice surrounded by low brick walls or hedges. There are no Australian, Canadian or New Zealand cemeteries, although some may contain large numbers of soldiers from those nations. The armies of the Empire fighting in the First World War and their dead are all buried in the same ground.

Large memorials were also erected to bear the names of fallen soldiers whose bodies were never recovered, like at Thiepval or Ypres' Menin Gate. Some Commonwealth nations have built their own specific memorials, though, like the Australians at Villers-Bretonneux, the Canadians at Vimy, the New Zealanders at Longueval and the South Africans at Delville Wood. Those memorials and cemeteries are commonly part of the same pilgrimage itineraries, travellers coming from Britain or overseas to visit the burial place of relatives or some local folks. No visitor will stop at every cemetery and memorial; the Canadians will focus on the Vimy area, the Australians and the Newfoundlanders will spend more time in the Somme and many descendants of the Empire's sons will make a call in the Ypres salient, but they will all concentrate almost exclusively on Commonwealth memorial sites.

Some museums and local interpretation centres will also be included in the typical First World War tour in northern France and Flanders. Although designed and managed by French or Belgian organisations, these institutions often give a large place to the British element, as visitors from the British Isles and the former dominions make up most of their business. The Historial at Péronne and the new Interpretation Centre at Souchez adopt a well-balanced approach in trying to give their fair share of the story to all belligerents, including the Germans, but other places, like the Wellington Quarry in

Arras, clearly target the British public, as the focus is almost exclusively put on the experience of the Tommy in those places.[4] Even In Flanders Fields and the Passchendaele Experience museums in Belgium devote a large portion of their exhibits to the Commonwealth soldiers.

More and more now, cemeteries, memorials, monuments, museums and interpretation centres are integrated into so-called remembrance trails (see Zimet, 2011). The French region Nord-Pas-de-Calais has developed very comprehensive 'Chemins de mémoire' for northern France and even part of Belgium.[5] With the upcoming centennial, some nations decided to set up their own specific remembrance trail. Australia allotted 10 million dollars to an Australian Remembrance Trail for the Western Front. Old memorials were renovated, new plaques were installed on various sites and museums were funded anew. Visitors are encouraged to follow those trails in order to learn about the experience of the First World War. There is a clear distinction, though, between the various national sites and circuits, on the one hand, and the more widely open French and Belgian organisations on the other. The Historial at Péronne, the In Flanders Fields Museum at Ypres and the Musée de la Grande Guerre du Pays de Meaux all have the ambition to tell the whole story of the Great War, relevant to all participating countries. The narrative is more comprehensive, and not restricted to one nation only.

A Call to Nationalism

In France and Belgium, the First World War is still a reality. Their landscape is deeply marked by its effects, unexploded ordnances are regularly unearthed and the population still holds vivid memories of the event.[6] The memory of the war in those two countries is not exclusively military. The whole of the population experienced this war and carries its memory with them to the present day. The story of the Great War in those areas is not only one of battles, it is a story of destruction and suffering, but also of a great movement of people, of an arduous reconstruction and of an ongoing healing process. Tens of thousands of soldiers from all of the continents came to northern France and Belgium and shared the life of the local populations during the First World War. The association with all those young men from Africa, Australia, Asia, North America and other European countries changed the way the local people looked at the outside world, and they still keep dear memories of those years. They made friends with those soldiers and they welcome the return of their descendants today.

This can clearly be seen in the museums and other interpretation centres they have built. They give a large place to the Tommies and to their weapons and equipment. They also devote significant space to the experience of the civilian population: the various restrictions, the evacuation of villages and towns, life under German occupation, the arduous reconstruction of destroyed cities, and all that made the global experience of the First World War – all aspects of the war that are totally absent from the interpretation centres at foreign national memorials. The Australian, Canadian, New Zealand, South African as well as the British armies were expeditionary forces; they were not defence forces fighting to protect their homeland. Only soldiers went to France and Belgium, and their memory of the war focuses exclusively on the soldiers' experience, on their own soldiers. There might be a few words and pictures to present in passing their 'home front', with the impact on the economy and women playing a larger part in industry, but the real focus of British and Commonwealth memory of the First World War is the Tommy and his experience in the trenches.

The history of the First World War in those countries is mostly the business of military historians, and military historians are mainly concerned with military operations. The result is an excessive interest in battles. Contrary to popular belief, fighting is but a small part of the soldier's life. 'War is a long waiting': this impression can be found, in one form or another, in many personal accounts of the First World War. Soldiers spent rarely more than a few days every month in the frontline trenches, and even then, raids and major offensives were fairly uncommon occurrences. Most of the time was spent waiting and taking part in various fatigues between stand-to at dawn and the night watch.[7] When in divisional, corps or army reserve, the soldiers would train, play sports, lots of sports, join in more fatigues, visit towns and villages, share a meal with local inhabitants and have a drink at one of the countless 'estaminets' held frequently by French and Belgian women. In the four years the Canadians spent on the Western Front, for instance, not more than nine months was occupied with serious fighting; between the end of the battle of Passchendaele in November 1917 and the opening of the battle of Amiens, eight months later, they were engaged in no major offensive and were only marginally involved in the defensive fighting around Arras. Yet what made the lives of the soldiers in those long periods of time separating each battle is scarcely documented (for one rare exception, see Gibson, 2014).

This results in a sharp contrast between local initiatives and foreign endeavours in the field of memory of the First World War in France and Belgium. While French and Belgian sites speak of a global experience, national memorials and interpretation centres tell an essentially military story. Since the military is the epitome of all state organs, the message becomes intrinsically nationalised. Visitors in Australian or Canadian memorials on the Western Front are not there to learn of the First World War; the real object of those sites is the exaltation of the Australian or Canadian armies and, ultimately, of their national identity. The South African memorial at Delville Wood even stands as the main military memorial for all wars fought by this country in the 20th century. The nation in those memorials, not the war, is the real focus, hence the legend that took form regarding the birth of certain of those nations on the Western Front, when it is actually their national armies that were born in the First World War, not the nations themselves (see also the works of Winter (2006, 2011) about the way the First World War was used by the former colonies of British Empire to define their 'birth').

The Canadian Case

Although very few historians would support this idea, it is often claimed that the Canadian nation was born on the slopes of Vimy Ridge on 9 April 1917 (see Martin (2011) about this debate). This is a fairly new idea, never expressed during the war years, and mostly advocated in certain neo-nationalist circles now, but it grows in popularity with every anniversary of the battle and it will no doubt be loudly stated by many English-speaking media for the centennial of the battle in 2017.[8] Some people like to believe that the Canadian Expeditionary Force, which was largely composed of recent immigrants in 1914 and 1915, was wielded in combat into a solid corps by the end of the war, giving birth to the Canadian nation of today. This, of course, does not take into account the fact that the 400,000 men who went to fight overseas represented merely 5% of the country's population and that a fair share of those men chose to stay in Britain rather than return to Canada after the war. For example, Nicholson (1962) explains that more than 22,000 Canadian soldiers, among some 250,000 who were offered repatriation (at least 50,000 of them were French Canadians), decided to stay in Britain after the war. So most of those men were first and foremost proud British subjects and they certainly never had the ambition to establish a new nation, but the myth has built up over the years and it will probably endure and even prosper in the future.[9]

It is a fact, though, that nowhere perhaps is the Canadian nation so loudly praised today as at Vimy (see Hayes et al., 2007). The Canadian memorials overseas are owned and managed by the state, and the government is free to shape the message it wishes to broadcast in those sites. There is no room for debate at Vimy. Historians and other analysts may argue over the meaning of the battle and of the whole war back in Canada, but only the state, its representatives and their occasional guests have a voice on the slope of Vimy Ridge and there is no argument allowed there. At every new official ceremony held on the site, the same simple message is repeated: the whole Canadian nation, united, fought at Vimy and achieved there a victory that had escaped all others who had dared to attempt it in the past.[10] Even if historians publish books that do not necessarily agree with the official views on the battle, those books will be read by a fairly small proportion of the population and they can never successfully challenge the official interpretation expressed in every ceremony and conveyed by all the national media. The endless repetition, for every anniversary, keeps reinforcing this interpretation in the eye of the public, and with passing time, the official message on Vimy and Canada in the First World War emerges as the irrefutable truth.[11]

Vimy is not the only First World War memorial site on the Western Front, but it is by far the best known; too many times it is even the only one known in Canada. Although there are 12 other Canadian and Newfoundland official memorials throughout northern France and Belgium, Vimy is most commonly the only one visited, with the Newfoundland memorial at Beaumont-Hamel, in the Somme. Those two sites are the only sites where part of the battlefield was preserved and where guided tours are offered to the visitors. Because of that, more than for the importance of the battle, those two sites are the first (and often the last) to be visited. Some Canadians may venture to the Ypres salient for a quick visit at Passchendaele and Sint-Juliaan, but very few people even know about the memorials at Le Quesnel, Bourlon Wood or Masnières.[12] While visitors go to Beaumont-Hamel because of the fairly well preserved battlefield, the only portion of the Somme battle-field still relatively unspoiled today, it is the impressive, and photogenic, monument that attracts most visitors at Vimy.

It is tempting to believe that the main Canadian memorial was erected at Vimy because of the extraordinary importance of the battle, but it should rather be remembered that it is the presence of the monument that has largely contributed to the disproportionate increase in the importance of the site over the past 80 years. Other sites were considered when it was decided to build one much larger memorial than the others in the late 1920s, and one can reasonably surmise that, had the monument been erected at Sint-Juliaan or Bourlon Wood, for example, it would be one of those two battles, more than any other, that would be most celebrated today in Canada. Vimy was chosen for various reasons, the natural advantage of its geography ranking higher than the military value of the battle among them. From the top of Vimy Ridge the monument can be observed from kilometres around, and it attracts to the site many visitors who are not even aware of the battle that was fought there by the Canadian Corps in 1917. Those visitors come to look at the monument, one of the most beautiful on the Western Front. Canadians like to believe that the many thousands of visitors all go to Vimy to pay tribute to the courage and sacrifice of the Canadian soldiers, but the truth is that a good share of them come first to admire an impressive work of art.

The memorial at Vimy Ridge is, by far, the most visited and celebrated memorial site in the French region of Nord-Pas-de-Calais. According to the Belgian tourism organisation Westhoek, Vimy welcomes over 200,000 visitors every year, which is between two and four times more visitors than the second most popular site in the area, the Wellington Quarry in Arras (Berger, 2015; La Voix du Nord, 2014). The power of attraction of the monument at Vimy Ridge is obvious when one considers that it is pictured on nearly all tourism publications in the area (see e.g. *Les Chemins de mémoire 14–18*, published in 2014 by the regional council). The elegant and impressive lines of the Canadian monument are the most easily recognisable features of the landscape in Artois. The Belfrey in Arras, for example, is another very attractive monument in that area, but it can only be seen when one has already entered the city. The monument at Vimy Ridge, on the contrary, can be clearly seen from kilometres away by people driving on one of the many highways in the area, and its imposing presence attracts many visitors. This Canadian monument has definitely emerged in the past decades as one prominent landmark of northern France.

The two Canadian sites of Vimy and Beaumont-Hamel are among the very few memorial sites that offer free guided tours, which is another powerful incentive for the tour operators to include it in their battlefield tours. Those tours will take their guests to other interesting sites, such as the necropolis and the new Ring of Memory at Notre-Dame-de-Lorette, but only at Vimy Ridge will they be offered free guided tours of part of a First World War battlefield by young Canadian students. The new interpretation centre that has recently opened in the nearby town of Souchez and the Wellington Quarry, for example, also offer guided tours, albeit for a fee and only within the confines of their building or underground exhibit.[13] A new interpretation centre will also open at Vimy Ridge in 2017, for the centennial of the battle, which will no doubt enrich the experience of the visit.

Canadian visitors are but a minority at Vimy. It is a long way for them to travel to this part of France, and military pilgrimage is not a very popular activity in Canada. Most visitors at Vimy come either from France or Britain, with a fair share originating also from Australia and from the other former dominions. Therefore, the memorial's main purpose is to proclaim and acclaim the Canadian nation in the face of the whole world, and this image will be reflected, as in a mirror, to the Canadian public back home. It is consequently essential that the impression made on the visitor conforms to the ideology and principles promoted by the Canadian State. Thus, Vimy must be the symbol of this new nation that the state wants to originate in 1917, to replace any other ideas of a nation that might have preceded it.

Vimy: Symbol of an Invented Nation

The 3,500 Canadians who died at Vimy in April 1917 represent only one out of 15 Canadians who fell on the Western Front during the First World War. Yet most people in France believe that Vimy was the only battle fought by the Canadians in the First World War. Contrary to the Australians, who put plaques and monuments every place they went and open museums and interpretation centres in a few locations, the Canadians decided to concentrate the whole memory of the Canadian participation in the war into one single symbolic site. Vimy Ridge is a naturally impressive feature of the regional landscape, it is conveniently located near some attracting urban centres and Vimy represents a 'great' victory. It is a particularly significant aspect of the Canadian memory of the First World War that it focuses on the idea of victory (Vance, 1997; McKane, n.d.).

Australia commemorates costly operations at Gallipoli and Fromelles, which did not conclude with great victories; even the monument at Pozières reminds more of the huge losses suffered after the capture of the village in late July 1916.[14] For the Canadians, all memorials are placed on the sites of what they regard as victories; even their participation in the Second Battle of Ypres, commemorated at Sint-Juliaan, is presented as a significant defensive victory, despite the loss of one-third of the 1st Canadian Division.[15] So while most other memorials of the First World War emphasise the sense of loss and grief, the Canadians have tended to put the accent on the idea of victory in their memorials, emphasising a victorious, almost conquering, Canadian nation. The impression left after a visit at the site of Vimy Ridge is too often that of a nation that crossed the Atlantic Ocean to conquer a piece of the French soil.

It is remarkable that barely any word is said at the Vimy interpretation centre about the tremendous efforts that were effected in 1915 by the French to allow the Canadians to open their offensive from a tremendously more advantageous position in 1917 (see Martin, 2014). The French eliminated several strong German defences and took the frontline from a distance of several kilometres to the very foot of the ridge. Two French divisions even occupied the top of the ridge for a few hours and a monument still stands today just a few dozen metres from the big Canadian monument to honour the men of one of those divisions. The French army lost some 80,000 men in the various offensives that were launched in this sector in the first two years of the war. Yet the story told today by the government of Canada at Vimy says nearly nothing of the deeds of those who did not belong to the Canadian army corps, not even of the thousands of British soldiers who fought alongside the Canadians in April 1917. The legend that is taking form has it that Canada sent its best young men to capture almost singlehandedly this 'most heavily defended position on the Western Front'.[16]

Conclusion

Visitors coming to Vimy today are invited to encounter an invented nation, one that started to build up years after the battle in the minds of a class of propagandists. This nation actually appears as an utterly male and militaristic body, which is quite separate from the actual diverse and complex Canadian nation.[17] In 1917, the real Canadian nation was massively busy in agriculture and industry in Canada and barely 1% of it, all male, was concentrated at the foot of Vimy Ridge on 9 April, fighting as part of the

First British Army. The Canadian memorial at Vimy Ridge is a major tourist attraction, not only for the French region of Nord-Pas-de-Calais, but also for a large pool of tourists interested in the memory of wars in general, in all parts of the world. Those tourists will find at Vimy a certain idea of the Canadian nation.

Vimy is fully participating in the 'invention' of the Canadian identity and the Canadian nation (cf. Hobsbawm & Ranger, 2012). The story told at Vimy is that of an imagined nation that would be born in April 1917. This event is being voluntarily recalled by rituals and symbolic practices. Repeated in unison, these rituals finally establish consensus. The battle of Vimy Ridge was fought 50 years after the Confederation of 1867.[18] The first centennial of the Confederation coincided with the 50th anniversary of the battle in 1967, and the forthcoming centennial of the battle will be commemorated concurrently with the celebration of the 150th anniversary of the Confederation. The Canadian nation will no doubt be highly acclaimed at the next commemorating ceremonies of the battle in 2017.

The monument's physical presence and its iconography of suffering, its proportions, its whiteness, its narrative of reconciliation, and its ideals of liberty provide a place to gather. The great park, the dramatic height and its geographically dominant position make it ideal for gathering. Urry (2002: 261) recalls that there is a further sense of co-presence, physically walking or seeing or touching or hearing or smelling a place. Vimy, as a central touristic place and as a pilgrimage site, offers this kind of encounter with a 'Canadian nation' (see also the works of Osborne, 2001; Winter, 2011). It is such a perfect place that other sites will be forgotten. The encounter goes even further in everyday life. The Bank of Canada decided to immortalise the event by printing the image of the monument on the 20 dollar bill. Since 2012, every Canadian has kept the Monument in their wallet, and should be keeping it in their heart.

Finally, Vimy's story, like other mythological narratives, occupies a particularly important place in the collective imagination. The ritualisation process (celebration, remembrance, pilgrim, image reproductions), and the sacralisation made the myth undeniable (Bouchard & Andrès, 2007), and finally created an 'imagined Canada' (cf. Anderson, 1991). One hundred years later, the Canadian state still holds part of the ground that was captured that day and uses it to present a certain idea of the Canadian nation. It is a decidedly nationalistic image that is offered there. The whole story of the war is not to be found in this site, not even the full story of the war for the Canadians.

Notes

(1)   The famous French movie *Bienvenue chez les Ch'tis* (Pathé, 2008; director Dany Boon) tells exactly this story of a man whose employer, as a punishment, ships him to northern France where, after an initial period of despair, he discovers the human appeal of the region.

(2) Newfoundland was a separate dominion in the First World War, but it has since joined the Canadian confederation.

(3) Funded by the Conseil franco-québécois de coopération universitaire, this research seeks to understand the turning of some sites of the First World War into tourist attractions. Data was collected from visits and interviews with managers of battle sites and tourist organisations, and from content analysis of tourism brochures and websites.

(4) Tommy was the general nickname of the British soldiers in the First World War, and this was sometimes extended to other white colonial troops.

(5) Remembrance trail would translate in French as 'sentier du souvenir', not 'mémoire', which shows a substantial difference in approach, the focus being set more on the concept of memory in this instance.

(6) A total of about one billion artillery shells were fired on the Western Front and it is estimated that at least 20% of them were duds. It is still a very common occurrence today to find British 18 pounder or German 77 cm shells in the fields between the Somme and the Belgian coast.

(7) Stand-to was the usual one-hour period around sunrise when the soldiers would stand ready for an eventual enemy attack, which only rarely materialised.

(8) French Canadians do not attribute the same nation-founding value to the event, the perception of a national identity among Canadian Francophones going back much further in time than the early 20th century.

(9) It is not that uncommon to read on headstones of Canadian soldiers buried in France or Belgium inscriptions like 'For England' or 'Tell England we died for her'.

(10) The French had tried twice in 1915 to capture Vimy Ridge and the Canadians like to claim that they succeeded where others had failed before. They forget to mention that the French actually eliminated all of the obstacles before the ridge, pushing the frontline nearly 4 km forward to provide the British and later the Canadians who relieved them with a much more favourable position to attack from.

(11) Although this idea of 'the birth of a nation' at Vimy was first expressed in 1967 (see Macintyre, 1967), 50 years after the battle, it is systematically repeated in official and semi-official accounts of the event. See for example the Canadian War Museum website (http://www.warmuseum.ca/cwm/exhibitions/vimy/index_e.shtml) and the Canadian Encyclopedia (http://www.thecanadianencyclopedia.ca/en/article/vimy-ridge-and-the-birth-of-a-nation/.)

(12) The Canadians fought at Saint-Julien (Sint-Juliaan) after the first German gas attack in 1915, and they achieved a costly victory at Paschendaele in 1917. The memorials at Le Quesnel and Bourlon Wood stand for two of the most successful actions of the Canadian Corps during the battle of Amiens (early August 1918) and the crossing of the Canal du Nord (late September 1918). The Caribou at Masnières commemorates the part played by the Newfoundland regiment in the First Battle of Cambrai (late 1917), after which the title 'Royal' was bestowed on the regiment.

(13) The Ring of Memory was inaugurated in November 2014 and the interpretation centre at Souchez was opened in early 2015. The Ring of Memory bears the names of nearly 600,000 soldiers of all nations who died in Nord-Pas-de-Calais during the First World War.

(14) The 1st, 2nd and 4th Australian Divisions lost nearly 23,000 men in the capture and defence of the little village of Pozières in July and August 1916.

(15) The Second Battle of Ypres was launched with the first use of combat gas by the Germans on 22 April 1915 and dragged on until the end of the month. The Canadians helped the French and the Belgians to prevent the German break-through, but it is generally presented as a largely Canadian victory in the Canadian historiography.

(16) This assertion can unfortunately too often be heard, although the strategic importance of Vimy Ridge in the spring of 1917 was no longer what it had been in 1915.

(17) This can be explained by the fact that Canada is made up of three territories and 10 provinces, one of which is francophone and another one bilingual. Furthermore, its population is largely made up of fairly recent immigrants or their descendants coming from a wide array of countries, and the parents and grandparents of a very large proportion of the Canadian population today did not even live in Canada during the First World War.

(18) The origin of the Canadian state can be found in the confederation that united four provinces in 1867. Six more provinces and three territories either joined or were created after that date.

References

Anderson, B. (1991) *Imagined Communities: Reflections on the Origins and Spread of Nationalism* (2nd edn). London: Verso.

Berger, C. (2015) *Le centenaire de la grande guerre premiers impacts et mobilisation des acteurs touristiques, Les rencontre du tourisme de mémoire*. See http://www.entreprises. gouv.fr/files/files/directions_services/tourisme/territoires/img/tourisme_de_memoire/ TR1_Quel_impact_des_commemorations_sur_l'economie_touristique_des_territoires. pdf (accessed 14 February 2016).

Boon, D. (2008) *Bienvenue chez les Ch'tis*. France: Pathé-Renn, 106 minutes.

Bouchard, G. and Andrès, B. (2007) *Mythes et Sociétés des Amériques.* Montréal: Les éditions Québec Amérique.

Gibson, G. (2014) *Behind the Front. British Soldiers and French Civilians, 1914–1918.* Cambridge: Cambridge University Press.

Hayes, G., Iarocci A. and Bechthold, M. (2007) *Vimy Ridge: A Canadian Reassessment.* Waterloo: Wilfrid Laurier University Press, Laurier Centre for Military Strategic and Disarmament Studies.

Hobsbawm, E. and Ranger, T. (eds) (2012) *L'invention de la tradition* (new augmented edn). Amsterdam: Paris Éditions.

La Voix du Nord (2014) *Tourisme de mémoire: la victoire du mémorial de Vimy,* 12 October 2014. See http://www.lavoixdunord.fr/region/tourisme-de-memoire-la-victoire-du-memorial-de-vimy-ia0b0n2430293 (accessed 14 February 2016).

Macintyre, D.E. (1967) *Canada at Vimy.* Toronto: Peter Martin Associates.

Martin, J. (2011) Vimy, April 1917: The birth of which nation? *Canadian Military Journal,* 11 (2). See http://www.journal.forces.gc.ca/vol11/no2/06-martin-eng.asp (accessed 2 August 2014).

Martin, J. (2014) Vimy, 9 avril 1917 une histoire à compléter. In J. Martin, *Un siècle d'oubli: les Canadiens et la Première Guerre mondiale (1914-2014)* (pp. 39–64). Outremont: Athéna Éditions.

McKane, B. (n.d.) Remembering the Great War in the Dominions of the British Empire. How have the contribution of the British dominions of Australia and Canada been memorialised in the aftermath of the First World War? (S1128469). MA thesis, Leiden University.

Nicholson, G.W.L. (1962) *Canadian Expeditionary Force, 1914–1919. Official History of the Canadian Army in the First World War.* Ottawa: R. Duhamel, Queen's Printer and Controller of Stationery.

Osborne, B.S. (2001) Landscapes, memory, monuments, and commemoration: Putting identity in its place. *Canadian Ethnic Studies Journal* 33 (3), 39–61.

Urry, J. (2002) Mobility and proximity. *Sociology* 46 (2), 255–274.

Vance, J. (1997) *Death so Noble: Memory, Meaning, and the First World War.* Vancouver: UBC Press.

Winter, C. (2011) Battlefield tourism and Australian national identity. In E. Frew and L. White (eds) *Tourism and National Identities* (pp. 176–189). London: Routledge.

Winter, J. (2006) *Remembering War: The Great War between Memory and History in the Twentieth Century.* New Haven, CT: Yale University Press.

Zimet, J. (2011) *Commémorer la Grande Guerre (2014–2020): propositions pour centenaire international.* Rapport au Président de la République, Secrétariat général pour l'administration, Direction de la mémoire, du patrimoine et des archives.

17 'Daddy, Why do we Celebrate SG50?' A Response to a Child Regarding Singapore's Golden Jubilee

Aaron Tham

Introduction

My daughter, Germaine, asked me, 'Daddy, why do we celebrate SG50?' over the dinner table one night in July 2015 after I had mentioned that I had ordered tickets to attend Singapore's Golden Jubilee event (hereafter abbreviated as SG50) in Brisbane on Sunday, 9 August 2015. This question became the catalyst for drafting this chapter as I recall the subsequent conversations and explanations of why the year's birthday celebrations was of such importance to Singapore. Drawing from a mixed methods approach of participant observation and content analysis from online sources leading up to SG50, this investigation has witnessed how commercial nationalism can apply to the notion of hot authenticity within tourism and events.

Singapore is one of the world's smallest countries and one that has a very short history of independence. The country only institutionalised independence following separation from Malaysia (then known as British Malaya) on 9 August 1965 (Siddique, 1990). Since then, Singapore has enjoyed a period of economic growth brought about by strong governance and a highly skilled labour force (Huff, 1995). These core ingredients have led various nations around the world to respect the country that has achieved much success within such a short time frame (Hamilton-Hart, 2000). Singapore has one of the highest GDPs per capita in the world, and is seen as a role model for, among other indicators, governmental integrity, ease of conducting business and a world-class educational system (Haley & Low, 1998; Haque, 2004; Marginson, 2011).

Its Golden Jubilee, better known as SG50, therefore provides the stage to showcase what the country has achieved over the past 50 years. SG50 took more than two years to plan and execute because of the consultative approach taken by all stakeholders to ensure that the country's success story is reflective of the multi-racial fabric of its citizens and the various sectors that have brought such outcomes to fruition (Halliday et al., 2015). For this reason, SG50 seemed to be a fitting showcase to investigate commercial nationalism on the back of such a commemorative event.

Commercial Nationalism

The notion of commercial nationalism needs to be disentangled from other relevant yet seemingly interchangeable terms. Primarily, the term commercial nationalism comprises two parts. The first, and perhaps most crucial, is that of nationalism. This is where nationalism can be understood across several domains, including national identity, national image and national brand (Stock, 2009). While most scholars are in general agreement of what constitutes national identity and image, a nation's brand is perhaps most difficult to conceptualise to a large, global audience (Fan, 2010). Nonetheless, some useful work exists to help shed light as to how one might interpret nation branding (see Caldwell & Freire, 2004; Gudjonsson, 2005; Kaneva, 2011; White, 2004). Derived from these scholarly works is an adopted definition of nationalism to represent a shared identity belonging to a community of persons and the portrayal of their unique attributes to the outside world (Conversi, 1995).

If we accept this definition of nationalism, then the second part involving the commercialisation process should be understood in terms of commoditising the celebrated identities, where this could take various symbols and artefacts, as well as tourism and commemorative events (Volcic & Andrejevic, 2011). As such, there can be various points in history or heritage that can be utilised in the evolution of commercial nationalism. For instance, White (2009) showed how the famous Australian bush story *The Man from Snowy River* can be a tool to celebrate Australianness and the spirit of the country. In 2015, the centenary of the Gallipoli battle commemorative event was likewise argued from a commercial nationalism perspective to be a highly emotive experience from visitors to the destination (Gibson, 2015). Yet detractors point to the flaws of commercial nationalism in profiteering from the hype of the festivities rather than providing authentic re-enactments of past events (Balmer, 2011). The nexus between the value of commercial nationalism and the tipping point of commodification is certainly one that I needed to reflect on in my narrative to Germaine given her inquisitive mind and how the SG50 event in Brisbane would unfold.

SG50 in Singapore and Brisbane

The acronym SG50 is a well-known term for the Singaporean community because of its immersion into the everyday landscape of the country. On its official website (https://www.singapore50.sg), one can ascertain the pride and celebratory tone of the event in showcasing Singapore's success to its citizens and the world. From advertising campaigns of household appliances to identifying faces synonymous with Singapore, it appeared that no stone was left unturned as the country sought an all-out approach to ensure that no Singaporeans were left behind in this commemorative event.

The year 2015 was indeed a year to remember for Singapore. A month prior to the SG50 celebrations, the country received its first UNESCO World Heritage site at the Singapore Botanic Gardens (Kotwani & Ariffin, 2015). This announcement was certainly a timely one to celebrate at SG50, but hardly anyone would have forgotten the death of Singapore's founding Prime Minister, Mr Lee Kuan Yew in March 2015. His passing, at the age of 91, resulted in more than one million individuals queuing to pay their final respects, resulting in the government having to allocate a full week for well-wishes to be complete before conducting the funeral (Ng, 2015). Few would argue that Singapore would not be where it is today if not for Lee Kuan Yew's legacy (Hong, 2002). 2015 was a year of significant gains and losses for Singapore, but the SG50 factor certainly played a pivotal factor in the ruling government's strong political showing in the September 2015 elections (Chew, 2015).

SG50 would therefore provide a milestone to encapsulate the journey that the country has taken to be where it is today. This was the catalyst for the government, via its Overseas Singaporean Unit (https://www.overseass-ingaporean.sg) to reach out to its diaspora all over the world, ensuring that they too can be part of this event. It was from this initiative that I learnt about the SG50 Brisbane event through the Singapore Club of Queensland (https://www.facebook.com/SingaporeClubBrIsbane). Other initiatives in partnership with the SG50 campaign included Jetstar running an online competition to fly home 50 individuals from around the world to be part of the SG50 activities (Hee, 2015). While the Jetstar competition was appealing, other commitments meant that this was not likely to be one that I could realistically undertake. However, subconsciously, without discussing it with my spouse, I decided to get the family tickets to attend the SG50 Brisbane event immediately after receiving notification on Facebook. This decision, I must admit, is somewhat out of the ordinary, given that I have not actively sourced for opportunities to attend any of the prior National Day celebrations, even though I have lived in the country for more than three decades.

Hence, I found the question posed by Germaine to be a hard one, and struggled to articulate why my decision to attend the event in Brisbane was justified instead of watching the event online via live streaming.

These questions lingered in my headspace for some time, without necessarily having answers, leading up to the event:

(1)   Is the motivation to attend SG50 in Brisbane because of the nostalgia associated with the Golden Jubilee?
(2)   What should I be expecting at the SG50 Brisbane event?
(3)   What will I use to ascertain satisfaction or authenticity cues related to the SG50 event?
(4)   What does SG50 mean to me?
(5)   How should I provide an informed and reasoned answer to Germaine?
(6)   How will I share with others the symbolism of SG50?

Prior to the event, the Brisbane organisers provided timely updates as to what one might anticipate through their Facebook page. Looking at these retrospective links, I gleaned the excitement and pride for the pool of volunteers in playing an instrumental role in the SG50 story. Organisers foregrounded the anticipation by notifying its Facebook community that the numbers had exceeded its preliminary expectations and that a revised police clearance application had to be sought owing to the enlarged attendee base. Little did I realise that this Brisbane edition of the event was to become the largest SG50 event outside Singapore. There were also several posts to showcase the types of Southeast Asian cuisine prepared by a few select food and beverage operators in the city. After all, Singapore takes pride in offering locals and visitors an array of food options and cultures to choose from (Henderson, 2004). Consistent with the appeal that food is part of the Singaporean culture, SG50 Brisbane featured the placement of key culinary treats as part of its narrative.

No effort was spared by the organisers in replicating the same types of experiences in an offshore SG50 event as the one held concurrently in Singapore. With the help of various ministries, the organisers managed to secure two key memorabilia of the SG50 event, namely LEGO sets for children and SG50 fun packs for attendees. The SG50 LEGO set is a specially designed toy that is issued to all teachers and children at educational institutions in Singapore (Khoo, 2015). While more than 600,000 commemorative sets were issued free of charge as part of the SG50 event, it was reported that some individuals had decided to make their sets available for sale to others, thereby profiteering from the cause (Abu Baker, 2015). It therefore came as a pleasant surprise when we were notified of the potential availability of such LEGO sets to Singaporean children overseas, including those in Brisbane. At the SG50 Brisbane registration desk, Germaine smiled when she was in receipt of one such set, as illustrated in Figure 17.1.

However, we did not manage to secure any SG50 fun packs as they had all been issued to others in the queue before us. Nonetheless, a request to another attendee at the event provided a glimpse of the contents in the fun

Figure 17.1 SG50 commemorative LEGO set

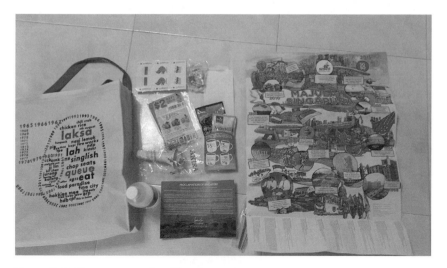

Figure 17.2 The contents of an SG50 fun pack

packs, as presented in Figure 17.2. Issued to each household in Singapore, each SG50 fun pack contained some snacks, a bottle of mineral water, historical fact sheets of Singapore and a *Singa* figurine that is associated with the kindness movement within the country (Chow, 2015). Similar to the SG50 LEGO sets, these fun packs have likewise become objects for sale on some online websites (Hwei, 2015). While not exclusive to SG50, souvenirs are emblematic of any event and can provide some tangible cues to heighten the attendee experience (Gordon, 1986).

Other cues at the SG50 Brisbane event provided some further exemplars as to how the Singapore story was reproduced for the diaspora living in the city. Figure 17.3 provides a brief synopsis of these exemplars and how they contribute towards commercial nationalism.

The six aspects present at the SG50 Brisbane event not only emphasise how commercial nationalism can be packaged, but also contribute to the notion that such commemorative events are an endorsement for the notion of hot authenticity. According to Cohen and Cohen (2012), the notion of hot authenticity is characterised by informal attempts through participation and the performance of rituals. Emanating from the SG50 Brisbane event are various exemplars of how hot authenticity embodies the immersive experience of celebrating such a momentous occasion with other like-minded Singaporeans. These include the role of a large pool of volunteers providing an impetus for the Singapore diaspora to show up and support one another's identity and celebrating the Singapore story.

I vividly recall the journey back home and the conversations I had with Germaine as to why SG50 was such a big deal. This was more than just the gift of an SG50 LEGO set. Rather, it was about celebrating what the country

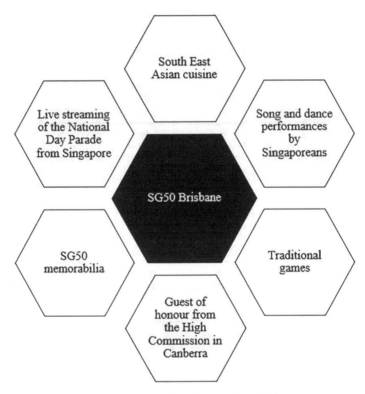

Figure 17.3 Elements of commercial nationalism at SG50 Brisbane

has achieved, and the pride of being a Singaporean at this point in history. As she moved to Australia at the age of 2, the memories of Singapore are perhaps fairly distant apart from knowing that her grandparents live there and that she was born in the country. To me, SG50 Brisbane provided an opportunity for Singaporeans located overseas to celebrate their identities with other citizens back home by providing a time and place to converge as an expression of commercial nationalism.

Deconstructing the SG50 Brisbane experience was therefore a very reflexive experience for me. There were moments where nostalgia set in, especially when watching the live stream of the National Day Parade and singing along to familiar tunes that had graced previous years' editions. I had expected a sizeable turnout at the Brisbane event, although the large number of attendees who chose to be there and immerse themselves with others sharing a common bond brought a smile to my face. While there were occasions when it appeared that some performances were highly staged, I was perhaps a little more accommodating given that SG50 would only occur once in Singapore's lifetime. The event in Brisbane had its imperfections, such as long waiting times for meals and also beverages that were issued past their expiry dates. Despite these blemishes, I purchased a t-shirt at the event to remind myself of the powerful symbol of having taken part in a chapter of Singapore's history. This t-shirt (see Figure 17.4), when worn occasionally, becomes a conversation topic with friends and often evokes a sense of pride in being a Singaporean.

As one might anticipate, it was unlikely that SG50 Brisbane would replicate all events that were part of the Golden Jubilee celebrations in Singapore. One of the most surprising and yet well-received announcements to Singaporeans was that 7 August 2015 was to be accorded a public holiday in Singapore (Hio, 2015). This announcement by the President of Singapore epitomised the importance of the event in declaring a one-off public holiday. The country is one that is extremely careful with giving extra days for public holidays, especially when the religious festival of Thaipusam was removed as a public holiday in 1968 (Tan, 2015). Consideration for the 11 gazetted public holidays in Singapore has been given on the basis of two public holidays for each of the ethnic groups, with the three remaining public holidays (New Year's Day, Labour Day and National Day) celebrated as a country. Therefore, to carve out a regular working day as an additional public holiday was certainly a reflection of the importance of SG50.

The extra-long weekend not only created an exodus of residents leaving for short getaways, but also generated greater visitor numbers to local attractions. These included free entry to the island of Sentosa, museums and the Science Centre, among others (Loo, 2015). Chan (2015) highlighted that hotels were also jumping onto the SG50 bandwagon, offering staycation packages throughout the year. According to Dodds (2012), the term 'staycation' describes a low-involvement decision to have a vacation in the local

Figure 17.4 SG50 Brisbane t-shirt

area. This is different from domestic tourism, as staycations are about the choice of having overnight accommodation in a commercial provider within one's city of residence (Caletrio, 2012).

These activities, among others, reiterate the heightened nature of commercial nationalism by amplifying the pride and national identity associated with SG50 to give citizens a reason to celebrate. Aside from the anticipated National Day Parade, the diversity of activities in conjunction with the SG50 image has provided citizens with ample opportunities to commemorate the event. However, the rampant use of SG50 has led some individuals to become suspicious as to the legitimacy of using SG50, and the drivers behind such promotions (Lay, 2015). In a country whose reputation in intellectual property is widely acknowledged around the world (see Lim, 2015), it would be perhaps surprising if the government was to press charges against any individual or organisation regarding violation of SG50 brand copyright. After all, SG50 was meant for every Singaporean in an extremely celebratory tone. Hence, any business or group appears to be able to use SG50 as an endorsement of their products or services. This is perhaps commercial nationalism taken to another level.

The differences between SG50 in Singapore and SG50 Brisbane go beyond geographical space. More pertinently, SG50 operated in a highly pervasive environment in Singapore, where one was unlikely to avoid any attachment to the event throughout 2015. There were numerous symbols, banners and advertisements of SG50 dispersed throughout the country and it almost appeared to be what Guo *et al.* (2007) termed 'nationalist indoctrination'. In contrast, SG50 Brisbane was an event that a large group of overseas Singaporeans dedicated to come together in unity to celebrate a commemorative event. By forming the largest offshore SG50 event, the 1,500 individuals could lay claim to a pivotal point in Singapore's history. The Brisbane event was not so much about a re-enactment of Singapore's success story, but more a case of weaving a narrative as a collective group celebrating a common identity.

Conclusion

In conclusion, the review of SG50 events in Singapore and Brisbane raises the need for future studies to critically evaluate the manifestation of commercial nationalism. While SG50 has led to a nuanced understanding of hot authenticity related to commemorative events, there remain very few studies to date that have probed the 'tipping point' as to when commercial gains outweigh national pride. Qiu (2006) argues that a perpetual state of tension exists between embedding citizenry identities within commercial practices, and calls for questioning of motives and equity. In spite of the goodwill in bringing all Singaporeans to be united as one nation, issues of relevancy and legitimacy have surfaced when SG50 became a tool for organisations cashing in on nationalistic allegiance.

As with any research, this response to Germaine is not without its limitations. SG50 is perhaps one of many different exemplars of commercial nationalism. Other countries or contexts may provide a different perspective of commercial nationalism. As exploratory research, the sample was limited to primary data collected through participant observation in Brisbane and secondary data collated via the internet. Surveys or interviews with citizens in Singapore, Brisbane or other cities may provide further insights as to what SG50 evokes in terms of commercial nationalism. These limitations notwithstanding, the chapter has constructed an appreciation of commercial nationalism from an Asian perspective. The emergence of Asia as a pillar of today's economy will undoubtedly compel other nations to strengthen their national brand and perhaps reap commercial returns accordingly (Duara, 2010).

At a personal level, it has been some time since SG50 elapsed. Germaine and I sometimes bring this topic up and recall what happened. During these conversations, it seems strange that the story appears to be one that I am narrating to myself, and the meanings of SG50 that I had ascribed. I do not know how she will further the conversation to her family and loved ones in the generations to come when Singapore celebrates its Diamond Jubilee (75 years) in 2040 or even its Centennial in 2065. Much will have changed by then, but as now, SG50 and its manifestations of commercial nationalism seem to be etched in our hearts and minds.

References

Abu Baker, J. (2015) *Free SG50 commemorative Lego sets from MOE being sold online for $100 and more.* See http://www.straitstimes.com/singapore/free-sg50-commemorative-lego-sets-from-moe-being-sold-online-for-100-and-more (accessed 5 October 2015).

Balmer, J.M.T. (2011) Corporate heritage brands and the precepts of heritage brand management: Insights from the British monarchy on the eve of the royal wedding of Prince William (April 2011) and Queen Elizabeth II's diamond jubilee. *Journal of Brand Management* 18 (8), 517–544.

Caldwell, N. and Freire, J.R. (2004) The differences between branding a country, a region and a city: Applying the Brand Box Model. Journal of *Brand Management* 12 (1), 50–61.

Caletrio, J. (2012) Simple living and tourism in times of 'austerity'. *Current Issues in Tourism* 15 (3), 275–279.

Chan, D. (2015) 15 SG50 staycation packages to book this year. See http://www.herworldplus.com/solutions/solutions/10-sg50-staycation-packages-book-year (accessed 16 October 2015).

Chew, H.M. (2015) GE2015 has assured Singapore's future beyond SG50. See http://news.asiaone.com/news/general-election/ge2015-has-assured-singapores-future-beyond-sg50-pm-lee (accessed 5 October 2015).

Chow, J. (2015) National Day goodie bags to be distributed to households from July. See http://www.straitstimes.com/singapore/national-day-goodie-bags-to-be-distributed-to-households-from-july (accessed 5 October 2015).

Cohen, E. and Cohen, S.A. (2012) Authentication: Hot and cool. *Annals of Tourism Research* 39 (3), 1295–1314.

Conversi, D. (1995) Reassessing current theories of nationalism as boundary maintenance and creation. *Nationalism and Ethnic Politics* 1 (1), 73–85.

Dodds, R. (2012) Questioning slow as sustainable. *Tourism Recreation Research* 37 (1), 81–83.

Duara, P. (2010) Asia redux: Conceptualizing a region for our times. *The Journal of Asian Studies* 69 (4), 963–983.

Fan, Y. (2010) Branding the nation: Towards a better understanding. *Place Branding and Public Diplomacy* 6 (2), 97–103.

Gibson, P.J. (2015) Imperialism, ANZAC nationalism and the Aboriginal experience of warfare. *Cosmopolitan Civil Societies: An Interdisciplinary Journal* 6 (3), 63–82.

Gordon, B. (1986) The souvenir: Messenger of the extraordinary. *The Journal of Popular Culture* 20 (3), 135–146.

Gudjonsson, H. (2005) Nation branding. *Place Branding* 1 (3), 283–298.

Guo, Z., Cheong, W.H. and Chen, H. (2007) Nationalism as public imagination: The media's routine contribution to latent and manifest nationalism in China. *International Communication Gazette* 69 (5), 467–480.

Haley, U.C.V. and Low, L. (1998) Crafted culture: Governmental sculpting of modern Singapore and effects on business environments. *Journal of Organizational Change Management* 11 (6), 530–553.

Halliday, L., Robertson, H. and Tan, R. (2015) Country branding: Singapore. *Research World* 52 (May–June), 28–29.

Hamilton-Hart, N. (2000) The Singapore state revisited. *The Pacific Review* 13 (2), 195–216.

Haque, M.S. (2004) Governance and bureaucracy in Singapore: Contemporary reforms and implications. *International Political Science Review* 25 (2), 227–240.

Hee, J. (2015) For SG50, Jetstar Asia is flying overseas Singaporeans home for free. See https://vulcanpost.com/214761/sg50-jetstar-asia-flying-overseas-singaporeans-home-free/ (accessed 5 October 2015).

Henderson, J. (2004) Food as a tourism resource: A view from Singapore. *Tourism Recreation Research* 29 (3), 69–74.

Hio, L. (2015) Aug 7 declared a holiday as part of Singapore's 50th birthday celebrations. See http://www.straitstimes.com/singapore/aug-7-declared-a-holiday-as-part-of-singapores-50th-birthday-celebrations (accessed 16 October 2015).

Hong, L. (2002) The Lee Kuan Yew story as Singapore's history. *Journal of the Southeast Asian Studies* 33 (3), 545–557.

Huff, W.G. (1995) The developmental state, government, and Singapore's economic development since 1960. *World Development* 23 (8), 1421–1438.

Hwei, L. (2015) First wave of SG50 funpacks hit Carousell, and we're not surprised. See https://vulcanpost.com/316811/sg50-funpacks-on-carousell/ (accessed 5 October 2015).

Kaneva, N. (2011) Nation branding: Toward an agenda for critical research. *International Journal of Communication* 5, 117–141.

Khoo, J.W.T. (2015) All MOE students, teachers to get SG50 LEGO sets. See http://www.todayonline.com/singapore/students-teachers-receive-special-lego-sets-sg50 (accessed 5 October 2015).

Kotwani, M. and Ariffin, N.A. (2015) Singapore Botanic Gardens declared UNESCO World Heritage Site. See http://www.channelnewsasia.com/news/singapore/singapore-botanic-gardens/1960028.html (accessed 5 October 2015).

Lay, B. (2015) Simi Sai Also SG50 blog will show you why the SG50 messaging is overkill. See http://mothership.sg/2015/02/simi-sai-also-sg50-blog-will-show-you-why-the-sg50-messaging-is-overkill/ (accessed 16 October 2015).

Lim, H. (2015) Singapore's IP ranking. See http://www.ipos.gov.sg/MediaEvents/SingaporesIPRanking.aspx (accessed 16 October 2015).

Loo, G. (2015) Here are 7 things to do during the SG50 long weekend. See http://www.tnp.sg/news/here-are-7-things-do-during-sg50-long-weekend (accessed 16 October 2015).

Marginson, S. (2011) Higher education in East Asia and Singapore: Rise of the Confucian model. *Higher Education* 61 (5), 587–611.

Ng, K. (2015) Mr Lee Kuan Yew's state funeral will be a moment for all to share together: PM Lee. See http://www.todayonline.com/rememberinglky/mr-lee-kuan-yews-state-funeral-will-be-moment-all-share-together-pm-lee (accessed 5 October 2015).

Qiu, J.L. (2006) The changing web of Chinese nationalism. *Global Media and Communication* 2 (1), 125–128.

Siddique, S. (1990) The phenomenology of ethnicity: A Singapore case-study. *Sojourn: Journal of Social Issues in Southeast Asia* 5 (1), 35–62.

Stock, F. (2009) Identity, image and brand: A conceptual framework. *Place Branding and Public Diplomacy* 5 (2), 118–125.

Tan, J. (2015) Why Thaipusam is no longer a public holiday in Singapore. See https://sg.news.yahoo.com/why-thaipusam-is-no-longer-a-public-holiday-in-singapore-050043065.html (accessed 16 October 2015).

Volcic, Z. and Andrejevic, M. (2011) Nation branding in the era of commercial nationalism. *International Journal of Communication* 5, 598–618.

White, L. (2004) Australia: The Bicentenary of Australia: Celebration of a nation. In L.K. Fuller (ed.) *National Days/National Ways: Historical, Political and Religious Celebrations around the World* (pp. 25–39). Westport, CT: Praeger.

White, L. (2009) The Man from Snowy River: Australia's bush legend and commercial nationalism. *Tourism Review International* 13 (2), 139–146.

18 Covering 'Captain America' and (Re)Imagining the United States during the 2014 FIFA World Cup

Nicholas Wise and John Harris

Introduction

Few sports are as truly global as association football (Giulianotti & Robertson, 2009), and many leading players are internationally renowned. Association football does not have the same profile or prestige in the United States as in many other parts of the world and this has been described as a kind of 'American exceptionalism' (Markovits & Hellerman, 2001). Every four years when the US competes in the Fédération Internationale de Football Association (FIFA) World Cup, the national media seems more interested in what is otherwise referred to as the 'other type of football' – *soccer*. In the US and particularly, it could be suggested, in places such as Texas, the global impulse of football has been resisted and sports fans celebrate their own (American) football heroes and icons. A soccer player from Texas, Clint Dempsey, was referred to as 'Captain America' based on his role and performance during the 2014 FIFA World Cup in Brazil. Indeed, Captain America is a fictional Marvel Comics superhero (or super soldier) who leads and defends the nation in international disputes (Dittmer, 2010). Therefore, it might be difficult to imagine an American athlete carrying the title of 'Captain America' in a sport that ranks quite low among the country's sporting milieu, but Dempsey is the captain of the nation in a truly global sporting competition.

The FIFA World Cup is a mega-event, recognised as a truly global competition. However, given the global popularity of football, the sport is not one that often features prominently in the US media – although recent research has pointed to a more visible role during FIFA World Cup every four years in wider sport media discourse (Novak & Billings, 2012). While the US represents global power politically and economically, and is home to several top professional sporting leagues, the most prestigious and financially powerful football leagues are in Europe. Major League Soccer (MLS) was launched in 1996 and was a condition of the nation's successful bid to stage the 1994 World Cup since there was no elite men's league in place at the time of the bid. There had been earlier attempts to develop a top-level men's professional soccer league in the country, such as the North American Soccer League (NASL) in the 1970s, but these had run into financial difficulties. To (re)imagine that brief period of time where the US competes in the FIFA World Cup, we may consider the role of Clint Dempsey as the nation's captain and how the nation (re)imagined to better understand the ways in which an international sporting event is used as a site for a particular representation of national identity. Given the semantics, 'football' and 'soccer' will be used interchangeably in this chapter although this does not overlook the contested place of soccer in a football world (see Harris, 2014). Rather, we attempt to highlight and understand the interchange between local, national and international discourse within and around a particular sporting body that represents his nation on what is arguably the biggest stage in international sport.

Media analyses take on contemporary sociological and geographic issues relevant to national identities and constructed imaginations (Lehtonen, 2000). This chapter assesses online textual content in articles and images where Clint Dempsey is mentioned in the nation's national newspaper: *USA Today*. The US played their first match in the 2014 FIFA World Cup on 16 June and were eliminated from the competition by Belgium on 1 July. This paper follows narratives concerning Clint Dempsey in *USA Today* from 16 June to 2 July 2014. The openly accessible online version of *USA Today* published 60 articles that mentioned Clint Dempsey between these dates. Of these articles, 45 were used in this longitudinal narrative content analysis and 15 were deemed not useful if they only included Dempsey in a list of starting players with no narrative alongside his role/performance. The analysis is structured longitudinally based on content around each match played. A brief discussion of the literature concerning the role of individual athletes and national identity is where this chapter now turns.

Athletes and National Identities

Andrews and Jackson (2001: 2–3) suggested that 'what is new about contemporary culture is the scale and scope with which variously celebrated individuals infuse and inform every facet of everyday existence'. There has been much development in the academic literature focusing on individual athletes, including those from international football (e.g. Cashmore & Parker, 2003; Dauncey & Morrey, 2008; Harris & Clayton, 2007; Wise & Harris, 2010). Bale (2003: 165) noted that sports stars in some cases 'are the only members of a particular nation (or region or city for that matter) known to people from other places, [and] may be taken to be representative of the whole nationality'. Therefore, many football players have become synony-mous with their respective nation, for instance: Diego Maradona and Argentina (e.g. Archetti, 2001) or David Beckham and England (Harris & Clayton, 2007). This has led to the rise of the 'postmodern athlete', cele-brated for their heroism and perceived as an iconic figure alongside narratives of their nation or the specific place they identify with.

Globalisation, politics and changing consumer patterns influence the identity athletes come to represent – such as being symbols of their nation during times of competition. When the media directs attention to particular athletes and their performance(s), academics have assessed pertinent narra-tives and representations to interpret elements of celebrity or heroism (e.g. Cashmore & Parker, 2003; Harris & Clayton, 2007; Wise & Harris, 2010). Based on the narratives in this analysis, this case observes how one fades from the narrative. Individuals not only help shape imaginations and percep-tions of their nation, but we must also consider how nations are (re)imagined (Bale, 2003). Moreover, Wise and Harris (2010: 323) suggested that 'we must (re)assemble the perceptions and interpretations of the athlete (in focus), supporting actors, and the places they represent or contest based on media presentations'.

Sport and national identity are also part of this geographical discourse presented through the media. The notion of imagined communities (Anderson, 1983) helps reinforce associations that position how nations are identified. Bale (2003) argued that this idea of imaginative geographies, rel-evant to sport, is linked to how we imagine and perceive regions, nations and national identity. While each nation is often defined by a particular sporting identity, we also need to understand the role of individual athletes as part of this discourse and consider the ways in which they themselves become rep-resentatives of the nation.

Clint Dempsey and US Soccer

Clint Dempsey hails from Nacogdoches, Texas and currently plays for the Seattle Sounders in the MLS where he is currently the league's highest paid player. Prior to moving back to the US in 2014 to join the MLS, Dempsey played in the English Premier League (EPL) from 2006 for Fulham and Tottenham Hotspur. His move back to the US sparked some criticism when he departed one of the best professional leagues in the world, although it should also be noted that a number of high-profile athletes from other nations have also moved to MLS in recent years as the league continues to develop and evolve. Some of the most high-profile of these have also come from the top level of English football towards the end of their careers (e.g. Frank Lampard and Steven Gerrard most recently), but other foreign players in the league include those who were good enough to play in the top leagues of international football (see Elliott & Harris, 2011).

Football (soccer), despite its downplayed presence in the media in the American sporting landscape, is a very popular sport among youths in the country, although it is also important to note its appeal amongst females, for whom the US has long been one of the leading nations in the world as most recently evidenced by their success in the 2015 FIFA Football Women's World Cup. While Dempsey and a number of other members of the US men's team play, or have played, in the EPL, they are not always widely recognised back home. Dempsey and his teammates are acknowledged and celebrated more every four years, when the nation and some parts of the national media show more interest in the game (Novak & Billings, 2012). In an age of accelerated globalisation, while the US is not one of the leading nations for men's football globally and the top players from the nation, including Dempsey, have moved abroad to further their professional careers, the MLS has developed markedly in the last two decades. The increased movement of athletes between nations, and the conservative growth of the MLS has also seen many leading figures from the international football world such as David Beckham (England), Thierry Henry (France) and Robbie Keane (Republic of Ireland) move to the US to compete in the league.

Analysis

There were clear transitions observed with varying degrees of focus on Dempsey over the course of the 2014 FIFA World Cup. The sections below longitudinally outline content specific to each match (see Table 18.1) in the form of a narrative analysis. There are a number of extended narratives on Dempsey at the start, but over the course of 17 days under analysis, around Matches 2 and 3, the narrative and focus on Dempsey abruptly shifts. At the start, Dempsey is the focus and is highlighted for his on-field performance and his popularity. His presence then begins to fade from the narrative in the build-up to Match 3. At the end of the second match, the US is silenced by Portugal's late goal that negates Dempsey's would-be game winner. Dempsey does not score another goal in the competition thereafter, and so more emphasis is put on the nation and the narrative of the team in addition to observations of soccer in the US. Since the analysis looks at the sole national

Table 18.1 Dates of content analysed in *USA Today*

Match (Date)	Dates of Content	Articles	Focus
1 (16 June)	16–19 June	18	Strong focus on Dempsey as a hero/celebrity
2 (22 June)	21–22 June	5	Dempsey part of the build-up but soon silenced
3 (26 June)	22–26 June	10	Focus on Dempsey fades but the nation unites
4 (1 July)	27 June to 2 July	12	Aspirations, hype and (re)imagining US sport

newspaper in the US, *USA Today*, only the date is provided after each quote below.

Match 1: The (new) national hero

It seems every four years the US has a new soccer hero. In 2010 it was Landon Donovan who captured the spotlight towards the end of the competition, scoring crucial goals to see Team USA advance. With Donovan not making the final squad in 2014, a new captain and national hero emerged. While Clint Dempsey was commonly referred to as 'Captain America' on the television and in numerous online discourses, he was not described specifically as this in *USA Today*. His image as a new hero was clear and the narratives were framed to position him as the key representative of the nation. Another element of this match was that Dempsey and Team USA needed to reign victorious against Ghana, as this victory 'gave the Americans a measure of revenge against the tiny West African county that knocked them out of the previous two World Cups' (16 June). It was a uniting focus that reinforced the imagined community: 'US players ran onto the field to celebrate at the final whistle, jumping as supporters chanted "U-S-A! U-S-A!"' (17 June).

The highest numbers of online articles published by *USA Today* featuring Dempsey (11 articles) was on 16 June. The image presented of Dempsey was clear – a hero has emerged and his audacious performance and actions are amplified. The headline 'US Emerges Bloodied and Victorious against Ghana' was complemented by an image of Dempsey continuing to play after breaking his nose. Immediately following the first match, stories focused on Dempsey's broken nose, stating that he 'returned to the field three minutes later, playing with tissue in his nose to stop the bleeding' (16 June), and in another story a quote from Dempsey notes ' 'I just had trouble breathing' ... 'I was coughing up blood a little bit. Hopefully I'll be able to breathe through my nose again before the next game'' (16 June). However, this heroic sentiment was overshadowed by the fact that Dempsey scored less than

30 seconds into the match. Each of the 11 articles focused on this feat by placing him in the World Cup history books. Emphasis added on 16 June around this goal highlighted:

Dempsey scores after 29 seconds vs Ghana.

Well, that didn't take long. US national team captain Clint Dempsey kicked off the American World Cup campaign by scoring a left-footed goal 29 seconds in the opening game against Ghana.

Dempsey became the first American to score in three World Cups.

Clint Dempsey scored fifth-fastest goal in World Cup history.

Clint Dempsey wasted no time in ending the goal drought by US forwards at the World Cup. The Americans' captain scored in the first minute of their opener against Ghana on Monday – the fastest World Cup goal in his country's history.

Dempsey's goal made him the first US player to score in three different World Cups and ranks as the fifth-quickest goal in World Cup history [… and] showed the kind of technical flair seldom seen from a squad that typically scores through set pieces.

… he blasted in a left-footed shot 29 seconds in to the game to give the United States a 1–0 lead against Ghana.

This 'dream start to [the] World Cup' along with his image was the headline story. In addition, it was noted that 'American World Cup fans lost their minds' (16 June), and videos were uploaded showing Americans back home watching from stadiums and live zones reacting to Dempsey's goal. It also did not take long after the first match win, alongside the focus on Dempsey, to reinforce the newly found national interest in soccer and for the country to get 'this football bug' once again, as noted:

The quick goal set off raucous cheers from the red, white and blue-clad American fans at the other end of Arena das Dunas, who had just drowned out the recording of 'The Star-Spangled Banner'. (16 June)

The match drew 11.09 million viewers on ESPN, a record for men's soccer on the network. And after decades when US soccer fans felt outnumbered – even at home games – players took notice of the raucous red, white and blue-clad crowd at Arena das Dunas in Natal. (18 June)

New-ish fans drawn into the World Cup via the South African games four years ago are tuning in again. (18 June).

This last quote reinforces this focus on sport, and how soccer really only plays a role in (re)imagining the nation every four years.

By 18 June, the hype of Dempsey's early goal and broken nose was still in focus, but the narrative of Dempsey transitioned to his off-field ambitions. With some downtime between the first and second matches, Dempsey's aspiring music career was discussed and rooted were semblances of soccer and Texas in his lyrics. Dempsey had actually long been pursuing a music career with his first album released in 2006. Amid the hype surrounding his on-field performance, a story on the same day noted, 'Clint Dempsey – the first single from his new rap album' (18 June). The story echoed his performances: 'Dempsey raps faster than a 30-second goal' before discussing the significance between his work/life balance of 'scoring Gs out on the green [and] his humble Texas roots' (18 June). While many (American) football stars are applauded for their efforts, Dempsey will donate proceeds to an East Texas Food Bank. Moreover, like many sports stars pursuing music careers, he spent his offseason free time in Los Angeles, and his producer left a comment with the *Wall Street Journal* picked up by *USA Today* to include in the story, stating 'we're not known as a soccer powerhouse – we're almost known for being soft. But Clint has this edge' (18 June).

Dempsey's next match reference builds on the story of the previous day, highlighting that 'Clint Dempsey went all gangbusters on Ghana's keeper in the first 30 seconds of the game on Monday night' (19 June). The album story was one of two articles that focused attention away from the World Cup and the team. The other was written on 19 June when a story broke that 'Rip Hamilton [a former professional basketball player] is out to convince Clint of the medical (and perhaps magical?) benefits of wearing a face mask'. This was reported because Hamilton notoriously wore a mask during the prime and successful heights of his career. Still, two group stage matches remained, but with the captain leading the nation's charge, they had momentum and the nation's attention after the first match in what was touted the 'group of death.'

Match 2: Carrying his weight before a nation silenced

Ahead of the second match it was noted that 'Clint Dempsey will play after his nose was broken against Ghana' (21 June), but it was the Amazon heat and humidity that ultimately represented the new challenge for Team USA. Dempsey was not a part of the narrative in articles following the second match, with only four stories covering him and his performance. While stories from 22 June did involve Dempsey – his sole defining moment was his goal that was thought to be the clincher in the 81st minute – the team and nation again began to celebrate:

> Dempsey's goal was his fourth at a World Cup and second at this year's tournament.

> Clint Dempsey, playing with a broken nose, then put the Americans ahead in the 81st. The United States captain used his stomach to direct the ball into the net.

> Clint Dempsey scored a go-ahead goal in the TKth minute to give the United States a 2–1 lead over Portugal, and US manager Jurgen Klinsmann lost his mind. The best part is all the players running past him to go celebrate.

However, this would be the peak of Dempsey's success and focus on him as the nation's hero. What happened minutes later in the match caused the narrative to abruptly change: 'they were less than a minute away from a huge win, the humidity was oppressive and the Americans were gassed' (22 June). At the end of the match, Cristiano Ronaldo and Portugal temporarily became the villains stopping the US from securing a definite spot in the knockout stage. Had Portugal not secured the draw, the narrative on Dempsey in the days following and for the remainder of the tournament would probably have continued to focus on him and wider narratives/performances. Dempsey's presence in *USA Today* as the national hero and an emerging celebrity was in a way tarnished by the draw. An image of Dempsey on 22 June showed an exhausted and defeated captain.

A clear transition concerning the focus on Clint Dempsey occured on 22 June. While it was only a matter of minutes at the end of the match, the articles in *USA Today* mentioning Dempsey began to see his emphasis fade as his go ahead goal was overshadowed by a draw. Almost immediately, the focus on the team and other players took precedence over Dempsey and he was only really mentioned briefly thereafter. There was a sense of trying to unite by focusing on the significance of the third match against Germany to make it through to the knockout stage.

Match 3: Dempsey fades but the nation unites

Jürgen Klinsmann, the US head coach, is a former German international who represented Germany in international football for many years and also coached the national team before taking up his position in the US. The US is regarded as a cultural melting pot, and this is reflected in the national team. 'German will be spoken on the field more than English' (22 June) was the focus ahead of the match against Germany, with five German-Americans on the US team. There were numerous discussions ahead of the match against Germany, distracting the focus from Dempsey. Dempsey was not fully forgotten – mentions of his late goal against Portugal and his EPL experience entered narratives – but more of the focus centred on what was going on at home. His main appearance in the articles was in response to the weather situation, which affected fans and family members not able to make the match, and how the elements impacted the performance of both teams.

The headline 'Klinsmann says US wants win, not tie, vs Germany' (23 June) brought the nation's coach into focus, whereas prior articles featuring Dempsey saw very little on the coach. Similarly, Dempsey was not featured in any of the images alongside the text, but midfielder Michael Bradley was featured in images and headlines commenting on the team's high expectations. Following the German match, Dempsey faded in popularity among the nation, as *USA Today* noted:

> As the din from the USA game disappeared, the team chewed over the two most salient trends from the match. One was goalie Tim Howard eclipsing Clint Dempsey as the team's most searched player, no doubt the result of the stellar performance in keeping the Germany attackers largely at bay.

What took precedence was how the shift in focus from Dempsey was now on the nation and a reinforced (re)imagined community, as detailed before and after the match:

> Will soccer score more US fans? #tellusatoday. (25 June)

> Across America, youngsters and athletes are turning into avid soccer supporters. San Francisco Giants pitcher Tim Lincecum wore a US jersey Wednesday after his no-hotter against San Diego, and Adam Wainwright had the American flag painted on his face when he went out to stretch with his St. Louis Cardinals teammates last weekend. Actor Will Ferrell came to Recife for Thursday's match, and the Empire State Building was illuminated in red, white and blue. (26 June)

Given the role of Team USA, a quote by US Soccer Federation President, Sunil Gulati, noted that success at the world stage 'translates into more fans, more casual fans, more kids that get turned onto the sport and may turn out to want to play'. Making it to the next stage continues the narrative, and exposure and success gained momentum back at home. However, was this (re)imagined presence raising the sports profile in the sporting landscape – or simply just a timely media spectacle?

Match 4: The hype, the team and (re)imagining the US

Dempsey's celebrity and heroic figure image were now removed to make way for the focus on the nation and the pride of making it out of the notorious 'group of death' and onto the knockout stage of the competition. Pre-match, Dempsey's focus in *USA Today* was merely dependent on his success on the field, which led to subsequent discussions of him. However, it was this time again when the nation was ready to support soccer as the US prepared for the knockout stage against Belgium. There was a four day gap between the third and fourth matches. Again the focus on Dempsey was minimal, with only brief mentions of his broken nose (27 June) and lone striker position as part of the team's reconfigured formation with the captain upfront (28 June). A much larger weight was placed on the national team, and that was not only the match but for the benefit of the sport back home:

> With support reaching fever pitch back home, American players realize the increased attention that comes with each match is an opportunity not to be missed to promote the sport in the United States. (29 June)

Following the loss to Belgium, Dempsey was brought back into attention, but his efforts did not reinforce the intended heroic image. Similar to the second match where Ronaldo and Portugal stole the show, this time the Belgian goalkeeper completed the narrative:

> With six minutes to go, the Americans almost got the equalizer. A free kick move set Clint Dempsey free in the center with only Courtois to beat. But the Belgium keeper proved he is one of the world's best by spreading his giant body to smother the shot. With almost no work at all in 120 minutes, Courtois turned out to be more decisive than Howard had been. (1 July)

Still, the broader narrative was on the nation, in articles published just prior and immediately following the match on 1 July:

> A lot more people are following now. The US averaged more than 18 million viewers on ESPN and Spanish-language Univision for its three first-round games, and viewing parties are scheduled for Tuesday ranging from Solider Field in Chicago to Veteran's Park in Redondo Beach, California.

> With waves of chants of 'USA, USA' echoing around the 48,000-seat stadium, the reinvigorated Americans kept searching for a late goal right up until the final whistle.

They captured the hearts of America – from coast to coast, big towns and small, all the way to the White House. At the final whistle, the US players fell to the field in their all-white uniforms like so many crumpled tissues. 'They made their country proud with this performance and also with their entire performance in this World Cup,' said Jurgen Klinsmann.

Back home, millions watched in offices, homes and public gatherings that included a huge crowd at Chicago's Soldier Field. President Barack Obama joined about 200 staffers in an Executive Office Building auditorium to watch the second half.

President Barack Obama was featured in five articles on 1 and 2 July. Some focused on the president following the match and others brought Dempsey back into focus concerning discussions of the two leaders, the nation's president and the nation's captain. On 2 July, the following article appeared:

President Barack Obama spoke to Clint Dempsey and goalkeeper Tim Howard on Wednesday to congratulate the team on its performance. Obama 'commended them not only for their work on the field, but for carrying themselves in a way that made the country proud,' the White House said in a statement. (2 July)

The president was quoted as saying:

I just wanted to call to say you guys did us proud. You guys did great, and as somebody whose first sport was soccer, although I was never that good, to see the way you guys captured the hearts and the imaginations of the whole country is unbelievable. (2 July)

When the US was eliminated, 'the growing legion of US soccer fans who have been chanting "I believe that we can win" will chant no longer. That newfound level of American enthusiasm for the World Cup ended' (2 July). If only momentarily over the course of 17 days in June and July, the focus on the nation's involvement in the 2014 FIFA World Cup gained support 'from Wall Street to the White House to the West Coast, Americans watched their national team on television in record numbers' (2 July).

Conclusion

In terms of (re)imagining the US in the national media, it seems that every four years the US increasingly puts men's soccer closer to the centre of sports media discourse, although there is still evidence of a strong resistance to the sport in general (Novak & Billings, 2012). The sport ranks well below the top four domestic sports leagues (Major League Baseball, National Basketball Association, National Football League, National Hockey League) in terms of media coverage but it is one of the fastest growing sports in the nation; participation levels have been healthy for a number of years and the game has continued to develop at the professional level (Harris, 2014; Markovits & Hellerman, 2001). With Dempsey as an elite international American soccer player returning to play professionally in the US, he is perhaps assisting efforts to inspire more male youths to play the sport. He was celebrated in the national media during the international event when he scored crucial goals and for leading his nation as captain.

This chapter has looked at media coverage of what is arguably the most popular sporting event in the world in a nation that has largely been positioned outside of the hegemonic core. By focusing on the representations of one player in particular, it has attempted to tease out the ways in which the nation and a particular imagined national identity is positioned and perceived. Again, Dempsey was recognised as a key player in the first two matches, but the following two matches focused more on team building and national unity. Developing an image of the US through the performance of its men's soccer team provides an interesting site to unpack narratives of the nation. However, in unpacking these narratives, it was apparent that this came to a rather abrupt end shortly after the US was eliminated from the competition. It will probably not be until the next FIFA World Cup in Russia (2018) that the men's national soccer team will once again be celebrated for their role in promoting the nation in an international context should they qualify for the finals. The next captain may well be compared with Dempsey as the nation seeks another 'Captain America'. Future work will consider representations of Dempsey during the 2014 FIFA World Cup in a wider range of discourses. The intention is to further examine the visibility of other players as the sport (arguably) grows in significance within the US and becomes a more central narrative surrounding wider discourses of the nation.

References

Anderson, B. (1983) *Imagined Communities*. London: Verso.
Andrews, D. and Jackson, S. (eds) (2001) *Sports Stars: The Cultural Politics of Sporting Celebrity*. London: Routledge.
Archetti, E. (2001) The spectacle of a heroic life: The case of Diego Maradona. In D. Andrews and S. Jackson (eds) *Sports Stars: The Cultural Politics of Sporting Celebrity* (pp. 151–163). London: Routledge.
Bale, J. (2003) *Sports Geography*. London: Routledge.
Cashmore, E. and Parker, A. (2003) One David Beckham? Celebrity, masculinity, and the soccerati. *Sociology of Sport Journal* 20 (3), 214–231.
Dauncey, H. and Morrey, D. (2008) Quiet contradictions of celebrity: Zinedine Zidane, image, sound, silence and fury. *International Journal of Cultural Studies* 11 (3), 301–320.

Dittmer, J. (2010) *Popular Culture, Geopolitics, and Identity*. New York: Rowman & Littlefield.

Elliott, R. and Harris, J. (2011) Crossing the Atlantic from football to soccer: Preliminary observations on the migration of English players and the internationalization of Major League Soccer. *WorkingUSA: The Journal of Labor and Society* 14 (4), 557–570.

Giulianotti, R. and Robertson, R. (2009) *Globalization and Football*. London: Sage.

Harris, J. (2014) Migration and soccer in a football world: The United States of America and the global game. In R. Elliott and J. Harris (eds) *Football and Migration: Perspectives, Places, Players* (pp. 47–60). London: Routledge.

Harris, J. and Clayton, B. (2007) David Beckham and the changing (re)presentations of English identity. *International Journal of Sport Management and Marketing* 2 (3), 208–220.

Lehtonen, M. (2000) *The Cultural Analysis of Texts*. London: Sage.

Markovits, A. and Hellerman, S. (2001) *Offside: Soccer and American Exceptionalism*. Princeton, NJ: Princeton University Press.

Novak, D. and Billings, A. (2012) The fervent, the ambivalent and the great gap between: American print-media coverage of the 2010 FIFA World Cup. *International Journal of Sport Communication* 5 (1), 35–50.

Wise, N. and Harris, J. (2010) Reading Carlos Tevez: Football, geography, and contested identities in Manchester. *International Journal of Sport Communication* 3 (3), 322–335.

19 Promoting Canada's Cultural Mosaic: John Murray Gibbon and Folk Music Festivals

Leighann Neilson

Introduction

Nation branding, understood as the self-sustaining myths that nations create to build a coherent identity, is a politico-cultural phenomenon that can be directed at internal as well as external publics or markets (Kaneva, 2011; Olins, 2002). In Canada, the expression 'Canadian mosaic' suggests a way of thinking about citizenship and belonging that marks the nation as distinct from other nations, in particular, the 'melting pot' of the United States. Although they acknowledge that the ideal is not attainable, many Canadians still choose to see their country as a place where multiple cultures live in relative unity, each contributing the best of its ethnic heritage to the brand equity that inheres in being Canadian. Most Canadians, however, would be surprised to learn that the self-sustaining myth of 'nation as cultural mosaic' was popularised not by a politician or cultural policy maker, but by a marketer – John Murray Gibbon, general publicity agent for the Canadian Pacific Railway (CPR).

Railways, and in particular the Canadian Pacific Railway, figure prominently in the popular imagining of the nation: without railways there would be no Canada.[1] If commercial nationalism is understood as 'the phenomenon whereby commercial institutions take on an increasingly important role in framing issues of national identity and promulgating branded forms of nationalisms and nationalist brand identities' (Volcic & Andrejevic, 2001: 612), then the relationship between the Canadian state and the CPR provides an important historical case study.[2] From a financial viability perspective, the construction and operation of railways were rarely, if ever, profitable (Chodos, 1973), requiring extensive government subvention. And from a political, nation-building perspective, railways provided the literal and figurative 'glue', linking the various provinces of Canada from east to west, defying the perhaps more natural north–south connections.

In his critique, Robert Chodos (1973: 3) notes that 'Nationalism is one essential component of the CPR myth, and there is one other. This is the concept of the public-spirited capitalist, the businessman whose activities, while perhaps providing profits for himself, are principally directed toward benefitting the great masses of people'. Here, Chodos provides a practical definition of commercial nationalism – business transactions that serve the dual purpose of nation-building and profit accumulation. The CPR enacted commercial nationalism through its business policies with respect to both tourism and immigration; its corporate objectives have often been seen as compatible with the policies pursued by successive national governments (Chodos, 1973; Ham, 1921). Just as the CPR played a lead role in enticing immigrants to the 'newly opened' lands along its routes in western Canada (Eagle, 1989; Gulka-Tiechko, 1991), its efforts were indispensable in attracting both international and domestic tourists (Hart, 1984a, 1984b).[3] In particular, as Becker (2005) argues, the nationalistic messaging in the company's brochures for its transcontinental rail service equated the act of travelling with that of nation-building.

As the literature linking tourism with national identity continues to grow, specific attention has been paid to the role of festivals (Nelles, 1999), music festivals in particular (Cristall, 2012; Satterwhite, 2005) and even to the distinctive properties of sound (Revill, 2000) in the constitution of nations and nationalism. This chapter discusses the contribution of a series of folk music festivals sponsored by the CPR and organised by their General Publicity Agent, John Murray Gibbon (see Figure 19.1), to the structuring of Canada's brand image as a 'cultural mosaic'.

As General Publicity Agent, Gibbon's duties included both attracting new immigrants and promoting the CPR's hotels as tourist destinations. Between the years 1928 and 1930, Gibbon was the driving force behind a series of 16 CPR-sponsored folk music and handicraft festivals, staged at hotel locations across Canada and showcasing the cultural traditions of various ethnic groups (Henderson, 2005; Kines, 1988; McNaughton, 1981, 1982). As Lazarevich (1996: 6) has commented, the scope of the festivals far exceeded their publicity purposes, 'This was the beginning of nation-building – that the arts and cultures of Canada can serve as unifying elements and as a means of communicating across cultures'. Thus, the branding of Canada as a cultural mosaic served not only the immigration and tourism promotion goals of the CPR but also functioned as a form of commercial nationalism, shaping national identity and constructing an 'imagined community' (Anderson, 1991).

This chapter will focus on how Gibbon and the CPR influenced ideas about new immigrants through these folk festivals, the actions that led to

Figure 19.1 John Murray Gibbon
Source: Whyte Museum of the Canadian Rockies.

the publication of Gibbon's award-winning book *Canadian Mosaic*, and the subsequent influence of the book on Canadian culture, politicians and immigration policy.

The CPR-sponsored Folk Music and Handicrafts Festivals

The CPR's early marketing efforts were directed at attracting settlers to the Canadian West. While it maintained a focus on its two immigration-related markets, new immigrants to Canada and Canadians resettling from central Canada to the western provinces, the CPR soon identified a third market: wealthy tourists from Canada, the US, the UK and continental Europe (Gibbon, 1951; Jones, 2003).[4] At the beginning of his career, while stationed in the UK, Gibbon was responsible for presenting Canada and the CPR effectively to Europeans contemplating emigration (Elson, 1935; Wallace, 1963). Once he made the move to Canada and became General Publicity Agent, Gibbon's duties expanded. Along with a focus on promoting Canada as a tourist destination and the CPR as carrier and hotelier of choice,

Gibbon also became involved in the company's efforts to smooth the acceptance of non-British immigrants.[5] In service of this goal, 'Gibbon set out to promote Canada itself, particularly the diversity of cultural traditions among the country's many ethnic groups' (Jones, 2003: 13).

In 1926, Gibbon was tasked with publicising the opening of a new wing of the Chateau Frontenac hotel in Quebec City. He suggested hosting a number of newspaper editors from the US, Toronto and Montreal at a dinner during which folksongs would be performed, illustrating traditional Quebecois culture (Gibbon, 1951). Gibbon does not record whether that evening was a success except to reveal that, on the train returning to Toronto, Fred Jacobs of the *Toronto Mail and Empire* suggested that 'if Ontario were to hear these songs [which Gibbon had translated into English] there would be much better understanding of Quebec in that Province' (Gibbon, 1951: 143). A seed was planted. From 1928 until the onset of the Depression forced an end to the events,[6] Gibbon played an integral role in staging massive festivals involving as many as 400 performers (McNaughton, 1981) that showcased the folk music and handicrafts of Canada's various ethnic communities.[7] In Gibbon's words (Composers, Authors and Publishers Association of Canada, CAPAC, 1946: 22–27):

> The next move resulted from the desire of the General Manager of Canadian Pacific Railway Hotels to find some early spring attraction for the Chateau Frontenac. I suggested a Folklore Festival lasting four days, to be combined with an exhibition of Quebec handicrafts with spinners and weavers at work, and with fiddlers and dancers if we could get them.

Thus, the first festival was held at the CPR's Chateau Frontenac hotel in Quebec City, 20–21 May 1927. Special trains brought visitors from Toronto and across Quebec to the festival; it 'drew much larger audiences than … expected' (Gibbon, 1951: 146) and received extensive and positive press coverage (McNaughton, 1982). The reviewer from *Le Devoir* stated that 'it was laudable to see an English (anglophone) company become instrumental in the continuance of francophone traditions, and that the CPR could not be thanked or congratulated enough' (cited in McNaughton, 1982: 92).

For years scholars and others have debated what counts as folk music (Tsai, 2007 and 2008) and multiple understandings exist of who the word 'folk' references (McKay, 1994). For Gibbon (1938: xi), there were two types of music: '(1) the folksong and folkdance tunes of the people; [and] (2) composed instrumental music or art song'. By the 'people' he was not referring to the group typically referenced by the term 'folk' – impoverished, illiterate, largely uncultured tillers of the soil (McKay, 1994: 23; McNaughton, 1981), nor was he necessarily adopting a Leftist understanding of the folk as working class, ordinary people longing for justice under an unfair political system (McKay, 1994: 26). Influenced no doubt by his extensive travel, Gibbon was open and respectful of other cultures. He sought to portray new immigrants as highly cultured people who brought with them to Canada musical and other traditions with which to enrich their new home country. In *Cultural Mosaic* Gibbon (1938: v) was to argue that, 'each racial group has brought with it some qualities which are worth-while contributions to Canadian culture'. His strategy during the festivals which involved multiple ethnic groups seemed to be to 'celebrate the [surface] differences in order to recognise the [underlying] similarities' to paraphrase Henderson (2005: 142).

As a student at Oxford, Gibbon was influenced by Fabian socialism, describing himself as an 'active' Fabian (Gibbon, 1951: 22). The Fabians believed that 'folk music could be used as a means not only of expressing the unique aspects of a nation's culture, but also of bringing people of different cultures together in mutual appreciation' (McNaughton, 1981: 69). Gibbon did not believe that folk and art music were immiscible. He thought that it was not only possible but desirable to construct art music for Canada on the foundation of the folk music traditions of the various immigrant groups (McNaughton, 1981).[8] This belief influenced the content of the festivals.

The success of the first festival led to the design of other festivals which can be grouped into three thematic categories: French-Canadian, European and British-oriented (McNaughton, 1981). Individual festivals featured themes appropriate to the cultural background of the local population (Lazarevich, 1996).

> After our second Festival at Quebec, [CPR President, Sir Edward Beatty] asked me what else I could suggest on the same lines. I recommended a Folksong and Handicraft Festival for the New Canadians at Winnipeg, so this was organized with the assistance of the Colonization Department of the Canadian Pacific Railway ... The success of the Winnipeg Festival resulted in an invitation from the Hon. James Gardiner, then Premier of Saskatchewan, to stage a similar affair in Regina ... Then [Premier] Brownlee invited us to do the same thing for Alberta, so we staged a Festival at Calgary... It seemed only natural that we should stage a Scottish Music Festival with Highland Games for Banff. This was repeated for a succession of years till the Depression of the 'thirties called a halt ... Vancouver had a Sea Music Festival and Victoria a Christmas Music Festival, both of which were highly successful. Then the opening of the Royal York Hotel in Toronto suggested an English Folksong Festival. (Gibbon in CAPAC, 1946: 27)

Professional musicians appeared alongside the folk musicians. Well-known composers such as Sir Ernest MacMillan, the 'most important musician in Canada during the first half of [the 20th] century' (Forster, 1996: 214), arranged folk music and composed music especially for the festivals.

Although well-known and highly respected musicians participated in the festivals alongside local talent, the festivals did not always meet with acceptance and understanding. An article in the *Winnipeg Free Press*, describing the 'New Canadians' festival held at the Royal Alexandra hotel in 1928 illustrates the author's ambivalence:

> Blazing in colours, the hotel rotunda presents a motley scene. Garbed in seemingly grotesque clothes of many bright hues, the European mingles with the conservatively-clad westerner. The new Canadian seems perfectly at home in this setting, for it is that of his native land. But the westerner is bewildered, there are many things that arouses (sic) his interest. (Quoted in Jones, 1988/1989)

Yet, in at least one case, the festival appears to have engendered an abrupt about-face in attitudes toward immigrants. The Reverend Charles W. Gordon, better known by his pen name Ralph Connor, attended the Winnipeg festival. Gibbon sat beside Connor during a 20 minute performance of the Polish National Dance and reports his reaction (Gibbon, 1951: 152):

> Do you know, these are some of the finest, most cultured people I have met since I have come to Winnipeg. But I have something on my conscience – I feel that I have done them an injustice. Recently I wrote a book called *The Foreigner*, in which I indicated that these immigrants were lousy and drunken. I should like to make amends.

Reflecting on his experience organising the music festivals, Gibbon was convinced that Connor's reaction was not an isolated case, but that 'in music these racial groups found contacts which helped greatly in making them understand each other, and in creating good will for themselves among Canadians of British stock' (Gibbon, 1938: x).

Canadian Mosaic

Gibbon's book, *Canadian Mosaic: The Making of a Northern Nation*, was published in 1938. Gibbon (1938: vii) believed that 'to know a people, you must know its history and origins' and since the Canadian people had not yet become assimilated into one culture, that 'to understand the Canadian people ... [w]e must ... study their racial origins'. Thus the reader is presented with 17 chapters each dealing with a specific ethnic group (or 'race' in the parlance of the time), providing a brief synopsis of their history, the geography and climate of their homeland, a discussion of the 'character' or 'social qualities' of the people, their rationale for emigration to Canada, and an accounting of their efforts at settlement in their new home. Each chapter is illustrated with black and white photographs or drawings of important historical figures along with artists, musicians or dancers in folk costumes and full-colour illustrations of a typical homestead, religious building or individual in folk costume.

The book was an outgrowth of and elaboration on the text prepared to accompany a series of 10 musical radio programs that Gibbon organised and delivered over the Canadian Broadcasting Corporation network in early 1938 (Gibbon, 1938: x).

> One day, en route to Ottawa, I sat in a chair in the parlor car next to Leonard W. Brockington, who had been put at the head of the [Canadian Broadcasting] Corporation and who asked if I could give him any suggestions as to programs. Remembering our Folksong Festivals and his own co-operation in one of these when he was at Calgary, I said I thought the C.B.C. had a unique opportunity of spreading the gospel of mutual understanding among the many racial groups scattered throughout the country, and that a series of programs dealing with the folksongs and culture of these groups would find a large listening public. ... [T]hese were very soon on the air under the title of 'Canadian Mosaic'.

Among those who listened to the radio shows was John McClelland of the publishing house McClelland and Stewart, who asked Gibbon to write a book on the subject (Gibbon, 1951: 182).

Gibbon was not the first to use the metaphor of a mosaic to describe the Canada of his day. The American writer Victoria Hayward had described the scenery of the prairies as 'a mosaic of vast dimensions' in her book, *Romantic Canada* (cited in Gibbon, 1938: ix), and Kate Foster titled her 1926 survey of 'New Canadians' conducted for the Dominion Council of the Young Women's Christian Association (YWCA) *Our Canadian Mosaic*. Gibbon claims to have not known about Foster's work until he was nearing completion of his book. At this time, he offered to change the title of his book; however, 'Mrs. Foster and the Dominion Council of the YWCA generously agreed to let it stand' (Gibbon, 1938: ix). Although not the first to use the metaphor, Palmer (1976: 96) suggests that Gibbon was the first to 'attempt to explore its meaning in any significant way'.

That Gibbon's book was well received by literary critics of the day can be concluded from the fact that it won the Governor General's Literary Award for Non-fiction in 1938.[9] The book was also popular with politicians. At the time of its printing, Gibbon received congratulatory notes from Canadian Prime Minister W.L. Mackenzie King and from the Honourable O.D. Skelton, Undersecretary of State for External Affairs, who suggested that publication of the book would provide a 'stimulus' to efforts at better understanding 'new Canadians' (Gibbon, 1951: 183).

At a dinner celebrating Gibbon's retirement, H.R. Jackman, then Member of Parliament for Rosedale-Toronto and later Lieutenant Governor of Ontario, said:

I wonder... if even Mr. Gibbon knows that among his many contributions to Canadian folklore and literature, he is the author of a politician's handbook! I refer to *Canadian Mosaic*, which I found indispensable when I first canvassed my riding of Rosedale-Toronto and met many New Canadians, about whose cultural background I knew little or nothing. I commend Mr. Gibbon's book to all budding politicians, as well as senior statesmen, for an understanding of the great racial strains that go to make up our Canadian heritage! (CAPAC, 1946: 19)

Paul Martin, Sr, then Secretary of State, was quoted in the *Ottawa Evening Citizen* (March 22, 1946: page unknown) as addressing Gibbon with these words, 'By your writings you have done more to develop this country than many of the men who daily are in the headlines of the newspapers'. In his speech for the occasion, Martin commented further:

Dr. Gibbon's book *Canadian Mosaic* is an invaluable record of the Canadian scene. Here is a happy choice of phrase for that is exactly what Canada is – a mosaic. It is made up of many peoples, whose ethnic differences explain the existence of as many cultural and national traditions, all of which in a process of orderly co-mingling, can provide a Canadian tradition and culture that will come to be not only distinctive but may easily excel. All this, Dr. Gibbon in his writings – and in that particular writing – has shown us. (CAPAC, 1946: 17)

In his autobiography, Gibbon notes (1951: 184) that Martin requested a copy of the book to assist him with his preparation of a new legislative bill on Canadian Citizenship.

Motivations for Commercial Nationalism

Various commentators have remarked on the motivation for the festivals, noting both Gibbon's personal interests and the commercial interests of his employer. Thus, Barnard (1945: 10) suggests, 'His folksong festivals grew out of his love for that sort of thing and his keen interest in many peoples who make up the Canadian nation – the mosaic that is Canada; but it was good business, too', while an early biographer commented that 'A little analysis showed that all this remarkable fostering [of Canadian culture] would be of wonderful assistance to a railroad. It is culture first and last that makes a race great, it is culture that brings the proper immigrants and settles them – and thus adds immeasureably (sic) to a railroad's earning power' (Glynn, 1929: 21). Folklorist Janet McNaughton (1981: 71) provides a balanced perspective, 'It was clearly to the CPR's economic advantage to promote a positive attitude towards European immigrants, but Gibbon's approach of presenting native European folk culture as a desirable element in Canadian society was a fairly radical one for that time'.

Gibbon's suggestion of a folk festival to the General Manager of the Chateau Frontenac as a 'publicity tool', along with his commitment of an enormous amount of his time and energies to producing subsequent festivals and writing *Canadian Mosaic* clearly had a dual purpose. It was during his initial trip to Canada that Gibbon (1951: 51–52)

> began to realize that the prairies were Europe transplanted – there were not only the Britishers and the Canadian born, but there were Germans, Scandinavians, the 'men in sheepskin coats' from Galicia and the Ukraine ... This trip through the West threw new light on my vocation. I began to realize that the Canadian Pacific was not merely a railway carrying passengers and freight, but was through its colonization work helping to build up a new nation.

Gibbon's belief in the possibility of a railway company contributing to the imagination of a new nation was apparently shared by his employer. Reflecting back on the folk festivals, Gibbon commented (CAPAC, 1946: 22–27), 'All this required money, but [CPR President] Sir Edward Beatty never failed us ... He was not particularly interested in music as such, but he saw that we were creating a better mutual understanding between English-speaking and French-speaking Canadians'. This special role of the CPR, in the 'national interest', seems to have been an essential part of the company's self-image and culture, as it is also referred to in in-house publications (Canadian Pacific Staff Bulletin, 1935; Jones, 1988/1989). Without this corporate orientation, it is difficult to estimate how widespread Gibbon's ideas or successful his efforts would have been.

Conclusion

Gibbon's belief that 'once people of different nationalities saw each other's cultures, they would be sympathetic, understanding, and accepting of one another,' has since been characterised as 'somewhat naïve and optimistic' (Wyman, 1974: 58), however, it is arguably this same belief that has become entrenched in much of Canada's cultural policy, especially since the 1970s. Palmer argues that, rather than crediting the Royal Commission with giving birth to the idea, the rise of multiculturalism during the 1970s had actually been presaged by the publication of Gibbon's book *Canadian Mosaic* and the writings of University of Manitoba English professor Watson Kirkconnell, which he says marked the 'emergence of the first full-blown pluralist ideas' (Palmer, 1975, 1976: 95). It is true that Gibbon took particular pride in the contributions of his Scottish countrymen to the development of Canada. During his first trip to Canada he spent a week in a public library in Toronto researching Scottish settlements in Ontario and their influence on the development of the fur trade. After learning of the time and energies his countrymen had invested in the country, Gibbon said, 'I felt Canada could not be a foreign country, if circumstances were to turn in favour of making my home in this country' (Gibbon, 1951: 55). However, in Gibbon's (1938: viii) opinion,

> The Canadian people today presents itself as a decorated surface, bright with inlays of separate coloured pieces, not painted in colours blended with brush on palette. The original background in which the inlays are set is still visible, but these inlays cover more space than that background, and so the ensemble may truly be called a mosaic.

Both Gibbon and Kirkconnell were influenced by a liberalism that rejected the assumption of Anglo-Saxon superiority. Further, they believed that ethnic diversity was compatible with national unity. CPR's commercial nationalism served its own purposes, no doubt, but in the way that Gibbon chose to promote the company's tourist facilities, they also shaped national identity.

Professor of Musicology, Gordana Lazarevich (1996), puts the CPR's contribution into historical context when she notes that, in Canada, government subsidy of the arts and artists was not provided until the second half of the 20th century. Her research details

> A remarkable chapter in Canada's cultural history ... during the period ca. 1925 to the late 1930s, when a business corporation provided sponsorship in the form of employment of artists, publicity for cultural events, broadcasting on one of the early radio networks, commissioning Canadian compositions through competitions at which major prizes were offered and the presentation of massive folk arts and folk music festivals. The corporation was the Canadian Pacific Railway (CPR), which promoted cultural events as a means of promoting itself in order to attract tourism to its hotels and railway services.

In Canada today sponsorship of the arts continues to be seen as a way of projecting an image of good corporate citizenship (Colbert *et al.*, 2005); however, it trails behind both professional and amateur sports as the investment of choice. A recent survey of sponsors indicates that only 10.5% of sponsors chose to invest in the arts compared with 22.2% for amateur and 27.2% for professional sports (O'Reilly & Beselt, 2013). These results underscore Lazarevich's use of the word 'remarkable' to describe the CPR's investment as event sponsor.

The CPR festivals were not the first events to feature folk content; the 300th anniversary of the founding of Quebec City was celebrated with a two week festival in 1908 (Nelles, 1999), and Marius Barbeau had organised two 'Veilées du bon vieux temps' featuring folk music in Montreal in the spring of 1919 (Keillor, 2008). The CPR festivals were, however, some of the first folk festivals to be staged in North America, part of the 'first wave' that influenced subsequent festivals such as the (US) National Folk Festival (McNaughton, 1981), the Winnipeg Folk Festival (MacDonald, 2008) and the Vancouver Folk Song and Dance Festival (Cristall, 2012). It is possible, therefore, to conceptualise Gibbon's and the CPR's actions as having both an ongoing and widespread influence.

Acknowledgement

The author would like to acknowledge the outstanding efforts of two highly skilled research assistants, Nicole Ives-Allison and Lauren Wheeler, along with the helpful assistance of staff at the Canadian Museum of Civilization, the Whyte Museum of the Canadian Rockies, Library and Archives Canada, and the Canadian Pacific Archives.

Notes

(1) Thus, railways have been duly mythologised in Canadian song, verse and literature. See for example songwriter Gordon Lightfoot's (1967) *Canadian Railroad Trilogy*, E.J. Pratt's (1952) epic poem, *Towards the Last Spike* and Pierre Burton's (1970, 1971) popular books on 'The Great Railway'.

(2) For readers not familiar with the Canadian case, it is helpful to understand the special relationship between a private company, the Canadian Pacific Railway, and the Canadian government. The construction of CPR lines across the Canadian West was heavily government subsidised and included the transfer of ownership to vast tracts of land. The CPR shared with the Canadian government responsibility for attracting immigrants. Long-time CPR publicity man, George Ham (1921: 267–268) commented on this relationship in his autobiography: The policy of the company has of necessity been somewhat broader, by reason of the variety of its activities, than that of a purely railway enterprise ... its affairs have been administered with what Sir John Willison terms 'A National Vision,' and this is largely responsible not only for the company's own success, but for the unique position which it occupies in Canada and abroad ... The policy of the future will be an extension of the policies of the past, namely that the company should be a good citizen of Canada, which means contributing to Canada's advancement and its own success, and taking, as it always has, its share of the country's burden.

(3) For more on the CPR's role with respect to tourism, see Ted Hart's (1984a) *The Selling of Canada: The CPR and the Beginnings of Canadian Tourism*; the Choko and Jones (2004) catalogue of the *Posters of the Canadian Pacific*; John Marsh's (1985) discussion of the positioning of western Canadian mountains in the CPR's tourism literature,

The Rocky and Selkirk Mountains and the Swiss Connection 1885–1914; and Courtney Mason's (2008) discussion of the CPR's influence in the Banff area, including in the formation of Banff National Park.

(4) The CPR's efforts to attract tourists date to the mid-1880s, when the President of the company, William Van Horne, decided to write the advertising script himself (Ham, 1921; Hart, 1984b).

(5) During the period when Gibbon organised the festivals an increasing number of immigrants were coming to Canada from European countries, rather than from Great Britain, and were often viewed with distrust and great distaste. For those who believed that assimilation and anglo-conformity were essential to the nation's future, it seemed impossible that these 'foreigners' could ever become truly Canadian (truly British). One of Gibbon's goals was to help others see new immigrants as cultured and valuable additions to Canada (McNaughton, 1981). See Palmer (1975, 1976) for a more thorough discussion of various perspectives on the acculturation of immigrants to Canadian life and Avery (1979) for a discussion of attitudes toward European immigrant workers.

(6) In his autobiography, Gibbon speaks only of the influence of the economic depression of the 1930s; however, McNaughton (1981) points to the expense of the festivals at a time when huge debts were incurred by the CPR as a result of the curtailing of immigration.

(7) Janet McNaughton (1981) and Stuart Henderson (2005) have both noted that non-European cultures, and in particular Asian cultures, were not included in these festivals and, in spite of the important role played by Chinese labourers in building the transcontinental railroad, *Canadian Mosaic* does not contain a chapter on Chinese immigrants and their culture. Although Gibbon does not provide a rationale for this, in 1923, the Canadian government passed the Chinese Immigration Act which effectively halted Chinese immigration to Canada. Closer to the time the book was published, immigration from China was so effectively restricted that only three Chinese immigrants were able to enter Canada between 1930 and 1935 (Kukushkin, 2006).

(8) In 1939, Gibbon published *New World Ballads*, songs written to the tune of European and British folk songs but featuring Canadian content, his personal contribution to creating national music for Canada.

(9) The Governor General's Literary Awards were established by the Governor General of Canada, Lord Tweedsmuir of Elsfield (John Buchan), and were first awarded for books published in 1936. Since that time, the Governor General's Literary Awards have evolved into Canada's premiere national literary awards (Canada Council for the Arts, 2006).

References

Anderson, B. (1991) *Imagined Communities: Reflections on the Origin and Spread of Nationalism.* London: Verso.

Avery, D. (1979) *'Dangerous Foreigners' European Immigrant Workers and Labour Radicalism in Canada, 1896 to 1932.* Toronto: McClelland and Stewart.

Barnard, L.G. (1945) John Murray Gibbon: An appreciation. *Canadian Review of Music and Art* 4 (1–2), 10–11, 19.

Becker, A. (2005) The layout of the land; the Canadian Pacific Railway's photographic advertising and the travels of Frank Randall Clarke, 1920–1929. MA thesis, McGill University, Montreal.

Burton, P. (1970) *The National Dream: The Great Railway, 1871–1881.* Toronto: McClelland.

Burton, P. (1971) *The Last Spike: The Great Railway, 1881–1885.* Toronto: McClelland.

Canada Council for the Arts (2006) *History of the Governor General's Literary Awards*. See http://www.canadacouncil.ca/prizes/ggla/ww128020470294038311.htm (accessed 24 December 2010).

Canadian Pacific Staff Bulletin (1935) New book on Canadian Pacific history comes from pen of J. Murray Gibbon, 1 October, unnumbered, File B-07.15. Canadian Pacific Archives, Montreal.

CAPAC (1946) *Tribute to a Nation Builder*. Toronto: Composers, Authors and Publishers Association of Canada.

Chodos, R. (1973) *The CPR: A Century of Corporate Welfare*. Toronto: James Lewis & Samuel.

Choko, M.H. and Jones, D.L. (2004) *Posters of the Canadian Pacific*. Richmond Hill, ON: Firefly Books.

Colbert, F., d'Astous, A. and Parmentier, M. (2005) Consumer perception of private versus public sponsorship of the arts. *International Journal of Arts Management* 8 (1), 48–60.

Cristall, G. (2012) The Vancouver Folk Song and Dance Festival with Arts and Crafts Exhibition: The first ongoing multicultural festival in Canada. *Canadian Folk Music* 46 (2), 19–27.

Eagle, J.A. (1989) *The Canadian Pacific Railway and the Development of Western Canada, 1896–1914*. Kingston: McGill-Queen's University Press.

Elson, J.M. (1935) Famous Canadian authors: John Murray Gibbon. *Onward* 45 (10), 73.

Forster, A. (1996) From the CPR to the Canada Council. In G. Carruthers and G. Lazarevich (eds) *A Celebration of Canada's Arts, 1930–1970* (pp. 213–225). Toronto: Canadian Scholars Press.

Gibbon, J.M. (1938) *Canadian Mosaic: The Making of a Northern Nation*. Toronto: McClelland & Stewart.

Gibbon, J.M. (1939) *New World Ballads*. Toronto: Ryerson Press.

Gibbon, J.M. (1951) 'Scot to Canadian – One of more than a million', unfinished and unpublished autobiography (photocopy). Whyte Museum of the Canadian Rockies, Banff.

Glynn, W. (1929) A man with a plan but little to say. *The Canadian Magazine* 72 (4), 21.

Gulka-Tiechko, M. (1991) Ukrainian immigration to Canada under the Railways Agreement, 1925–30. *Journal of Ukrainian Studies* 12 (1–2), 29–60.

Ham, G.H. (1921) *Reminiscences of a Raconteur: Between the '40s and the '20s*. Toronto: Musson.

Hart, E.J. (1984a) *The Selling of Canada: The CPR and the Beginnings of Canadian Tourism*. Banff, AB: Altitude Publishing.

Hart, E.J. (1984b) See this world before the next: Tourism and the CPR. In H.A. Dempsey (ed.) *The CPR West: The Iron Road and the Making of a Nation* (pp. 151–169). Vancouver & Toronto: Douglas & McIntyre.

Henderson, S. (2005) 'While there is still time ...': J. Murray Gibbon and the spectacle of difference in three CPR folk festivals, 1928–1931. *Journal of Canadian Studies* 29 (1), 139–174.

Jones, D. (1988/1989) C.P.R.'s Gibbon celebrated 'mosaic'. *CP Rail News* December/January, 5. File B-07.15, Canadian Pacific Archives, Montreal.

Jones, V. (2003) Surfacing value: The transformation of Canadian Pacific hotels and resorts. *Proceedings of the Administrative Studies Association of Canada (ASAC)* 24, Business History Division, 10–18.

Kaneva, N. (2011) National branding: Toward an agenda for critical research. *International Journal of Communication* 5, 117–141.

Keillor, E. (2008) Marius Barbeau as a promoter of folk music performance and composition. In L. Jessup, A. Nurse and G.E. Smith (eds) *Around and About Marius Barbeau* (pp. 137–155). Gatineau, Quebec: Canadian Museum of Civilization, Mercury Series.

Kines, G.B. (1988) Chief man-of-many sides: John Murray Gibbon and his contributions to the development of tourism and the arts in Canada. MA thesis, Carleton University, Ottawa.

Kukushkin, V. (2006) *Radical Policies*. Library and Archives Canada. See http://www.collectionscanada.gc.ca/immigrants/021017-2511-e.html (accessed 16 July 2015).

Lazarevich, G. (1996) The role of the Canadian Pacific Railway in promoting Canadian culture. In G. Carruthers and G. Lazarevich (eds) *A Celebration of Canada's Arts, 1930-1970* (pp. 3–11). Toronto: Canadian Scholars Press.

Lightfoot, G. (1967) *Canadian Railroad Trilogy*. For lyrics see http://gordonlightfoot.com/Lyrics/CRT.txt

MacDonald, M.B. (2008) 'The best laid plans of Marx and Men': Mitch Podolak, revolution, and the Winnipeg Folk Festival. *Ethnologies* 30 (2), 73–91.

Marsh, J. (1985) The Rocky and Selkirk mountains and the Swiss connection 1885–1914. *Annals of Tourism Research* 12 (3), 417–433.

Mason, C.W. (2008) The construction of Banff as a 'natural' environment: Sporting festivals, tourism, and representations of Aboriginal peoples. *Journal of Sport History* 35 (2), 221–239.

McKay, I. (1994) *The Quest of the Folk: Antimodernism and Cultural Selection in Twentieth-Century Nova Scotia*. Montreal: McGill-Queen's University Press.

McNaughton, J. (1981) John Murray Gibbon and the inter-war folk festivals. *Canadian Folklore Canadien* 3 (1), 67–73.

McNaughton, J.E. (1982) A study of the CPR-sponsored Quebec folk song and handicraft festivals, 1927–1930. MA thesis, Memorial University of Newfoundland, St John's.

Nelles, H.V. (1999) *The Art of Nation-building. Pageantry and Spectacle at Quebec's Tercentenary*. Toronto: University of Toronto Press.

Olins, W. (2002) Branding the nation – The historical context. *Brand Management* 9 (4–5), 241–248.

O'Reilly, N. and Beselt, E. (2013) 7th Annual Canadian Sponsorship Landscape Study. See http://sirc.ca/sites/default/files/content/docs/webinars/pdf/csls_rev_gen_1.pdf (accessed 16 July 2015).

Palmer, H. (ed.) (1975) *Immigration and the Rise of Mulculturalism*. Toronto: Copp Clark.

Palmer, H. (1976) Reluctant hosts: Anglo-Canadian views of multiculturalism in the twentieth century. In *Conference Report: Second Canadian Conference on Multiculturalism* (pp. 81–118), 13–15 February, Ottawa.

Pratt, E.J. (1952) *Towards the Last Spike*. Toronto: Macmillan of Canada.

Revill, G. (2000) Music and the politics of sound: nationalism, citizenship, and auditory space. *Environment and Planning D: Society and Space* 18, 597–613.

Satterwhite, E. (2005) 'That's what they're all singing about': Appalachian heritage, Celtic Pride, and American nationalism at the 2003 Smithsonian Folklife Festival. *Appalachian Journal* 32 (3), 302–338.

Tsai, S. (2007 and 2008) Electric picking, ethnic spinning: (Re)defining the 'folk' at the Winnipeg Folk Festival. *Musicultures* 34–35, 71–94.

Volcic, Z. and Andrejevic, M. (2011) Nation branding in the era of commercial nationalism. *International Journal of Communications* 5, 598–618.

Wallace, W.S. (ed.) (1963) John Murray Gibbon. In *The Macmillan Dictionary of Canadian Biography* (3rd edn, p. 263). London: Macmillan.

Wyman, G. (1974) John Murray Gibbon, 1975–1952. National Historic Parks and Sites Branch, manuscript report 160 (pp. 52–66). Call #08.1 G35w Pam, Whyte Museum of the Canadian Rockies, Banff.

Conclusion

20 Commercial Nationalism Research Directions: Negotiating New National Narratives

Leanne White

Introduction

When I announced the call for chapter abstracts in 2014, I welcomed a broad range of topics from contributors around the world. The chapters in this book were selected from more than 40 abstracts. This collection has considered what happens when commercial nationalism, tourism and events meet. The three main themes of National Narratives, Heritage and Tourism; Tourism Branding and Promotion; and Festivals, Events and National Identity, were addressed by examining a variety of case studies from around the world.

Many of the chapters in this book take the commercial nationalism discussion to another level. They reinforce the critical intersecting domains of commercial nationalism and tourism and highlight the importance of understanding this connection for researchers, tourists, destination managers and a range of other key stakeholders. This book builds upon two earlier books which I co-edited: *Tourism and National Identities: An International Perspective* (Frew & White, 2011) and *Dark Tourism and Place Identity: Managing and Interpreting Dark Places* (White & Frew, 2013) by narrowing the focus of study to commercial nationalism while broadening the discussion of national identity to encompass both tourism and events. This book is a reference text aimed principally at the academic market. It is designed to address the void that currently exists in the discursive space where commercial nationalism and tourism intersect. When tourists visit a country they encounter many forms of commerce and nation, which occasionally intersect (see Figure 20.1).

Figure 20.1 Visitors to Istanbul can purchase Turkish nationalism from the flag vendor

While the focus of this book was on commercial nationalism and tourism, some of the connected terms that have also been discussed in the volume include battlefield tourism, heritage tourism, cultural tourism, dissonant heritage, conflict heritage, place perception, place branding and destination marketing. This book incorporates a solid understanding of commercial nationalism, tourism and events while exposing these areas to both a multidisciplinary and an international approach.

In Chapter 1, an overview of the sections and chapters was provided along with some background to nationalism in tourism and events, and particularly the concept of commercial nationalism.

National Narratives, Heritage and Tourism

In the first section of the book on National Narratives, Heritage and Tourism, each of the six chapters demonstrated how commercial nationalism relates to national stories and traditions. The authors in this section discussed case studies in Canada, Bosnia–Herzegovina, Croatia, Ukraine, China and India.

In Chapter 2, Rettie argued that national parks fulfil important positions in relation to the national and the international stage. She argued that national parks matter to Canadians. They value access to their national parks and all that the parks have to offer. Even those who do not directly access national parks have a strong affiliation through a sense of pride in their nation's choice and ability to showcase and protect their country's natural treasures.

In the following chapter, Naef presented some of the elements of the touristic and museum landscape in the former Yugoslavia. The tourism promotion of Vukovar and the Alija Izetbegović Museum cases showed that the tourism sector can produce strong nationalist narratives. In Chapter 3, Naef threw light on specific mechanisms associated with nationalism and tourism, especially in relation to war heritage.

In Chapter 4, Iarmolenko, Kerstetter and Shahvali revealed how national stories and nationalistic sentiments are commonly used by the tourism industry to promote nations. The authors demonstrated how stories reflecting nationalistic feelings of diaspora can be built into a promotional campaign. They found that, apart from the economic benefits of promoting tourism, such travels benefit communities who have been removed from their original national identity. The authors also argued that documenting such enhancement in psychological well-being as a result of diaspora tourism calls for further research.

In Chapter 5, Zhu and Yang found that the story of Xi'an contributes to the understanding of the interplay between cultural heritage, tourism and Chinese nationalism. The authors claimed that local and central governments have combined to orchestrate nationalism through commercialising heritage. Zhu and Yang argued that nationalism is not an abstract ideology – it can be performed through embodied experience. It is an accumulative process with performative practices of creating, preserving and reinforcing the sense of originality, roots or authenticity.

In Chapter 6, Ranganathan argued the Bharatiya Janata Party (BJP) victory in 2014 allowed for a clear ideation of the nation as the BJP's term in power signals new directions for nation-building in India. The political and public discourse that has followed the BJP government's performance indicates a radical shift in nation-making, also supported by some of its initiatives. The BJP government's efforts form part of the many initiatives that may transform far more than the physical nation. The author claimed that these efforts are perhaps the first few pages of a new national story with the cultural icons under construction potentially emerging as the synecdoche for Indian nationalism.

In Chapter 7, Clarke showed how particular narratives are woven to tell a national story. He argued that, by deconstructing nationalist discourses, it is possible to see the Silk Road as a bridge from its legendary past to its commercialised present. Clarke suggested that the commercial nationalism of the Silk Road was not blameless and pointed to the development of trade and commerce along with cultural and heritage exchanges.

Tourism Branding and Promotion

In the second section of the book the authors discussed case studies in New Zealand, South Africa, Malta, Estonia, India and Colombia.

In Chapter 8, Hall argued that the commercial nationalism of Brand New Zealand is part of the wider neoliberal project in which places are competing for capital and people. The success of businesses, economies and brands is now a form of sport in which you can see your team's performance in the latest league table. Hall claimed that nation branding is not a neutral tool but a reflection of a set of assumptions about the way the world does and should run. In the New Zealand case, the country's formal branding process is part of a wider neoliberal discourse of competitiveness and a dominant stakeholder belief system that reinforces the commercial imaginaries of national branding.

In Chapter 9, Phelan argued that national identity is often difficult to articulate – and even more so in the case of the diverse continent of Africa. Much of the outside world views Africa as one cohesive entity. Yet even within those separate countries, national identity is not a simple philosophy to define as the diversity of its citizens is so great. Phelan claimed that national identity plays an important role in the tourism experience. It assists tourists with making sense of the community and locals with whom they interact. It serves as a guide for branding a destination, both domestically and internationally. National identity in Africa is a perplexing concept, but it is particularly valuable in aiding foreign tourists in comprehending the cultural variations in such a vast continent.

In the following chapter, Avelino Stewart and Cassar argued that the vestiges of Imperialism still linger in Maltese contemporary travel narratives and that it may take many decades before we see this neo-colonial reality subside. The authors suggested that Malta is now at a point where, while it looks forward to further development, it wants to make sure that it does not leave the safety zone of the European Union. Today's Malta is being branded as a welcoming destination for whoever wishes to join its people in an experience of relaxation, culture, good cuisine and an exciting stay.

In Chapter 11, McKenzie found that one of the expected results in his survey data was a great degree of similarity in terms of ethnic versus nationality identity measures of residents and diaspora. There was an expectation that the differences in terms of the findings from the survey data would

provide greater understanding of the Estonian nation brand, and by extension could be useful to both governmental agencies and tourism firms that
wish to attract investment and tourists. There was also the hope to provide
insights into how ethnicity, country of residence and country of origin of a
defined group of people can be used for comparisons in terms of non-culture-
related activities.

In Chapter 12, Singh found that commercial nationalism in India is not
necessarily a story of selling tourism, but, when carefully regulated, is a
viable means of earning income. What is required, however, is foresight on
how to circumvent a kind of tourism that is deleterious and not sustainable
in the medium term, both for the natural environment and for cultural and
spiritual heritage. Many of the advantages of commercial nationalism, used
as a ploy for tourism marketing, apparent from this chapter, are lost when
basic issues that affect the tourist receiving population have not been sorted
out or at least brought to a point where they can be reasonably managed.
Singh argued that rhetoric can fail whereas efficient administration and
proper inculcation of social values can bring better results in the medium to
long term.

In the final chapter of this section, Sanin examined narratives of
Colombianness created in the last decade through tourism promotion. The
Colombian case demonstrated how commercial technologies of nation
branding are utilised to reinvent the image of countries whose economies
have been affected by their negative international reputations. Sanin found
that, although these narratives build upon 'real' features of Colombia's
national culture, they are constructed using a fictional tone that overlooks
Colombian history and politics to emphasise the aesthetics of the country.
Seen from the perspective of commercial nationalism, the narratives developed in the last decade to sell Colombia as a tourist destination make evident
a series of interrelated shifts in the construction of the nation. These shifts
start with the adoption of commercial technologies as part of the machineries of nation-making. This use of marketing techniques demonstrates the
collaboration between governmental organisations and multinational advertising agencies to create commercial narratives aimed at selling the nation.

Festivals, Events and National Identity

In the final section of the book on Festivals, Events and National Identity,
the authors explored case studies in Hungary, Japan, Canada, Australia,
Singapore and the United States.

In Chapter 14, Rátz and Irimiás found that Hungary's National Gallop
media coverage confirmed that the narratives presented by the mass media
may significantly affect an event's ability to contribute to national identity
construction and reinforcement. The authors argued that, although the event

certainly contributes to increasing local pride in the community and its equestrian customs, in order to become able to gain further advantage from participation in the Gallop, most settlements would require expert assistance in destination marketing and brand development.

In Chapter 15, Basil examined a seasonal celebration in the form of cherry blossom festivals. Although it is virtually impossible to know if the Japanese celebration has become more commercialised over time, it is apparent that a number of commercial activities, such as the sale of food, are sanctioned at these events, many in the form of commercial consumption. Examining how the celebration changes in other cultures and climates demonstrates the extent to which the event is modified or 'glocalised' to each environment. Basil concluded that these international celebrations show evidence of globalisation through their worldwide celebration, but they also demonstrate glocalisation in the local adaptation and interpretation of the form of the celebration itself.

In Chapter 16, Martin and Marcotte found that visitors coming to Vimy Ridge are invited to encounter an invented nation – one that appears as an utterly male and militaristic body, which is quite separate from the actual diverse and complex Canadian nation. Vimy is fully participating in the 'invention' of the Canadian identity and the Canadian nation. The story told at Vimy is that of an imagined nation that was born in 1917. The Canadian nation will no doubt be highly acclaimed at the next commemorating ceremonies of the battle in 2017. Vimy's story, like other mythological narratives, occupies a particularly important place in the collective imagination. The ritualisation process (celebration, remembrance, pilgrim, image reproductions), and the sacralisation made the myth undeniable and created an 'imagined Canada'.

In the following chapter, Tham argued that, while the analysis of Singapore's Golden Jubilee event (SG50) has led to a nuanced understanding of hot authenticity related to commemorative events. Tham found that SG50 was perhaps one of many different exemplars of commercial nationalism. The chapter constructed an appreciation of commercial nationalism from an Asian perspective. The emergence of Asia as a pillar of today's economy will undoubtedly compel other nations to strengthen their national brand and perhaps reap commercial returns accordingly.

In Chapter 18, Wise and Harris looked at media coverage of what is arguably the most popular sporting event in the world. By focusing on the representations of one player in particular, the authors attempted to tease out the ways in which the nation and a particular imagined national identity is positioned and perceived. Developing an image of the US through the performance of its men's soccer team provides an interesting site to unpack narratives of the nation.

In the final chapter of this section, Neilson argued that the Canadian people today present as a decorated surface, bright with inlays of separate coloured pieces, not painted in colours blended with brush on palette. The original background in which the inlays are set is still visible, but these inlays cover more space than that background, and so the ensemble may truly be called a mosaic. Neilson found that the Canadian Pacific Railway's (CPR) commercial nationalism served its own purposes, no doubt, but in the way that Gibbon chose to promote the company's tourist facilities, it also shaped national identity. The CPR festivals were, however, some of the first folk festivals to be staged in North America, part of the 'first wave' that influenced subsequent festivals. It is possible, therefore, to conceptualise Gibbon's and the CPR's actions as having both an ongoing and widespread influence.

Conclusion

This collection has considered what happens when tourism and events meet commercial nationalism. The three main themes of national narratives, tourism branding and festivals and events were addressed by examining a variety of case studies from around the world. Many of the chapters in this book take the discussion of commercial nationalism to another level. They reinforce the critical intersecting domains of commerce and nation and, in particular, highlight the importance of understanding this connection for visitors, tourism operators, event managers and other key stakeholders. This book has focused on creating an awareness of the importance of commercial nationalism in a range of settings and regions in the world. The authors in this book have illustrated the importance of commercial nationalism within countries and communities. This relationship is of course complex and dynamic.

Gaining an improved understanding of commercial nationalism is a meaningful pursuit. Integrating such an undertaking with links to national stories, tourism branding and events adds significantly to the innovative nature of this book. The benefit of this awareness is likely to lead to better informed policies and procedures in the management and promotion of industries concerned with tourism and national identity. The linking of the significant issues of commercial nationalism and tourism has not been investigated before to such a degree. From a social, cultural, political, economic and historical perspective, this book helps us gain a deeper level of appreciation and understanding of the complicated connections across the globe between people, places, products and services.

This edited volume has explored the numerous ways in which aspects of commercial nationalism, tourism and events intersect and overlap. With the tourism and consumption experience, individuals and groups partake in diverse experiences and often reflect upon their own identity and the perception of the places visited. Commercial nationalism, as it has been discussed in this book, has increasingly broad appeal and increasing scholarly interest.

This book aims to address the void that currently exists in the place where commerce and the nation intersect.

Further research might examine whether new nations such as Australia, Canada and New Zealand have (or seem to require more) instances of commercial nationalism. In older countries (such as England) nationalism seems more of a taken for granted frame of reference. It may also be the case that manifestations of commercial nationalism are more common when nations are commemorating particular events such as Australia's Bicentenary of 1988 (White, 2004) or the celebration of Singapore's 50th anniversary of independence (Chapter 17). Nations market themselves in particular ways and when they tell and sell their story to the world in key global rituals such as an Opening Ceremony of an Olympic Games, commercial nationalism is more evident (White, 2006).

This book critically examined national images exploring the ways in which official nationalism and commercial nationalism intersect and overlap in what Cunningham referred to as the 'popular audiovisual grammar of national identity' (Cunningham, 1992: 83). Further research might attempt to explore why some national images continue to generate such distinct and unique meanings. A particular area worthy of further examination would be to determine the nature and intensity of national images in the domains of official nationalism and commercial nationalism as the world becomes increasingly more globalised, particularly in the social and cultural spheres.

I trust that you have been inspired and energised by the diverse international cases of commercial nationalism that have been explored in this volume. As the editor of this collaborative international body of work, I am delighted that from the tremendous collegial work of scholars around the globe, we have produced a volume that advances the academic debate surrounding commercial nationalism and tourism. All 26 contributors have combined an applied approach with solid academic and critical analysis.

References

Cunningham, S. (1992) *Framing Culture: Criticism and Policy in Australia*. Sydney: Allen and Unwin.

Frew, E. and White, L. (eds) (2011) *Tourism and National Identities: An International Perspective*. Abingdon: Routledge.

White, L. (2004) The bicentenary of Australia: Celebration of a nation. In L.K. Fuller (ed.) *National Days/National Ways: Historical, Political and Religious Celebrations around the World*. Westport, CT: Praeger.

White, L. (2006) The story of Australia: National identity and the Sydney 2000 Olympic Games opening ceremony. In M. Robertson (ed.) *Sporting Events and Event Tourism: Impacts, Plans and Opportunities*. Eastbourne: Leisure Studies Association.

White, L. and Frew, E. (eds) (2013) *Dark Tourism and Place Identity: Managing and Interpreting Dark Places*. Abingdon: Routledge.

Index

298 Commercial Nationalism and Tourism